Reinventing the Wheel

Reinventing the Wheel

Paintings of Rebirth in Medieval Buddhist Temples

STEPHEN F. TEISER

UNIVERSITY OF WASHINGTON PRESS *Seattle & London*

Published with the assistance of The Getty Foundation.

Printed in China
Designed by Veronica Seyd
12 11 10 09 08 07 06 5 4 3 2 1

University of Washington Press
PO Box 50096, Seattle, WA 98145
www.washington.edu/uwpress

Library of Congress Cataloging-in-Publication Data

Teiser, Stephen F.
Reinventing the wheel : paintings of rebirth in medieval Buddhist temples / Stephen F. Teiser.
p. cm.
Includes bibliographical references and index.
ISBN 0-295-98649-2 (hardback : alk. paper) ISBN 13: 978-0-295-98649-4
1. Reincarnation in art. 2. Art, Buddhist—Asia. 3. Reincarnation—Buddhism. 4. Transmigration—Buddhism. 5. Pratityasamutpada. I. Title.
N8193.3.R45T45 2006
704.9'48943—dc22 2006013867

The paper used in this publication meets the minimum requirements of American National Standard for Information Sciences–Permanence of Paper for Printed Library Materials, ANSI Z39.48–1984.

Cover: Based on Wheel of Rebirth. Relief carving. Dafowan Niche 3, Baodingshan, Sichuan, thirteenth century. After Bai Ziran, *Zhongguo Dazu shiku,* pl. 62.

Frontispiece: PLATE 1. Wheel of rebirth. Cotton painting. Tibet, nineteenth century. Rubin Museum of Art, item no. 65356. Photography: Bruce White.

For Wei

Contents

Preface and Acknowledgments *ix*

1. Picturing Life and Death as a Wheel *3*
2. The Canonical Version of the Wheel of Rebirth *50*
3. Temples and Legends: Western India, 350–550 C.E. *76*
4. King Rudrāyaṇa's Painting of the Twelve Conditions *104*
5. La roue imaginaire en Chine *120*
6. Wheels for Meditation: Kumtura, Central Asia, Ninth Century *146*
7. Wheels in Cave Temples: Yulin, Gansu, Tenth Century *163*
8. Wheels in Esoteric Temples: Tabo, Western Tibet, Eleventh Century *193*
9. Wheels for Pilgrims: Baodingshan, Sichuan, Thirteenth Century *221*
10. Conclusions *239*

Character Glossary *273*
Bibliography *278*
Index *309*

Preface and Acknowledgments

In art as in life, modest insight into one's motivations is acheived only gradually. In my case, I had begun working on the research for this book for several years before I figured out the experience that probably, in the troubled mist of adolescence, ignited my interest in the subject. My first encounter with a painting of the wheel of rebirth occurred not in a modern Tibetan temple or in the remains of a medieval cave shrine in India or China, but rather when reading Kipling's novel *Kim*, published in 1901. The memories of the book I carried into adulthood had to do with the title character, the India-born British boy who can pass himself off now as a native, now as a sahib, and whose adventures in espionage along the Grand Trunk Road and the Himalayas are only briefly, it seems, interrupted by the boredom and discipline of formal schooling.

What I had forgotten was that the image of the wheel of rebirth plays a key structuring role in the novel. Kim's spiritual teacher, the Teshoo Lama, uses the wheel of life constantly as a metaphor for the meaning of life. The *lama* invokes the wheel as a way of making sense out of the tide of events. In the Buddhist theory of reincarnation, each life is followed by another lifetime, and the turning of the wheel—one painful rebirth after another—is fueled by the egocentric propensities of anger, lust, and ignorance. The lama seeks release from the wheel, liberation from the cycle of rebirth. He is also searching for a mythical river, associated with the historical Buddha, that has curative powers. Near the beginning of the book the lama explains his quest to one of the many wise white men who appear in Kipling's unrepentantly rosy picture of British colonialism, the Keeper of Images at the "Wonder House," the Lahore Museum (a position that Kipling's father in fact held for many years). The two men chat amiably about the spread of the Buddhist religion across Asia, and the curator trots out the latest gems of Buddhological scholarship, books tracing the route of ancient travelers between India and China. Although the lama appreciates these scientific advances, he distinguishes between the curator's book knowledge and the kind of religious journey in which he, the lama, is engaged. He explains, "Your scholars, by these books, have followed the Blessed Feet in all their wanderings; but there are things which they have not sought out. I know nothing—nothing do I know—but I go to free myself from the wheel of things by a broad and open road."[1]

1. Kipling, *Kim*, p. 57.

I have to confess, at the very beginning of this book, that my current sympathies lie more with the scholars than the lama. Like the nineteenth-century founders of fields like Buddhist studies, I try to reassemble sources written in a variety of languages that most Buddhists would not command and to draw links between paintings spread farther across Asia than most traditional pilgrims could visit in a lifetime. Since the eighteenth century, the discipline of comparative philology has attempted to account for the dissemination of linguistic forms and religious ideas across cultures. Such breadth of coverage is surely fitting in the case of the wheel of rebirth, pictures and stories of which are found throughout the Buddhist world, from western India to the oases of central Asia, the Himalayas, China, Tibet, and more recently to Japan, Southeast Asia, and the West. As a researcher in the modern field of religious studies, I would also celebrate the recent divorce between studying and practicing religion. As the lama suggests, the interest of the practitioner is liberation from the cycle of painful rebirth, while mine as investigator is the creation of an edifying and accurate picture of Buddhism as a pan-Asian, international force. At the same time, I have to acknowledge that this very bifurcation, between the methods of the believer and those of the scholar, is itself a recent invention with its own set of problems and pretensions. While conforming to the canons of academic study and utilizing maps, history, context, translations, analysis, and so on, I also hope to say something important or essential about Buddhism. Questions of meaning and significance are as central to the humanities as they are to traditional religious undertakings. The two quests are closer than I would like to admit.

I have been influenced by *Kim* in another way as well, I think. The lama not only conceives of himself through the image of the wheel, he also produces paintings of the wheel, which he uses to instruct others. The lama employs a picture of the wheel he has drawn as a standardized teaching device. Kipling portrays the lama's tutelage of Kim this way:

> He drew from under the table a sheet of strangely scented yellow Chinese paper, the brushes, and slab of Indian ink. In cleanest, severest outline he had traced the Great Wheel with its six spokes, whose center is the conjoined Hog, Snake, and Dove (Ignorance, Anger, and Lust), and whose compartments are all the Heavens and Hells, and all the chances of human life. . . . Few can translate the picture-parable; there are not twenty in all the world who can draw it surely without a copy: of those who can both draw and expound are but three.[2]

Kipling's character of the lama alerts us, then, to the importance of the pictorial in the dissemination of religion. Rather than focusing merely on texts, I try in this book to devote more room than usual to visual evidence and the activity of preaching. The field of Buddhist studies has been moving in this direction for some time now. The alleged logocentrism of earlier models has been supplemented more recently by an interest in ritual, symbols, and artifacts. Where studies of texts, schools, and pure con-

2. Ibid., p. 240.

cepts once predominated, we now see more books treating texts as material objects, icons as subjects of Buddhist devotion, and monasteries as educational institutions. Although I lack the talents of a novelist, I follow Kipling's lead in attending wherever possible to the practice of painting, and I ask questions about who draws, who preaches, who observes, and who listens.

The lama's wheel of life is not only a metaphor and a pictorial practice, it also constitutes, in a literal way, the decisive rupture in the novel. Toward the end of the book Kim has rejoined the lama and they travel together up to Ladakh and the Himalayas. Dedicated again to the service of his guru, Kim is also surreptitiously shadowing a pair of Russian spies whose maps and letters he will soon succeed in stealing. When the two parties first meet, the Russians ask the lama to explain the wheel of rebirth. The lama obliges, removing the treasured drawing from his robes and beginning his sermon. The Russians are so taken with the lama's rendering that they ask to buy the painting from him. He objects, since the painting is a vessel of the Dharma—in Kipling's depiction the lama calls it "the Written Word"—and it is used only for instructing disciples. The Russian spy, as a representative of evil imperial designs (as opposed to the benign, civilizing aims of the British), waves some cash at the religious object, but the lama still resists. Finally the Russian simply grabs at the painting, tearing it almost in two. After defiling the holy teaching, he strikes the lama, and a nighttime tussle and long flight ensue. In ignorance, the Russians are sidetracked through a hundred mountain villages by one of Kim's fellow spies. The dénouement of the Russians' political failure is paralleled by the unfolding story of the lama's spiritual victory. The rip in the painting of the wheel is a signal to the lama. He interprets it as a sign that his life hangs simply by a thread and that he needs to reorient his search and look on the plains rather than in the mountains for the Buddha's river. Ultimately, he is successful:

> "And for my merit that I had acquired I gain yet another sign." He put his hand in his bosom, and drew forth the Wheel of Life. "Look! I considered this after I had meditated. There remains untorn by the idolator no more than the breadth of my fingernail."
>
> "I see."
>
> "So much, then, is the span of my life in this body. I have served the Wheel all my days. Now the Wheel serves me. But for the merit I have acquired in guiding thee upon the Way, there would have been added to me yet another life ere I had found my River. Is it plain, *chela?*"
>
> Kim stared at the brutally disfigured chart. From left to right diagonally the rent ran—from the Eleventh House where Desire gives birth to the Child (as it is drawn by Tibetans)—across the human and animal worlds, to the Fifth House—the empty House of the Senses. The logic was unanswerable.[3]

3. Ibid., pp. 310–11.

Kipling's portrayal of the rupture in the lama's painting captures a crucial insight into how paintings of the wheel of rebirth work in the history of Buddhism. In *Kim* as in Buddhist mythology, on the one hand people are bound to what the wheel represents, while on the other hand the wheel as representation is supposed to free people from that which it represents. My book takes up this question of the relationship between the viewer, the image, and what the image is supposed to represent. The tale in *Kim* also hints that we as interpreters can best make sense of pictures—and rips in pictures—by telling stories. This is what the lama (and through him, Kipling) does: he makes the tear redemptive by weaving it back into the quest that guides the narrative. My point is more than the simple claim that Buddhologists need to consider both pictorial and textual evidence. Rather, I am suggesting that we ought to attend to the hermeneutical issues raised by pictures and stories about pictures in Buddhism. In this process—again as *Kim* shows—a lot of evidence is, literally, torn in two or fragmentary, and much of the story involves a political subplot.

Although in the foregoing ways I adopt the orientalist pose, in other respects I am committed to the values of the more recent turn in Buddhist studies. I am interested more in exemplary than in comprehensive history. That is, I structure this book around examples of the wheel of rebirth that I believe are particularly instructive about Buddhism. I leave out a lot of evidence, particularly in Tibet and Japan after the medieval period and in modern Southeast Asia. In this sense, I try to make the book a historian's version of the kind of multi-sited fieldwork now practiced in American anthropology. Rather than defining my topic as Buddhism as a whole or a specific Buddhist culture, I intentionally choose the specific site as my unit of analysis. Buddhist studies has already made progress in moving from generalizations about Buddhism to considering Buddhist texts and practices in particular places like ancient India, medieval Japan, and modern Thailand. In this book I try to go one half step farther, treating "India" (and "China" and "Tibet" and the like) as needing explanation instead of as an unchanging political essence that explains why Buddhism here is unlike Buddhism there. I hope to contribute to a new picture of Buddhism as well as to a new picture of the meaning of pictures in Buddhism.

Most of my goals are spelled out more programmatically where the reader would expect, in the first and last chapters of this book. I have used a variety of methods and -ologies to explain the significance of representations that were spread across different cultural areas, in many of which I do not specialize. I am overreaching, and I hope that those whose toes I step upon will view these forays indulgently.

This book was originally conceived as one chapter in a longer book based on a seminar I taught at the École Pratique des Hautes Études, Quatrième Section, Sciences Historiques et Philologiques, in 1996. Thanks to a generous invitation from Jean-Pierre Drège, that course, entitled "La mort dans le bouddhisme chinois," helped me to narrow my topic to the wheel of rebirth and to expand my coverage beyond the borders of China. Snejana Vassiliev helped prepare a French translation of my lectures, in which I learned, at the first meeting, to distinguish clearly between *la mort* and *l'amour*. My colleagues in Paris—Li-ying Kuo, Christine Mollier, Richard Schneider, and Eric

Trombert—provided help and collaboration. Patricia B. Ebrey invited me to present the growing manuscript at a meeting of her seminar on visual culture when she was Visiting Faculty at the Institute for Advanced Study in 1998, and I received encouraging responses from Victor H. Mair, Nancy Schatzman Steinhardt, and Angela F. Howard. During 1998 Walter Spink graciously allowed me to join his site seminar at Ajaṇṭā (Maharashtra, India), where he introduced me to the joys of archaeology and architecture. In 1999 I joined a three-year Luce Foundation–funded research project organized by Sarah E. Fraser that brought together six American and six Chinese scholars. For one month we conducted research together in Sichuan and Gansu and then two years later reported back to one another at a conference in Beijing. The assistance I received from my Chinese colleagues (Ding Mingyi, Fan Jinshi, Hao Chunwen, Ma Shichang, Peng Jinzhang, Rong Xinjiang, Sun Xiushen), drawn from the fields of art, archaeology, and history, was invaluable. The American-based scholars on the team (Wendi L. Adamek, John Kieschnick, Wei Yang, and Brook Ziporyn) offered advice and support all along the way. During further field research in 2001 at the Yulin caves (Gansu, China), Ma Xiwu of the Dunhuang Research Institute was extremely helpful. At Kizil and Kumtura (Xinjiang, China), Li Li and Su Huiming worked with me and opened important doors for several days. In 2001 Wu Hung and Anthony C. Yu arranged a series of lectures at the University of Chicago. Their hospitality and feedback, plus that of Matthew Kapstein, Steven Collins, and Wendy Doniger, are much appreciated. In 2002 the Venerable Sheng-yen and Ch'en Hsiu-lan of the Chung-Hwa Institute of Buddhist Studies in Taiwan were wonderful hosts for a stint of research there. In 2003 Shimazono Susumu invited me to a stimulating conference, "The Co-Existence of the Dead and the Living," at Tokyo University, where I learned much from discussions with him, James H. Foard, Ikezawa Masaru, Osano Shigetoshi, Fabio Rambelli, Gaynor Sekimori, and Sueki Fumihiko. The Pro-Vice-Chancellor of the University of Hong Kong, C. F. Lee, graciously invited me to deliver a series of lectures in January 2004 at the Centre of Buddhist Studies, where I received much help from the Venerable Jingyin, Liu Ming Wood, Wang Bangwei, and Yao Zhihua.

Various draft chapters of this book were presented at several institutions, where I received helpful advice from many colleagues: Donald S. Lopez Jr., Robert H. Sharf, and Luis Gomez at the University of Michigan; Jo-shui Chen, Fu-shih Lin, and Mu-chou Poo at the Institute of History and Philology at the Academia Sinica in Taiwan; James Benn, Jinhua Chen, Phyllis Granoff, and Eugene Yuejin Wang at a conference held at the University of British Columbia; Ryuichi Abe, Wendi L. Adamek, Robert Hymes, Robert A. F. Thurman, Serinity Young, and Chün-fang Yü at Columbia University; Enomoto Fumio, Funayama Toru, Kominami Ichirō, Mimaki Katsumi, and Takata Tokio at Kyoto University; Robert Duquenne, Hubert Durt, François Lachaud, and Sylvio Vita at the Italian School of East Asian Studies and the École française d'Extrême-Orient in Kyoto; Ho Puay-Peng, Lai Chi Tim, Jenny Fong-suk So, Tam Wai Lun, and Franciscus Verellen at the Chinese University of Hong Kong. John Blazejewski contributed many of the photos in this book, often at short notice. The staff at the Princeton University East Asian Library, Marquand Library, and Interlibrary Loan were particularly cooperative. Others who have provided important advice along the way are Huaiyu Chen, Paul Copp, Lorraine Fuhrmann, Dorothy Ko, Cathy Cheng Mei Ku, Lothar Ledderose, Rob Linrothe, Yang Lu, Susan Naquin (who loaned me her childhood copy of *Kim*), Daniel L. Overmyer, Ruth Rogaski, Louisa Schein, Jacqueline I. Stone, and Jeffrey L. Stout.

Many people came to my assistance in the final stages of preparing this book for publication. John S. Strong wrote what every author looks for in a reader's report: sympathetic, thoughtful comments and dozens of suggestions for improvement. Gregory Schopen offered ten handwritten pages of meticulous, insightful comments on the book manuscript and shared several of his unpublished translations from the Sanskrit and Tibetan. Walter Spink and Monika Zin provided invaluable comments on the Ajaṇṭā material, and Bryan Cuevas, Deborah Klimburg-Salter, and Christian Luczanits helped tremendously with the chapter on western Tibet. All of their help saved me from many gaffes, although I am sure that many remain. Sorat Tungkasiri created several of the drawings and provided technical assistance with many of the illustrations. Tsering Wangyal Shawa offered expert help with historical geography and drew all of the maps. Several people and institutions were particularly generous in sharing illustrations; I am especially grateful to Lionel Fournier, Sadakane Keiji, Lucy L. Lo, and the Rubin Museum of Art. I extend my thanks to everyone else who helped me secure illustrations: Lisa Arcomano, Dina Bangdel, Holly Frisbee, Cory Grace, John C. Huntington, Ruth Janson, Laurel Kendall, Anne Rose Kitagawa, Elizabeth Knight, Michael W. Meister, U. S. Moorti, David Nelson, Angela Powell, Vandana Sinha, Janet Temos, Verena Widorn, and Leela Aditi Wood. At the University of Washington Press, Michael Duckworth's enthusiasm for this project has helped to keep it going, John Stevenson's oversight of production has made it look a lot better than I could have imagined, and Julie Van Pelt improved the final version with thoughtful and meticulous copyediting.

Any project that takes as long to complete as this one depends on input and support from nearly all of one's scholarly interlocutors and many of one's students. I hope members of this large group will not be offended if I do not name all of them individually.

For time and money I am grateful to two successive deans of the faculty at Princeton University. Amy Gutman gave me permission to teach in Paris at the beginning of the project, and Joseph Taylor helped fund a semester of writing near the end. The Chiang Ching-kuo Senior Scholars Fellowship provided a generous grant for a semester's leave, and Princeton's University Committee on Research in the Humanities and Social Sciences awarded crucial funding for travel, research assistance, photographic materials, and publication costs. I also wish to express my appreciation to the University Seminars at Columbia University for their help in publication. Material in this work was presented to the University Seminar on Buddhist Studies.

Most of all I have my family and friends to thank for their support and patience over the years. My three children have put up, seemingly without complaint, with my early morning hours, my need for quiet, and my summer research trips. My son,

Walker, in particular, shared adventures in Xinjiang while battling a dogged case of pneumonia that was eventually cured in Chengdu, thanks to the hospitality of our friend Jiang Zhaohui and his staff. I completed two large chunks of this book in the semitropical comforts of the Newman household on Yangmingshan, in Taipei, Taiwan. Charlie and Snow Newman provided great company, writing space, a cone of silence, mangoes, and good coffee for what remains, at base, a lonely endeavor. My greatest fortune in this project is to have had the support and inspiration of my wife, Wei Yang. She has supported me through hardship, shared her knowledge and ways of thinking throughout the book, placed her own research behind mine, and has been instrumental in building a life together that makes it possible to write books like this one.

Reinventing the Wheel

PLATE 2. Wheel of rebirth. Cotton painting. Tibet, nineteenth century. Shelley and Donald Rubin, item no. 78, acc. no. P1994.3.6.

Chapter 1

Picturing Life and Death as a Wheel

When Buddhists talk about what happens at the end of a person's life, one of the things they say is that until final deliverance is achieved, each death is followed by a rebirth. From this perspective, to conceive of death as a terminus is to commit a category mistake, to confuse the temporary suspension of an inauthentic life with the stillness of true cessation. Instead, the end of any single lifetime leads inevitably to the beginning of another. More specifically, the Buddhist theory states that forty-nine days after death, the person assumes bodily form again as a sentient being. Whether pleasantly as a god, demigod, or human being, or less happily as an animal, hungry ghost, or resident of hell, the person returns to that state characterized by impermanence, suffering, and lack of enduring substance. What I am calling the Buddhist notion of death thus stands in contrast to the scientific understanding, which views death as a unique event marking a permanent ending. What modern secularism prefers to think of as life is simply one small part of a broader process of re-death. The Buddhist notion of death is, then, inseparable from the idea of rebirth—but the opposite formulation is equally true.

In the language of Indian Buddhism the traditional term for the unenlightened life is *saṃsāra*, the verbal form of which (*saṃ√sri*) means "to flow together with," "to go about, wander or walk or roam through," "to walk or pass through (a succession of states)," or "to undergo transmigration." The most common Chinese translation of the word saṃsāra, *shengsi*, literally "birth and death," emphasizes the inescapable linkage of birth, death, and rebirth. The only possible release from the succession of unpleasant lives is an exceptional death, one that brings an end to egoism and clinging. In some forms of Buddhism the standard term for that salvation is *nirvāṇa*, literally "blowing out" or "extinction." Unlike mundane death, which merely projects the sufferer into a new mode of being within saṃsāra, the achieving of nirvāṇa means that recurrent death has been conquered. The historical Buddha, Śākyamuni, was one of the few individuals to break the cycle of transmigration. Buddhism claims that through his insight into the nature of spiritual thirst, the Buddha's death was utterly unlike that of unenlightened humans. Rather than leading to further incarnation, his death

Fig. 1.1. Parinirvāṇa scene. Statue and wall painting. South and west walls, Mogao Cave 158, late Tang dynasty. The Lo Archive.

was a definitive release from the pain and suffering of saṃsāra. That is why representations of the Buddha's passage into nirvāṇa portray him lying beatifically on his side. The atypical finality of his death also explains why some of his disciples grieve at the prospect of his passing. Figure 1.1 is a late Tang-dynasty (618–907) cave temple in the Mogao Caves at Dunhuang (Gansu) in northwestern China. It is dominated by a long statue of Śākyamuni entering nirvāṇa. Figure 1.2 is a detail of the scene painted on the wall by the Buddha's head. While the Buddha himself is dying in a calm, enlightened fashion, his disciples remain attached to their emotions. Kāśyapa, in this rendition, contorts his face in anguish.

The Buddha's achieving of true rest means that he will never again, at least in human embodiment, grace his followers with his wisdom or holy presence. Precisely how to conceive of the Buddha's post-nirvāṇic inaccessibility—or even whether to accept it—is a topic of heated debate in Buddhist circles. Many forms of Buddhist practice imply that he is not so absent after all: relics and *stūpas* (reliquary mounds or structures) are treated as the Buddha himself, icons do not so much represent as they do embody the Buddha, and books of the Dharma (the Law) are understood as the Buddha's body in literary form.

One of the most common ways to stress the repetitive nature of birth and death within saṃsāra is to use the metaphor of a wheel or circle. In historical perspective, this usage might predate the development of Buddhism in ancient India.[1] Early Buddhism inherited much of its cosmology, including the doctrine of *karma* (literally,

1. Sources like the *Maitrāyaṇīya Upaniṣad* invoke the expression "wheel of saṃsāra" (*saṃsāracakra*), although this particular text may well have been influenced by Buddhism. See Monier-Williams, *Sanskrit-English Dictionary*, p. 1119b–c; and van Buitenen, *Maitrāyaṇīya Upaniṣad*.

Fig. 1.2. Disciples distraught at passing of Buddha, detail of parinirvāṇa scene. Wall painting. South wall, Mogao Cave 158, late Tang dynasty. Dunhuang wenwu yanjiusuo, *Dunhuang Mogaoku*, vol. 4, pl. 64.

"action") and the goal of liberation from repeated rebirth, from the Brahmanical religion (an early form of what was later called Hinduism) dominant in that day. Nowadays modern Buddhists still invoke the metaphor of the wheel, often pointing to a picture of a wheel like the one in plate 1, a nineteenth- or early twentieth-century painting, about four feet in length, from Tibet.[2]

The construction of the Tibetan painting marks off a contrast between saṃsāra, the realm of birth and death depicted inside the wheel, and liberation from saṃsāra, suggested by the figures outside the wheel. The five sectors of the wheel define the five or six forms of life in which sentient beings can be reborn (represented in some versions of the wheel as Five Paths and in others as Six Paths). The top two segments of the painting (see fig. 1.3) represent the happier forms of rebirth. The top left segment actually pictures two forms of life, gods and demigods (called *asuras*), sharing one space. Gods are placed at the top right corner of the segment, where a musician stands in a palace and strums a lute. This figure is an incarnation of the Buddha, who assumes this form when he preaches to the gods; the gods' attentions are devoted to the pleasures of song and dance throughout their long lifetime in heaven. To the left of the palace, in the leaves of a tree, an army of gods engages in battle with warriors below. The warriors are *asuras*, hoping to gain entrance to heaven. One point of their contention is the right to enjoy the fruit growing on the large, magical *parijāta* tree whose roots, according to the picture, are in the realm of the demigods. A Buddha figure also appears in the realm of the *asuras*, in a green-skinned incarnation. Human beings are located in the top right segment of the painting. Their realm is dominated spatially by the large seated Buddha, who manifests himself as Śākyamuni. He is surrounded by several figures, monks and laypeople, in supplication. To the left is a monastery building with a procession of monks in front. At bottom right is another building representing the woes of life as a human. Inside the building a woman is lying down, perhaps dead. In front of the building a man offers an animal's heart to someone else, perhaps a practitioner of Bön or shamanism. On the left side of the human realm there is a procession of upper-class people, perhaps on their way to a wedding under a canopy. Their presents are stacked on a table. The highest-ranking couple is dressed in green, and their guest of honor, standing in front of them, is clearly cast as

2. One of the earliest Western studies of the wheel in Tibet is L. Augustine Waddell, "Buddhist Pictorial Wheel of Life"; see also his "Buddha's Secret from a Sixth-Century Pictorial Commentary and Tibetan Tradition." Other important studies of the wheel of rebirth include: Batt and Baird, *"Sipa Khorlo" (The Tibetan Wheel of Life)*; Dunnington, *Tibetan Wheel of Existence*; Govinda, *Foundations of Tibetan Mysticism*, pp. 234–47; Gyatso, *Meaning of Life*; Khantipalo, *Wheel of Birth and Death*; Lauf, *Tibetan Sacred Art*, pp. 140–43; Przyluski, "La roue de la vie à Ajaṇṭā"; Schlingloff, "Das Lebensrad in Ajaṇṭā"; idem, *Studies in the Ajaṇṭā Paintings*, pp. 167–74; Snellgrove, *Indo-Tibetan Buddhism*, 1:14–19; and Tharchin, *King Udrayana and the Wheel of Life*. Published examples of modern Tibetan paintings of the wheel are quite numerous. See, for example, Eracle, *L'art des thanka et le bouddhisme tantrique*, pp. 34–49; Essen and Thingo, *Die Götter des Himalaya*, vol. 1, pl. 28; Reynolds et al., *Catalogue of the Newark Museum Tibetan Collection*, vol. 3, *Sculpture and Painting*, cover illustration and pp. 195–96; Olschak, *Mystic Art of Ancient Tibet;* and the Web site of the Himalayan Art Project, http://www.himalayanart.org, search under "Wheel of Life."

FIG. 1.3. Top two segments of wheel of rebirth. Cotton painting. Tibet, nineteenth century. Rubin Museum of Art, item no. 65356. Photography: Bruce White.

a Westerner, dressed in hunting attire. These are the upper three paths of rebirth, here split between two segments of the wheel.

The three unfortunate forms of rebirth are depicted in the lower half of the painting (see fig. 1.4). Hell beings are placed at bottom center, undergoing a grisly assortment of tortures as retribution for deeds committed in previous lives. The punishments reflect the rich mythology in Buddhism concerning the netherworld. Nude and scantily clad figures are tormented by various demons. Some are shown in cold mountains and ravines, while others have nails sticking out of their bodies or are stabbing each other. A demon saws off a man's head, while guards stir two hot cauldrons full of sinners. The master of the infernal regions, King Yama, stands at the top left of the segment. His skin is red and his hair is adorned with five skulls. A Buddha with blue skin appears here, offering inmates the only chance of escape to a higher realm. To the left are forests of knives and people floundering in pools of filth. Only slightly less horrific are the sufferings of the hungry ghosts in the bottom right segment. In Buddhist lore hungry ghosts (*pretas*) have necks as thin as needles, so their stomachs swell due to hunger. This painting portrays their bodies almost like cocoons. Even the royalty among the ghosts, like the woman seated under a canopy at left, suffer from hunger. A Buddha manifests himself in the center of the scene, and sufferers receive further help from the *bodhisattva* pictured at top right. The lower left segment contains animals. Watery realms and their inhabitants are shown at the bottom of the segment. The royal figure standing in the sea under a canopy is evidently a princess of the *nāgas*,

FIG. 1.4. Lower three segments and center of wheel of rebirth. Cotton painting. Tibet, nineteenth century. Rubin Museum of Art, item no. 65356. Photography: Bruce White.

the giant, serpentlike creatures who rule the sea in Buddhism. Land animals are portrayed above, and yaks can be seen in the mountains at the top of the segment. A green-skinned Buddha appears at left.

It is no accident that a circle is used to lay out the Six Paths of rebirth. Arranging the six forms of life within a wheel relativizes the distinctions between them. The circular design suggests that gods and other inhabitants of the top part of the wheel are no different from those who suffer at the bottom: to the extent that their status is impermanent, they suffer, and after death they will be reborn in another body. The segments of the wheel specify in graphic detail the many possible forms of rebirth one could take in the next life.

Fig. 1.5. Twelve Conditions, wheel of rebirth. Cotton painting. Tibet, nineteenth century. Rubin Museum of Art, item no. 65356. Photography: Bruce White.

The six realms are surrounded by the outermost ring of the circle, divided into twelve segments. These twelve links depict stages in the life and death of the individual (see fig. 1.5 and table 1). The twelve stations are known as the Twelve Conditions or Underlying Factors (*nidānas*) in the cycle of dependent origination (or conditioned coarising, *pratītyasamutpāda*). At the one o'clock position there is a blind man, representing ignorance, which causes deluded beings to mistake the miseries of existence for true happiness. Proceeding clockwise, a potter comes next, his shaping of pots a symbol for actions that produce perishable objects (dispositions). The results of such actions lead to the playful, desire-driven monkey in the next segment, representing consciousness. Around four o'clock is a boat with a man inside, showing how name and form propel individual personalities through life. Next is a series of six houses, the six doors of which serve as a metaphor for the six sense organs that allow discrete perceptions to pass into the human body. Just before the six o'clock position is a couple

Table 1. Representations of causation. Twelve or Eighteen Conditions (*nidāna*) of dependent origination

List of 12 in the Vinaya (chapter 2)	List of 18 in the Vinaya (chapter 2)	Symbol in the Vinaya (chapter 2)
1. ignorance *(avidyā, wuming)*		1. *rakṣa*
2. dispositions *(saṃskāra, xing)*		2. potter
3. consciousness *(vijñāna, shi)*		3. monkey
4. name and form *(nāma rūpa, ming se)*		4. person in boat
5. six sense fields *(ṣaḍāyatana, liuchu)*		5. six sense organs
6. contact *(sparśa, chu)*		6. people embracing
7. feeling *(vedanā, shou)*		7. people feeling pleasure
8. desire *(tṛṣṇā, ai)*		8. woman holding child
9. appropriation *(upādāna, qu)*		9. person with bottle
10. becoming *(bhava, you)*		10. Brahmā
11. birth *(jāti, sheng)*		11. woman giving birth
12. old age and death *(jāra maraṇa, lao si)*		12. corpse
	12a. old age *(jāra, lao)*	12a. old people
	13a. sickness *(vyādhi, bing)*	13a. ill people
	14a. death *(maraṇa, si)*	14a. corpse
	15a. sadness *(śoka, you)*	15a. person grieving
	16a. malady *(parideva, bei)*	16a. person weeping
	17a. pain *(duḥkha, ku)*	17a. person suffering
	18a. difficulty *(durmanas, nao)*	18a. person pulling camel

embracing, a symbol of the contact that occurs between sense organs and sense objects. That contact gives rise to the experience of feelings, represented crudely in the next frame by a picture of the arrow striking a person in the eye. In the Buddhist view, feelings inevitably produce desire, as shown in the next picture, a hungry man consuming a drink. Desire is inevitably followed by appropriation, symbolized next by a monkey plucking fruit from a tree. Appropriation gives rise to the perpetuation of life, and so just under the ten o'clock position stands a bride, representing the potential for new life, followed by a woman having a baby, representing birth. The last symbol, at twelve o'clock, is a corpse being carried in a funeral sack. It stands for death, and through causation it is connected to the following link in the chain, the state of ignorance from which all individuals begin life. Thus, the twelve symbols demonstrate not only how the stages of a single lifetime are connected, but also how deluded actions in this lifetime bear fruit in the next. As a sentient being, whatever rank one holds in the Six Paths , life and death are inexorably ruled by the twelve links in the chain of causation.

Grasping the entire wheel in his claws is the Great Demon of Impermanence (see plate 1). This painting figures the demon as Yama, the overseer of the hell regions in (*pratītyasamutpāda*).

PAINTING, NINETEENTH-CENTURY TIBET, RUBIN MUSEUM (CHAPTER 1; PLATE 1)	PAINTING AT AJAṆṬĀ CAVE 17 (CHAPTER 3; PLATE 8)	SCULPTURE AT BAODINGSHAN (CHAPTER 9, PLATE 14)
1. blind man	1. demon outside wheel?	1. *rakṣa*
2. potter	2. potter	2. potter
3. monkey	3. monkey	3. meditating figure?
4. person in boat	4. people in boat?	4. person in boat
5. empty houses	5. mask	5. plump meditating figure
6. couple embracing	6.	6. people embracing
7. arrow striking eye	7.	7. seated and standing figures?
8. woman offering drink	8.	8. woman holding child
9. monkey plucking fruit	9.	9. robber?
10. bride	10.	10. Brahmā
11. woman giving birth	11.	11. woman giving birth
12. corpse	12.	
		12a. old man (supported by young person)
	13a.	13a. medicine administered to sick man
	14a.	14a. mourner weeping over coffin
	15a. woman kneeling?	15a. crying person being consoled?
	16a. person consoling another?	16a. person entreating?
	17a.	17a. person carrying load on back?
	18a. person pulling camel	18a. person pulling horse

Buddhist mythology. Tibetan iconography usually depicts him in the form of a savage, reddish-brown-skinned demon. He sports five skulls in his hair, indicating his rank in the pantheon of wrathful deities as Lord of Death (gShin-rje), the chief god in the nether regions. His third eye watches over everything, and his ferociousness is made plain by his fangs, the long nails on his fingers and toes, his tail, and his tiger pelt. By placing all Six Paths under the control of Yama, who rules the lowest realm of rebirth, the painting shows how all forms of life, even the long years of pleasure enjoyed by the gods, are unavoidably subject to pain as punishment for one's deeds.

Other indications about the quality of life within the wheel are placed at the axis. The three animals are supposed to stand for the Three Poisons, or basic psychological afflictions: the chicken (or its variant, a pigeon) represents greed, the snake hatred, and the pig delusion. These three attitudes condition all life within saṃsāra. They are all intertwined, just as the animals are shown here biting each others' tails.

The picture also announces that sentient beings can find ways to escape from the oblivion of repeated death. Some solutions appear within the realm of birth and death itself. Surrounding the three animals at the axis is a ring with two sets of figures. The

hopeful figures are in the white semicircle at the left: they are exemplars, either sages and monks who inspire progress, or pilgrims who make progress on the path by engaging in piety. They are matched on the right side by the demon who drags sinners into the lower stations of life. The Six Paths of rebirth also contain mechanisms of salvation attuned to each path. The most active agent of salvation is the Buddha (sometimes portrayed as Avalokiteśvara Bodhisattva), who as we have seen displays himself in the form best suited to the needs of sentient beings in each of the Six Paths.

The clearest intimation of release from saṃsāra is painted outside the wheel of transmigration altogether (fig. 1.6). At the top, on either side of the wheel and beyond the clutches of the demon, float two formations of clouds. On the right stand Śākyamuni Buddha and his disciple Maudgalyāyana. The Buddha is pointing to the monument enshrined in the clouds at left, a wheel of the Dharma (*dharmacakra*) on a platform, underneath of which are two stanzas of verse announcing the inevitability of karmic retribution, the importance of renunciation, and the possibility of achieving nirvāṇa. The wheel of the Dharma has eight spokes, probably representing the Eightfold Path, the specific practices that all Buddhists are supposed to follow. All of these figures at the top of the painting not only represent a means of escaping from suffering; they also serve as a pictorial reminder of the origin myth for the painting of the wheel of rebirth itself. The myth (discussed in more detail below) relates that the Buddha instructed his followers to paint a wheel of rebirth on the outer walls of monasteries. The Buddha directed the monks to appoint a lecturer to use the painting as a teaching device for explaining the laws of karma and the benefits of Buddhist morality to anyone who visited the temple. The Buddha explained to his disciples precisely what

FIG. 1.6. Top section of wheel of rebirth. Cotton painting. Tibet, nineteenth century. Rubin Museum of Art, item no. 65356. Photography: Bruce White.

symbols to paint inside the wheel, and he ended by reciting the words of the poem that should be inscribed beside the picture.

The painting of the wheel of the Six Paths makes a sophisticated statement about birth and death. By placing all paths within one circle, it shows how death in one form of existence leads to rebirth in another. It chooses paradigmatic experiences and stereotypical social classes to define what life is like in each of the six destinies. While admitting that some paths are better than others, the painting proclaims that all conceivable species of existence are marked by suffering. The painful and transitory nature of life within the Six Paths is the opposite of deliverance, agents for which intrude within the circumference of the wheel and promise to lead its inhabitants to the purity of nirvāṇa.

The same iconographic elements in the wheel—the Three Poisons, the Six Paths, the Twelve Conditions, the Demon of Impermanence, plus the symbols of nirvāṇa outside the wheel—are found in similar paintings throughout the modern Buddhist world. Even limiting our sample to paintings made in Tibet and China between 1700 and 1900, considerable variation is possible. The sampling of modern paintings offered here will help us gain a better idea of how the basic image of the wheel works, what kind of variations in iconography are possible, and the different meanings that can be wrought in interpreting the wheel.

Plate 2 is a nineteenth-century painting from Tibet, especially striking for the deep blue color in the upper background and the artist's use of curving lines in portraying details. Unlike the first wheel introduced above, this painting contains no Buddhas or other figures stationed outside of Yama's grasp. Buddhas do appear in some realms

FIG. 1.7. Realm of *asuras*, wheel of rebirth. Cotton painting. Tibet, nineteenth century. Shelley and Donald Rubin, item no. 78, acc. no. P1994.3.6.

within the wheel of transmigration, but not among hell dwellers, animals, or *asuras*. Some details reflect the local conditions under which the painting was executed. In the realm of the *asuras*, for instance, two warriors hold firearms in battle (see fig. 1.7). The one at the top is portrayed in a particularly difficult, ineffective posture for shoot-

FIG. 1.8. Scene of corpse, wheel of rebirth. Cotton painting. Tibet, nineteenth century. Shelley and Donald Rubin, item no. 78, acc. no. P1994.3.6.

ing, as if the artist had never seen rifles used in battle. The portrayal of the Twelve Conditions is also different from that of the first painting. In plate 2, although the twelve symbols for each link are largely the same, their layout is different. The first link, the blind man representing ignorance, is placed not at one o'clock but at seven o'clock, and the rest proceed clockwise. The portrayal of the last link, at the five o'clock position, also adds a new detail (see fig. 1.8). This more complex rendering shows a man carrying a corpse in a bag on his back as he walks toward a cemetery. The method of burial follows Tibetan custom: a corpse is shown set upon a hill, with a bird of prey and another animal ready to consume it.

Other paintings simplify the subject in some areas while making it more complex in others. The eighteenth-century painting from eastern Tibet shown in plate 3, less than half the size of the larger paintings discussed above, presents only a few significant scenes in each of the Six Paths of rebirth. The human realm contains only four people seated in front of three houses, and in the path of hungry ghosts there are only four *pretas*, fire escaping from their mouths to indicate that everything they eat turns to flame. At the same time, however, the composition includes three large, soteriologically significant figures. Outside the wheel at top right is seated the Buddha of the future, Maitreya, while to the left is a standing image of the current Buddha, Śākyamuni.

Positioned beyond the clutches of Yama, they are immune from the effects of the Three Poisons. Underneath the wheel of life and death is an image of a bodhisattva whose help might be called upon by those within the wheel. He is Avalokiteśvara in his form possessing a white face and four hands.

A nineteenth-century painting from Tibet portrays a group of five deities at the top of the composition (see plate 4). The chief deity, in the center, is Vajradhara Buddha, with Amitāyus to his left and four-faced Avalokiteśvara to his right. Flanking these figures are two larger deities, Uṣṇīṣavijaya on the left and White Tārā on the right. The bottom of the painting depicts two bodhisattvas, Sitātapatra on the left and Vasudhāra on the right, who answer the worldly wishes of devotees. This painting also offers a different interpretation of the center of the wheel. In the middle of the wheel of rebirth stands Śākyamuni Buddha. His presence there might be an antidote to the effects of the Three Poisons, which are also shown (along with a fourth figure, a seated sage). The outer ring of the painting suggests its own reading of the Twelve Conditions as well. The artist has chosen to place the first link in the chain in the top left, midway between the nine and ten o'clock positions. The Twelve Conditions proceed clockwise, with some interesting deviations from the canonical norm. The careful observer of this painting will note, for instance, that the fourth and fifth symbols are interchanged: after the third link (the monkey, representing consciousness) at one o'clock, the artist has painted the fifth link (an empty house, representing the six sense fields), followed by the fourth link (a person in a boat, for name and form), after which the normal sequence is resumed. Also, in place of a bride for the tenth link, this painting uses a bird roosting atop two eggs (at eight o'clock) to represent becoming (see fig. 1.9). Some of the mechanical features of a wheel, technically speaking, are also absent in this portrayal. The Six Paths are separated not by the spokes of a wheel but by topographical features of the cosmos: clouds and mountains in the upper paths of rebirth, water and the spiked walls of hell at the bottom.

We know more about the conditions under which some of the paintings were executed. Plate 5 is an early twentieth-century painting on paper commissioned by Berthold Laufer (1874–1934), a sinologist and curator at the American Museum of Natural History in New York and the Field Museum of Natural History in Chicago. This specimen was probably painted for Laufer by a Chinese artist in Beijing. It attempts to follow the Tibetan conventions for the wheel of rebirth, but it combines them with Chinese traditions as well. Some of the painting's more unusual features are found at its center. Rather than a white semicircle and a black semicircle, the painting shows people being yanked down to the hell regions directly from the center of the wheel and figures ascending directly to the realm of the gods. The painting lacks any reference to the realm of hungry ghosts as well. The most Sinicized designs are clear at the bottom of the wheel. The segment depicting hell (see fig. 1.10) draws on early modern Chinese

PLATE 3. Wheel of rebirth. Cotton painting. Eastern Tibet, eighteenth century. Rubin Museum of Art, item no. 591, acc. no. F1997.40.10.

PLATE 4. Wheel of rebirth. Cloth painting. Tibet, nineteenth century. Brooklyn Museum of Art, L25.5, lent by Dr. and Mrs. Frank L. Babbott Jr.

FIG. 1.9. Scene of bird on eggs, wheel of rebirth. Cloth painting. Tibet, nineteenth century. Brooklyn Museum of Art, L25.5, lent by Dr. and Mrs. Frank L. Babbott Jr.

motifs. It includes a red pond of blood (bottom left) to which women are consigned on account of menstrual fluids and the blood that accompanies childbirth; a banner presented by a guard to King Yama that reads, in Chinese, "Failure to think about good and evil deeds"; and a karma mirror placed directly in front of King Yama that unerringly reflects the deeds a person committed in his or her previous lifetime. The last link in the chain of causation (for death, at twelve o'clock) also supplies a good clue to the artist's background. In addition to a man carrying a corpse on the way to a Tibetan-style burial, it shows a wooden Chinese coffin with the word for longevity (*shou*) inscribed on the end and a simple scene depicting a formal memorial ceremony, with mourners on one side of the coffin. This painting also appears to be unfinished, since the white background in the outer rim, containing the Twelve Conditions, is not filled in with paint. Perhaps it was left incomplete because of the error made in portraying the Twelve Conditions out of their normal order: the cycle begins with the first link at the seven o'clock position but inserts number five after that, and then continues with the rest in clockwise order.

PLATE 5. Wheel of rebirth. Cotton painting. Tibet, early twentieth century. American Museum of Natural History 70/11044. Courtesy of the Division of Anthropology, American Museum of Natural History.

Still other elaborations are apparent in another nineteenth-century painting from Tibet (see plate 6). In the ring surrounding the center of the painting, the artist has added Sanskrit seed syllables to the six figures heading upward and downward in the hierarchy of rebirth. Two *oṃ* syllables are placed at top and bottom, two *hūṃ* syllables at top left and bottom right, and two *āḥ* syllables at top right and bottom left. The artist has also added a thirteenth link to the chain of causation, a beckoning figure located between eleven and twelve o'clock. One of the most interesting innovations in this painting is the delineation of a pathway leading from hell—from under King Yama's throne, in fact—to the top right of the painting (see fig. 1.11). That extracurricular space is a triangular container for the pure land of Amitāyus Buddha. Its status as a pure land, close to but not synonymous with nirvāṇa, is made clear by the babies being born in the lotus flowers in front of Amitāyus. According to Buddhist scripture, those who are reborn in Amitāyus's land of bliss are invariably born as male babies, and one's mode of birth, through a flower, is utterly free of the pollution that accompanies normal human birth. Thus, although this Buddha hovers, enshrined in

FIG. 1.10 Lower half of wheel of rebirth. Cotton painting. Tibet, early twentieth century. American Museum of Natural History 70/11044. Courtesy of the Division of Anthropology, American Museum of Natural History.

FIG. 1.11. Pure land at top right of wheel of rebirth. Cotton painting. Tibet, early nineteenth century. American Museum of Natural History 70.0/6931. Courtesy of the Division of Anthropology, American Museum of Natural History.

his paradise, outside the wheel of saṃsāra, he helps to rescue beings from hell; monks and pilgrims can be seen making their way up the white path leading from hell to the pure land. The bottom of this painting is also remarkable (see fig. 1.12). On the left is a scene of women playing Chinese chess, mirrored by a merry band of skeletons engaged in a similar board game at right. The juxtaposition of these scenes may have been intended as a comment about or by the commissioner, or it may be a statement about the humorous, lively side of the afterlife; but without further information about the artist and precise provenance of the painting, it is impossible to know.

Modern Tibetan paintings of the wheel of rebirth are not confined to museums, of course. Tourists in Lhasa and Khatmandu encounter them often in souvenir shops, and they are available for purchase through a variety of magazines and Web sites catering to modern Buddhist practitioners. The wheel of rebirth is also rendered in other media than just silk and paper. The Tibetan teacher and artist Losang Samten (b. 1953) made a representation of the wheel using colored sand at the Philadelphia Museum

PLATE 6. Wheel of rebirth. Cotton painting. Tibet, early nineteenth century. American Museum of Natural History 70.0/6931. Courtesy of the Division of Anthropology, American Museum of Natural History.

FIG. 1.12. Bottom section of wheel of rebirth. Cotton painting. Tibet, early nineteenth century. American Museum of Natural History 70.0/6931. Courtesy of the Division of Anthropology, American Museum of Natural History.

of Art over a weeklong period in July, 1999.[3] The construction of the painting was carried out in public view, as was its ritual dissolution. On July 16, 1999, the painter disassembled the painting by collecting the sand into an urn, leading a procession to the banks of the Schuylkill River, and pouring the sand into the river (see plate 7 and fig. 1.13).

Portable paintings of the wheel of life and death have been used by itinerant storytellers (Tib.: *'das-log*, pron.: *délok*) in Tibet for at least the past few centuries. These lay entertainers, who base their tales on their near-death experiences, unfurl the *saṃsāracakra* (wheel of rebirth) and explain its figures to audiences throughout the Himalayas. This tradition, part narrative and part pictorial, may be the historical basis for the fictionalized account of the itinerant Tibetan lama in Kipling's novel *Kim*,

3. Photos of the sand painting, its construction, and dissolution are available online at http://www.philamuseum.org/exhibitions/exhibits/mandala (accessed Jan. 17, 2005).

PLATE 7. Losang Samten disassembling sand painting of the wheel of rebirth. Dispersion Ceremony of Sand Maṇḍala, Philadelphia Museum of Art, July 16, 1999. Photography: Lynn Rosenthal.

FIG. 1.13. Losang Samten dispersing sand from painting of the wheel of rebirth into the Schuylkill River. Dispersion Ceremony of Sand Maṇḍala, Philadelphia Museum of Art, July 16, 1999. Photography: Lynn Rosenthal.

discussed in the preface.[4] Roving teachers, many of them unordained women, used similar paintings in late medieval Japan. These "picture explainers" (Ja.: *etoki*) incorporated the wheel of rebirth into scrolls depicting the sacred history of important temples and pilgrimage centers.[5]

Whereas the examples of the wheel of rebirth discussed so far are quite impermanent or at least portable, most of the paintings examined in this book are stationary: they are wall paintings in Buddhist temples. For the modern paintings hung in museums, we have had to speculate about their creators and imagine the original conditions of their use. We have had to guess at the place and date of their composition. By contrast, although murals of the saṃsāracakra are usually anonymous, the overall design of the temples in which they are located provides important clues about how they were used and how their viewers understood them.

Stories invoked to explain the authenticity and origin of the painting of the wheel of rebirth have to be treated critically. Popular tradition in Tibet credits a long, impressive list of ancient Buddhist philosopher-heroes with transmitting the wheel of rebirth, beginning with Śākyamuni and extending through Nāgārjuna (second century), Asaṅga (sixth century), and Atiśa (eleventh century). In this account, the modern Tibetan painting is supposed to be a faithful reproduction of a tradition begun by the Buddha and transmitted accurately from Indian masters to Tibetan ones. Measured against the literary, archaeological, and artistic evidence, however, the veracity of this account, except perhaps concerning Atiśa, is highly unlikely. Paintings of the wheel of rebirth may not have been in existence in Nāgārjuna's day, and no early evidence links either him or Asaṅga to such paintings. Atiśa, an Indian teacher responsible for spreading a second wave of Buddhist teachings to western Tibet, may well have known the wheel of rebirth, since it was painted in some Tibetan temples as early as the late tenth century.[6]

The first surviving reference to the wheel of rebirth does not date from the time of Śākyamuni (fifth to fourth centuries B.C.E.). Rather, the earliest surviving origin myth, discussed at length in the next chapter, is contained in the canonical literature governing monastic life (*vinaya*) in India written in the second century C.E., many hundreds of years after the death of the Buddha. The story of the wheel's origin contained in the vinaya is itself anachronistic. The tale legitimates the painting of a wheel of rebirth on monastery walls by claiming that the historical Buddha himself ordained the practice. The narrative explains that one of the Buddha's disciples, Maudgalyāyana, was

---

4. See Pommaret, *Les revenants de l'au-delà dans le monde tibétain*, esp. p. 121, figs. 14, 24–25, 26–27. For Kipling's possible reliance on early Tibetological scholarship and the importance of Buddhism in the novel, see Leoshko, "What Is in *Kim*?," esp. pp. 66–73.

5. See Hagiwara, *Miko to bukkyō shi*, pp. 36–130.

6. For the traditional account of the transmission of the wheel of rebirth, see Waddell, "Buddhist Pictorial Wheel of Life," pp. 134–35. Modern Tibetans also associate the wheel with the story of King Udrāyaṇa (Rudrāyaṇa), a ruler who lived during the time of the Buddha; see Tharchin, *King Udrayana and the Wheel of Life*. The connection, however, is tenuous, since the content of Rudrāyaṇa's painting did not, according to legend, include the figure of a wheel or symbols of the Five Paths. For details, see chapter 4 in the present volume.

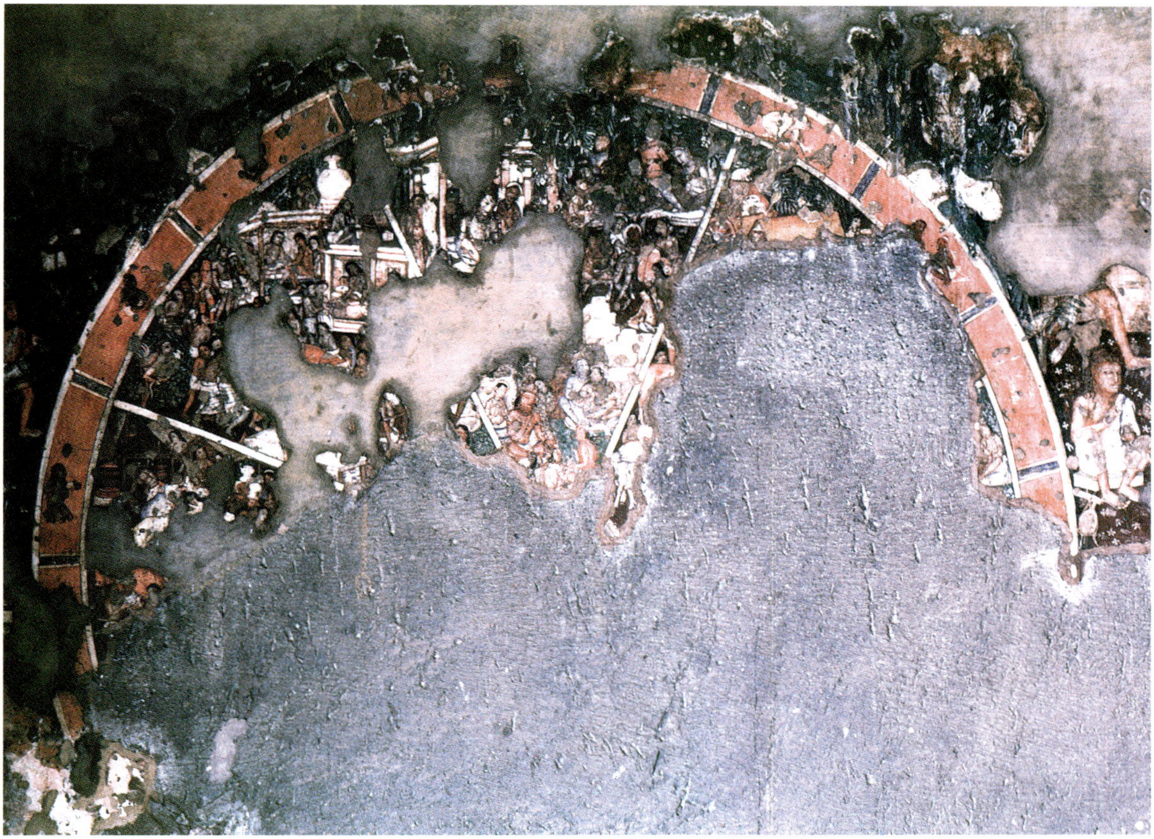

PLATE 8. Wheel of rebirth, Ajaṇṭā Cave 17. Wall painting, fifth century. Photo courtesy of Sadakane Keiji.

extremely successful in luring large crowds to hear about his adventures in the other world. Śākyamuni encourages the monks to propagate the doctrines of karma, rebirth, and morality. He insists that, rather than following Maudgalyāyana's example and relying on their own experience of the Six Paths , the other monks should paint a picture of the wheel of rebirth on the porch walls of Buddhist temples. Śākyamuni specifies how the painting is to be constructed, what symbols to portray, and which monks should be appointed to lecture about the image. This is the story that the figures in the top of the modern Tibetan painting, discussed above, appear to be enacting, with Śākyamuni directing Maudgalyāyana's attention to a wheel of Dharma (see fig. 1.6).

The Buddha's instructions occur in the vinaya of the Mūlasarvāstivāda sect, which may have been a subsect of the Sarvāstivāda. The original vinaya was written in Sanskrit sometime between the second and fifth centuries. It was translated into Chinese in the early eighth century and then into Tibetan in the early ninth century. Thus, in the Indian context, the story connecting the wheel of rebirth to the Buddha of the current world, Śākyamuni, provides no firm evidence about early Buddhism. (By

Plate 9. Meditating monk. Wall painting. Rear wall, Kumtura Cave 75, ca. ninth century. Xinjiang Weiwu'er zizhiqu wenwu guanli weiyuanhui et al., *Kumutula shiku*, pl. 178.

Facing page:

Plate 10. Wheels of rebirth. Wall painting, left wall, Kumtura Cave 75, ca. ninth century. Photography: Stephen F. Teiser.

Plate 11. Wheel of rebirth. Wall painting. Right wall of corridor, Yulin Cave 19, tenth century. Fan, *Dunhuang shiku*, p. 117.

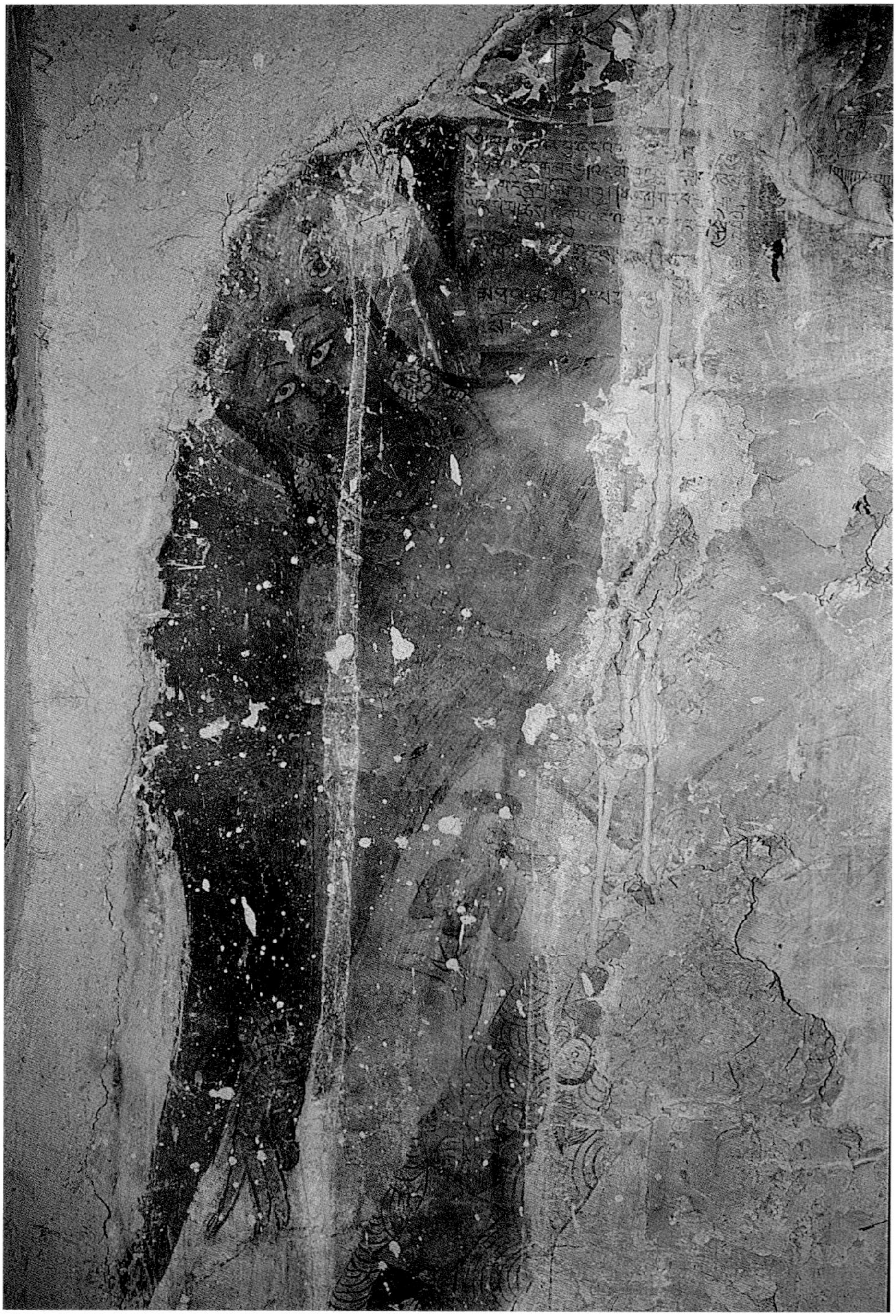

PLATE 12. Red deity outside wheel. Wall painting. East wall, entry hall. Tabo main temple, eleventh century. Photo courtesy of Christian Luczanits, 1994, Western Himalaya Archive Vienna.

PLATE 13. Wheel of rebirth. Wall painting. Entrance corridor, Pedongpo cave temple, twelfth century. Photo courtesy of Lionel Fournier.

extension, the Tibetan lineage proffered for the painting tradition offers even less certainty about the early Indian tradition.) Rather, the vinaya account reflects the concerns of the Buddhist community living in northwest India sometime between the second and fifth centuries, a time when donors probably underwrote the production of many temple paintings and monks preached to laypeople gathered at temples.

I would like to extend the general question of historical accuracy to virtually all versions of the wheel of rebirth. The problem, simply put, is that using the wheel as a metaphor for life and death is not universal in Buddhism. When did Buddhist sources first start using a wheel to symbolize saṃsāra? Early compilations of Buddhist scriptures, the Āgamas (Collections), include a short *sūtra* in which the Buddha invokes two metaphors to explain saṃsāra: a long night and a wheel. The untitled sūtra reads:

> Thus have I heard. Once the Buddha was in Śrāvastī in the garden of Anāthapiṇḍika. At that time the World-Honored One said to the various *bhikṣus* [monks], "Sentient beings turn about without beginning [or end] in the long night of birth and death [saṃsāra], without knowing the ultimate cause of suffering. It is as if, oh *bhikṣus*, there were a strong man turning a wheel with five sections. The wheel turns constantly, without stopping. In the same way, sentient beings turn about in the wheel of Five Paths [*pañcagati*], falling into the path of hell, of animals, of hungry

PLATE 14. Wheel of rebirth. Relief carving. Dafowan Niche 3, Baodingshan, Sichuan, thirteenth century. Bai Ziran, *Zhongguo Dazu shiku*, pl. 62.

ghosts, or of humans or gods. It turns constantly, without stopping. In the same way, they turn about without beginning [or end] in the long night of birth and death, without knowing the ultimate cause of suffering.

"Therefore, oh *bhikṣus*, you must practice like this: cut off all states of existence and do not cause them to increase."

After the Buddha preached this sūtra, all the *bhikṣus* heard what the Buddha preached, became joyous, and put it into practice.[7]

A wide range of Buddhist sources postdating the Āgamas compare reincarnation to the turning of a wheel. One late Mahāyāna sūtra emphasizes that rebirth in bodily form has potentially no beginning or end. In *The Mahāyāna Scripture on Previous Lives and the Contemplation of the Stages of Mindfulness*, the Buddha states: "Sentient beings circle round and round, assuming rebirth in the Six Paths / Just as the wheels of a cart have no beginning or end."[8] The verse reflects basic Buddhist teachings about the woes of sentient existence. It analyzes the geometrical properties of the wheel, suggesting that the lack of any definitive starting point or terminus characterizes saṃsāra as well. Other pieces of common wisdom draw attention to the regularity or inescapability of the revolving of the wheel. Their thinking is based on one of the natural phenomena invoked most commonly as an equivalent for a wheel, the sun. In one such text, the Buddha preaches about the importance of non-killing. This most fundamental of precepts is justified, he says, because the animals one consumes as a carnivore or the people one kills in warfare could have been one's relatives in a previous lifetime: "Sentient beings in the Three Realms circle back and forth through the Six Paths like the turning of the fire wheel [i.e., the sun]. Some become your parents, some your brothers, some your extended family. Since among the Three Realms there are none who are not your relatives, how could you develop the intention of taking life or acting violently?"[9]

We can delimit the use of the wheel to represent saṃsāra even further by comparing it to the wealth of non-wheel metaphors used for saṃsāra in early Buddhist sources. The cycle of birth and death is compared to a long night, as noted above. Other metaphors include a cloud, a mountain, the wilderness, a great ocean, a river, an abyss, a cliff, mud, a deep ravine, a tree, a forest, a prison, a walled city, a net or snare, an army, a fire, and a serious illness.[10] Some of these figures are features of the natural world. In deploying them as symbols for saṃsāra, Buddhist authors draw attention to their impermanence, their threatening nature, or the difficulty people have in passing through them. Like a wheel, some metaphors on this list (e.g., prison, nets,

---

7. Translation from *Za ahan jing* (*Saṃyuktāgama*), trans. Guṇabhadra (Qiunabatuoluo, 394–468), *T* no. 99, 2:243b. For another version, see *Bieza ahan jing* (*Saṃyuktāgama*), anon. (350–431), *T* no. 100, 2:844c.

8. Translation from *Dasheng bensheng xindi guan jing*, trans. Prajñā (Bore, 744–ca. 810), *T* no. 159, 3:302b.

9. Translation from *Guanfo sanmei hai jing* (**Buddhānusmṛti samādhisāgara sūtra*), trans. Buddhabhadra (Fotuobatuoluo, 359–429), *T* no. 643, 15:674b.

10. See the list of metaphors in Mori, *Bukkyō hiyū reiwa jiten*, pp. 232–35.

armies) are human contrivances, but they carry a stronger denotation of punishment, capture, or organized violence than does the symbol of the wheel. The wheel is the only figure used for saṃsāra that emphasizes the quality of repetition. The list is also instructive because it shows that a wheel is just one metaphor among many used to characterize the process of rebirth in the Buddhist world.

In none of these sources does Śākyamuni suggest that anyone paint a wheel to represent the Six Paths and the Twelve Conditions, but he does use the figure of the wheel to demonstrate the recurring nature of rebirth. The wheel metaphor, then, is relatively old and fairly well established in Buddhist sources, but even the oldest Buddhist canons are relatively recent. We have to remember how distant the earliest Buddhist literature remains from the time of the historical Buddha. Although the Āgamas (and their Pāli counterparts, the Nikāyas) were probably passed down in oral traditions for several hundred years, they were not cast in written form until roughly 50 B.C.E., about three hundred years after the death of the historical Buddha. And the current versions of these written texts, both Pāli Nikāyas and Chinese Āgamas, date from the fifth century C.E. at the earliest. Thus, we have no way of knowing—and good grounds for doubting—if the idea of painting a wheel to represent saṃsāra goes back to the time of the Buddha.

History does provide solid evidence of the use of the wheel metaphor before the first canonical account, but in those cases the wheel does not symbolize saṃsāra. Wheels were used to represent many different kinds of things in ancient India, preeminently the sun.[11] The regular course (*ṛta*) of the sun was symbolized by the metaphor of the wheel. Its progression across the sky was formulated discursively as the law of the Vedic god Varuṇa and later Viṣṇu. In concrete terms, wheels belonged to vehicles or they were weapons. The physiological or psychic centers of the body, spheres of existence, groups of people, and the artistic form known as *maṇḍala* were also analogized to wheels (*cakra*). Early Buddhist sources invoke the wheel or the wheel of a vehicle as a symbol for a wide range of doctrines: action, emptiness, the Four Proselytizing Deeds, the Twelve Conditions, the causal chain in general, the authentic vow, the world, the perpetuation of moments of consciousness, beginninglessness and endlessness, merit, seeing the path, the perpetuation of energy over lifetimes, sentient beings, wisdom, the Eightfold Noble Path, the afflictions, marklessness, transmigration, and the Dharma. Writing in the fifth century, Buddhaghosa defines the understanding of the wheel in the Theravāda tradition of South India and Śrī Lanka. He lists eight kinds of wheels recognized in Buddhist literature: the wheel of happiness, the wheel on the soles of the Buddha's feet, the wheel of a chariot, the wheel of postures, the wheel of charity, the wheel of the universal monarch, the wheel of the Dharma, and the wheel of torture.[12] Buddhaghosa does use two terms for the wheel of rebirth, *bhavacakra*

11. See Brown, *Dvāravatī Wheels of the Law*, pp. 160–66; Karunaratne, *Buddhist Wheel Symbol*; Malalasekera et al., *Encyclopaedia of Buddhism*, s.v. *cakra*, ; and Mori, *Bukkyō hiyū reiwa jiten*, s.v. *sharin*, *rin*, index pp. 593b, 591b.

12. Karunaratne, *Buddhist Wheel Symbol*, p. 1. Gurulogami adds four more: the discus, the wheel of the thunderbolt, the wheelwright's wooden wheel, and the wheel of life; ibid.

and saṃsāracakra, but in these cases he is not referring to a picture of a wheel that represents the Three Poisons and Five Paths. Instead, Buddhaghosa understands the wheel to refer to rebirth in general and the process of dependent origination in particular. He writes, "Ignorance is its hub because it is its root. Ageing-and-death is its rim because it terminates it. The remaining ten states of dependent origination are its spokes. . . ."[13]

The reasons why the wheel was used so frequently to symbolize the Dharma are probably overdetermined. Like the sun, the Law illuminates the world and moves with a regularity that can be made the measure of all things. Some portrayals of the Law as a wheel (*dharmacakra*) concern King Aśoka (r. 273–232 B.C.E.). In later mythology Aśoka is depicted as the ideal Buddhist monarch, one who ruled through righteousness; he was a wheel-turning king (*cakravartin rāja*), whose possession of the wheel of Dharma both proved and assured his legitimacy. In art one of the earliest representations of the wheel linked to Aśoka is the lion capital, perhaps constructed under his reign, dating from the third century B.C.E. and located in Sārnāth (Uttar Pradesh; see fig. 1.14).

The wheel of Dharma came to be associated more specifically with the Buddha in later Buddhist art, such as narrative scenes depicting events in the life of Śākyamuni. Figure 1.15, for instance, is a limestone relief carving from the railing around a stūpa from Amāravatī (Andhra Pradesh), dating from the second century C.E. It depicts gods and humans venerating the wheel, perhaps a stand-in for the Buddha himself. It was also around this time that the *dharmacakra* came to be a regular marker of the Buddha's first sermon.[14]

Above and beyond these uses of the wheel as a symbol representing a specific doctrine or event in Buddhism, the wheel was also used as a complex root metaphor for a variety of things in Buddhism. The various parts of the wheel (spokes, outer rim, hub, axle, etc.) could be separated analytically and then analogized to specific doctrines. In one early account of the Buddha's first sermon at Benares, the Buddha preaches: "The spokes of the wheel are the rules of pure conduct; justice is the uniformity of their length; wisdom is the tire; modesty and thoughtfulness are the hub in which the immovable axle of truth is fixed."[15] Functioning like the numerical lists of Buddhist teachings (Three Jewels, Four Noble Truths, etc.), the metaphor of the wheel was used as a mnemonic teaching device in early Buddhism.

This book takes seriously the multiplicity of meanings of representations of the wheel of rebirth in some of the premodern cultures of Asia. I am motivated by concerns with the history of Buddhism, with contemporary Buddhism, and with the academic field of Buddhist studies. One point I want to make is that cosmology—ideas about time and space, rebirth and causality—is central to Buddhism. I am thus implicitly

13. Ñyāṇamoli, *Path of Purification*, p. 207. See also the preceding passage on p. 207, and pp. 666–68.

14. See Karetsky, "First Sermon."

15. Translated from "First Sermon," in Stryk, *World of the Buddha*, p. 51.

Fig. 1.14. Lion capital. Stone sculpture. Sārnāth (Uttar Pradesh), third century B.C.E. Sārnāth Museum. Courtesy of the John C. and Susan L. Huntington Archive of Buddhist and Related Art.

FIG. 1.15. Worship of the wheel of Dharma (*dharmacakra*). Limestone relief carving, 62 × 53 × 12 cm. Amāravatī stūpa (Andhra Pradesh), second century C.E. Gift of the Government Museum, Madras, 21.1505. Photograph © 2006 Museum of Fine Arts, Boston.

arguing against modernist or "Protestant" understandings of Buddhism.[16] According to these recent forms of Buddhism, both Asian and Western, the teaching of Śākyamuni resembles a philosophy more than a religion. It is primarily concerned with mental cultivation and personal experience. It is ultimately about cultivating a certain kind of spirituality or psychological attitude. In the eyes of one of its most influential international interpreters, D. T. Suzuki (1870–1966), Buddhism is grounded in an ineffable experience that lies outside words and symbols. In Suzuki's view, "Buddhism

16. For assessments and critiques of the nineteenth-century construction of Buddhist "modernism," see Almond, *British Discovery of Buddhism*; Blackburn, *Buddhist Learning and Textual Prac-*

is nothing else than the inner life and spirit of the Buddha himself; Buddhism is the structure erected around the inmost consciousness of its founder."[17] Within such a paradigm, doctrines like the Six Paths are deemed inessential to the more important task of privately developing a mode of awareness that cannot be put into creedal form.

Modern Buddhists after Suzuki remain divided over the question of rebirth and the interpretation of Buddhist cosmology.[18] Some believers construe "science" and Buddhist beliefs as constituting two overlapping orders, and they admit that anything proven by science must be accepted by Buddhism. Responding to questions about modern physics, for instance, Tenzin Gyatso, the fourteenth Dalai Lama, states, "Buddhists believe in rebirth. But suppose that through various investigative means, science one day comes to the definite conclusion that there is no rebirth. If this is definitively proven, then we must accept it and we *will* accept it."[19] From this perspective, as science encroaches on the tradition-bound, dated forms of Buddhist belief such as the Six Paths of rebirth, modern Buddhists should jettison discredited theories and retreat to a core composed of safer, seemingly incontrovertible tenets. Reporting on a lecture by the Dalai Lama in 1972, Jeffrey Hopkins explains that the Dalai Lama discussed the structure of Buddhist hells and considered the possibility that traditional calculations of their size and location could be proven wrong by modern scientific investigation. The Dalai Lama said that Buddhists should not be disturbed by possible discrepancies. According to Hopkins, the Dalai Lama explained, "We do not celebrate Buddha as a land surveyor or maker of external maps. . . .The Dalai Lama said that what matters is whether Buddha was right about the Four Noble Truths, the Two Truths, and the like."[20]

The problem with such attempts to demythologize Buddhism is that elements of the rebirth cosmology pop up in unexpectedly crucial places. Some interpretations of the Four Noble Truths, for instance, explicate the first truth of *duḥkha* (suffering) by pointing to the pain beings undergo when they are reborn in the lower paths, and some explanations of the Two Truths stipulate that conventional truth (*saṃvṛti satya*) applies, in limited but valid ways, to the structuring of the universe in the Six Paths. Even the position of the Dalai Lama in the modern world is hard to disentangle from the traditional Buddhist worldview. The current Dalai Lama is believed to be the incarnation of the previous Dalai Lama, in a line stretching back fourteen generations. If rebirth from one lifetime to the next is jettisoned because it contradicts scientific discoveries, then traditional Tibetan ideas about divine rulership are also thrown into question. The Dalai Lama himself finds it difficult to deny the rebirth cosmology in

---

tice in Eighteenth-Century Lankan Monastic Culture; Gombrich and Obeyesekere, *Buddhism Transformed*; Holt, "Protestant Buddhism?"; Lopez, *Curators of the Buddha*; idem, *A Modern Buddhist Bible*, esp. pp. vii–xli; and Sharf, "Buddhist Modernism and the Rhetoric of Meditative Experience."

17. Suzuki, "Zen as Chinese Interpretation of the Doctrine of Enlightenment," p. 53.

18. The two standard positions are nicely summarized in a published debate between Stephen Batchelor (agnostic or against rebirth) and Robert Thurman (for) in Tworkov, "Reincarnation: A Debate, Batchelor v. Thurman." For more recent views on the subject, see Kornman, "Forum: The Law of Karma."

19. Tenzin Gyatso, *Answers: Discussions with Western Buddhists*, p. 25.

20. Hopkins, *Tantric Distinction*, p. 23, capitalization added.

its entirety. In one published conversation, a questioner suggests that ideas of transmigration must possess enough validity to justify the belief that the fourteenth Dalai Lama is a reincarnation of his predecessor. The questioner asserts that knowledge acquired in a previous lifetime must have helped the Dalai Lama to master the intricacies of Buddhist philosophy so quickly in this lifetime. The Dalai Lama responds, "In relatively little time and with little effort I am usually able to understand difficult subjects. This indicates that perhaps in my past lives I may have pursued some studies. Otherwise, I am just an ordinary person—like you—so that is that!"[21] On the one hand, he seems to be saying that in the cosmic scheme of things, his status is no more exalted than that of other human beings, a claim often made about Buddhas and other holy beings in Buddhism. On the other hand, he still makes use of the belief in rebirth in order to make sense of his unusual abilities.

Some modern Buddhists adopt a psychological reading of traditional cosmology. In this view, a symbol like a hungry ghost is supposed to be read as a concrete metaphor for a state of mind dominated by thirst that can never be satisfied. Francesca Freemantle writes, "Many Western Buddhists have difficulties with the concept of rebirth in the Six Realms, or even with rebirth at all. No one can prove to us what lies beyond death. However, we *can* investigate our minds here and now and discover all the worlds contained within."[22] Freemantle's opinion has many precedents in the history of Buddhism, east and west. It is based on the position that all forms of existence—mental, emotional, and physical, conditioned and unconditioned—depend on the generative powers of consciousness. But the traditional Buddhist view differs significantly from a modern psychologistic understanding in stressing the provisional reality of the world. That is, the Six Paths (or the Eighteen Realms or the Seventy-five Constituents of Existence) are recognized as both delusory, impermanent, and marked by suffering on the one hand, but also as unavoidable and real enough to matter on the other. As Chögyam Trungpa has said about the monkey, used as a metaphor for the ego, "The point is that in the perception of ego the phenomenal world is very real, overwhelming, solid. It may in fact be hallucinatory, but as far as the monkey is concerned the hallucination is quite real and solid."[23]

One item on this book's agenda, then, is the importance of ideas about rebirth and karma in Buddhism. I hope to direct attention to the prevalence, if not the ubiquity, of cosmological notions in the history of Buddhism. The rebirth cosmology, I believe, deserves to be added to the growing list of problems deemed central to Buddhism: nirvāṇa, the status of the Buddha and his relics, no-self, *dharmas* or the analysis of existence into its constituent parts, causality, monasticism and renunciation, the soteriological orientation of morality, and so on. This is not to suggest that the saṃsāra-nirvāṇa dyad has the same valence everywhere in Buddhism, much less that it is represented universally in the same way. As we have seen, there is no clear evidence

21. Gyatso, *World of Tibetan Buddhism*, p. 51.
22. Freemantle, *Luminous Emptiness*, p. 143, capitalization added.
23. Trungpa, *Cutting through Spiritual Materialism*, p. 148.

that paintings of the wheel of rebirth were executed in Indian temples prior to the fifth century. But I would claim that many forms of Buddhism are better understood when we attend seriously to concepts of the afterlife. This is especially true in those times and places where Buddhism comes into contact with non-Indian worldviews. In such settings, outside of Brahmanical hegemony, the Buddhist solution provided by the Eightfold Path cannot easily take hold until the Buddhist problem situation has first been comprehended. That is, release from saṃsāra makes better sense when rebirth in the Six Paths is first understood as a painful, repetitive process. Paintings of the wheel of life and death are one of the most important means of propagating the Buddhist analysis of suffering and of establishing the need for release from the cycle of rebirth.

Another assumption I hope to validate is that Buddhist ideas are not essentially bound to textual embodiment. Visual representations occupy a significant number of pages in this book because in premodern Asia, far more people were literate in images than in the written language. This is hardly news to social historians and scholars of art, and even to many Buddhologists, but its methodological implications have yet to make a very big impact on how scholars of Buddhism go about writing books.[24] In medieval Asia, reading and writing were skills limited to a tiny percentage of the population. In India the literate were members of the *kṣatriya varna* or Brahmins who knew how to write down the sacred sounds in which they specialized. In central Asia merchants regularly possessed rudimentary literacy. All across Asia other small groups of men and women learned the basics of writing as part of their training in monasteries and nunneries. For most people, images, not written words, were crucial.

Standing in third place, perhaps, after the practices of family religion and the festivals celebrated in the community, painting and sculpture were some of the most common media for learning about religion. Religious art was pervasive. The walls of most Buddhist temples, large and small, were covered with brightly colored wall paintings. Paintings executed on paper and silk were hung in temples as well as in private homes. Colossal statues stood in their own buildings in the larger temples, medium-sized carvings of gods were placed separately and as attendants to more magnificent Buddhas and bodhisattvas, and small, hand-sized statues were lodged in the homes of the well-to-do. Temple architecture—not just the design of buildings but also pagodas containing Buddha relics and sūtra towers that enshrined the words of the Buddha—carried its own form of visual meaning. So too did relief sculptures, complex narrative scenes carved onto open rock faces at pilgrimage sites. Another kind of religious image was the set of paintings used by itinerant entertainers, who unfurled their scrolls in front of an audience and sang about the saints, heroes, and monsters

24. Important exceptions include the pioneering work of Mus, *Barabuḍur: Sketch of a History of Buddhism*; and Tucci, *Tibetan Painted Scrolls* and the various volumes of *Indo-Tibetica*. For more recent work combining Buddhist studies and art history, see Klimburg-Salter, *Tabo: A Lamp for the Kingdom*; Sharf and Sharf, *Living Images*; and Weidner, *Latter Days of the Law*.

depicted therein. It is particularly notable that in all of these settings except that of the home, common people were likely to encounter visual images and oral teaching at the same time. Monks often gave public lectures in monasteries, and on ritual occasions they led groups of laypeople through cave temples. Pilgrims sometimes traveled with guides who provided oral commentary, and many relief sculptures contained quotations from holy scripture and short hymns in the local language, inscribed directly above the scene. Storytellers worked from memory to narrate the story line connecting the episodes depicted in different scrolls. In almost all of these situations, then, painting is conjoined to preaching, and the canonical text, around which the discipline of Buddhist studies continues to circumambulate, is at the margins.

This is not to deny the necessity or importance of using textual material. This book is full of translations and citations of Buddhist canonical sources, historical accounts, and written inscriptions. Rather, I try to use both visual and written evidence to understand better the lived religion of the past. Images and texts are important here because they enable us to imagine social action. Hence it is entirely fitting that in this enterprise—nowadays found throughout the academic world, among art specialists, scholars of religion, anthropologists, historians, and literary scholars—the category of ritual plays a prominent role. I aim to place each piece of visual and textual documentation in its original performative setting, since the meaning of any single representation of the wheel of rebirth is determined partly by its ritual context. It makes a difference, for instance, whether a painting of the wheel is hidden in a cave temple visited only by a few prominent clans or whether it is sculpted onto towering rock cliffs at a popular pilgrimage site. Similarly, the implications of placing the wheel of rebirth in a small cloister within a large temple complex are different from those of positioning a painting of the wheel of rebirth in the entryway of a cave temple that leads the viewer into a small, self-contained paradise.

In addition to the importance of artistic evidence and the centrality of ritual, another claim I try to substantiate is that the things transmitted by Buddhism are more like discursive practices than prepackaged ideas. By "discursive practice" I mean two things. First are the conceptual or representational properties of the wheel of rebirth. What ideas were made possible, for instance, and which ones were ruled out, by using a wheel rather than another figure (a river, a prison, an abyss, a bubble) to understand rebirth? I am interested in how the metaphor of the wheel was interpreted in different places. Even when a painting uses standard symbols like the Three Poisons, how they were understood is still an open question. As the title of this book suggests, the wheel was reinvented each time it was represented. As a "discourse" or representation in the first sense, then, the wheel of rebirth placed limits on interpretation at the same time that its meaning was subject to continuing negotiation. The second sense of discursive practice has more to do with power than with knowledge. As a discursive practice, the wheel of rebirth was painted by some groups of people and viewed by other groups. Commissioners and patrons of the saṃsāracakra sometimes had interests different from those of its viewers. As suggested by using the language of power and interest, my point is that artistic representations take part in social institutions. The concept of discursive practice draws attention to who authorizes paintings of the wheel of rebirth and to the process of legitimation.

The last item on my agenda is to clear a path for dealing with a pan-Buddhist symbol like the wheel of rebirth in a manner that does justice to the local contexts in which the symbol is found. On the one hand it is undeniable that the wheel rolled—that the picture of the wheel of life and death was spread across many Buddhist cultures. Speaking of the wheel as a pan-Buddhist symbol or formulating generalizations about a single Buddhist understanding of life and death does make sense, but only up to a point. Evoking the wheel as a metaphor for both the Dharma and the process of rebirth, Henry Alabaster chose the title *The Wheel of the Law* for his 1871 book. His preface advertises the universality of the idea:

> All Buddhists, throughout the wide range of countries where the doctrines of Buddha prevail, call their religion the doctrine of "The Wheel of the Law." I have adopted the name for this book, because it is peculiarly appropriate to a theory of Buddhism, which the book in some degree illustrates. I refer to the theory that all existence of which we have any conception is but a part of an endless chain, or circle, of causes and effects; that so long as we remain in that wheel there is no rest and no peace; and that rest can only be obtained by escaping from that wheel into the incomprehensible Nirwana. Buddha taught a religion of which the wheel was the only proper symbol. . . .[25]

On the other hand, there are crucial senses in which it is misleading to say that the wheel rolled. If "the wheel" is understood as the Dharma, then it is difficult to specify with any degree of concreteness precisely what content moved—undisturbed, unmodified, without depreciation—from one country to the next. More is at stake here than the truism that every understanding of the wheel of rebirth is specific to its time and place. In Buddhist history the question of interpretation entered as soon as the historical Buddha preached the first of many sermons, and the problem of interlingual dissemination ballooned as soon as the teaching was formulated in languages other than the Buddha's native dialect (probably Magadhi). Early texts portray the Buddhist community as vitally concerned with such hermeneutical issues. Buddhist studies as an academic discipline often has recourse to metaphors that easily but inappropriately imply the solidity, the naturalness, the fetishism of the object of study. Witness the importance of ideas like development, growth, decline, spread, dissemination, assimilation, and so on. Such paradigms of transmission are faulty because they trick us into presuming that the thing being passed down does not change, that its meaning is singular or stable, and that the process of transmission is similar everywhere that it occurs. Despite their opposing claims, the two reigning hypotheses about Chinese Buddhism, for instance—that it represents the "Indianization" of Chinese

25. Alabaster, *Wheel of the Law*, p. iii.

traditions or the "Sinification" of Indian Buddhism—are both constructed on the model of transmission.[26]

Not only must we guard against reifying the thing being transmitted, we must increasingly take note that the entities performing the transmission are not the simple, conventional givens we once thought they were. To say, for instance, that Buddhism was made more Tibetan through the creation of paintings of the wheel of life in temples in the Himalayas during the eleventh century is to beg the question of what regulative concepts like "Tibet" and "Tibetan" really mean. Many of the constructions on which Buddhist studies is based suffer from the projection backward in time of the form of the modern nation-state.

Snapshots of the political situation obtaining during three key eras discussed in this book, though crude, demonstrate how much our usual ideas of nation and culture can obscure our vision. Reading the rushed political survey presented in the next few pages, one should keep in mind how unhelpful the modern geopolitical map of Asia is for understanding medieval history. Around the year 450, a wall painting of the wheel of rebirth was executed on the porch of a magnificent monastic residence and shrine chiseled out of the cliffs at Ajaṇṭā, which is in the modern Indian state of Maharashtra (see map 1). Calling that form of the saṃsāracakra "Indian" helps only a little: it places the painting on the Indian subcontinent, helps us imagine a Hindu-Buddhist context, and signals that its creators would have spoken a Middle Indic precursor to Marāṭhī and used Sanskrit as a literary language. But beyond that, Indianness provides only illusory explanatory comfort. Ajaṇṭā was a part of the Vākāṭaka empire then ruling the central part of India on the Deccan Plateau. To the north lay lands that had long been controlled by the Gupta family, whose relatively long reign (ca. 320–540) was increasingly threatened by incursions by various Hun groups. The Vākāṭaka house, itself divided into an eastern and western branch, was sandwiched between the Gupta to the north and a succession of kingdoms in the south, where the Pallavas often dominated. Looking northward and eastward to sites where the wheel of rebirth was painted later, we see only more political disaggregation in the fifth century. East of the Pamirs and the Hindu Kush and north of the Kunlun Mountains lay the Tarim Basin, the oases of which provided key watering holes and cultural entrepôts for the caravans plying the silk trade between Europe and China. The area as a whole escaped the long-range domination of any single power: its various city-states fell alternately under Chinese hegemony and the sway of the Huns, Kushans, and various Turkish groups. Far to the north of the Deccan, in the Himalayas, strong families ruled the more highly settled river valleys in the fifth century, but the area of medieval and modern Tibet had not been unified in either theory or practice. To the far east, China lay divided. The Liu-Song dynasty (420–479), which prided itself on preserving Han culture, ruled in the south, its capital at Jiankang (modern Nanjing, Jiangsu) on the Yangtze River. North China had been ruled by a succession of non-

26. See Gimello, "Random Reflections on the 'Sinicization' of Buddhism"; Sharf, *Coming to Terms with Chinese Buddhism*, pp. 1–30; and Teiser, "Chinese Buddhism before China."

Han groups, including the Xiongnu, Xianbei (proto-Mongolians), and Di and Qiang (perhaps proto-Tibetan). The Tuoba, a proto-Turkish nomadic group, established the Northern Wei dynasty in 386 and held control until 534.

Jumping ahead on the timeline to the year 850 or so, the wheel of rebirth appears elsewhere: certainly in the kindgdom of Kucha in central Asia, perhaps in monasteries in northern India, and probably in the metropolitan temples and cave temples of Tang-dynasty China (see map 2). Kucha, which contained the town of Kumtura in which a representation of the wheel of rebirth was painted in a tiny cave shrine around the year 850, had seen various rulers, including local families, Chinese and Uighur forces, and Tibetan armies. When the wheel was painted there, the town was under the control of the Uighurs, a Turkish-speaking people. The Uighurs had arisen as a political force in the sixth century on the steppes north of China, and their armies exercised control over much of north China and the Tarim Basin. When the Kirghiz conquered Mongolia in the middle of the ninth century, the Uighurs moved westward and established a kingdom centered at Qočo (Gaochang, Xinjiang) that lasted roughly from 850 to 1250. There is no clear evidence of paintings of the wheel in the Indian subcontinent in the year 850, but it is possible that Buddhist temples in the north contained them. Beginning in the eighth century, three strong families struggled over control of the Ganges River valley: the Pratihāra to the west, the Rāṣṭrakūṭa in the center, and the Pāla to the east. The Uighurs were a growing power in the Punjab (modern Afghanistan), while beginning around 850 south India was dominated by the Cola dynasty for over four hundred years. Buddhist temples in Tibet probably did not have paintings of the wheel of rebirth in the year 850. The idea of Tibet as a federation may have taken shape in the seventh century under the Yarlung dynasty, which unified much territory, engaged in war, and pursued marriage alliances with the Tang court. They controlled significant stretches of the Tarim Basin late in the seventh century and then again, taking advantage of China's military decrepitude after the An Lushan rebellion, from the middle of the eighth to the middle of the ninth century. During these periods of domination, Tibetan armies pursued peace and war, alternately, with both local rulers and with the other extensive empires in Asia—the Chinese, the Uighurs, and the Arabs. Tibetan kings adopted Buddhism as a state religion early in the seventh century, but beginning around 850, Tibetan rulers embarked on a suppression of Buddhist institutions. The earliest undisputable evidence of a painting of the wheel of rebirth in Tibet dates only from the late tenth to early eleventh century at a monastery in Tabo (medieval western Tibet, modern Himachal Pradesh, India). By that time the Tibetan empire was again in abeyance, and Tabo owed its glory to the local kings in the area of Guge and Purang, their authority limited to western Tibet. Wheels of rebirth had probably been painted in China by the year 850. Chinese pilgrims knew about Ajaṇṭā and had traveled to the great Indian monastic academies, and the Buddha's commandment to paint a wheel of saṃsāra had been translated into Chinese early in the eighth century. Large temples in the capital cities of Luoyang and Chang'an blended Chinese, Indian, and central Asian influences. Similarly, by 850 the idea of the cave temple had already undergone five hundred years of development in China, since the

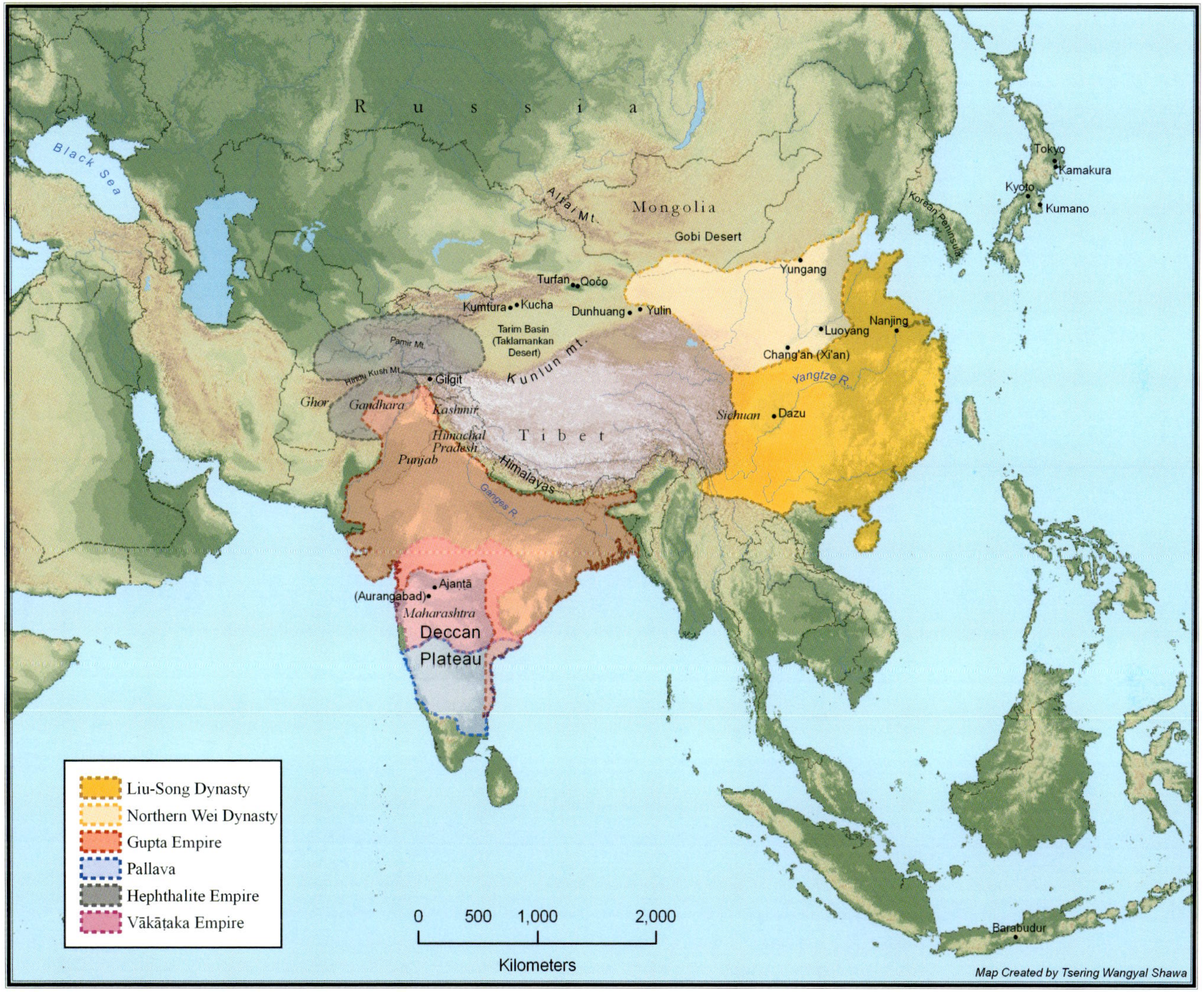

MAP 1. Asia, ca. 450.

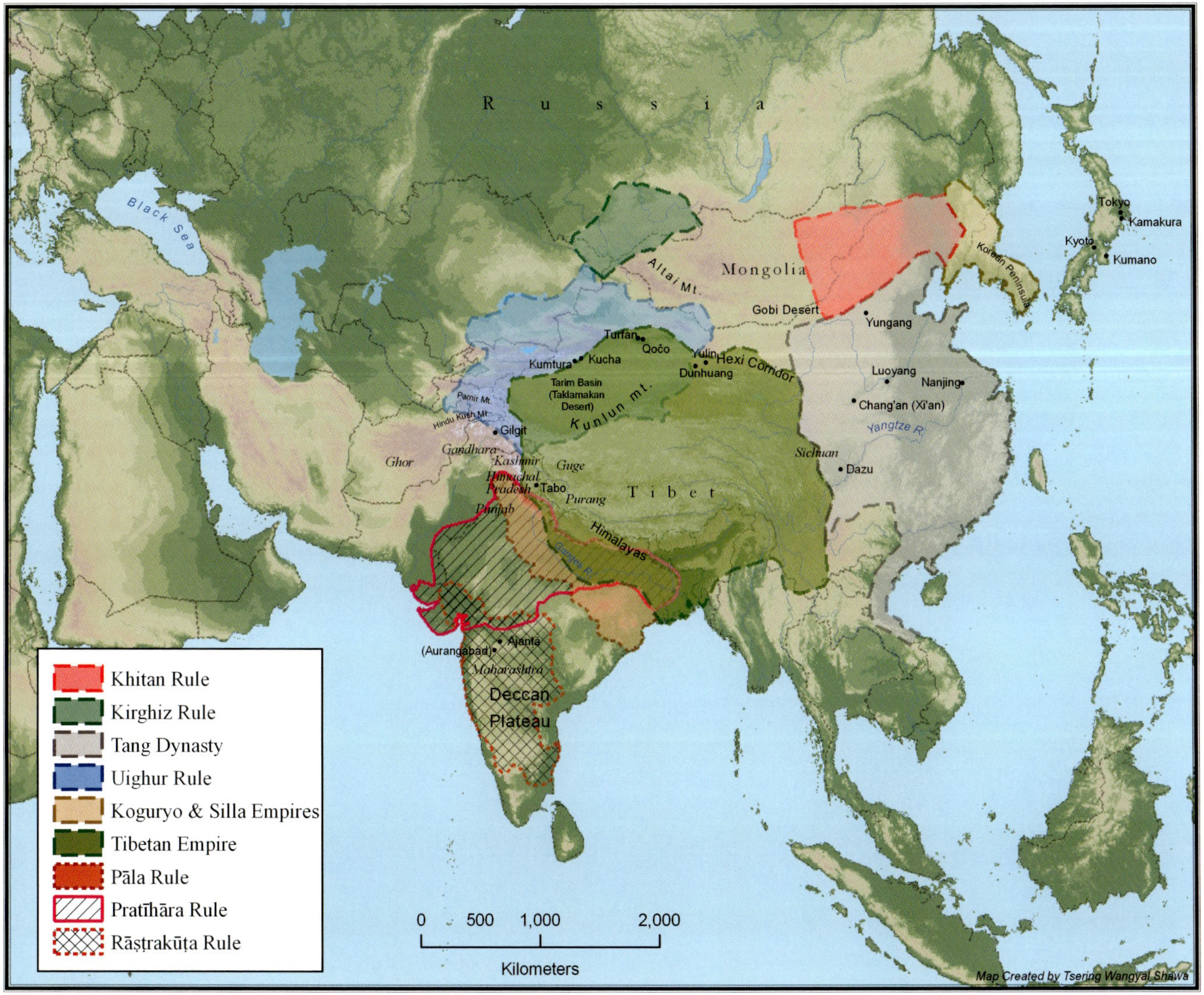

Map 2. Asia, ca. 850.

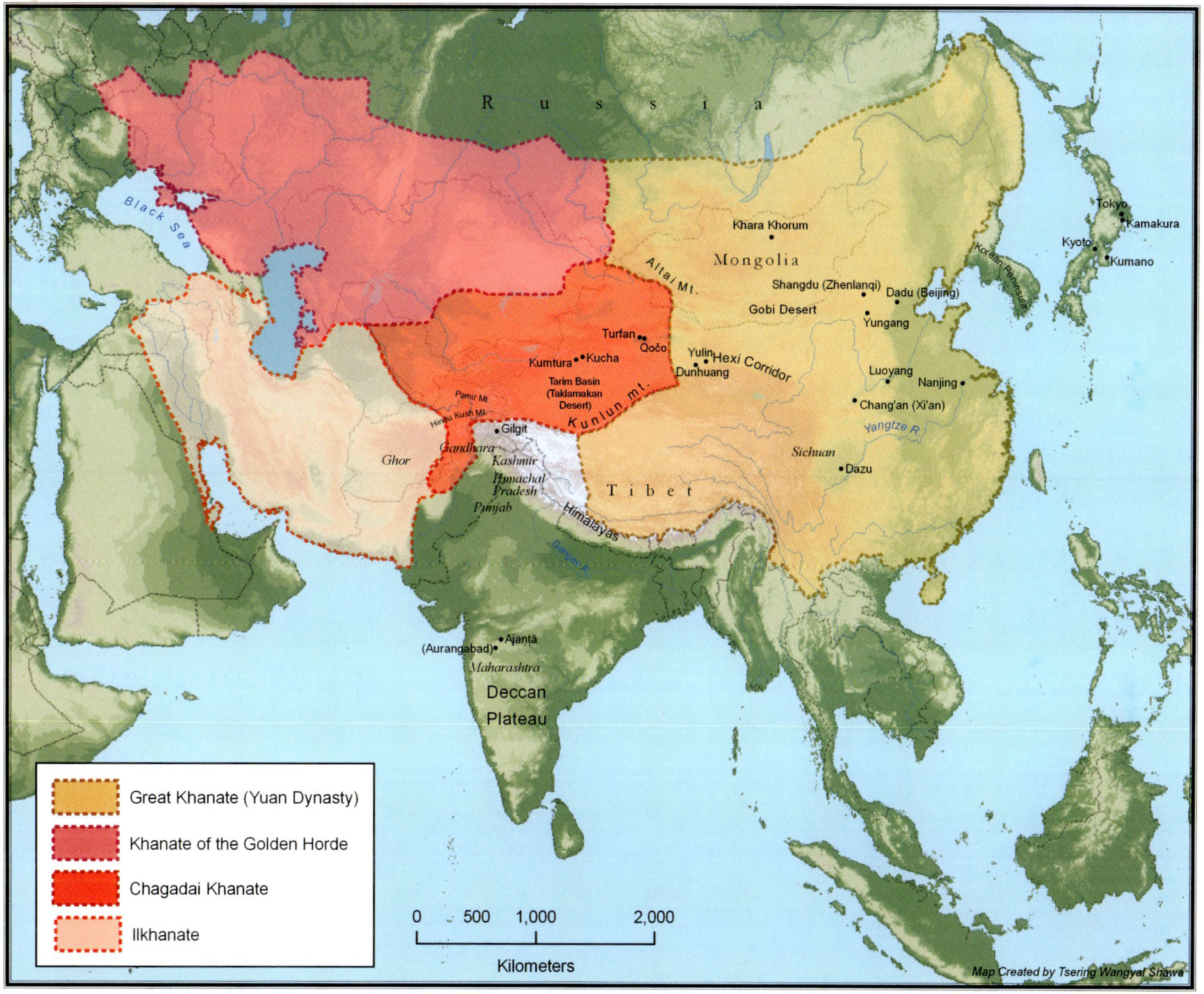

Map 3. Asia, ca. 1250.

first temples were hollowed out in Yungang (Shanxi) around 330. The earliest proof that paintings of the wheel of rebirth were made in China is later, in a tenth-century cave-temple complex at Yulin (Gansu). The temple containing that painting was commissioned by the local ruler, Cao Yuanzhong, whose family had controlled the western portion of the Gansu corridor during much of the long period in which central Chinese rule was nonexistent.

Moving forward another four hundred years to the year 1250, we find representations of the wheel of rebirth carved into the cliffs at Baodingshan, a popular pilgrimage center near the town of Dazu in central Sichuan (see map 3). To construe that wheel, however, as a "Chinese" appropriation of Buddhist ideals would miss most of its significance. The site as a whole is a proof text for the miracles performed by an indigenous holy man some five centuries earlier. The saint, Liu Benzun, was known for his public acts of self-mortification and his dedication to a localized version of the Tantric pantheon. The thirteenth-century planner of the complex displayed little interest in advertising its connections to parts of the empire beyond Sichuan. And, if he had, we should not forget that the empire in question was as much Mongolian as it was Chinese. Genghis Khan (1155–1227) had pioneered the military defeat of the Liao- and Jin-dynasty rulers of north China, and his grandson Kublai Khan (r. 1260–1294) extended Mongol control southward and founded the Yuan dynasty. Mongol rule represented not only the control of government by a non-Han ethnic group—which was, after all, more common than not since the founding of the Qin dynasty in 221 B.C.E. Mongolian domination also marked the englobement of the former Chinese empire within the vast Mongolian empire, which stretched from Iran and the Black Sea in the west to Russia in the north and the Korean peninsula in the east. The rulers of the Tibetan plateau had submitted proleptically to Mongol superiority several decades before 1250, and their peaceful alliance and symbolic submission enabled them to continue developing a Buddhicized confederation. Soon after the thirteenth century, Tibet developed the architectural and iconographic program for Buddhist temples that would be practiced into modern times. In that design, the temple resembles a fortress. One enters the monastery through a courtyard, moves through a circumambulatory passage, and then walks into an entrance portico linking the outer precincts and the inner sanctum of the temple. The entrance portico usually contains a wall painting of the wheel of rebirth. The several independent kingdoms on the Indian subcontinent had begun to feel pressure from Muslim armies already in the eighth century, and invasions and the destruction of Buddhist institutions accelerated in the eleventh century. Soon Turkish rulers from Ghor (modern Afghanistan) established the Delhi Sultanate in the north, and by the early thirteenth century Muslim dynasties dominated most of India, effectively putting an end to the large-scale patronage of Buddhism.

What, then, is the purpose of this whirlwind survey of medieval Asian history? My point is not simply that such tours are, like the Mongol attempt to control half the Eurasian continent, stretched perilously thin. Nor do I hope to construct a new set of smaller culturelike containers (Vākāṭaka, Uighur, Sichuanese) that could be used to conceptually capture the important transitions in the history of Buddhism. Rather, this chronological exercise is intended to help complicate the usual model of transmission in Buddhist studies. Not only was the thing transmitted (the picture of the wheel of rebirth) not very thinglike—as my use of "discursive practice" suggests—but the entities between which the thing was transmitted were rather unlike what we usually imagine them to be.

We tend to forget that notions (and nations) like "India," "Tibet," and "China" came into existence only recently, and we usually ignore the statelike formations that did not survive into the present. Very few books and conferences are dedicated to topics like the Uighurizing or the Gugefication or the Purangicization of Buddhism, or to Buddhism and the Silla (or Mon, or Bactrian, or Nanzhao) state. The problem is hardly more tractable when the agents of transmission are defined as cultures rather than national identities. Buddhism is an intercultural phenomenon not only because it has been involved in the contact of cultures and has given rise to new, less culturally bound forms. It is also intercultural because it helps draw attention to the "constitutively hybrid nature" of any given culture—to show the ways in which specific claims to cultural homogeneity are usually products of conflict and debate.[27]

Rather than relying on the paradigm of transmission, this book construes pictures of the wheel of rebirth in terms of the interplay between the canonical and the local, between transregional or pan-Buddhist forces and specific sites. Even with this formulation, however, I want to emphasize the dialectical, ultimately unstable nature of both "canonical" and "local" meanings. Although knowledge of the wheel of rebirth was publicized through translation of the canonical vinaya account from Sanskrit into Chinese and Tibetan, "canon" must nevertheless be understood in the plural. Rendered into different languages, the allegedly standardized wheel of rebirth existed in different versions and was always susceptible to different readings, as the following pages show. Furthermore, as an authoritative body of knowledge, the canon was as much a visual tradition as a written corpus. Thus, I want to break down and diversify what we mean by "canonical." Nor does the category of the "local" constitute simple, empirical bedrock. Like each painting or text, each context is of course different, but over and above that variation, the local setting is what the analyst makes of it. My hermeneutics are, like the wheel of rebirth, circular. I seek the meaning of any local example of the wheel in how it combines a reinterpretation of the canonical possibilities with the site-specific construal of meaning and the juggling of political forces.

27. See Hay, "Toward a Theory of the Intercultural," p. 5.

Chapter 2

The Canonical Version of the Wheel of Rebirth

The *locus classicus* of the Buddha's instructions about the wheel of life and death is the voluminous canon of monastic discipline (vinaya) of one of the schools of Indian Buddhism, the Mūlasarvāstivāda (Genbenshuoyiqieyoubu). Like other so-called sects of Indian Buddhism, the Mūlasarvāstivāda is best thought of not simply as a group of people united by explicit articles of faith, but more fundamentally as a community of monks that distinguished itself from other Buddhist groups by adherence to a specific set of rules and rationales for communal living. The formal justification for those rules—stories from the past, decisions by the Buddha, other monastic precedents—were compiled in written form in the vast collection known as vinaya. The original Mūlasarvāstivāda vinaya was written in Sanskrit. Scholars have recently arrived at the conclusion that the original vinaya in Sanskrit was formed in northwestern India in the first or second century.[1] Many of the texts comprising the Mūlasarvāstivāda vinaya were translated into Chinese between 700 and 712 by the pilgrim and monk Yijing

1. Erich Frauwallner (*Earliest Vinaya*, pp. 24–41) believes that the Mūlasarvāstivāda vinaya in its hypothetical original form represents the earliest vinaya of any Buddhist school. He places it at Mathurā prior to Aśoka. Sylvain Lévi ("Les éléments de formation du *Divyāvadāna*," p. 121) estimates that some portions of the text were written between the second and fourth centuries. The earliest surviving texts (manuscripts discovered at Gilgit and the Chinese translation by Yijing) are based on recensions that probably crystallized in the fifth century. Enomoto Fumio ("'Mūlasarvāstivādin' and 'Sarvāstivādin'") substantiates the claim that each so-called sect could have many subsects, each with its own vinaya. In this view, the Mūlasarvāstivāda was not separate from the Sarvāstivāda in reality, despite the fact that later writers treated the two separate vinaya canons as proof of the existence of two opposed social groups. See also Bareau, *Les sectes bouddhiques du petit véhicule*, pp. 153–54; Clarke, "*Mūlasarvāstivāda Vinaya Muktaka*"; Gnoli, *Gilgit Manuscripts of the Saṅghabhedavastu*, 1:xvii–xxii; Hirakawa, *Ritsuzō no kenkyū*, pp. 153–54, 95–98, 147–51, and 365–415; Huber, "Études bouddhiques"; de Jong, "Les *Sūtrapiṭaka* des Sarvāstivādin et des Mūlasarvāstivāda"; Mukherjee, "On the Relationship between the Sarvāstivāda Vinaya and the Mūlasarvāstivāda Vinaya"; Panglung, *Die Erzählstoffe des Mūlasarvāstivāda-Vinaya*; Prebish, "Theories concerning the *Skandhaka*"; Przyluski, "Le nord-ouest de l'Inde dans le *Vinaya* des Mūla-sarvāstivādin"; and Wille, *Die handschriftliche Überlieferung des Vinayavastu*. For the most complete recent study of the

(635–713). The entire vinaya was also translated into Tibetan in the early ninth century.[2]

To comprehend the specificity and significance of the account of the wheel of rebirth in the Mūlasarvāstivāda vinaya, it is important to examine the social history of the vinaya across Asia. The earliest monastic communities in India were relatively small Saṃghas that passed down their teachings orally. At the beginning, their vinaya probably consisted of *pratimokṣa* rules, which they recited semimonthly in public gatherings. The vinaya literature as it survives now comes from a much later period in Indian Buddhist history, when Saṃghas had become corporate institutions with endowments of land, monks numbering in the hundreds or thousands at the largest centers, and voluminous written canons divided into the three baskets of sūtra, vinaya, and *abhidharma* (treatises on the Dharma). The Mūlasarvāstivāda vinaya dates from this later period. It was not really a guide for a life of quiet, individualized contemplation, as the misnomer "monastic"—from the Greek *monazein*, "to live alone"—might lead one to believe. Rather, as the canonical story of the wheel of rebirth shows, the vinaya provided the narrative authority for a collective enterprise that drew laypeople to Buddhist temples and sent monks and nuns out into the lay community. Vinaya literature demonstrates how strongly social the lives of *bhikṣus* and *bhikṣuṇīs* really were. Each Saṃgha maintained its own vinaya, and as Buddhism expanded beyond its homeland in north-central India, groups of monks carried their vinayas—undergoing change all the while—with them. A key point to remember about this picture of the developing canons of Buddhism is that the Buddha's direction to paint the wheel of rebirth was found in only one of the many vinayas (the Mūlasarvāstivāda) in use across Asia.

The Chinese translation of the Mūlasarvāstivāda vinaya was undertaken by the eminent monk Yijing (635–713) after his travels in Southeast Asia and India.[3] Prior to that time, Chinese monks possessed four relatively complete translations of various vinaya canons, all completed in the early fifth century: the Dharmagupta (412), Sarvāstivāda

Mūlasarvāstivāda vinaya, based largely on Tibetan and Sanskrit sources, see the studies by Gregory Schopen, including "Bones of a Buddha and the Business of a Monk"; "Death, Funerals, and the Division of Property"; "Hierarchy and Housing in a Buddhist Monastic Code"; "Lay Ownership of Monasteries and the Role of the Monk in Mūlasarvāstivādin Monasticism"; "On Avoiding Ghosts and Social Censure"; and "Ritual Rights and Bones of Contention." Schopen generously shared his draft translations of several sections of related texts in Sanskrit and Tibetan, including the Tibetan version of the vinaya dealing with the wheel, Guṇaprabha's compilation of vinaya material (*Vinayasūtra*), and later commentaries on the latter text. In this chapter and the next I rely on this unpublished work in my comparison of the Chinese, Sanskrit, and Tibetan. I am much indebted to his work, although I do not follow all of his conclusions.

2. For a full listing of Yijing's works on vinaya, see Hirakawa, *Ritsuzō no kenkyū*, pp. 147–51. J. W. de Jong ("Les *Sūtrapiṭaka* des Sarvāstivādin et des Mūlasarvāstivāda," p. 401) believes that the original on which Yijing based his translation was shorter than the Sanskrit version translated into Tibetan one century later. The Tibetan translation was done by Sarvajñadeva, Vidyādaraprabha, Dharmakara, and dPal-gyis Lhun-po and was revised by Vidyādaraprabha and dPal-brtsegs.

3. Primary sources on Yijing include *Song gaoseng zhuan*, Zanning (919–1001), *T* no. 2061, 50:710b–11b; *Datang xiyu qiufa gaoseng zhuan*, Yijing (635–712), *T* no. 2066, 51:7c ff.; and *Kaiyuan shijiao lu*, Zhisheng (669–740), *T* no. 2154, 55:568b–69b. For secondary studies, see Tso, "Transformation of Buddhist Vinaya in China," pp. 46–51; Takakusu *Record of the Buddhist Religion as Practised in India*, pp. xxv–xxviii; and Wang Bangwei, *Nanhai jigui neifa zhuan jiaozhu*, pp. 1–187.

(413), Mahāsāṃghika (418), and Mahīśāsaka (424). In China in his youth, Yijing had studied the Dharmagupta vinaya and was probably a witness to the magnificent honors accorded to the pilgrim-translator Xuanzang, including the latter's funeral rites held in Chang'an in 664. Long desirous of making the journey to the homeland of his faith, Yijing set out for India by sea from Guangdong in 671. His first and last port of call on his twenty-five-year journey was Sumatra, where he began the study of Sanskrit. His time on the Indian subcontinent was spent mostly in eastern and central India. He made pilgrimages to key sites associated with the Buddha, studied at the great monastic academies of the day, and collected Sanskrit texts to bring home to China. Empress Wu granted him honors and lent him support upon his return to China in 695, and he was patronized by her son, Emperor Zhongzong (r. 705–710) as well. He was appointed to assist the Khotanese monk Śikṣānanda (652–710) in the translation of many texts, including the *Avataṃsaka.* Later, as a chief translator of vinaya texts in his own right, he was chairman of literary committees composed of Indian and central Asian monks who verified the original text and Chinese monks and literati who polished and proofread the final product. Although his own specialization was the vinaya of the Mūlasarvāstivāda, from which he translated eighteen separate works, he always considered himself a follower of the Dharmagupta vinaya. It was that school's vinaya corpus that he studied in his early years in China, and that was also the vinaya in vogue in the Tang capital cities and the Yellow River valley. According to Tso Sze-bong, the dominance of the Dharmagupta vinaya over that of other schools was secured in the year 709—precisely when Yijing was engaged in translating an alternative vinaya—when proponents of the Dharmagupta convinced the emperor to issue an edict encouraging adherence to it.[4] In China, then, the account of the wheel of rebirth is found in a vinaya text that was known as only one—and not the most authoritative—version of the vinaya.

The kingdoms and oasis towns of central Asia apparently knew of two major vinayas, although the evidence for all aspects of social life there is more limited than for China. Xuanzang reports that the Sarvāstivāda vinaya was followed all across the region, and manuscript versions have been found along the eastern and northern edges (Kizil and Duldur-aqur near Kuche, and Murtuq near Turfan).[5] Evidence for the Mūlasarvāstivāda vinaya is found at the western end of central Asia (Gandhāra) as well as at Bezeklik (near Turfan) and Miran.[6]

The plurality of vinaya canons in India, central Asia, and China stands in contrast to the situation in Tibet, which knew only the rich vinaya tradition of the Mūla-

4. See Tso, "Transformation of Buddhist Vinaya in China," pp. 4–117. The edict is mentioned in only one source, *Song gaoseng zhuan*, *T* 51:793c. For other explanations of the dominance of the Dharmagupta vinaya, see Funayama, "Acceptance of Buddhist Precepts by the Chinese in the Fifth Century," pp. 12–13; and Hirakawa, "Shibunrisshū no shutsugen to jūjuritsu."

5. See de Jong, "Les Sūtrapiṭaka des Sarvāstivāda et des Mūlasarvāstivādin"; and Lamotte, *Histoire du bouddhisme indien*, p. 598.

6. See Tso, "Transformation of Buddhist Vinaya in China," pp. 46–51; and Murakami, *Seiiki no bukkyō*.

sarvāstivāda. The monks who translated the Mūlasarvāstivāda vinaya from Sanskrit into Tibetan in the early ninth century were part of the revival of Buddhism there. The retrieval of authoritative texts on monastic life from India and their translation into Tibetan were important parts of the development of an indigenous Saṃgha in Tibet at the time. The relative univocality of the vinaya tradition in Tibet made it possible—in theory, at least—for the painting of the wheel of rebirth to later assume an unquestioned and widespread status.

The story of the wheel occurs in the part of the vinaya entitled *Mūlasarvāstivāda vinaya vibhaṅga* (literally, *Analysis of the Vinaya of the Mūlasarvāstivāda*). The original Sanskrit does not survive, and I base my translation on Yijing's Chinese version, translated in 703, entitled *Genbenshuoyiqieyoubu pinaiye*.[7] The story initiates a discussion of rules governing the taking of meals by monks. It begins with Maudgalyāyana's tours of the cosmos:

> At that time the Bhagavat [Lord, i.e., Śākyamuni] was in Rājagṛha, in the park of the bamboo grove of the lake of Kalandaka. The Great Maudgalyāyana, Possessed of Long Life [Āyuṣmat], would often out of compassion carry out inspections of all the paths of rebirth—of *naraka* [hell], animals, hungry ghosts, humans, and gods. In *naraka* he saw sentient beings undergoing such sufferings as having their bodies carved by knives, being cooked in excrement, and being roasted and boiled in fierce ashes and blazing embers. Among the animals, he saw them devouring one another and other sufferings. Among the hungry ghosts he saw such sufferings as being afflicted by all kinds of hunger and thirst. Among the gods he saw the sufferings of falling lower in the next rebirth and being separated from what they loved. In the path of humans he saw that they had various difficulties, searching for the necessities of life and food and clothing, undergoing death and punishment, and other sufferings.

---

7. The text is *T* no. 1442, 23:810c–11c. For a French translation, see Przyluski, "La roue de la vie à Ajaṇṭā." For a Japanese rendering, see Nishimoto, "Konponsetsuissaiubu binaya," pp. 654–56. For the date of Yijing's translation, see *Kaiyuan shijiao lu*, Zhisheng (669–740), completed in 730, *T* no. 2154, 55:567c. Although many Sanskrit manuscripts of texts in the Mūlasarvāstivāda canon were discovered at Gilgit (northwestern India), this text is not among them; see Prebish, *Survey of Vinaya Literature*, pp. 84–113; and Daizōkyō gakujutsu yōgo kenkyūkai, *Taishō shinshū daizōkyō sakuin*, vol. 12a, "Shūroku tenseki kaidai," pp. 5–6. I have chosen to construct a picture of "the canonical version" of the wheel of life and death in this chapter based largely on the Chinese vinaya, rather than related versions in Sanskrit and Tibetan. The advantage of this approach is that among the surviving versions of this story in the vinaya, the original translation by Yijing was made a full century before the Tibetan translation (of an original Sanskrit that may well have been different from the source text used by Yijing). Furthermore, some of Yijing's works survive among the Dunhuang manuscripts (e.g., Stein nos. 2516, 4742, Pelliot nos. 3314b, 3791), thus significantly predating the current versions of the related texts in Sanskrit and Tibetan. The disadvantage of this approach is that it might imply erroneously that the Chinese version was closer to the original Sanskrit than it actually was or that non-Chinese versions of the same text were inconsequential. I hope that future scholarship will be able to utilize both the Chinese texts on which I focus and the Sanskrit and Tibetan materials studied by Schopen to move in new directions.

Having seen this, the Great Maudgalyāyana would explain it all to the Four Orders,[8] announcing, "All people should know that, as I have seen, the Five Paths are quite distinct. The retribution of pleasure and pain is not empty—you must believe and not doubt. The receiving of painful retribution is called forth by evil deeds. Evil deeds are killing, stealing, lying, adultery, and so on up to maintaining heterodox views;[9] not venerating the Three Jewels; cheating respectable people and one's family; having no compassion; and not upholding the precepts. The fruit of pain ripens as a result[10] of these evil deeds. The receiving of pleasurable retribution is stimulated by good deeds. Good deeds are not killing, not stealing, and so on, up to not maintaining heterodox views; venerating the Three Jewels; honoring respectable people and one's family; perfecting compassion; and upholding the precepts. The fruit of pleasure ripens as a result of these good deeds."

When everyone heard this, they would exclaim that it was amazing. They would all raise their hands and sing out loudly, "Wonderful! On behalf of those blind in the dark like us, who see only the present and never the future, the Sage is familiar with the Five Paths; he observes good and evil and then returns to inform us. We are beginning to understand that retribution is like shadows and echoes and should not be denied. From now on we will correct our evil ways, cultivate blessings, seek rebirth in the paths of goodness, and not fall into the evil paths."

At that time, after hearing the Great Maudgalyāyana preach, the Four Orders would all think, "Our sons, daughters, and disciples are always performing evil deeds. They are not diligent in cultivating the pure conduct of a Brahmin."[11] Because they wanted to make them give up their evil deeds, they would bring them to the Sage, the Great Maudgalyāyana, and have them listen to the Law [Dharma]. After hearing the Law, they would aspire to cultivate good deeds, to avoid falling into the evil paths, and to achieve the supreme fruit.[12]

At that time the Four Orders gathered like clouds to come hear the essentials of the Law. The crowds made an uproar. The World-Honored One [Lokajyeṣṭha, i.e., Śākyamuni] knew this, so he asked Ānanda, Possessed of Long Life, "Why do the Four Orders gather like clouds wherever the Great Maudgalyāyana is?" Ānanda told the Buddha, "World-Honored One, the Great Maudgalyāyana, Possessed of Long Life, makes tours of the Five Paths and observes the various forms of suffering, and he explains it all to the Four Orders. Thus, everyone comes together in order to hear the Law."

---

8. The Four Orders (*sizhong, catasraḥ parṣadaḥ*) are monks (*bhikṣu*), nuns (*bhikṣuṇī*), laymen (*upāsaka*), and laywomen (*upāsikā*).

9. The Ten Evil Deeds (*shi'e, daśākuśala*), here abbreviated, are killing, stealing, adultery, lying, coarse language, double tongue, foul language, desire, anger, and heterodox views.

10. "Ripens as a result" renders *yishu* (*vipāka*).

11. "Pure conduct of a Brahmin" renders *fanxing* (*brahmacaryā*).

12. "The supreme fruit" (*shengguo*) is becoming an *arhat* (worthy one or saint), one destined to achieve nirvāṇa in this lifetime. See the discussion of the Four Fruits in this chapter, below.

At that time the World-Honored One told Ānanda, "The Great Maudgalyāyana will not always be everywhere. This kind of phenomenon is truly rare. For this reason I command all *bhikṣus* [monks] to paint a wheel of birth and death beneath the room at the gate of the temple."

At that time the various *bhikṣus* did not know how to paint one. The World-Honored One told them: "Being careful of the proportions, draw an image of a circle. Place the hub in the middle and then place five spokes to represent the Five Paths. Beneath the hub paint *naraka*, and on its two sides paint animals and hungry ghosts. Then on the top paint humans and gods. In the path of humans make the Four Continents: [Pūrva]videha to the east, the Jambu continent [Jambudvīpa] to the south, [Apara]godānī to the west, the [Uttara]kuru continent [Uttarakurudvīpa] to the north. In the hub make a white circle and paint an image of the Buddha in the center. In front of the Buddha image paint three symbols.[13] First make a pigeon to symbolize greed. Next make a snake to symbolize hatred. Last make a pig to symbolize delusion. Around the rim make the image of a wheel for carrying water. Put on many water pails and draw images of sentient beings dead and alive: the live ones have their heads poking out of the pail, the dead ones have their feet poking out. Within each of the Five Paths make their respective symbols."

"All around this you should then paint the Twelve Conditions[14] and the signs of life and the extinction of life, which means ignorance, dispositions, and so on, up to old age and death. For the ignorance branch make an image of a *rakṣa* [demon]. For the dispositions branch make an image of a potter's wheel. For the consciousness branch make an image of a monkey. For the name-and-form branch make an image of people riding in a boat. For the six sense fields branch make an image of the six sense organs. For the contact segment make an image of men and women embracing. For the feeling branch make an image of a man and woman experiencing pain and pleasure. For the desire branch make an image of a woman holding a child in her arms. For the appropriation branch make an image of a man holding a bottle fetching water. For the becoming branch make an image of the great god Brahmā. For the birth branch make an image of a woman giving birth. For the old age branch make an image of old, decrepit men and women. For sickness make an image of men and women who are ill. For the death branch make an image of a dead person on a bier. For sadness make an image of men and women grieving. For malady make an image of men and women weeping. For pain make

---

13. The Three Symbols (*sanzhongxing*) are also known as the Three Poisons (*sandu, tridoṣāpaha*): greed (*rāga, tanran*), hatred (*dveṣa, chenhui*), and delusion (*moha, yuchi*). In some artistic representations, the pigeon is replaced by a chicken.

14. "The Twelve Conditions" (*shi'eryuan*) go by several other names, including the "Twelve Branches of Dependent Origination" (*shi'erzhi yuanqi, dvādaśāṅga pratītyasamutpāda*). See Mochizuki, *Bukkyō daijiten*, pp. 2321c–25c. As discussed below, the list given here contains eighteen elements, not twelve. For a comparison of the two lists and their artistic forms, see table 1 in chapter 1.

an image of men and women suffering. For difficulty make an image of a man and woman pulling a camel that is hard to tame.

"Above the wheel make the Great Demon of Impermanence with disheveled hair and a gaping mouth. In his outstretched arms he holds the wheel of life and death. To the two sides of the demon's head write two *gāthās* [verses]:

> You should seek renunciation[15]
> And apply yourself to the practice of the Buddha's teaching.
> Conquer the army of life and death
> As an elephant smashes a thatched hut.
>
> Within the Law [Dharma] and the Discipline [Vinaya]
> Constantly practice—don't give up,
> And you will be able to exhaust the sea of afflictions
> And arrive at the point where suffering ends.

"Next, above the Great Demon of Impermanence, you should make a round, white altar, in order to symbolize the perfection and purity of nirvāṇa. [Thus] as I have instructed, you should make a wheel of birth and death beneath the room at the gate."

Then the various *bhikṣus* put the teachings into practice and made one. All of the believers, Brahmins and laypeople, out of faith and respect, saw the images painted in the wheel and asked, "Oh Sage, what are you trying to represent in painting the wheel?" The *bhikṣu* replied, "I don't know what it represents either." Everyone responded, "If you don't understand, then why draw a painting?"

All of the *bhikṣus* were silent then, with nothing to reply. They told the whole story to the World-Honored One. The World-Honored One told them, "You should station a *bhikṣu* beneath the room at the gate and have him point out the reasons for the turning of the wheel of birth and death to all visitors and Brahmins. [Thus] as I have instructed, you should order someone to offer an explanation."

Then the *bhikṣus* made a poor choice: they appointed someone who lacked understanding to give instruction in the matter, which failed to produce faith among anyone[16] and gave rise to criticism as well. The Buddha said, "Appoint someone who understands to offer an explanation to people."

In portraying the wheel painted on monastery walls as a pale reflection of Maudgalyāyana's tours of the other world, the vinaya text draws on a rich tradition of mythology

15. "Renunciation" renders *chuli* (*naiṣkramya*). As I suggest below, the phrasing is interesting because it avoids specific mention of leaving the family and becoming a monk.

16. "Faith among anyone" is my uncertain rendering of *wuxin*. The closest analogue I can find is *wulun*, "everyone's opinion"; see Luo et al., *Hanyu dacidian*, 6:256a.

about the disciples of the Buddha. Maudgalyāyana's manifestations in the Buddhist world are quite diverse; here I confine the discussion to how he appears in the literature of the Mūlasarvāstivāda.[17] Maudgalyāyana is often paired with another leading disciple, Śāriputra. The two were friends even before becoming monks. Together they became followers of one of the famous non-Brahmanical teachers of their day, Sañjaya-Vairaīputra, and amassed a following of their own. Then, while visiting Rājagṛha, they met a disciple of Śākyamuni who taught them his master's doctrine of causality, which turned them to the Buddhist path. Upon their entry into the Buddhist order, they achieved the status of *arhat* (worthy one or saint), and the Buddha proclaimed that they would each be foremost in a particular skill. Śāriputra, he said, would excel at wisdom (*prajñā, zhihui*), Maudgalyāyana at special forms of knowledge (*abhijñā, shentong*).[18]

Among the powers Maudgalyāyana exercises, it is the use of his "spiritual feet" (*ṛddhi pādāḥ, shenzu*) for which he is best known. They enable him to travel to distant parts of the cosmos. Other vinaya texts describe his journeys to various compartments of hell, where he encounters non-Buddhist teachers and erroneous disciples of the Buddha suffering what is portrayed as their just desserts.[19] Maudgalyāyana's powers grow out of the technology of meditation, and his earthbound brothers view them as a threat. In Buddhist mythology he is often called to account for displaying his achievements to the laity. In an earlier chapter of the vinaya text describing the wheel of life and death, the monks ask the Buddha to decide whether Maudgalyāyana is guilty of breaking the monastic code. The story goes that Maudgalyāyana has convinced the great lay patron of Buddhism, Anāthapiṇḍika, to let him instruct his sons in the religion of Śākyamuni, rather than having the boys follow their usual Vedic and secular studies. The boys receive their instruction in Maudgalyāyana's quarters, an arrangement that works well until thieves discover the arrangement and kidnap the young boys in hopes of gaining a royal ransom. Rather than admitting his quandary to the Buddha or alarming the boys' powerful father, Maudgalyāyana resorts to his own devices. Through supernatural abilities he turns himself into an army of a powerful general in the area (Viḍūḍabha, who serves King Prasenajit), and in that form Maudgalyāyana routs the bandits and rescues the boys. Having used his own, potentially transgressive authority to solve a problem, Maudgalyāyana must now submit to the judgment of the Buddha. A discussion ensues over whether Maudgalyāyana has violated the precepts by displaying his powers in front of laypeople, but the Buddha settles the issue

17. Except for work focusing narrowly on medieval Chinese materials, Maudgalyāyana remains little studied. General overviews are available in Bareau, *Recherches sur la biographie du Bouddha*, 1:348–54; Migot, "Un grand disciple du Bouddha: Śāriputra"; and Nyanaponika and Hecker, *Great Disciples of the Buddha*, pp. 67–106. On the legend of Maudgalyāyana in China, see Chen Fangying, *Mulian jiumu gushi zhi yanjin ji qi youguan wenxue zhi yanjiu*; Iwamoto, *Jigoku meguri no bungaku*; and Teiser, *Ghost Festival in Medieval China*.

18. See *Genbenshuoyiqieyoubu pinaiye chujia shi* (*Mūlasarvāstivāda pravrajyāvastu*), trans. Yijing (635–713), *T* no. 1444, 23:1023c–31a.

19. See, for example, *Genbenshuoyiqieyoubu pinaiye poseng shi* (*Mūlasarvāstivāda saṃghabhedakavastu*), trans. Yijing (635–713), *T* no. 1450, 24:149b–51b.

in Maudgalyāyana's favor by pointing to the intention that motivated the deed: "The Buddha told the *bhikṣus*, 'For the *bhikṣu* Maudgalyāyana to display spiritual powers (*xian shenli*) with this intent is not an offense.'"[20]

Maudgalyāyana's other association is with the virtue of filial piety. The Mūlasarvāstivāda canon situates him especially closely to his mother. One text describes his motivation for seeking out his mother's place of rebirth: if he can arrange for her to hear the Law, even in another reincarnation, then she will be able to achieve liberation. The text reads:

> Maudgalyāyana, Possessed of Long Life, had this thought, "The World-Honored One has explained what parents do for children. They do what is difficult to do. They nurse them and take care of them. They teach them about the various affairs of the Jambu continent. If there were a person who carried his father on one shoulder and his mother on the other for a full one hundred years, still he would not be able to repay his parents' kindness. Or if he offered items decorated with the valuables of the whole earth to his parents, still he would not be able to repay them. . . . But if his parents do not believe in the Buddha, Dharma, or Saṃgha, and he gradually converts them to belief in the Buddha, Dharma, or Saṃgha, then that is repaying their kindness. If his parents at first do not act in accord with the precepts and he gradually teaches them to uphold the precepts; or if his parents are greedy and he convinces them to practice charity; or if they lack wisdom and he causes them to be wise; then all of these cases can truly be called repaying kindness."[21]

Maudgalyāyana proceeds to search for his mother, who has died and been reborn. By clairvoyance he sees her in her new abode, the realm of the goddess Marīci. He asks for the Buddha's help, and together they embark, arriving in Marīci's kingdom after seven days. Mother and son are reunited, much to the surprise of the other residents of Marīci's realm. They wonder how such a young, newly reborn woman could be addressing a man like Maudgalyāyana as her son, so Maudgalyāyana dispels their confusion by explaining that in her previous lifetime she was his mother. Then the Buddha turns to the main purpose of his visit, which is to preach to Maudgalyāyana's mother. After hearing the Dharma from the mouth of the Buddha, she achieves the fruit of stream-enterer, becomes a laywoman, and makes offerings to the Three Jewels.

All of these accounts corroborate what the story of the wheel of existence assumes, that Maudgalyāyana is, preeminently among the disciples of the Buddha, best suited to entertain audiences with stories about what happens to people after death. His tales are based on his own experience. He uses paranormal abilities to travel up and down

---

20. The story is in *Genbenshuoyiqieyoubu pinaiye* (*Mūlasarvāstivāda vinaya vibhaṅga*), trans. Yijing (635–713), *T* no. 1442, 23:649b–50b, translation from 23:650b.

21. Translated from *Genbenshuoyiqieyoubu pinaiye yaoshi* (*Mūlasarvāstivāda bhaiṣajyavastu*), trans. Yijing (635–713), *T* no. 1448, 24:16a; the story continues, 16a–c. For translations from the corresponding passages in the *Divyāvadāna*, see Strong, "Filial Piety and Buddhism," p. 180; and Tatelman, *Glorious Deeds of Pūrna*, pp. 76–78.

in the cosmos and to report back with the results. Whether seeking his own relatives or those of others, he assuages the fears of living family members by telling them where their ancestors have been reborn and how they are faring. In the *Vinaya vibhaṅga*, Maudgalyāyana is credited with knowledge of all Five Paths of rebirth. Maudgalyāyana is especially concerned with narrating the sufferings generic to each realm. Rather than describing the pleasures that gods experience, for instance, Maudgalyāyana draws attention to the anxiety they feel. The delights they enjoy are undermined by the nagging awareness that they will inevitably be reborn lower, rather than higher, in their next lifetime.

One of the themes in Maudgalyāyana's sermons is retribution. All deeds have results, a doctrine he explains with metaphors drawn from plant life and with such figures as echoes and shadows. He also offers his audience details about what kind of actions are considered "good" and which are "evil." In the process, he runs through basic Buddhist morality, including performing the Ten Good Deeds, honoring the Three Jewels, supporting the values of the family and society, keeping the precepts of lay Buddhism, and observing days of fasting each month. The narrator leaves no doubt about the effectiveness of Maudgalyāyana's abilities: he attracts great crowds of people to hear his stories, and when they become Buddhist lay followers, they bring along their unenlightened sons and daughters, who in turn are converted too. The phrasing of the text, which mentions the "Four Orders," makes clear that laypeople as well as monks and nuns make up Maudgalyāyana's audience, and that their ultimate goal is to become *arhats*.

Even before the wheel of rebirth is mentioned, the narrative raises the issue of salvation. According to the text, the lay disciples attracted by Maudgalyāyana resolve to gain "the supreme fruit" (*shengguo*), which is the state of *arhat*. In the other portion of the *Vinaya vibhaṅga* mentioned above, Maudgalyāyana's mother achieves the first of the Four Fruits, the state of stream-enterer. The text plots salvation on the map of the Four Fruits, an important component of Buddhist soteriology.[22] According to this theory, existence as a human being is simply one of six possible forms of rebirth. Although reincarnation as a human (on Jambudvīpa) or as a god (in heaven) is relatively pleasurable, such existences still lead to further rebirth. The more noble option is to try to achieve release from the cycle of rebirth altogether. Unconditional release is achieved with four different degrees of certitude. The first rank is that of stream-enterer (*śrotāpati*). Someone who achieves it will eventually, after an unspecified number of rebirths, achieve nirvāṇa (extinction). The second fruit ("once-returner," *sakṛdāgāmi*) and third fruit ("non-returner," *anāgāmi*) involve one or zero further reincarnations before achieving deliverance. The highest fruit is that of *arhat*, who is assured of nirvāṇa at the end of the current lifetime. Although in theory all sentient beings could eventually achieve the Four Fruits, the Four Fruits are not equally accessible to

---

22. For a traditional overview of the Four Fruits (*catvāri śramaṇa-phalāni*), see Mochizuki, *Bukkyō daijiten*, pp. 1799b–1800a. For more recent studies, see Masefield, *Divine Revelation in Pali Buddhism*, pp. 1–36; and Strong, *Legend and Cult of Upagupta*, pp. 75–92.

all. They are achieved most often by beings reborn as human. The Four Fruits are usually triggered—and certified—by an encounter with a Buddha, one of the Buddha's advanced disciples, or, as we will see in the accounts of other paintings, simply by viewing an image of the Awakened One. Achieving any one of the Four Fruits is an assurance that one will achieve nirvāṇa; the only difference between the four is the speed with which one is liberated. What is certified in the encounter with the Buddha is not so much a condition or spiritual status as a causal nexus: hearing a disciple preach the Law is identified as the cause, from which the result of nirvāṇa naturally follows. The Four Fruits are consistently ranked above unenlightened life in the Five Paths, but they are not wholly separate from the lower paths either, since they are the results ("fruits") of causes or seeds planted during one's life as a human being. In the vinaya text on the wheel of rebirth, hearing the sermons preached by Maudgalyāyana causes laypeople to aspire for the highest of the Four Fruits. The text assumes a soteriological hierarchy linking the early and later stages. Non-Buddhists can be led, by sermons or viewing paintings of karmic retribution, to enter the Buddhist path and follow the basic system of morality. That step, in turn, can lead eventually to achieving the Four Fruits, from which the goal of final liberation is assured.

It is only at this point in the story—after crowds swell, like clouds, to hear Maudgalyāyana preach—that the Buddha intervenes. Because Maudgalyāyana cannot be everywhere at once, the Buddha instructs his disciples to institutionalize a method for teaching people about life and death. In the vinaya the Buddha calls it a "wheel of birth and death" (*shengsi lun*, which may be reconstructed as *saṃsāracakra*), and he orders that it be painted "beneath the room at the gate of the temple" (*simen wu xia*).[23] According to the story line of the vinaya text, the idea for such a wheel is novel, since none of the Buddha's followers knows how to paint one. The Buddha's explanation of the wheel of rebirth encapsulates some of the most important Buddhist doctrines about the nature of existence. The basic structure of the painting is a wheel with five spokes meeting in a hub. In Sanskrit the wheel is often described as having five parts (*pañcgaṇḍaka*). The five spokes do not mark off equal areas. Instead, the wheel is divided into five qualitatively different wedges, representing the Five Paths (*wuqu*, *pañcagatayaḥ*). Gods and humans are above, while the bottom semicircle is composed of animals, ghosts, and hell beings. The precise number of paths is clearly specified in the vinaya as five, but other versions of the wheel of rebirth have variations. Sometimes the number is six, with *asuras*—the titans jealous of the gods' unequalled pleasures, including the right to enjoy the fruit of the *parijāta* tree that is rooted in the realm of the *asuras*—added below the gods.[24] Another rendering, visible in the Ajaṇṭā caves (Maharashtra, India; see plate 8 and figs. 3.4–3.5, discussed in the next chapter),

23. Later in the text the wheel is referred to as "the wheel of rebirth in the Five Paths" (*wuqu shengsi lun*), located "below the gate of the temple" (*simen xia*); see below. For parallel wording in the *Divyāvadāna*, see chapter 3.

24. Mibu Taishun ("Rokudōsetsu ni kan suru nisan no mondai ni tsuite") offers good evidence of the range of opinion concerning the number of paths and the order in which they are presented in a wide range of Buddhist texts.

divides the wheel into eight sections, each realm marking a specific mixture of reward and punishment. Despite their differences, these representations of the possibilities of rebirth share two key features. In the first place, they all portray the higher realms as more pleasurable than the lower ones. The greatest contrast within the wheel is between the gods at the top and the denizens of hell at the bottom. Gods lead longer lives, they hear music wherever they go, and, like royalty, they live in palaces. The inhabitants of the lowest path are subject to constant torture, usually infernal. If they are consumed by flames or if they are incinerated by internal heat after being forced to consume red-hot balls of iron, their bodies are magically reconstituted for more rounds of punishment. Secondly, residents of all the realms share the same fate after death: they will be reborn within the wheel, still subject to karmic retribution, impermanence, and suffering.

Śākyamuni directs his disciples to paint a Buddha in the center of the wheel (a detail lacking in the Tibetan translation of the vinaya). Later tradition gives us little basis for interpreting this particular figure, since most surviving representations do not include him in the picture. (Exceptions include the modern Tibetan painting in plate 4 and the Sichuan sculpture shown in fig. 9.4, discussed in chapters 1 and 9.) Also in the hub are three animals, who are supposed to represent what is known as the Three Poisons (*tridoṣāpaha*). By being placed at the center of the wheel, greed, hatred, and delusion are construed as energizing the entire cycle of rebirth. Śākyamuni gives very careful directions to painters and preachers. First he tells them to paint the three symbols, then he explains in doctrinal terms what each animal is supposed to represent. Some modern versions of the wheel emphasize the interrelation of the Three Poisons by depicting the three animals as linked, each holding in its mouth the tail of the animal in front of it (see plate 1).

Śākyamuni tells the monks to paint another circle just outside the hub. It is supposed to be a water wheel, with human beings carried in its buckets. By portraying some people head-up and others head-down, the water pails reinforce the idea that one can move upward or downward in the circle. The placement of a second, moving wheel inside of a chariot wheel emphasizes the recurring nature of life within saṃsāra. The earliest surviving paintings of the saṃsāracakra, at Ajaṇṭā and Kumtura (Xinjiang, China), omit this ring of the wheel. Later medieval versions (Yulin, in Gansu, China; Pedongpo in western Tibet; Baodingshan in Sichuan, China) contain something like it, a series of barrels through which creatures are jumping. The barrel conceals the main part of their bodies, so that only their heads and feet are visible. The barrel marks the moment of trans-specification in the process of rebirth. In figure 9.5, for example, a snake is undergoing rebirth: its head has changed into a fish while its tail remains that of a snake. Most recent paintings from Tibet (e.g., plates 1–4, 7) use light and dark shading to represent movement upward and downward. Within the band, there are saints and other good influences on the right side, while demons with their victims are located on the left, shaded side.

The outer ring of the circle is supposed to contain symbols representing the twelve stages in the cycle of dependent origination (*pratītyasamutpāda*, also translated as "conditioned coarising"). The doctrine has an interesting history in Buddhism, the details of which are still imperfectly understood.[25] In some contexts the list contains six, eight, or other numbers of stages; the standardized list of Twelve Conditions so well known in modern Buddhist studies had not yet developed in the earliest Buddhist texts. To further complicate matters, the various schools of Indian Buddhism offered different interpretations of the doctrine. Early texts do, however, make clear that the sequence was read both forward (ignorance gives rise to dispositions, dispositions give rise to consciousness, and so on) and backward (old age and death depend on birth, birth depends on becoming, and so on). They also show that quite early in the history of Buddhist thought, the doctrine was used to make sense of continuity between lives. In addition to its embodiment in the wheel of rebirth and in early texts, the idea of dependent origination was expressed in a variety of other media in Indian Buddhism. Dependent origination was sometimes understood as the most effective encapsulation of the entire Buddhist Dharma. The *Rice-Seedling Scripture*, for instance, quotes the Buddha as saying, "For a *bhikṣu* to see dependent origination is to see the Dharma, and seeing the Dharma is to see me."[26] Not only is the entire Law of Buddhism crystallized in the teaching of dependent origination. In this text the Buddha goes further and promises that anyone who truly understands causality will also see—encounter—the Buddha. This equivalence also helps to explain how and why short verses on dependent origination were often inscribed on statues of the Buddha in medieval Indian Buddhism: they were one more method for making the Buddha himself (and the Dharma itself) present.[27] Another virtue of the notion of dependent origination is that it explains the process of living, dying, and being reborn without recourse to the concept of a soul that endures from one lifetime to the next.[28] Modern Buddhists also portray the Twelve Conditions as stages of consciousness within one lifetime.[29]

The vinaya account in Chinese is complicated somewhat because after referring to the Twelve Conditions, the Buddha in fact proceeds to name eighteen of them, each

25. See, for example, Bucknell, "Conditioned Arising Evolves"; Conze, *Buddhist Thought in India*, pp. 156–58; La Vallée Poussin, "Deux notes sur le Pratîtyasamutpâda"; and Oltramare, *La formule bouddhique des douze causes*.

26. Translation from *Liaoben shengsi jing* (*Śālistambhaka sūtra*), trans. Zhi Qian (ca. 220–252), *T* no. 708, 16:815a. For later versions of the text, see Ono, *Bussho kaisetsu daijiten* 11:239a–b. Zhi Qian's version, entitled *Scripture on Understanding the Fundamentals of Birth and Death*, repeatedly invokes the metaphor of the growth of rice to explain various aspects of the process of causation. Later versions in Chinese, and probably their Sanskrit analogues, explicitly refer to "rice seedling" in their titles.

27. See Boucher, "The *Pratītyasamutpāda gāthā*"; and Leoshko, "About Looking at Buddha Images in Eastern India."

28. Among the Nikāyas, see the *Mahānidāna suttanta*, in Rhys Davids and Rhys Davids, *Dialogues of the Buddha*, 2:50–70; and chapter 12 of the *Nidāna vagga*, in Rhys Davids, Woodward, and Thera, *Sanyutta-Nikaya*, 2:1–94. For Chinese parallels to the latter text, see *Za ahan jing* (*Saṃyuktāgama*), trans. Guṇabhadra (Qiunabatuoluo, 394–468), *T* no. 99, 2:80b–81a; and *Zengyi ahan jing* (*Ekottarāgama*), trans. Gautama Saṃghadeva (Qutan Sengqietipo, fl. 383–398), *T* no. 125, 2:718a–c. See also *Beiduoshuxia siwei shi'eryinyuan jing*, trans. Zhi Qian (ca. 220–252), *T* no. 713; *Yuanqi shengdao jing*, trans. Xuanzang (602–664), *T* no. 714; and *Jiucheng yu jing*, trans. Faxian (aka Tianxizai, fl. 980–1000), *T* no. 715.

29. See, for example, Govinda, *Foundations of Tibetan Mysticism*, pp. 234–47.

with a separate symbol. The longer list is composed of the original Twelve Conditions, with the last one split into two (old age and death), plus five more. While some scholars have found the discrepancy between twelve and eighteen quite vexing,[30] I find the text less troubling. The Tibetan translation of the vinaya omits a listing of the causes (twelve or eighteen) altogether,[31] and the Chinese text itself recognizes twelve as the more authoritative number, since it refers to each as "the XXX branch" (XXX *zhi, aṅga*), while deleting the word "branch" in referring to the extracanonical six. Dividing up the causal conditions into a list of eighteen is attested in numerous Indian texts.[32] Most of the pictorial representations of the wheel contain twelve segments, but some portray eighteen (see table 1 in chapter 1). The spatial arrangement of the causes around the wheel also varies considerably. Some paintings portray them consecutively, others in balanced groups of three; some move clockwise, others counterclockwise.

In the vinaya text, Śākyamuni seems to be especially interested in questions of pedagogy, as he insists that monks paint easily recognized symbols for each link in the causal chain. The symbols he assigns were undoubtedly widespread in medieval India. Many of them are used, with the same associations, in early Upaniṣadic literature.[33] Like other symbols in the wheel of life (the animals representing the Three Poisons, the white altar for nirvāṇa, etc.), the Twelve Conditions stand in need of explanation: understanding requires either prior knowledge of their significance, creative reflection on the part of the viewer, the exegesis of a preacher, or some combination of all three. When modern Buddhist teachers talk about the wheel of rebirth in Dharma lectures, they often concentrate on the Twelve Conditions.[34] They adopt an analytical attitude, distinguishing clearly between each of the twelve stages in order to explain Buddhist psychology. In contrast to this attitude toward the Twelve Conditions, some modern scholars view the teaching more as an article of faith rather than a theological exercise. David Snellgrove, for instance, writes, "The twelvefold causal nexus (*pratītyasamutpāda*) announced at the time of Enlightenment as the formal expression of a Buddha's intuitive insight into the whole process of saṃsāra is by its very nature a kind of dogmatic statement, which requires no proof for believers. Thus it is a form of revelation, and efforts by Buddhist commentators as well as non-Buddhist scholars to discover a logical relationship between the various terms of the nexus are probably misdirected."[35]

Interpreters of dependent origination—whether artists or preachers, traditional or modern—have thus adopted a number of perspectives on the Twelve Conditions. What unites these modes of interpretation is that they all begin by trying to make sense of

30. See, for example, Przyluski, "La roue de la vie à Ajaṇṭā," pp. 322–31.

31. See Nishimoto, "Konponsetsuissaiubu binaya," p. 656, n. 15.

32. See La Vallée Poussin, "Théorie des douzes causes," pp. 31–33.

33. See Hartmann, "Symbols of the *Nidānas* in Tibetan Drawings of the Wheel of Life."

34. See, for example, Dunnington, *Tibetan Wheel of Existence*, pp. 73–86; Govinda, *Foundations of Tibetan Mysticism*, pp. 234–47; Gyatso, *Meaning of Life*, p. 13–38; Lauf, *Tibetan Sacred Art*, pp. 140–43; and Tharchin, *King Udrayaṇa and the Wheel of Life*, pp. 82–159.

35. Snellgrove, *Indo-Tibetan Buddhism*, 1:14.

the referential properties of the symbol in question. They discuss what each element means and take different approaches to the process of representation. They take advantage of the pedagogical possibilities ordained by the Buddha in the founding legend of the wheel. Their variety demonstrates that the Twelve Conditions in the wheel of rebirth are both an inalterable dogma and, at the same time, a site of production of further elaboration and logical analysis.

Next in the vinaya story, the Buddha suggests a way of drawing a conceptual border between what lies inside the circle of life and death and what lies outside it. He instructs his followers to draw a "Great Demon of Impermanence" (Wuchang dagui), who holds the entire wheel in his clutches. Impermanence (*anitya*) is, of course, another key doctrine in early Buddhism. In formulaic terms it is the first of the Three Marks (*trilakṣana*)—impermanence, suffering (*duḥkha*), and lack of soul (*anātman*)—that characterize all phenomena. Explanations of impermanence in Buddhist philosophy emphasize the lack of an enduring substance, the constructed nature, the arising and extinction, and the unpleasantness of all things short of nirvāṇa. The major metaphorical use of the term, especially in liturgies and didactic poetry, is as a euphemism for death.[36] In the Indian Buddhist context, the Mūlasarvāstivāda corpus is one of the few places that impermanence seems to have been personified as a threatening, animated being. In the vinaya text he is clearly categorized as a demon. One other section of the Mūlasarvāstivāda vinaya refers to the "Demon of Impermanence" (Wuchang gui), describing him as a being who arrogates fearlessness and power.[37]

The next place to look for clues to the interpretation of the Great Demon of Impermanence, after the second- through fourth-century textual background, is the earliest surviving painting of the wheel of rebirth, at Ajaṇṭā (fifth century). Although that painting has deteriorated badly over the years, enough of it remained in the nineteenth century to show that the monster's body was, like that of other demons painted at Ajaṇṭā, rendered in green.[38] The demon's arms are adorned with jewelry, and he grasps the wheel in his hands and mouth. Medieval Chinese paintings and sculptures (at Yulin and Baodingshan) depict the demon as part human and part animal, while a twelfth-century western Tibetan cave painting (Pedongpo, Tibet) shows four female deities, not very wrathful in appearance, holding the wheel. The early modern painting tradition in Tibet casts the demon in the form of King Yama, Lord of Death. The fourteenth Dalai Lama reports that he once commissioned a painting of the saṃsāracakra held not by Yama but by a skeleton.[39] Although this most recent version does not interpret impermanence in wrathful or animated form, it does maintain the canonical tradition of viewing death as the underlying principle of rebirth.

---

36. See, for example, Morohashi, *Dai kan wa jiten*, no. 19113.426–30. In Tang-dynasty usage, "The Cloister of Impermanence" (Wuchang yuan) was the part of the temple where last rites were performed; see *Fayuan zhulin*, Daoshi (d. 683), *T* no. 2122, 53:987a, citing a text by Daoxuan (596–667).

37. See *Genbenshuoyiqieyoubu pinaiye zashi* (*Mūlasarvāstivāda vinaya kṣudrakavastu*), trans. Yijing (635–713) in 710, *T* no. 1451, 24:403b.

38. See the citations in Schlingloff, *Studies in the Ajaṇṭā Paintings*, p. 169.

39. Gyatso, *Meaning of Life*, p. 12.

The two verses that Śākyamuni says should be inscribed beside the demon are significant for several reasons. First, they constitute the only written element in the whole composition. The rest of the wheel consists of images, the interpretation of which the Buddha assigns to a knowledgeable monk. In contrast to these visual and oral modes, the Buddha here adds a textual element. Compared to the picture and its verbal exegesis, the verses claim more independence from an interpretive community. Notwithstanding the fact that the stanzas are written rather than spoken, and hence assume a literate audience where the pictures do not, the language of the stanzas is, like much didactic Buddhist verse, easily accessible. There are uncomplicated metaphors for important Buddhist teachings (army of life and death, sea of afflictions), similes (the elephant smashing a grass hut to describe the Buddhist's attitude toward saṃsāra), and the most basic words of Buddhist piety (Dharma and vinaya).

The wording of the stanzas takes on added significance when compared to several other versions of the same two stanzas. The two circulated widely in the Buddhist world, appearing in early sources like the Nikāyas (Collections), the many versions of the *Dharmapāda* (*Verses on the Law*, also entitled *Udānavarga*), the *Vinaya vibhaṅga*, and the *Theragāthā*.[40] All of the versions share a certain stock of ideas and images, but the variations are also interesting. The version in the vinaya exhorts people to seek "renunciation" (*chuli*, *naiṣkramya*), a general term connecting the desire to dispense with attachments and seek liberation. Most versions adopt the same wording, but one uses the word denoting the renunciation specific to monks, "giving up the family" (here *shejia*, rather than the more usual *chujia*, both rendering *pravrajya*). "Army of life and death" (*shengsi jun*, *macuno sena*) in our version appears as "hosts of death" (*sizhong*) and "army of impermanence" (*wuchang jun*) in other accounts, and the figure for the defeat of saṃsāra varies as well. In our version it is defeated "like an elephant smashes a thatched hut," but other readings are "like an elephant leaves a house of flowers" and "like an elephant emerges from a lotus pond." Variations in the last two lines may also be significant. Our vinaya text refers generally to the process of rebirth and alludes to nirvāṇa without naming it. By contrast, the Chinese versions of the *Udānavarga* specify "the wheel of birth and death" (*shengsi lun*, *saṃsāracakra*) and the "other shore" (*bi'an*, *pārimaṃtīraṃ*), a stock figure for nirvāṇa.[41]

The two stanzas accompany the Buddha's revelation of the structure of the cosmos in other Buddhist literature as well. *The Legend of King Aśoka* (*Aśokāvadāna*), for

---

40. For a comparison of the two verses in the Nikāyas to Sanskrit, Tibetan, and Chinese versions of the *Udānavarga* and to the *Divyāvadāna* (but not to the Mūlasarvāstivāda vinaya), see Lévi, "L'*Apramāda-varga*," pp. 286–88. The stanzas in the two Chinese versions of the *Udānavarga* discussed below are *Chuyao jing*, trans. Buddhasmṛti (Zhu Fonian, ca. 365), *T* no. 212, 4:649a–b; and *Fa jiyao song jing*, trans. Fajiu (Dharmatrāta?, dates unknown) and Tianxizai (fl. 980–1000), *T* no. 213, 4:779c. For a translation and discussion of the latter, see Willemen, *Chinese Udānavarga*, p. 19. For the *Theragāthā* version, see Norman, *Poems of Early Buddhist Monks*, pp. 33–34.

41. The last two lines of *Chuyao jing* (*T* 4:649b) read: "Break off from birth, old age, sickness, and death, / Transcend suffering and cross to the other shore." The last two lines of *Fa jiyao song jing* (*T* 4:779c) read: "Get rid of the wheel of life and death, / And permanently put an end to the affliction of suffering."

instance, contains a scene well known in Buddhist mythology: the Buddha smiles, and light rays emerge from his mouth.[42] The differently colored rays not only illuminate different realms; they also take a tour of the Buddhist universe. Some travel to the hells and relieve the suffering of beings who live there. The Buddha further creates apparitions of himself, so that the hell beings can generate enough faith to be reborn among gods and humans. Other rays move upward, penetrating the various heavens. There, the light beams are transformed into sound: they declare the two stanzas of the vinaya for the sake of the gods. After completing this salvific tour of the highest and lowest levels of the world, the rays reenter the Buddha's body. Their point of reentry depends upon the kind of prophecy the Buddha wishes to announce: if he wants to predict someone's rebirth as a hungry ghost, for instance, the light is absorbed back into his body through his big toe; future birth as a righteous king is indicated by the light returning to the Buddha's right palm; and so on. Thus, the two stanzas contained in the vinaya account seem to have been common tools of salvation, utilized by the Buddha in dramatic scenes of cosmic disclosure.

Nirvāṇa enters the prose of the vinaya account when the Buddha explains the last component of the picture. The Buddha makes clear that the round, white altar is supposed to refer to nirvāṇa. According to later understandings of the vinaya, in fact, the Buddha's act of referring to nirvāṇa should be drawn directly into the picture itself. Guṇaprabha (sixth-century?) writes, "Above, the Buddha should show the white circle of nirvāṇa."[43] Whether the symbol is a moon or an altar, its roundness symbolizes the perfection of complete extinction, and its whiteness stands for the purity traditionally attributed to the state of nirvāṇa.[44]

Having explained the Buddha's command to replace Maudgalyāyana's dramatic journeys with a complex pictorial representation of the workings of rebirth, the narrative moves on to discuss how the Buddha's followers implement his instructions. The story is one of repeated failures, in which monks unschooled in the interpretation of the diagram are unable to respond to simple questions from laypeople. The episode ends with the seemingly obvious command, attributed to the Buddha, to appoint a monk who understands the symbolism of the wheel to fill the post of preacher.

Up to this point I have treated the vinaya account as an isolated, self-contained story, which of course it is not. It occurs as a pericope in a text entitled *Vibhaṅga* (literally, *Analysis*), which is an explanation of a class of much shorter texts on the vinaya called *pratimokṣa* (literally, "emancipation"). Pratimokṣa texts contain inventories of

---

42. John Strong (personal communication, Sept. 2004) alerted me to this important theme, which I hope he will explore at greater length. For a translation from the Sanskrit, see Strong, *Legend of King Aśoka*, pp. 201–2. In the Chinese version, the rays emerge not from the Buddha's mouth, but from different parts of his body; *Eyuwang jing* (*Aśokarājasūtra*?), trans. Saṃghabhara? (Sengqiepoluo, 460–524), *T* no. 2043, 50:131c–32a.

43. I am here citing the draft translation of a portion of Guṇaprabha's *Vinayasūtra*, graciously given to me by Gregory Schopen. See also Sopa, "Tibetan 'Wheel of Life,'" p. 125.

44. The Tibetan translation and the *Divyāvadāna* read "*nirvāṇa maṇḍala*" (circle or altar of nirvāṇa); see Nishimoto, "Konponsetsuissaiubu binaya," p. 65, n. 15.

offenses deemed significant by the Saṃgha. The list, classified according to the gravity of the crime, was supposed to be recited at semimonthly gatherings. The particular offense to which the story of the wheel is attached is "eating out of turn" (*zhanzhuan shi*), which in the Mūlasarvāstivāda *Pratimokṣa* is number thirty-one in a list of ninety *pāyantika* (Ch.: *poyidijia*) offenses, all of which can be expiated by being confessed in front of other monks.[45] The text of the offense reads, "If a *bhikṣu* eats out of turn, unless it is at an exceptional time, that is a *pāyantika*. Exceptional times are during illness, working, travelling, or the bestowal of robes."[46]

The *Vibhaṅga* contains a number of stories that all involve questions of how monks should behave in accepting offerings of food from lay donors. The story about the wheel of life and death simply serves to introduce a tale, the longest in the chapter, about a boy named Pinsheng, literally meaning "Born in Poverty."[47] All of the major karmic twists in the boy's life—and, as we will see, in his past lives—have to do with vegetarian feasts given by laypeople for monks. An encounter with the wheel of rebirth inaugurates the spiritual life of Born in Poverty. As a boy he visits a temple and sees a picture of the wheel of rebirth. Intrigued, he seeks instruction from the resident monk, asking, "Oh, Sage, what is the name of this thing?" The *bhikṣu* responds, "This is the wheel of life and death in the Five Paths [*wuqu shengsi zhi lun*]," and proceeds to explain what life is like in each of the Five Paths and what deeds people commit to earn rebirth in each of them. The boy is especially interested in being reborn in heaven, so the monk explains what the boy must do to enjoy the pleasures of the gods. First, the monk says, the boy needs to join the Saṃgha, but Born in Poverty responds that that option is impossible. The second option, becoming a layman and observing the five precepts, is also out of the question. Again the boy asks, "What acts can I perform to achieve rebirth in heaven?" and this time the monk holds out a slightly more realistic goal. "If," the monk replies, "you offer food and drink to the Buddha and the Saṃgha, then due to this meritorious cause you shall be reborn in heaven." The boy asks how much the feast will cost, and the monk tells him that five hundred gold pieces will suffice.

Having defined the terms of the boy's salvation, the story then tells how Born in Poverty earns the money needed for a good rebirth. At first he is rejected for work as a day laborer, but he convinces a wealthy man to hire him as a construction worker by agreeing to forego wages if his work does not match that of the stronger men. The

---

45. Authors disagree over the precise rendering of the Sanksrit term *pāyantika* (or *pāyattika*). Some understand it to mean "falling into fire," because those who fail to confess transgressions of this class will fall into the fires of hell. Other readings of the Sanskrit include *pātayantika* (cause to fall) and *prāyaścittikaḥ* (must be confessed). See Edgerton, *Buddhist Hybrid Sanskrit Grammar and Dictionary*, s.v. *pātayantika*, 2:340a–b; and Mochizuki, *Bukkyō daijiten*, pp. 4178c–79b.

46. Translated from *Genbenshuoyiqieyoubu jie jing* (*Mūlasarvāstivāda prātimokṣa sūtra*), trans. Yijing (635–713) in 710, *T* no. 1454, 24:504c. For an English translation of the corresponding Sanskrit, see Prebish, *Buddhist Monastic Discipline*, p. 79. For a comparison to other versions of the rule, see Pachow, "Comparative Study of the Prātimokṣa," p. 157.

47. The story is in *Genbenshuoyiqieyoubu pinaiye*, *T* 23:811c–13c. In the Tibetan version the boy's disadvantaged background is noted, but he is not named; see Nishimoto, "Konponsetsuissaiubu binaya," p. 657, n. 17. For more on the boy's name, see later in this chapter.

boy succeeds admirably: not only does his dedication allow him to finish more work than the others, but everyone on the work crew accomplishes more because the youth entertains them with stories while they labor. The patron returns at the end of the first day and discovers that construction on his new house is much farther along than he thought. He offers to pay Born in Poverty twice the usual amount, but the boy instead negotiates a long-term contract: the man will employ him every day until the house is completed, and if the man is satisfied with the new house, only then does he need to pay the boy's accumulated wages.

When the house is finished, the owner is delighted. He pays Born in Poverty his wages, totaling 450 gold pieces. At this the boy breaks into tears, explaining that he had been hoping to earn 500 gold pieces to use as a gift to the Buddha. The owner proposes to make up the difference of 50 gold pieces, but the boy is concerned that because it includes contributions from others, the total offering will not count as his own meritorious deed. The boy goes to the Buddha, seeking clarification of the proper conditions for making offerings to the Buddhist institution. The Buddha allows that, since the boy's intentions are pure, he need not forego the offer of 50 gold pieces from the owner.

Although he now has enough money to buy the necessary food, the boy still lacks the eating utensils and fine seating required to serve a proper meal to guests. The owner of the new house makes up for this problem too, loaning his new home to Born in Poverty for the day of the feast.

Now that he has accumulated enough money and prepared a fitting meal, Born in Poverty is ready to host the Buddha and the Saṃgha. When they arrive at the elder's house, the boy personally serves the Buddha with his own hands. After the meal the Buddha preaches the Dharma, with the boy seated in front.

Although the offering that motivates the boy's actions from the beginning of the story seems to have been completed, the narrative does not end there. It just so happens that on the day of the feast, a party of five hundred merchants comes to Rājagṛha from overseas. Hoping to trade their goods for food and other supplies, they go to the market but find it deserted. The merchants proceed to the home of the elder and offer to purchase the leftovers from the feast held in honor of the Saṃgha. Born in Poverty refuses to accept their money and instead shares freely everything left from the Saṃgha's meal. The head of the merchants expresses his gratitude for such kind treatment by trying to bestow jewels on Born in Poverty. At first he refuses, saying, "You, kind sir, are very generous, but I cannot accept your gift. I don't want it to obstruct my rebirth in heaven." Faced with another dilemma over the terms of his offering, the boy again asks the Buddha for help. The Buddha advises the boy to accept the merchant's gift, classifying it as immediate compensation, which will not devalue the long-term result the boy seeks.

Having amassed great wealth as a corollary to his devotion, Born in Poverty receives another boon, social prestige. The leading merchant in the city stands on the verge of death. He is old and decrepit, but he has no son to inherit his position. So he organizes a lottery to find an heir: the person who draws a colored seed from a box will be his legal heir and become the next leading elder. When Born in Poverty picks the winning piece, everyone objects, insisting that the rules be changed to best out of three, since Born in Poverty, despite his newly found wealth, is a mere laborer. He of course wins the next drawing as well, which convinces everyone in the city of his suitability for the post. The other elders of Rājagṛha pay their respects to their new leader and give him their daughters in marriage. Treasures miraculously appear in his house, on account of which people call him by a new name, Birth of Good.[48]

After gaining wealth, status, and family, Born in Poverty is finally ready to complete his offering. He invites the Buddha and the Saṃgha to his home for a banquet. He prepares a meal of delicacies and serves the Buddha with his own hands. After the meal the Buddha preaches the Dharma, which causes Born in Poverty and his wife to achieve the first of the Four Fruits, that of stream-enterer. As far as the narrative is concerned, however, becoming a stream-enterer exceeds the ritual frame of the story, which is defined by Born in Poverty's boyhood resolution to achieve rebirth in heaven by making an offering to the Buddha. To achieve the status of a stream-enterer is to go beyond any of the Five Paths of rebirth, including heaven. So the story, in effect, backpedals, stressing the complementarity of the worldly goal of rebirth in heaven and the otherworldly goal of transcendence. While Born in Poverty does not deny that he will eventually achieve nirvāṇa or ultimate release, he circumscribes it, subordinating it to the program of lay Buddhism. The story describes how Born in Poverty reaches an understanding of the Four Noble Truths and achieves the fruit of streamwinner. Then the young man addresses the Buddha:

> Oh, World-Honored One. Because of the Buddha we have achieved the fruit of salvation, which is not something that can be done for us by parents, ancestors, rulers, the hosts of heaven, *śramaṇas*, *brahmins*, relatives, friends, or households. Because we were lucky enough to experience the great, compassionate wisdom of the Buddha, we will be rescued from being reborn in the paths of hell, animals, and hungry ghosts, and will be placed in the exceedingly fine abode of gods and humans. We will arrive at the border where suffering ends, dry up the sea of blood, and pass over the mountain of bones. All of the illusions of a real self that we have built up without end will be extinguished, and we will achieve the first fruit.

---

48. "Birth of Good" translates Shansheng, which would normally be used for the Sanskrit Sujāta. The corresponding Sanskrit in the *Divyāvadāna*, Sahasodgata (from *sahasā abhudgata*), has a slightly different meaning: Suddenly Arisen; see Nishimoto, "Konponsetsuissaiubu binaya," p. 663, n. 27, and Huber, "Études de litterature bouddhique," pp. 27–29. I think it is likely that Yijing or a later Chinese editor was responsible for adding the boyhood name of Born in Poverty to the narrative in its Chinese version. First is the divergence between the meaning of his adult name in Sanskrit (Suddenly Arisen) and in Chinese (Birth of Good). Second is the fact that his boyhood name, which does not occur in the Tibetan version, parallels the Chinese (rather than the Sanskrit) reading of his adult name. Furthermore, the Chinese version is not consistent in its use of the boyhood name, and it often uses a related term, *pinren* (the poor person), to refer to the boy. In other texts, the Chinese name Shansheng renders Sujāta and Siṅgālaka; see Akanuma, *Indo bukkyō koyū meishi jiten*, pp. 649, 620, and Muller, *Digital Dictionary of Buddhism*, s.v. *shansheng shijiaoluoyue*.

Now we take refuge in the Three Jewels of Buddha, Dharma, and Saṃgha. We pray that the World-Honored One acknowledge us as *upāsaka* [layman] and *upāsika* [laywoman]. From now until the end of our lives we will uphold the Five Precepts, from not taking life all the way up to not drinking alcoholic beverages.[49]

The Buddha's disciples have a hard time comprehending the remarkable fortune of Born in Poverty. In answer to their questions, the Buddha makes sense of his rise from servant to stream-enterer by revealing past events.[50] Five hundred lifetimes ago, says the Buddha, during the time of a *pratyekabuddha*, there lived a rich elder. Although people were unable to achieve the Four Fruits (because a full-fledged Buddha was not present), still the *pratyekabuddha* showed great compassion to people. He granted them the opportunity to amass great merit for the future by serving as a field of merit—which is to say, he gave up the isolation for which *pratyekabuddhas* are famous and allowed people to make offerings to him. The elder and his wife are portrayed as pious people who make frequent offerings. All goes well until one day their son sees his mother giving food to the mendicant *pratyekabuddha*. Outraged, the son calls the *pratyekabuddha* "a loafer who accepts other people's food." The boy's parents immediately realize their son's error, which, they fear, will cause him to be reborn in an unpleasant state. The elder leads his son to the *pratyekabuddha*, who displays such great feats of magic that the boy is radically affected. The son bows at the feet of the *pratyekabuddha* and makes an offering. The boy prays that the merit from the act will counterbalance the evil effects of calling the *pratyekabuddha* lazy and that he will be reborn in a rich family. After telling this story, the Buddha explains how the slanderous boy is none other than Born in Poverty. His complicated situation in this life is due to his mixed karma in the past. Long ago he criticized a *pratyekabuddha* but then made a sincere offering. The former deed caused him to be reborn as a servant for five hundred incarnations. But now, says the Buddha, that evil karma has been exhausted, and he has achieved his vow.

The story of Born in Poverty and his past life takes up over two-thirds of the chapter on eating out of turn in the vinaya text. The last third of the chapter contains four more stories, plus the Buddha's clarifications of the rules and exceptions in each case.[51] The incidents all involve questions of how monks should behave when accepting invitations from laypeople to attend vegetarian feasts. The Buddha outlines the circumstances under which other members of the Saṃgha should attend feasts in place of the Buddha, when monks may decline invitations due to illness or travel, how to resolve scheduling conflicts when two donors plan banquets for the same time, and how to prioritize attendance at banquets depending on what offerings (food, cloth, or both) are promised by laypeople.

49. Translation from *T* 25:813c.
50. I summarize the story of the past lives of Born in Poverty from *T* 23:813c–14b.
51. *T* 24:814b–16a.

What is the significance of the wheel of rebirth in this chapter of the vinaya? In the story of Born in Poverty, the wheel functions as a karmic epiphany. Upon seeing pictures of the sufferings of hell and the pleasures of heaven, the boy resolves to seek rebirth in the highest of the Five Paths. In this story, the painting of the wheel seems to fulfill the purpose for which the Buddha designed it. The monk stationed beside the wheel not only elaborates on the conditions of life in each segment, he also establishes the requirements for the boy's reward: if the boy sponsors a vegetarian feast for the Buddha and the Saṃgha, then he will be reborn in heaven. The boy asks the monk to clarify the terms of the bargain, and the monk settles on five hundred gold pieces. That amount—or perhaps the entire ritual transaction, including both offering and result—becomes the boy's focus in life. The problem is: how can a person born in poverty make so much money? The amount cannot be earned through immoral means, and the boy cannot break the terms of the initial deal. Every new development in the story brings the boy closer to his goal, but also threatens to sink the whole agreement. At each critical juncture the boy goes to the Buddha to resolve questions over the interpretation of the transaction, and each time the Buddha allows other people's contributions to be used to raise the necessary funds. The Buddha's flexibility enriches everyone in the story: the boy, who rises literally from rags to riches and eventually to heaven and nirvāṇa; the city of Rājagṛha, which enjoys a reputation for the circulation of wealth; and the Buddhist institution, for which a feast is organized on every possible occasion. The boy uses his own skill to earn money; he enjoys the loan of a house to hold the ritual; his kindness to foreign merchants nets him still more money; and he gains a new station in life thanks to his luck in a lottery.

It is also interesting to view the story of Born in Poverty as one particular reading of the wealth of possibilities pictured in the painting of the wheel of life and death. In the version ordained by the Buddha, the wheel presents several options for rebirth: in addition to the Five Paths, it also contains an altar representing nirvāṇa. Among those alternatives, the one on which Born in Poverty focuses is rebirth in heaven, a choice reinforced by the preacher in the temple. Although birth as a god remains his goal throughout, the narrative still attempts to keep the other destinies within view. In my reading, at the end of the story Born in Poverty postpones the promise of nirvāṇa he has already earned, choosing instead to talk about the practices of lay Buddhism. His unending commitment to the practice of charity brings a superabundance of benefits. In his final speech to the Buddha he verifies that his prospects are a pleasant rebirth, release from saṃsāra, and the eventual attainment of nirvāṇa, but he closes with the ritual formula of the householder. The story of his past life appended to the tale explains that such mixed results are in harmony with the mixed causes of a previous lifetime.

I have suggested that the story of Born in Poverty can be understood as an interpretation of the wheel of birth and death, but the relationship between the two tales is worth clarifying further. We might ask, first, why they are linked in the same vinaya text. I would begin by distinguishing between two principles of order in Buddhist narrative, narrative order and karmic order. The chronological order of the narrative is the sequence of events as the narrative unfolds. There are four important stories, each marked by its own time frame. Maudgalyāyana's tours and preaching come first, marked off as occurring in the past. Second is the story in which the Buddha explains how to construct the wheel of samsāra and the monks try to paint one. The story of the wheel is narrated, as it were, in the imperfect tense. It begins in the past but continues into the present; it constitutes the immediate past of the main action. The third story tells of the boyhood of Born in Poverty, his resolve to sponsor a feast after seeing the wheel of rebirth, and the certification of his salvation. It is framed in the present, although the boundaries encompass nearly the whole lifetime of Born in Poverty. Perhaps we could say that it covers his soteriologically relevant lifetime, beginning with the circumstances of his birth, focusing on how he overcomes the various impediments to fulfilling his agreement to provide a feast, and ending not with his demise, but with his achieving of the first fruit. The fourth story tells of the actions of Born in Poverty five hundred lifetimes earlier, when he set in motion the process that accounts for his current status. Its tense could be called pluperfect, in that its action was completed long ago—except that in Buddhism, the results of past actions are still being felt. In the narrative, the story of the wheel (including the story of Maudgalyāyana) comes first, and the narrative flows in chronological order up until the last story, an addendum explaining how Born in Poverty came to be born in poverty.

Analyzed under a different principle of order, however, the story of the present life of Born in Poverty constitutes the central part of the text, of which the other stories are explanations. In the karmic order of the tale, the main story is presented as a conundrum that the other stories attempt to solve. The puzzle is this: how could a boy born poor become so rich and powerful that his offerings to the Buddha earn him the promise of a better rebirth? The story of his past lives, placed at the end of the narrative, is a stock Buddhist device for interpreting unusual or complicated situations. Long ago Born in Poverty performed both good and bad deeds. He slandered a *pratyekabuddha*, and in questioning the motivation of mendicants who accept food offerings, he cast doubt on the *modus vivendi* of the Buddhist order, the cycle of exchange between laypeople and monks. Those evil deeds explain why Born in Poverty was reborn as a servant five hundred times in a row. Yet the evil was also mixed with good: five hundred lifetimes ago, the boy was, after all, born into a wealthy family; his derision of the *pratyekabuddha* was founded on youthful ignorance; and he tried to repair the damage by apologizing and carrying out an offering. In the karmic order of the text, the story about the wheel of rebirth performs a function analogous to that of the boy's past life—it helps to explain how Born in Poverty could achieve salvation. By telling the story of how the wheel of life and death came into being, the vinaya text helps make sense of the boy's unusual success in conquering saṃsāra.

The stories of the wheel of existence and of Born in Poverty are not found independently in other early texts, so it is hard to guess the shape of the two original stories that the authors of the Mūlasarvāstivāda vinaya had at their disposal. We can comment further, though, on how the two stories are linked in the surviving vinaya text. As noted above, the chapter in which the stories occur constitutes an analysis of one particular offense that was codified in the rules (pratimokṣa) recited by monks at semimonthly gatherings. Such analyses typically contain four parts:

1. A story (or stories) explaining the circumstances under which the rule was pronounced.
2. The pratimokṣa rule.
3. A word-for-word commentary on the rule.
4. Stories indicating mitigating circumstances in which exceptions to the rule or deviations in punishment might be made.[52]

Another interesting feature of the chapter is that the story of the wheel of birth and death is, independently of the rest of the narrative, shaped very much like a standard vinaya analysis. Although the language used to describe the Buddha's directions to paint a wheel is that of "command" (*ci*) rather than "instituting a rule" (*zhi jie*, Pāli: *sikkhāpadaṃ paññāpeti*) for monastic life, in other respects the pericope about the wheel of saṃsāra follows the structure noted above. The four parts of the story of the wheel of rebirth are:

1. The story explaining the circumstances in which the Buddha commanded that wheels be painted in monasteries (as a substitute for Maudgalyāyana's preaching).
2. The command to paint the wheel.
3. A piece-by-piece description of what the wheel should look like.
4. Stories of the successful and unsuccessful implementation of the command.

I am not suggesting that the Buddha's order to paint a wheel of existence in monasteries and to appoint a monk to preach about the wheel was part of the pratimokṣa offenses. Rather, my claim is that insofar as the structure of the surviving story about the wheel follows the pattern of other vinaya vibhaṅga texts, the painting of a wheel and the appointing of a preacher were understood as authoritative commands of the Buddha.

Since the authors of the Mūlasarvāstivāda vinaya viewed the wheel and preacher as "canonical," we would expect to find the Buddha's command listed elsewhere in their vinaya. The *Vibhaṅga* is, after all, an analysis of the pratimokṣa offenses, and there is nothing in the story of the painting of the wheel that could be construed as an offense against the rules of monastic life. Instead, the wheel would be described in prescriptive, rather than prohibitive, terms. Following this line of reasoning, we would expect the command to occur in the two sections of the vinaya dealing with the Saṃgha as a large institution, the structures of communal life (*karmavācanā*) or the discussion and adjudication of those monastic institutions (*skandhaka*). Happily, the *skandhaka* portion of the Mūlasarvāstivāda vinaya does contain a reference to the wheel

52. Quoting Prebish, "The Vinaya Piṭaka," p. 51; see also Hirakawa, *Ritsuzō no kenkyū*, pp. 353–65.

of life and death. It occurs in a text entitled *Miscellaneous Matters* (*Kṣudrakavastu*, Ch.: *Zashi*), which, as its title suggests, was a collection of stories not united by a common theme.[53] The *Kṣudrakavastu*, translated into Chinese by Yijing in 710, contains a section on the art of Buddhist temples.[54] The story begins with Anāthapiṇḍika, the donor of the famous Jetavana monastery in Śrāvastī. Anāthapiṇḍika is concerned that the monastery does not look proper without paintings decorating its walls, so he asks the Buddha for permission to hire artisans. The Buddha grants the layman's request, but Anāthapiṇḍika does not know what subjects should be painted. The Buddha then explains, "Elder, on the two halves of the gate make a *yakṣa* [ogre] holding a club. Beside that, on one side make the great miracle [at Śrāvastī], and on the other side make a wheel of birth and death in the Five Paths [*wuqu shengsi zhi lun*]." Other scenes, the Buddha directs, should be appropriate to their location. The lecture hall should have a picture of an old monk preaching; *yakṣas* serving food ought to be seen in the dining hall; and *yakṣas* carrying jewels should adorn the doors of the treasury. We can assume that because it is mentioned near the beginning of the account of the temple gate, the wheel was supposed to be at or near the main entrance to the temple. Aside from that, though, no details are given about the content of the painting of the wheel of existence, nor do we learn anything about its effect on viewers. We can be certain, however, that the compilers of the Mūlasarvāstivāda vinaya regarded pictures of the wheel of birth and death as an important part of Buddhist life.

Attention must also be paid to the sectarian affiliation of the texts that we have been examining. Mention of the wheel of rebirth occurs only in the vinaya of the Mūlasarvāstivāda school and, as we will see in chapter 3, in the *Divyāvadāna*, which drew extensively from that vinaya. Both in name and in explicit articles of doctrine the Sarvāstivāda and Mūlasarvāstivāda schools were very close, the Mūlasarvāstivāda having grown out of—or perhaps presenting itself as a different version of—the Sarvāstivāda. What is especially interesting for our purposes is that both schools defined themselves, in part, by the position they held on the fate of the dead. The Sarvāstivāda school took its name from the claim that "All exists" (*sarvam asti*, Ch.: *yiqieyou*). According to this doctrine, the three times of past, present, and future must all exist at the same time, since otherwise there would be no causal connection between action (in the past) and consequence (in the future).[55] As a corollary, the Sarvāstivāda maintained that between this life and the next, there is a state of intermediate existence (*antarābhava*, Ch.: *zhongyou*).[56] Upon death a person is not immediately reborn in another path. Rather, one enters a liminal period, usually lasting forty-nine days, during which one assumes bodily form and experiences pain and uncertainty. The karmic

53. For a discussion of the *Mūlasarvāstivāda vinaya kṣudrakavastu*, see Frauwallner, *Earliest Vinaya*, pp. 125–27; and the essays by Schopen cited in note 1 of this chapter.

54. *Genbenshuoyiqieyoubu pinaiye zashi*, *T* 24:283a–b; see also Zürcher, "Buddhist Art in Medieval China," pp. 6–7.

55. Bareau, *Les sectes bouddhiques du petit véhicule*, p. 137; and Willemen, Dessein, and Cox, *Sarvāstivāda Buddhist Scholasticism*.

56. See Bareau, *Les sectes bouddhiques du petit véhicule*, pp. 142–43; and idem, "Chūu."

consequences of actions during one's previous life, as well as the merit created in funerary rituals by one's descendants, are borne by this intermediary existence and then achieve fruition in a subsequent rebirth. Similarly, the Mūlasarvāstivāda based itself on the claim that all of the constituents of being exist during past, present, and future.[57] The Mūlasarvāstivāda theory about personal continuity from one rebirth to the next was perfectly consistent, then, with the school's interest in the wheel of life and death. The philosophical problems about the continuity between lifetimes expressed themselves in later doxographical discussions of time, causality, and selfhood. In art, the same concern is clear in the Mūlasarvāstivāda focus, alone among the medieval schools, on pictorial representations of the process of rebirth.

57. According to Vinītadeva, writing in the eighth century, the first thesis of the Mūlasarvāstivāda was, "Tous les composés (*samskrta*) sont compris (*saṃgrhita*) dans les trois temps, le nom (*nāman*) et la matière (*rūpa*)"; see Bareau, *Les sectes bouddhiques du petit véhicule*, p. 154.

Chapter 3

Temples and Legends

Western India, 350–550 C.E.

The previous chapter may have fostered the illusion that the vinaya of the Mūlasarvāstivāda provides a precise and indisputable norm for all later depictions of the wheel of rebirth. The point of this chapter is to demonstrate not only how influential that account was in establishing a reference for later artists and authors concerned with the saṃsāracakra, but also how indeterminate the canonical versions were. The stupendous cave temples carved into the cliffs at Ajaṇṭā (Maharashtra) are proof that the Buddha's instructions to paint a wheel of rebirth on the walls of monastery porches were taken seriously by members of the aristocracy in western India. Cave 17 at Ajaṇṭā, commissioned in the second half of the fifth century, preserves a painting of the saṃsāracakra on its veranda. The authors and editors of Buddhist texts from the period 350 to 550 also reflected on the significance of the story of the wheel's creation and offered their own versions of it. Rather than giving unquestioned priority to the canonical accounts, this chapter argues that the very definition of what constituted the wheel of rebirth in the Five Paths was always a matter of debate. Literary evidence proves that there were several different versions of the wheel of rebirth. Even the different editions of the vinaya account—in Sanskrit, Chinese, and later, Tibetan—varied in their details, as each vinaya circulated in different Buddhist communities. In addition, the artistic remains show that, despite the Buddha's seemingly straightforward instructions in the vinaya, the iconography of the wheel of rebirth was constantly evolving. Artists still had to struggle with how to divide the wheel into segments, how many of the Twelve Conditions (*nidānas*) to include, and what scenes to paint. Temples could not be built without the involvement of people with different motivations for painting the wheel than those announced by the Buddha in the vinaya. According to the vinaya, monks are supposed to have the wheel painted and then appoint one of their members to explain the painting to others. At Ajaṇṭā, like most of the temple sites discussed in this book, wealthy lay donors commissioned a lavish temple painted by professional artists in order to gain merit for and announce the prominence of the donor's family.

The vinaya account is paralleled, with interesting variations, in the *Divyāvadāna* (*Avadānas of Gods*), a long collection of Sanskrit tales compiled around the year 350.[1] The story of the wheel of existence is one example of a broader pattern: over two-thirds of the thirty-eight stories in the *Divyāvadāna* are excerpted from the Mūlasarvāstivāda vinaya.[2] As a technical term in Buddhist literature, *avadāna* (from *ava√dā*, literally "cutting off" and hence "exploit" or "meritorious act") refers to legends about deeds of people in the past or future that have a morally relevant result. They often contain a story of the present, a story of the past, and an identification of how past deeds are related to current results.[3]

Like the account in the vinaya, the narrative in the *Divyāvadāna* is based on the story of the boy who, though born into poverty, becomes a member of the village elite, makes good on his vow as a youth to provide a large feast for the Buddha and the Saṃgha, and thereby achieves a glimpse of nirvāṇa. The figure of a monk explaining the wheel of rebirth appears early in the story, providing an impetus for the boy to aspire to pious deeds. Rather than calling the boy "Born in Poverty," the *avadāna* account supplies the character's name only after he inherits the elder's wealth, calling him Sahasodgata (Suddenly Arisen). Like the vinaya, the *Divyāvadāna* begins with the story of Maudgalyāyana and how the Buddha institutes the painting of a wheel in the monastery. It follows the boy's progress through life as he strives to fulfill his part of the ritual bargain struck with the preacher who explains the wheel. It also concludes the same way as does the segment of the vinaya: it relates the story of how an elder's son insulted a *pratyekabuddha* in a past life, and it identifies the slanderous son from long ago as an earlier incarnation of Sahasodgata.

The commonalities in the two accounts demonstrate, in general terms, some of the concerns over the representation of life and death that were current in Indian Buddhist circles during this time. In both texts, saṃsāra is best explained by a preacher using an illustration as a teaching aid. The picture is a combination of symbols requiring exegesis on the one hand and words on the other. The preacher must be knowledgeable, and he is seen as taking the place of Maudgalyāyana. The anachronism of the two versions is also interesting, since even if the Mūlasarvāstivāda vinaya was first formed as early as the second century C.E., still both texts are working with a mythologized recollection—not an experience—of Maudgalyāyana. From this perspective,

1. On the date of the text, see Okano, "Chūki Avadaana bunken no kenkyū shi"; Vaidya, *Divyāvadāna*, p. xii; and Winternitz, *History of Indian Literature*, 2:284–90. For translations of the passage in question, see Khantipalo, *Wheel of Birth and Death*, pp. 11–14; Nara, "Shigo no sekai," pp. 78–79; and Rotman, "Wheel of Existence." I am also indebted to Gregory Schopen for sending me his unpublished translation of the account in the *Divyāvadāna*.

2. For the sources of the *Divyāvadāna* and its relation to the Mūlasarvāstivāda vinaya, see Satoshi Hiraoka, "Relation between the *Divyāvadāna* and the *Mūlasarvāstivāda vinaya*"; Huber, "Études de littérature bouddhique"; Lévi, "Les éléments de formation du Divyāvadāna"; Okano, "Chūki Avadaana bunken no kenkyū shi"; and Przyluski, "Fables in the Vinaya-Piṭaka of the Sarvāstivādin School."

3. See, for example, Malalasekera et al., *Encyclopaedia of Buddhism*, s.v. *avadāna*, 2:395–98; and Tatelman, *Glorious Deeds of Pūrna*, pp. 4–12.

Maudgalyāyana functions more as an example of a charismatic preacher than as a disciple of the Buddha. Similarly, the Buddha does not appear in the role of teacher or sage. Rather, in both texts he serves as an assurance of the validity of the painting of the wheel of existence. Constructed by later Buddhist communities long after the Buddha and Maudgalyāyana had become stock figures for authority and transgression, respectively, the story functions as a charter for a practice of talking about death.

The differences between the two accounts are also interesting. The *Divyāvadāna*, like the later Tibetan translation of the vinaya, consistently credits both Śāriputra and Maudgalyāyana, working together, with the forte of traveling to other realms and returning to educate people about karmic retribution. Yijing's Chinese translation of the vinaya, by contrast, usually portrays Maudgalyāyana alone in this role. The texts also differ in how they refer to the wheel. Where the *Divyāvadāna* calls it a "wheel having five sections" (*pañcagaṇḍaka cakra*), the Chinese vinaya refers to a "wheel of birth and death" (*shengsi lun*, corresponding to Skt.: *saṃsāracakra*) and a "wheel of birth and death in the five paths" (*wuqu shengsi lun*, corresponding to Skt.: *pañcagati saṃsāracakra*). In the Chinese vinaya the wheel is supposed to be painted "beneath the room at the gate of the temple" (*simen wu xia*), while the *Divyāvadāna* reads "in the entrance hall" (*dvārakoṣṭake*).[4] For the cycle of origination depicted in the outer ring of the wheel, the *Divyāvadāna* simply refers to the twelve stages of dependent origination (*pratītyasamutpāda*) without explaining which symbols to use, while the vinaya (in Chinese but not Tibetan) specifies eighteen causes and their proper symbols.

The accounts also diverge systematically over the role of lay Buddhists. The Chinese vinaya offers a long description, not included in the *Divyāvadāna*, of the content of Maudgalyāyana's sermons to laypeople, including his teachings on karmic retribution, specific precepts to follow, and the metaphor of ripening. The Chinese vinaya notes that in addition to monks and nuns bringing their disciples, laypeople would bring their sons and daughters to attend Maudgalyāyana's performances. The *Divyāvadāna* states merely that monks would bring their "coresidential pupils" (*sārdhaṃ vihārin*) and "disciples" (*antevāsin*). The Chinese vinaya betrays a heightened concern over the relationship between monks and laypeople; in its eyes, the audience for preaching about life and death was largely composed of laypeople. This difference in emphasis is particularly interesting for what it might say about the concerns of the monastic establishment in medieval India. Current scholarly opinion is divided over the authorship and audience of the *Divyāvadāna*: some believe that it was directed at laypeople, others regard it as a largely monastic text.[5]

---

4. See Schopen, "Hierarchy and Housing in a Buddhist Monastic Code," pp. 173–75; cf. Edgerton, *Buddhist Hybrid Sanskrit Grammar and Dictionary*, 2:273b–74a.

5. Compare Upreti, *India as Reflected in the Divyāvadāna*, p. 21—"The style and contents of the book make it evident that it was essentially compiled for the consumption of the masses. The use of popular language, the deep religiosity and the frequent use of stock-phrases all point in that direction. The compiler's main objective was to arouse interest and respect for Buddhism among the laity"—with Vaidya, *Divyāvadāna*, p. xii, which says that the stories seem to have been "put

The other literary account of the saṃsāracakra is much more fragmentary than the account in the *Divyāvadāna*, and its dating is uncertain. I place it in this discussion of the early Indian milieu because it seems closest to the other sources treated here. The source is an untitled set of seven Sanskrit fragments retrieved from Duldur-aqur (part of ancient Kucha, modern Xinjiang) by Paul Pelliot. In 1959 Bernard Pauly realized their significance, reassembled the fragments, and transcribed and translated them.[6]

The content of the text is close to that of the vinaya account. Maudgalyāyana's tours are mentioned, and most of the text is a detailed prescription of how to paint the wheel, which it explicitly refers to as a "circle of the wheel of rebirth" (*saṃsāracakrasya maṇḍala*). The wheel is divided into five parts. Like the vinaya, the text lists eighteen links in the chain of causation and specifies what symbols should be used to represent them (see table 1 in chapter 1). One link differs from those listed in the vinaya, and most of the symbols are the same. The text is notable for placing a depiction of the Buddha above and outside the wheel of rebirth. Other interesting additions are also stationed outside the wheel. The text states that figures representing each of the Four Fruits (stream-enterer, once-returner, non-returner, and *arhat*) should be painted outside the circle. In addition to these four advanced practitioners of Buddhism, ancient worthies and sages of Brahmanism (doctors, astronomers, etc.) should be portrayed. The whole construction is supposed to be grasped by Impermanence, shown in the form of a three-headed *rakṣa*. In another variation, the text explains that Māra, the personification of death, should be shown in his different forms turning the wheel.

Comparing this fragmentary, undated text to the Mūlasarvāstivāda vinaya, of which it is probably a variant version, yields some important observations. Both texts seem to concur about the connection between Maudgalyāyana and the wheel of rebirth, and their depictions of the interior of the wheel are nearly identical. The undated text shows the greatest innovation in its discussion of figures painted outside of the wheel. Not only the Buddha, but virtuous models like *arhats* should be depicted. These paragons of good are matched, in a way, by the proliferation of Māra-like figures who cause the cycle of rebirth to continue. The inclusion of people famous for their technical achievements suggests that other, less ultimate issues could be joined to the soteriological program of the composition.

An even richer sense of the varieties of Buddhist cosmology at the time is apparent in the wall painting in the Buddhist cave temple complex at Ajaṇṭā. The caves at Ajaṇṭā are an immense monument to the flourishing state of western Indian political and religious culture in the late fifth century (see map 4). For most of the fifth century the Gupta empire dominated northern India, while the Vākāṭaka house ruled in the central part of the subcontinent. The Vākāṭakas were subdivided into eastern and

together for ease and convenience of instruction to young monks." Given that "young monks" had only recently been members of the "laity," perhaps the difference is purely perspectival.

6. Pauly, "Fragments sanskrits de Haute Asie (Mission Pelliot)," pp. 228–40; analyzed also in Zin, *Devotionale und ornamentale Malereien*, 1:442–45.

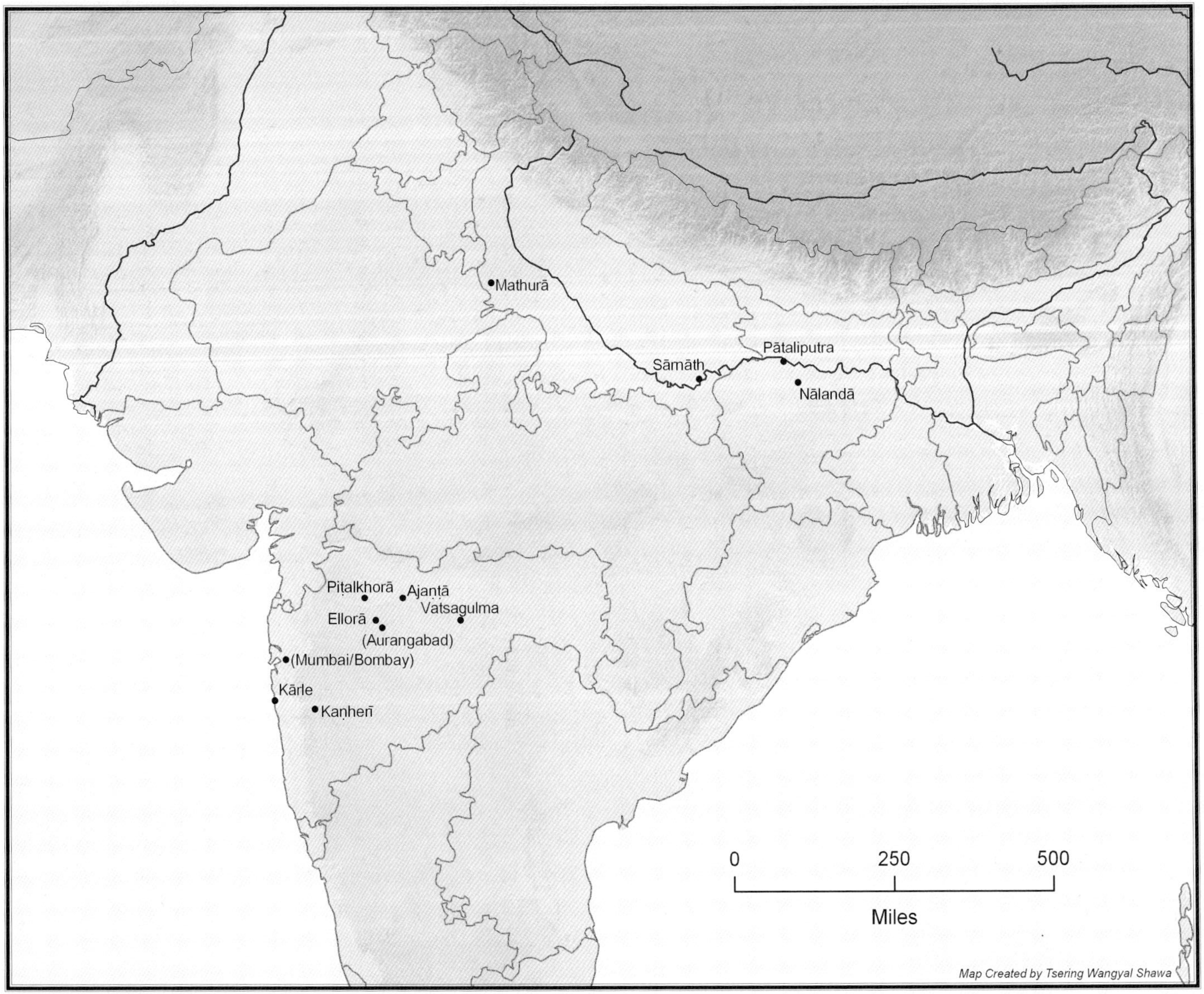

Map 4. Western India, ca. 500.

western branches, the balance of power between them changing more than once. The western Vākāṭaka were based in the capital of Vatsagulma, located some 160 kilometers east of the Ajaṇṭā caves, on the eastern edge of the Ajaṇṭā plateau. Relative to their eastern cousins, the western branch of the Vākāṭakas, who were responsible for the fifth-century cave temples at Ajaṇṭā, were more wealthy and their art more indulgent. According to Hans Bakker, their inscriptions compare their rulers not to righteous human heroes of the past, but to gods like Indra and Rāma. Dedications to Buddhist temples erected by the western Vākāṭakas refer to their kings as "great kings of the Dharma" (*dharmamahārāja*). Bakker writes that the Buddhist murals at Ajaṇṭā are distinguished by representations of "sensuous pleasures and sophisticated refinement. . . . They reflect the very world of leisure and affluence that enabled their donors to be magnanimous."[7] In art, religion, and literature, the western Vākāṭakas shared much with the Gupta empire to the north and the branch of the Vākāṭaka family to the east. Members of both branches made pious donations both to Hindu sites (dedicated to Maheśvara/Śiva or Bhagavat/Viṣṇu) and to Buddhist institutions, although Buddhist inclinations appear especially strong in the west. Under their reign other important cave temples in the modern Maharashtra state were excavated at Ghaṭōtkacha, Gulwāḍā, Kaṇherī, Kārle, and Piṭalkhorā.

The Ajaṇṭā caves are located along a basalt cliff formed by volcanoes and the cutting action of the Waghora River (see fig. 3.1). The site attracted human attention as early as the first century B.C.E., when a few caves were carved out of the rock and used for monastic residences. These early caves are common all across the Deccan Plateau. Beginning as early as Aśoka's time, merchant princes in the area sponsored the excavation of cave temples near the capitals, many of which lay on or near important caravan routes. In early Indian thinking, such retreats were designed for quiet meditation. As one source puts it, "an ideal place for the contemplation of the Divine is a hidden cave protected from wind, situated in surroundings made favourable to the mind by the sound of water and other features and not offensive to the eye."[8] Like most of the thousands of surviving paintings at Ajaṇṭā, the wheel of rebirth (located in Cave 17) was executed later, near the end of the fifth century under the western Vākāṭaka dynasty, during the height of activity at the caves (see fig. 3.2).[9]

---

7. Bakker, *Vākāṭakas*, p. 58, 44. See also Williams, "Vākāṭaka Art and the Gupta Mainstream."
8. Deshpande, "Buddhist Art of Ajanta and Tabo," p. 3.
9. The dating of the cave in which the wheel of rebirth is located (Cave 17) is a difficult problem, enmeshed in the broader controversy over the dating of the whole Ajaṇṭā complex. Following the epigraphical studies of Vasudev Mirashi and the analysis of a Sanskrit play written 550–650 that reflects on earlier political events, most scholarship now dates the set of caves in which the wheel is located to the years 475–500. See Mirashi, *Inscriptions of the Vākāṭakas*; and idem, "Historical Data in Daṇḍin's *Daśakumāra charita*." For the *Daśakumāracarita*, see Ryder, *Ten Princes*; and De Caroli, "An Analysis of Daṇḍin's *Daśakumāracarita*." More recently, relying on a closer archaeological analysis, Walter Spink has suggested that most of the Ajaṇṭā caves were completed in a flurry of activity between 462 and 480. Spink dates Cave 17 to 463–471, while his critics place it slightly later, 490–505. See Spink, *Ajaṇṭā*; idem, "Ajaṇṭā's Chronology"; idem, "Archaeology of Ajaṇṭā"; and idem, "Vākāṭaka's Flowering and Fall." For other opinions, see Gupta, "Authorship

FIG. 3.1. Ajaṇṭā Cave 16 (right) and Cave 17 (left) in cliff face. Photo courtesy of American Institute of Indian Studies, 1393/72 and 1392/72.

The structure and patronage of the cave temples at Ajaṇṭā are important for understanding the painting of the wheel of rebirth located there. Most of the caves follow one of two architectural models, a hall for worship (*caitya*) or a residence for monks (*vihāra*).[10] The *caityas* at Ajaṇṭā (Caves 9, 10, 19, and 26 in the site map, fig. 3.2) are oblong structures that emulate wooden halls with vaulted ceilings, often including real timber ribs and stone pillars. Their liturgical focus is a stūpa located near the back of the hall. Like earlier earthen mounds containing relics of the Buddha or of monks,

of Ajaṇṭā Caves 17 to 20"; Khandalavala, "Chronology of Caves 16, 17, 19, 26, and 2 at Ajaṇṭā and the Ghatotkacha Cave"; Weiner, *Ajaṇṭā: Its Place in Buddhist Art*; and Williams, *Art of Gupta India*, pp. 181–87.

10. For the evolution of *caitya* and *vihāra* forms, see Percy Brown, *Indian Architecture*, pp. 6–74; Dehejia, *Early Buddhist Rock Temples*; Harle, *Art and Architecture of the Indian Subcontinent*, pp. 43–58, 118–22; Li, *Zhong Yin fojiao shikusi bijiao yanjiu*, pp. 35–130; and Sadakane, "Indo bukkyō kaiga no tenkai."

the monolithic stūpas at Ajaṇṭā are usually round at the top. In some of them a Buddha statue is carved into the front of the stūpa. The rear of the *caitya* is round, allowing ritual circumambulation of the stūpa.

By contrast, the other major architectural type at Ajaṇṭā, that in which the wheel of rebirth is located, is a square residence hall or *vihāra* (see fig. 3.3). The main hall is entered from a door in a vestibule or porch. Around the walls of the hall are cut doorways leading into square cells that serve as residences for monks. The cave in which the wheel of rebirth is found follows the model of later *vihāras* at Ajaṇṭā. Compared to earlier *vihāras*, the later ones expanded the space at the rear of the hall previously used for monastic cells and placed a Buddha statue inside. The icon became the new ritual focus of the cave. As Percy Brown writes, "The appropriation of these cells originally serving as dormitories for the monks and their conversion into sanctuaries for the reception of images of the Buddha is significant of the alteration in the belief as a whole. It meant, firstly, that the *vihāra* was now fulfilling the functions of both abbey and church, secondly, that relic worship was being supplanted by image worship, and

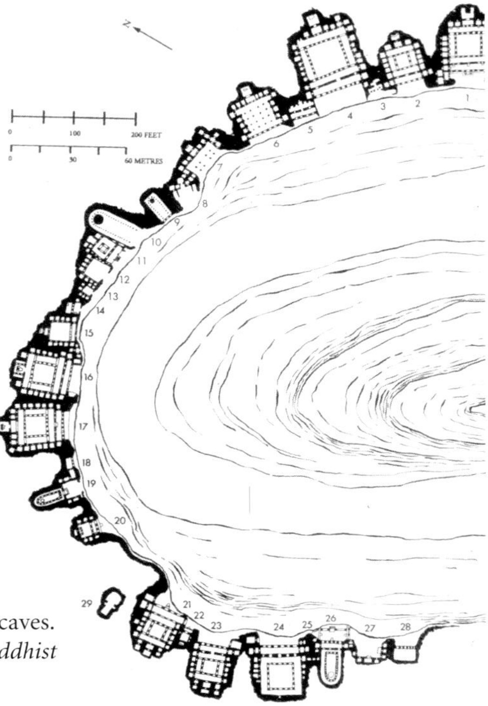

FIG. 3.2. Sketch map of Ajaṇṭā caves. After Burgess, *Report on the Buddhist Cave Temples.*

thirdly, that the dominating cult of Hinduism was not only influencing the Buddhist doctrine, but also was vitally affecting its art and architectural practice."[11]

The center of these *vihāras* is a shrine room located in the rear center, containing a large image of the Buddha. For donors, this image, the largest in the hall, was the main purpose for commissioning a cave. The dedication of the Buddha statue marked the completion of the cave and the actualization of the patron's merit. In the eyes of the commissioners of such caves, the main Buddha image did not simply represent the Awakened One. Rather, as Lisa Owen and Gregory Schopen have suggested, the sculpted Buddha was itself considered to be the living Buddha. Most of the dedications at Ajaṇṭā refer to the main Buddha statue not as an "image" of some kind (*biṃba*, *pratikṛti*, or *pratimā*), but as a kind of person: a Thus Come One (Tathāgata), a teacher, or, as in Cave 17, the king of ascetics (*munirāja*).[12] The main shrine containing the Buddha was sometimes flanked by two minor shrines dedicated to *yakṣas*. The central part of the *vihāra* at Ajaṇṭā is an open square hall, marked off by pillars. The actual residences for monks are small rooms carved out of the side and back walls. Judging from their current condition, the cells originally contained a bed and a shelf and had wooden

11. Percy Brown, *Indian Architecture*, p. 68.

12. See Owen, "Constructing Another Perspective for Ajaṇṭā's Fifth-Century Excavations," pp. 30–31, 44; building on Schopen, "The Buddha as an Owner of Property and Permanent Resident in Medieval Indian Monasteries."

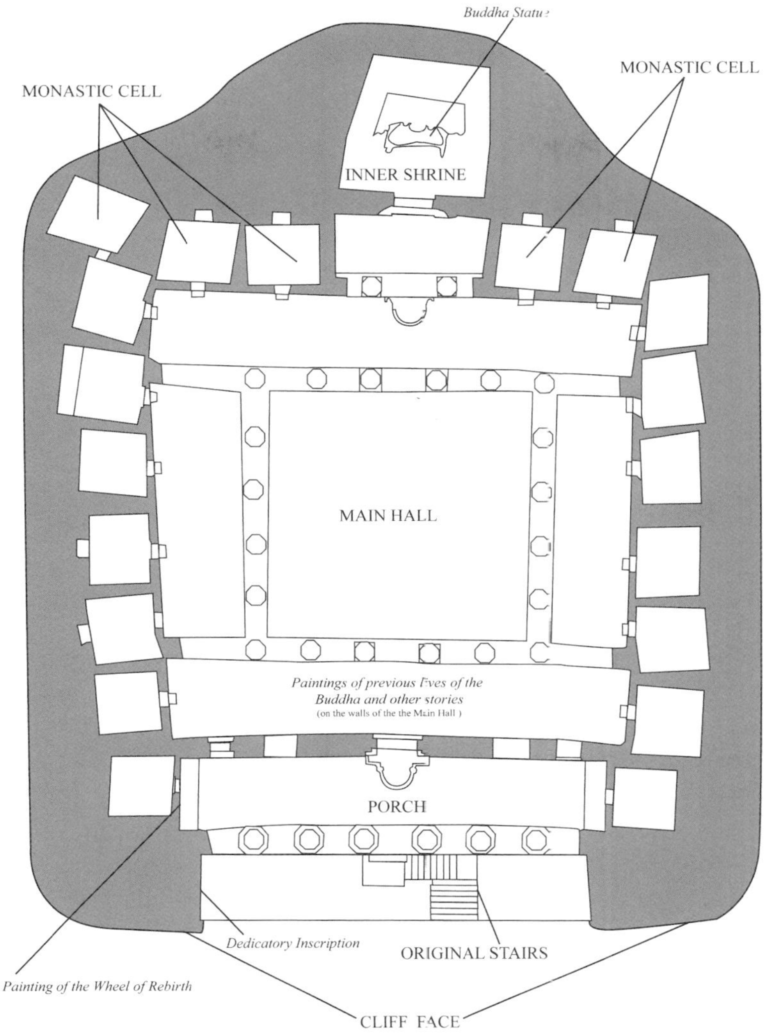

FIG. 3.3. Plan of Ajaṇṭā Cave 17. After Fergusson and Burgess, *Cave Temples of India*, fig. 33, right. Drawn by Sorat Tungkasiri and Stephen F. Teiser.

doors that could be closed and latched. Running along the front of the *vihāra* was a long porch, often with small rooms excavated at either end.

After the caves were carved out and smoothed, the walls and ceilings were plastered and then painted. The ceilings were decorated with geometric designs, flowers, and some mythical figures, but the richest images were the paintings on the walls. Their subject matter covers a wide range of Buddhist mythology. The vast majority of the paintings have parallel narratives in two specific texts that were well known in western India at the time. The first is Ārya Śūra's (third century?) *Jātakamāla*, a postcanonical collection of tales of the previous lives of the Buddha. Many of them depict the

Bodhisattva as an animal, and many of them involve royal characters. The second text (or, rather, set of texts) is the vinaya of the Mūlasarvāstivāda, which, as noted above, provides a *locus classicus* for the painting of the wheel of rebirth. The question of where the later Ajaṇṭā donors stand in relation to the divergence between Mahāyāna and Hīnayāna is largely irrelevant.[13] Some of the monastic donors place themselves consciously in the lineage of monks that began with the Buddha's son, Rahula. In scenes from the life of the Buddha at Ajaṇṭā, emphasis is placed on the miracles performed at Śrāvastī and on the Buddha's descent to earth to preach to human beings after having spread the Dharma to the gods (and his mother) residing in the Heaven of Thirty-three.

In the heyday of Ajaṇṭā, the entrance to each cave was a grand sight. In modern times the caves are linked by a cement walkway added to the front of the caves high above the river valley. Originally, however, many caves had their own set of stairs leading up from the river. The entryways (like the one still standing at Cave 16) attracted the attention of medieval pilgrims. Xuanzang (602–664), who did not actually visit Ajaṇṭā, cites the lore he heard:

> On the eastern frontier of the country is a great mountain with towering crags and a continuous stretch of piled-up rocks and scarped precipice. In this there is a *saṃghārāma* constructed, in a dark valley. Its lofty halls and deep side-aisles stretch through the face of the rocks—story above story they are backed by the crag and face the valley. . . .
>
> On the four sides of the *vihāra*, on the stone walls, are painted different scenes in the life of the Tathāgata's preparatory life as a bodhisattva: the wondrous signs of good fortune which attended his acquirement of the holy fruit, and the spiritual manifestations accompanying his nirvāṇa. These scenes have been cut out with the greatest accuracy and fineness. On the outside of the gate of the *saṃghārāma*, on the north and south side, at the right hand and the left, there is a stone elephant. The common report says that sometimes these elephants make a great cry and the earth shakes throughout.[14]

Like other large monuments, the Ajaṇṭā caves may be said to have monumentalized more than one thing. The *vihāras* enshrined a large image of the Buddha, which served as a focus of devotion for all and a generator of merit for its commissioner. The Dharma was evident in the paintings that advertised the most important stories of Buddhism, supplying a rich environment for the resident monks and a topic of reflection for any visitors. The *vihāras* also housed monks, the support of whom was simultaneously a duty of the rich and an index of their wealth. Thus, the Ajaṇṭā caves, like other Bud-

---

13. See Cohen, "Setting the Three Jewels," esp. chaps. 4–6.
14. *Datang xiyu ji*, Xuanzang (602–664), *T* no. 2087, 51:935b, translated in Beal, *Si-yu-ki*, 2:257–59.

dhist centers, testified to the importance of the Three Jewels as well as to the prominence of the donors who supported the Three Jewels.

Thanks to the preservation of a long inscription at Cave 17, we know a fair amount about the announced intentions of the person who donated the *vihāra* in which the wheel of rebirth is located. The inscription, part of which is damaged, begins, "Having bowed to the sage [Buddha] who has completely mastered the three laws and who is a thunderbolt to the tree of worldly existence, . . . I will set forth a description of the excellences of the donor of the *vihāra*, whose deeds are pure."[15] The text goes on to mention a lineage of kings, which has led some interpreters to identify the local ruler, Upendragupta, as donor of the cave.[16] The inscription also mentions Hariṣena, the king of the Vākāṭaka dynasty, whom Upendragupta served, as well as one of the competing kingdoms (Aṣmaka). The inscription also states that the donor planned for a cistern to be built at the cave, "pleasing to the eyes and filled with sweet, light, clear, cold, and copious water." The inscription closes by assigning the merit resulting from the construction of the *vihāra*:

> Let all the blessings so highly desired in the world [possessed by this donor], who undertakes his every deed for the benefit of living beings . . . , serve to complete his vow to become a Lord of Sages.
>
> May this pavilion [presented] with affection . . . help good people to produce merit as long as the sun dispels darkness by its rays. Amen.[17]

The preceding discussion has suggested some answers to the question of who made the wheel of life at Ajaṇṭā and what purposes it served. It remains to consider the picture itself, but that task is complicated by the ravages of time and modern stabs at preservation, which have caused serious deterioration. Shortly after the caves were rediscovered in 1819, early studies interpreted the wheel as an Indian zodiac, but scholars now agree that it represents the wheel of existence.[18] The painting has deteriorated so badly (sometimes at the hand of collectors) that a documentary oil painting of the scene, made late

---

15. Trans. Mirashi, *Inscriptions of the Vākāṭakas*, p. 127.

16. Chandrashekhar Gupta and Walter Spink identify Upendragupta as the donor; others are less certain. See Bakker, *Vākāṭakas*, pp. 38, 88–89; Khandalavala, "Chronology of Caves 16, 17, 19, 26, and 2 at Ajaṇṭā and the Ghatotkacha Cave"; Gupta, "Authorship of Ajaṇṭā Caves 17 to 20"; Mirashi, *Inscriptions of the Vākāṭakas*, pp. 120–29; Spink, *Ajaṇṭā: A Brief History and Guide*; idem, "Archaeology of Ajaṇṭā"; and idem, "Vākāṭaka's Flowering and Fall."

17. Trans. Cohen, "Setting the Three Jewels," pp. 367–71; cf. Mirashi, *Inscriptions of the Vākāṭakas*, p. 12a. Cohen interprets "becoming the Lord of Sages" as the desideratum of the Buddha on whom the donor meditates, whereas Mirashi believes that the donor himself desires to become the Lord of Sages. I have corrected typographical errors in Cohen's translation.

18. One of the earliest attempts to read the painting as a saṃsāracakra rather than a zodiac was by L. Augustine Waddell, who in 1892 based his exegesis of the Indian material on the paintings he had observed in Tibetan temples; see Waddell, "Buddhist Pictorial Wheel of Life"; and idem, "Buddha's Secret from a Sixth-Century Pictorial Commentary and Tibetan Tradition." A few years later, Caroline A. Foley (later known as Caroline A. F. Rhys David) linked the painting to the account

in the nineteenth century under the supervision of John Griffiths, now supplies a better idea of the whole wheel than the original painting that survives on-site.[19] Not only is the surface of the wall painting in tatters, the stone and plastering underneath it have also suffered much damage. A brief consideration of the archaeology and original architecture of Cave 17 is necessary before analyzing the content of the painting.

The wheel of saṃsāra is located not inside the main hall of the *vihāra* cave, but on the veranda outside the entrance to the cave (see fig. 3.3). There is a room at each end of the porch, accessible by a doorway. The wheel is located over one of these doorways, on the left wall. In its current condition, however, a 90-degree swatch at the bottom right of the wheel appears to have been left out, and the top of the hole cut for the doorway juts up into that space instead (see fig. 3.4). Studies based largely on iconography have tried to solve this apparent anomaly by suggesting that the artist, presented with a doorway cutting away a portion of his compositional space, adjusted to the physical limitations of the site by crowding the rest of the original circle into the remaining 270 degrees.[20] Others, however, believe that the original painting was a full circle comprising 360 degrees. As early as 1828, a British army officer, Captain Gresley, voiced the opinion that the top of the doorway had been patched up and that the original painting included a full, 360-degree wheel.

The account by Gresley's traveling companion, a Mr. Ralph, is worth quoting at length:

> . . . I left Aurungabad, and went seven marches eastward that I might join Captain Gresley, and induce him to come thither with me. . . . we came in two breakneck

---

in the *Divyāvadāna*; see Foley, "Correspondence." In my reading of the painting, I largely follow Sadakane, "Ajantā daijūshichikutsu no 'goshu shōjirin' hekiga." For other important studies of the iconography of the wheel, see Hiraoka Mihoko, "Indo no shōjirin zu"; Przyluski, "La roue de la vie à Ajaṇṭā"; Schlingloff, "Das Lebensrad in Ajaṇṭā"; idem, *Studies in the Ajaṇṭā Paintings*, pp. 167–74; Umezu, "Goshu shōjirin zu ni tsuite"; and Zin, *Devotionale und ornamentale Malereien*, 1:446–53.

19. The copy was made by a team of artists from the Jamshedji Jijibhai School of Art in Bombay working under Griffiths between 1872 and 1885; see Griffiths, *Paintings in the Buddhist Cave-Temples of Ajaṇṭā*, vol. 1, pl. 56. I have not seen the original copy and assume that it was burned along with more than half of the copies made by Griffiths's students in a fire in the Victoria and Albert Museum in 1885; see Schlingloff, *Studies in the Ajaṇṭā Paintings*, p. x. Already in the nineteenth century the original wall painting had been subject to serious destruction. In 1880, James Fergusson and James Burgess (*Cave Temples of India*, p. 310, n. 1) report on the condition of the wheel, then still understood as a zodiac, writing, "In 1828 Lieutenant Blake counted 73 figures in three divisions of this shield, varying from 5 to 7 inches in height, and apparently only about a third of it was then wanting. Dr. Bird is believed to have removed some of the figures from it, and a mere fragment now remains." For photographs of what remained of the original wall painting in the 1950s, see Yazdani, *Ajaṇṭā, Plates*, portfolio vol. 4, pls. 4a–7a.

20. See Schlingloff, *Studies in the Ajaṇṭā Paintings*, chap. 17, esp. figs. 1 and 2, pp. 383–84; Griffiths, *Paintings in the Buddhist Cave-Temples of Ajaṇṭā*, 1:35 ("It never could, however, have been a complete wheel, as the cell-door cuts into the lower part of it"); and Yazdani, *Ajaṇṭā, Text*, 4:21, n. 2 ("The circle of the wheel could never have been complete because its lower part is cut by the cell-door"). More recently, Dieter Schlingloff agrees that the original doorway was patched up and the circle made whole; see Schlingloff, *Guide to the Ajaṇṭā Paintings*, p. 39; and Zin, *Devotionale und ornamentale Malereien*, 1:440–56.

> marches, galloping over stony roads and rocky torrents at the rate of ten miles an hour. . . . During the last two days Gresley has been with me, and his exclamations of admiration and regret, the mere variations of wonder,—would fill three pages. The paintings, which are fast fading and falling away, demand consideration. There is nothing in India like them. They give us glimpses of a former world—but alas! how industriously these valuable and beautiful remains have been by violence destroyed! . . .
>
> These caves are becoming daily more difficult of access. You pass along narrow goat paths with a chasm of 50 or 80 feet below, the footing not nine inches broad, with scarce any thing to cling to. The rains yearly making the passages worse.[21]

Ralph's account continues with his and Gresley's impressions of the artwork in the caves, much of it viewed with the aid of torches made from dry grass. They were particularly interested in the wheel of rebirth in Cave 17, at that time still understood as a zodiac. Ralph, however, questions this identification:

> This zodiac, as they call it, is very elaborate. Why they call it zodiac I know not. There is in one part a bull, and in another scales. We must get a ladder to see it clearly. It might have been called the shield of Achilles as well as a zodiac. There have been eight grand compartments and sixteen smaller ones—how full of little figures! I think this is the best example in the whole series, and evidently done by the same painters who worked in what we call "*par excellence*" the painted caves. . . . [22]

Ralph believes that the original painting was incomplete, its bottom third cut out by the doorway. Gresley, however, disagrees. According to Gresley's notes, the conversation went as follows:

> Ralph: The zodiac is incomplete. I think about a third of it is wanting, and the lower part of the circle could never have been complete, for it must have been over this door of the cell.
>
> Gresley: Perhaps they covered the top of the doorway with something in order to complete the circle.
>
> Ralph: You admire it so much: you are willing to suppose it must have been complete.[23]

In keeping with Gresley's reasoning almost two hundred years ago, more recent archaeological evidence, gathered by Walter Spink, suggests that the artists filled in the upper

21. Ralph, cited in Prinsep, "Facsimiles of Ancient Inscriptions, Part IV," p. 557.
22. Ralph, cited in ibid., p. 559.
23. Ibid.

FIG. 3.4. Wall with painting of the wheel of rebirth. Porch of Ajaṇṭā Cave 17, fifth century. Courtesy of the John C. and Susan L. Huntington Archive of Buddhist and Related Art.

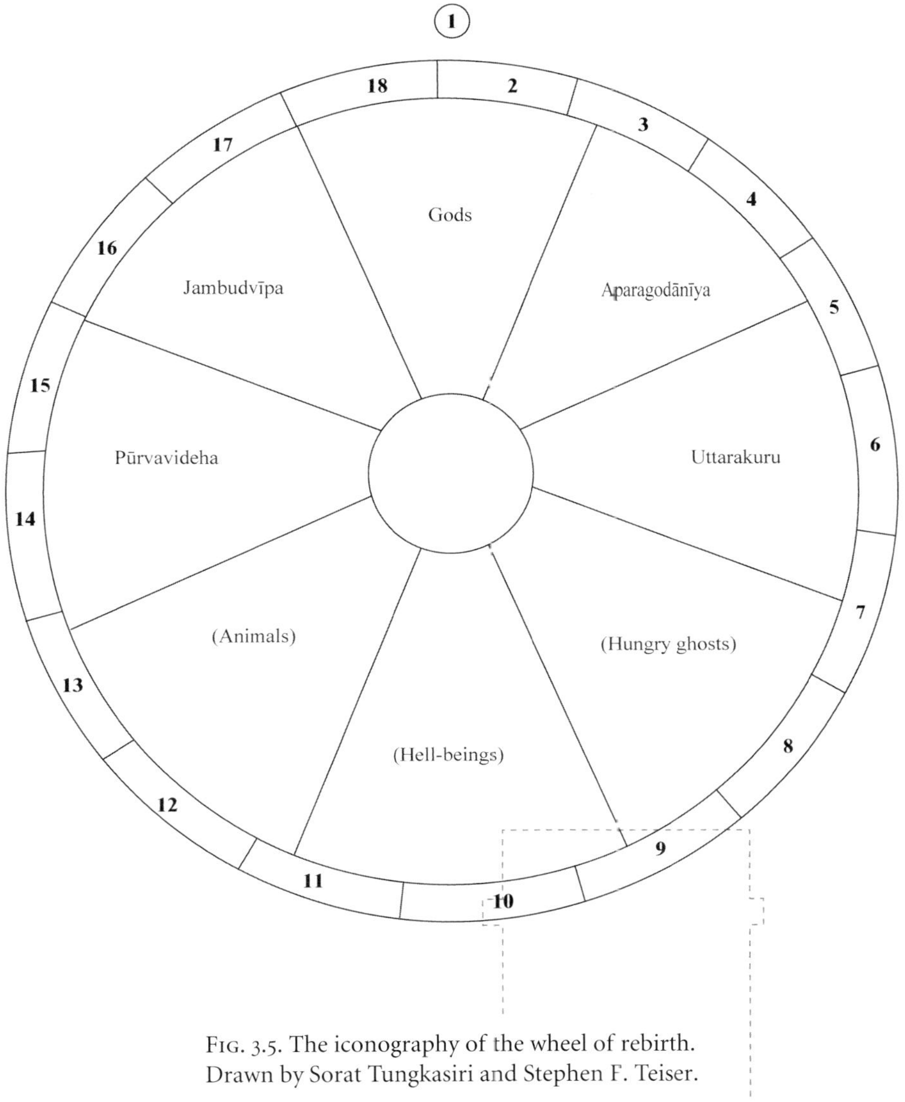

FIG. 3.5. The iconography of the wheel of rebirth. Drawn by Sorat Tungkasiri and Stephen F. Teiser.

part of the doorway in order to paint a complete circle.[24] The crucial piece of the puzzle is a pair of notches, three inches square, taken out of the doorway several inches

24. See the objections to Schlingloff's theory in Spink, "Review of *Ajaṇṭā Paintings*," p. 119. Spink has not yet published much on this particular problem. I am indebted to him for sharing his unparalleled knowledge of Ajaṇṭā during the August 1998 site seminar and for offering helpful comments on an earlier version of this chapter. The explanation of the archaeology of Cave 17 that follows is basically his. I am also grateful to Monika Zin for offering helpful comments and important references; to Sadakane Keiji for sharing his knowledge of the cave paintings and allowing me to use his color photograph, reproduced as plate 8; and to Leela Aditi Wood for offering helpful corrections and allowing me to use her photograph of the inner shrine of Cave 17, reproduced as fig. 3.8.

from the top (visible in fig. 3.4). The notches could not have been a setting for a door hinge, since hinges at Ajaṇṭā are mounted vertically on the side openings (not the top opening) of doorways. Nor could they be notches used for a lock bar, since the lock bars at Ajaṇṭā are located halfway up the door opening, which allows a wooden bar to prevent the opening of doors inward. The only possible purpose for the notches was to hold in place a piece of wood or stone, so that a packing of mud plaster could then fill in the upper part of the doorway. In this theory, once in place, the architectural repair was then painted over. This technique of solving slight miscalculations in construction is in fact found elsewhere at Ajaṇṭā. It was one of the tricks of the trade that afforded craftsmen and artists some leeway in working in an otherwise unforgiving medium.[25] As long as the cave was kept in good repair, the painting appeared whole, and the initial misjudgment of stone was hidden behind plaster and pigment.

Examining what does survive of the painting (see plate 8), and proceeding on the supposition that the original wheel ran a full 360 degrees, I would suggest that the wheel was composed of three concentric circles (see my projections in fig. 3.5, with the doorway outlined at the lower right). Although the content of the smallest circle at the center of the wheel is completely effaced, a fragment of the circle's circumference is evident at the two o'clock position. I hypothesize that the circle outside the central circle was divided into eight equal segments. Of the five segments that survive, each measures 45 degrees, so a total of eight symmetrical segments would compose a full circle. The felloe at the perimeter was probably divided into seventeen segments, an estimate based on measurement of the angles of the eight surviving segments in the outer ring ($21° \pm 1° \times 17$ segments $= 357°$).

The division of the middle circle into eight segments is somewhat unusual, since it seems to diverge from the canonical number of paths, which is five. This conundrum has constituted a fertile field of scholarly debate for over a century. When I first began work on the subject of this book, I would claim, in public lectures, that the eight segments of the wheel at Ajaṇṭā probably represent the Eight Unfortunate [Places] or Eight Difficulties (*aṣṭa akṣaṇāḥ*, Ch.: *banan*), the eight forms of rebirth in which it is impossible to see a Buddha. They are (1) hell; (2) realm of hungry ghosts; (3) animals; (4) the heaven of long life, in which beings live for five hundred *kalpas*; (5) Uttarakuru, an out-of-the-way paradise where people lead happy lives lasting one thousand years; (6) rebirth as a blind, deaf, or dumb person; (7) rebirth as a genius in

25. Similar attempts to restore a segment of wall surface in doorways are found in Caves 16 and 17. Other signs of miscalculation and revision in Cave 17 are evident in the location of the doorways to the two rooms of the porch. They are placed at two different levels, which is explicable by the hypothesis that one doorway was cut after the porch floor was excavated, but then the porch floor was lowered another foot or so, and the second door was cut. The doorway on the left side (under the wheel of rebirth) is positioned oddly in another sense: it is off-center with respect to the porch wall, whereas normally it would be in the center of the wall, symmetrical to the position of the doorway on the right wall of the porch. This discrepancy is consistent with the fact that the entire left room, which would normally be placed symmetrically to the room at the opposite end of the porch, is moved slightly back of center in order to accommodate the water cistern mentioned in the votive inscription. From the inside of the room, the door is on center (see fig. 3.3).

secular or non-Buddhist learning; and (8) rebirth during a period before or after the appearance of a Buddha.[26] The first three forms of rebirth are obviously unpleasant and entail so much suffering that one is unable to benefit from the presence of a Buddha. The same can be said for the sixth form of rebirth. The other four are difficulties of a different sort: although life in those incarnations can be filled—nearly interminably—with sensual delights, they are, in the ultimate scheme of things, undesirable, since one has to finish that lifetime and be reborn again in order to encounter a Buddha and achieve liberation. My stab at an explanation, based on reading every list of eight I could find in Buddhist literature, had the advantage of identifying a term that was probably known to the creators of Ajaṇṭā Cave 17. The concept of Eight Difficulties goes back to early Buddhism, and the authors of the Mūlasarvāstivāda vinaya were quite familiar with it, since they invoke it in at least a few places without providing a detailed enumeration.[27]

My early interpretation also had some grounding in the visual evidence. The segment occupying the top of the painting includes a throne at left, perhaps Indra's, and numerous dancers and magicians. Such scenes could depict life in heaven. Couples are shown seated together, possibly making love, at the top and at the bottom of the segment. The blocks in the center of the segment may be symbols of Mount Sumeru, atop which Indra's heaven is located. I found that the content of other segments was relatively comprehensible on a figure-by-figure basis, but I was unable to make the pieces add up to a sum that allowed me to identify which of the Eight Difficulties was being portrayed in any but the top segment.

Other solutions seemed equally problematic. As noted above, some scholars believe that the painters intentionally created an incomplete wheel to fit it around a space for the door, cramming the canonical five paths of rebirth into a truncated circle. On archaeological and geometrical grounds, however, I have argued that the wheel originally contained eight symmetrical segments. Monika Zin has recently suggested that the original wheel possessed six segments: a larger one at the bottom (now missing) representing hell, and five smaller segments above.[28] Another proposal comes from Jean Przyluski, who speculates that the wheel contains eight segments representing eight out of ten forms of life mentioned in the *Legend of King Aśoka*, a text forming part of the *Divyāvadāna*, some form of which was well known in the world of Ajaṇṭā.[29] Early in the text, when the Buddha predicts that a boy who has made an offering to him will in a future lifetime be reborn as King Aśoka and achieve sovereignty over the earth, the Buddha mentions ten forms of existence in which sentient beings can

26. See Nakamura, *Bukkyōgo daijiten*, pp. 1104d–05a.

27. For early citations, see *Zengyi ahan jing* (*Ekottarāgama*), trans. Gautama Saṃghadeva (Qutan Sengqietipo, fl. 383–398), *T* no. 125, 2:625c, 686a, 733a, 747b, 751b, 757a, 764b, etc. For citations in the Mūlasarvāstivāda vinaya, see *Genbenshuoyiqieyoubu pinaiye zashi* (*Mūlasarvāstivāda vinaya kṣudrakavastu*), trans. Yijing (635–713) in 710, *T* no. 1451, 24:211b, 367c, etc.

28. Zin, *Devotionale und ornamentale Malereien*, 1:446–48.

29. See Przyluski, "La roue de la vie à Ajaṇṭā," p. 321. A translation from the Sanskrit may be found in Strong, *Legend of King Aśoka*, p. 202.

be reborn. The last two are different kinds of Buddhas (a *pratyekabuddha* and a perfect Buddha), figures who have achieved liberation from saṃsāra, so it is natural, says Przyluski, that they would not be pictured inside the wheel. The first eight forms of life are (1) hell being; (2) animal; (3) hungry ghost; (4) human; (5) king of the iron wheel (*balacakravartin*); (6) king of the golden wheel (*cakravartin*); (7) god; and (8) voice-hearer (*śrāvaka*). The first three and the seventh overlap with the list of the Eight Difficulties. The unique elements in this listing are the two forms of wheel-rolling kings and the voice-hearer—none of which can be made out definitively, one way or the other, in the painting of the wheel of rebirth. Another possibility is raised by L. Augustine Waddell, who suggests that the eight segments of the wheel depict eight previous lifetimes of the Buddha.[30] Waddell's theory does not seem very strong, since within the very same cave, in the main chamber of the *vihāra*, the Buddha's previous incarnations are depicted in great detail. Nor is the number eight very important in general in the enumeration of the Buddha's previous lifetimes.

I am now convinced, however, that all of these interpretations of the iconography of the eight segments of the wheel, including mine, are wrong. In 1995 the Japanese scholar Sadakane Keiji published a definitive article identifying the main subjects in each sector of the wheel (see fig. 3.5). Beginning with the presupposition that the original painting defined a full circle of 360 degrees, Sadakane's key insight is that the realm of humans is subdivided into four sectors of the wheel, each depicting life on one of the Four Continents. The Five Paths become eight sectors: one of the paths is divided into four parts, so the entire wheel is made up of the gods, hungry ghosts, animals, and hell beings occupying one sector per species, plus four more sectors depicting the continents of the human realm.[31] The abode of the gods occupies the top segment (one of the few plausible points in my interpretation of the Eight Difficulties, above). The top segment pictures Indra, Mount Sumeru, musicians, dancers, and couples in sexual relations. The two sectors to the left of the gods in heaven depict two of the continents in the human realm, and the two sectors to the right depict the other two continents constituting realms in which humans are reborn. In fact, the ordering of the continents in Sadakane's interpretation of the painting follows the order in which they are enumerated in the vinaya text. Sadakane's explanation has the extra advantage that many of his readings of the figures shown in the human subrealms are supported by what was, prior to the sixth century, one of the longest and best-known mythological descriptions of the Buddhist cosmos, *The Sūtra on the Arising of the World* (**Loka-upapatti sūtra*). This text, now known through four surviving Chinese trans-

30. See Waddell, "Buddhist Pictorial Wheel of Life," p. 155. Waddell actually lists nine prior incarnations: as a Brahmin, Indra, *garuḍa*, elephant, deer, monkey, pigeon, thief, and ascetic.

31. Sadakane, "Ajantā daijūshichikutsu no 'goshu shōjirin' hekiga," esp. pp. 26–33. Various components of Sadakane's argument had been advanced earlier, but not so completely or convincingly, in my opinion. Several scholars, for instance, had proposed that the human realm was divided into four subrealms representing the Four Continents; see, for example, Hiraoka Mihoko, "Indo no shōjirin zu," pp. 283–84; Mochizuki, *Bukkyō daijiten*, p. 1222a; and Umezu, "Goshu shōjirin zu ni tsuite," p. 12.

lations made between the years 300 and 600, probably circulated in India and was loosely associated with Sarvāstivāda schools of thought.[32] While I do not agree with the interpretive strategy that puts textual evidence ahead of artistic evidence *a priori*, nevertheless Sadakane's visual analysis is often strengthened by his citation of historically relevant literary support.

After the gods pictured at the top of the Cave 17 wheel of rebirth, beginning from middle left and moving clockwise, the first segment is the eastern continent (Pūrvavideha), depicting domestic spaces with storage jars, cows, and a bare-headed monk toward the center of the wheel receiving offerings. Elsewhere in the segment are a cow and houses with women and pots. The next segment, at top left, pictures the southern continent of Jambudvīpa, which in Buddhist lore is the only continent on which Buddhas make their appearance. It contains two structures from town life, probably a house and a shop, above which is a white pot, otherwise downplayed in the composition, which some scholars interpret as a stūpa, a container of the cremated remains of a Buddha. The bottom part of the section is largely effaced, but at the top of the damaged portion one can discern a person riding atop a large animal, probably an elephant, facing left. Below the animal, people are crammed together, either fleeing or rushing toward it, and a *garuḍa*, a golden-feathered bird with a snake in its mouth, stands behind them in the corner (see fig. 3.6). Musicians and noble onlookers are crowded along the rim of the wheel. Continuing clockwise after the gods' realm, what remains in the upper right section are a monkey riding on top of a cart, birds roosting in a tree, and cattle. Following Sadakane's theory, this is the western continent (Aparagodānīya), abounding in animals and markets, a world where cattle are used as tokens of exchange. The last of the four human realms is at middle right, depicting the continent of Uttarakuru (Ptolemy's Ottorokorra).[33] Only one detail in this section is discernible in the wall painting as it survives now, a man with ornate headdress seated at right. The copy of the mural painted in the nineteenth century, however, shows a few more crucial details: a woman who appears to be seated in the man's lap and the foliage and branches of a luxuriant tree in front of them (see fig. 3.7). Following the mythology of the time as recorded in *The Sūtra on the Arising of the World*, this scene probably depicts a couple making love beneath the magical trees that grow only in Uttarakuru. On that continent, when men desire women, the men need not speak, and the male's intent is communicated telepathically to the woman, who comes to her suitor. If the match is inappropriate and the beckoned woman turns out to be a relative of the desirous male, then the tree announces the mismatch by remaining immobile. If the pairing is licit—if the woman is not a near or distant relative of the

32. The four Chinese translations are *Daloutan jing*, trans. Fali (ca. 290–306) and Faju (ca. 290–306), *T* no. 23; *Shiji jing*, trans. Buddhayaśas (Fotuoyeshe, ca. 384–417) and Buddhasmṛti (Zhu Fonian, ca. 365), in 412–413, in *Chang ahan jing* (*Dīrghāgama*), *T* no. 1; *Qishi jing*, trans. Jñānagupta (Shenajueduo, 523–600), *T* no. 24; and *Qishi yinben jing*, trans. Dharmagupta (Damojiduo, ca. 590–619), *T* no. 25. There is no corresponding text in the Pāli Nikāyas. See Ono, *Bussho kaisetsu daijiten*, 2:227b–d, 7:508c–d.

33. See La Vallée Poussin, "Cosmogony and Cosmology (Buddhist)," p. 133a, n. 2.

Fig. 3.6. Garuḍa with snake in its beak, detail of wheel of rebirth. Wall painting. Porch of Ajaṇṭā Cave 17, fifth century. Photo courtesy of American Institute of Indian Studies, 319.86.

FIG. 3.7. Couple and tree, detail of copy of painting of the wheel of rebirth at Ajaṇṭā Cave 17. Painting, nineteenth century. Griffiths, *Paintings in the Buddhist Cave-Temples of Ajaṇṭā*, vol. 1, pl. 56.

man—then the branches of this tree spontaneously bend over to form a shady welcome. Leaves grow, flowers bloom, and fruit ripens instantaneously, making a *rendezvous au naturel* in which the couple can lie down together.[34]

After the gods and humans depicted in the top half of the wheel, continuing with Sadakane's theory, the bottom half of the wheel, now entirely destroyed, must have portrayed what is universally regarded as the three lower paths of rebirth. The bottom hemisphere must have depicted hell at the very bottom/center, with the two realms of animals and hungry ghosts at either side.

Sadakane's theory of Five Paths depicted in eight segments builds on the explanation of how the builders of the porch filled in a doorway to allow the whole wheel to be painted. His theory focuses on the visual evidence in the painting itself, supplemented by other iconography and literary remains from medieval Indian sources. It also allows us to see how artists at Ajaṇṭā responded to a problem posed by the canon-

34. See, for example, *Qishi jing*, *T* 1:316b.

ical description of the wheel of rebirth and solved it creatively and convincingly. In the canon, the Buddha says that when painting the Five Paths, one should place two paths (gods and humans) in the top half and three paths in the bottom. If followed crudely, this way of representing the cosmological cycle leaves unclear the relationship between gods and humans. They both share the top half of the circle, but there is no indication of their relative ranking: the top two realms are interchangeable. The artists at Ajaṇṭā solve this difficulty by choosing pictorially to add more detail about the human realm: they divide it into four subrealms, and place them, in order, beside—but always below—the domain of the gods. The Ajaṇṭā composition thus resolves an asymmetry in the orthodox notion of the Five Paths, and it does so in a perfectly canonical fashion. The layout of the painting shows that the gods reside at the apex of saṃsāra and that the cosmological space occupied by humans, while located below the gods, is still situated above the more painful paths of rebirth. From this perspective, dividing the wheel into eight sectors is an elegant solution to the pictorial problem posed by the doctrine of the Five Paths.

The outer felloe of the wheel at Ajaṇṭā is also a conundrum. Based on the discussion of architecture and geometry above, the entire rim contains seventeen sectors, whereas the canonical numbers would mandate twelve or eighteen. I agree with Sadakane in believing that out of a hypothetical seventeen sections in the original wheel, seven can be identified with a fair degree of assurance (see fig. 3.5 in this chapter and table 1 in chapter 1). Starting at the top of the wheel in the one o'clock position, a man sitting in front of a potter's wheel is an indisputably canonical symbol for the second *nidāna*, dispositions. Next comes a monkey, the third link in the chain, representing consciousness. After that there are two figures, seated facing each other, sitting in or on something that cannot be made out—my guess is that they sit in a boat, which is what the Buddha decrees for the fourth *nidāna*, name and form. The next sector, number five in the canonical listing, depicts a face or mask, which seems to be shadowed by a second, lighter face above it. My guess is that the upper face was painted first and then the whole sector repainted a little bit lower. The paint has deteriorated to show the original undercomposition. This scene is a symbol for the six sense fields. Sectors six through fourteen have been destroyed completely. The next visible link is number fifteen, located just above the nine o'clock position, which possibly shows a woman kneeling. The vinaya stipulates a person grieving as a symbol for sadness. The next sector (sixteen) shows two people, perhaps one man consoling another, which seems close to the canonical description of malady, symbolized by a person weeping. The seventeenth sector is unclear in the Ajaṇṭā painting. According to the canon, it should be a person suffering, symbolizing pain. The last sector is clear and canonical: it shows a person pulling a camel, representing difficulty.

The missing piece here is the very first link in the chain of causation. In the vinaya, the Buddha names it as ignorance (*avidyā*) and says it should be symbolized by a *rakṣa*. It seems very odd that such an important concept—the condition of ignorance in Buddhist philosophy perhaps being comparable to the state of sin in Protestant theology—should be elided here. There is always the possibility, of course, that the link was intentionally dropped, for reasons unknowable to us now. The repainting and repositioning of the face, noted above, lend some credibility to the scenario in which the outer ring was at first planned with eighteen sectors but then reduced to seventeen.

But the question remains: why seventeen, and why drop the most crucial link? Sadakane's creative solution to this problem is not conclusively supported by the available evidence, but it is not contradicted either. He proposes that the artists at Ajaṇṭā chose the largest entity outside the wheel, the Demon of Impermanence, to symbolize ignorance.[35] Noting that the vinaya specifies a *rakṣa* as the proper icon of ignorance, Sadakane argues further that several attributes of the demon grasping the wheel also appear in paintings of *rakṣas* elsewhere at Ajaṇṭā, including skin color, shape and color of the fingernails, the monster's bracelets, and gendering the demon as female. It is as if the Ajaṇṭā artists considered ignorance so fundamental to the condition of sentient existence that they felt justified in amplifying its grip over the saṃsāracakra.

There are many scenes pictured around the wheel, but they are difficult to connect to the discourse of the wheel of rebirth. Recently Zin has identified four manifestations of Māra outside the wheel and linked these representations to the story of the wheel contained in the Sanskrit fragments of the vinaya discussed at the beginning of this chapter.[36] An early report mentions an inscription in the wheel, but this incomplete reference ("In the zodiac there is some writing"),[37] coupled with the deterioration of the picture, makes it hard to prove that the original representation included the two stanzas prescribed by the Buddha in the canonical account. Similarly, because the paint above the wheel has largely peeled away, it is impossible to know if the original contained a picture of a circle symbolizing nirvāṇa, as mandated in the vinaya.

The painting of the wheel of saṃsāra at Ajaṇṭā supplements what we know from the accounts in the vinaya and the *Divyāvadāna*. In the first place it shows that the prescriptions contained in written accounts were indeed carried out in fifth-century India. Judging from notes taken by James Burgess during a visit in the 1870s to the Kaṇherī caves 300 kilometers west of Ajaṇṭā, the porch of one of the stone *vihāras* at Kaṇherī also contained a painting of the wheel of rebirth. It had a Buddha image in the center and eight segments defining the wheel, just like the one at Ajaṇṭā.[38] This

35. See Sadakane, "Ajantā daijūshichikutsu no 'goshu shōjirin' hekiga," pp. 37–38; Hiraoka Mihoko, "Indo no shōjirin zu," p. 291; and Zin, *Devotionale und ornamentale Malereien*, 1:448–50.

36. Zin, *Devotionale und ornamentale Malereien*, 1:450–53.

37. See the comments of Mr. Ralph cited in Prinsep, "Facsimiles of Various Ancient Inscriptions, Part IV," p. 560.

38. See Burgess, *Report on the Buddhist Cave Temples*, p. 70. Burgess describes Kaṇherī Cave 86: "To the right of it, outside, are the traces of a large circular painting, like the so-called zodiac in Cave XVII at Ajaṇṭā. It has had a figure of the Buddha in the center, and the area was divided into eight sectors, in each of which, if we may judge from what remains of one, were numerous figures variously employed." Cited and misdated (1889) in Schlingloff, *Studies in the Ajaṇṭā Paintings*, pp. 171–72. Schlingloff (p. 172) also records that the painting had decayed and vanished by the time he visited in 1969: "At the designated place, however, we found nothing more than a blank wall that, instead of presenting us with an image of Transmigration, conveyed a striking symbol of Impermanence." Although I sympathize with Schlingloff's disappointment, perhaps the topics of transmigration and impermanence are more closely linked than he admits.

wealth of hard data, in texts and monuments, demonstrates that there was significant interest in paintings of the wheel of saṃsāra in western India. Coupled with the previous chapter's discussion of the vinaya story about the wheel, the survey presented here points up the diversity of opinions about what the wheel of rebirth meant and how it was supposed to be portrayed. There was considerable variation between the different versions of the vinaya alone, as our discussion of the Chinese translation, the Sanskrit fragments, and the Tibetan translation has shown. The *Divyāvadāna* tale presented yet other alternative readings. The surviving painting at Ajaṇṭā is stunning proof of just how many symbolic and narrative details could be fit into paintings of the wheel and of how artists exercised considerable freedom in thinking through the quandaries in the story of the wheel of rebirth.

We can also be confident that, because it was located in a monastic residence (*vihāra*) commissioned by a ruling family, resident monks and members of the patron's family saw the painting. Unfortunately, given the aristocratic background of the sponsors of the cave complex and our basic ignorance of other social classes at the time, we have little knowledge about other possible viewers of this particular representation. The vinaya account, at least, makes it sound as if monks are supposed to preach about the picture to a lay audience. Some scholars have jumped from this normative statement to the conclusion that members of the Saṃgha at Ajaṇṭā actually carried out the canonical instructions, functioning as Indian versions of the "picture-explainers" known as *etoki* in medieval Japan.[39] I think it is wiser to adopt a more critical attitude toward the sources and refrain from the conclusion that monks gave oral interpretations to laypeople at the Ajaṇṭā caves. Like the situation facing the social historian of other premodern cultures, medieval Buddhist sources (with some exceptions like inscriptions, material culture, and popular literature) provide few straightforward clues about the religious practice of ordinary people. Most of the cave temples at Ajaṇṭā were founded by members of the ruling elite, and there is little evidence to suggest they functioned more as public gathering spaces than as family temples. It is impossible to say decisively who, aside from donors, artists, and resident monks, had access to such temples.

Other conclusions can be derived from the relationship between the painting of the wheel and the larger program of artistic representations in Cave 17. To the extent that the *vihāra*-style caves at Ajaṇṭā simulated monastic residences, the wheel is located precisely where (in the Mūlasarvāstivāda vinaya) the Buddha says it should be: in the porch room just outside the main entrance to the temple. The wheel was positioned on the porch because it prepared the way for—and enticed the implied visitor into—the scenes portrayed inside the cave. The wheel of rebirth is located as far as possible from the inner sanctum of the temple. It offers a pictorial encapsulation, at the entrance

39. Sadakane ("Ajantā hekiga no sezokuteki seikaku") believes that monks served as "picture-explainers" (*etoki*) and that they supervised the construction of many temples and paintings at Ajaṇṭā. For his citation of other vinaya sources in support of these claims, see idem, "Ajantā hekiga wa dare no tame ni kakareta ka?" and idem, "Ajantā daijūshichikutsu no 'goshu shōjirin' hekiga," esp. pp. 39–40.

to the *vihāra*, of the Buddhist worldview. Passing through this exoteric, preambulatory space, the visitor proceeds through the parts of the temple narrating the gradual perfection of the Buddha-to-be over many lifetimes. The innermost space is the actual residence of the Buddha. Whatever interpretation we adopt of the sections in the Ajaṇṭā wheel—Five Paths in eight segments, Six Paths in six segments, Eight Difficulties in eight segments—Buddhas are not present within the wheel of saṃsāra. The painting on the porch, then, forms the perfect antithesis to the main shrine, where the Buddha himself resides.

We should note too that other images in Cave 17 match the content and location specified for them in the *Kṣudrakavastu* of the Mūlasarvāstivāda vinaya: the great miracle of Śrāvastī is portrayed on the right wall of the antechamber; the Buddha preaching to his mother and the gods of the Heaven of Thirty-three and then again after descending from heaven is on the antechamber's left wall; *yakṣas* holding garlands are carved at the entrance to the main shrine; and scenes from the previous lives of the Buddha (especially in the *Viśvantara jātaka* and the *Siṃhalāvadāna*) dominate the main interior walls of the cave.[40] The wheel of rebirth stands at the beginning of the path that leads to the dominating figure of the Buddha, the main statue in the inner shrine of the cave, seated on his throne in the Deer Park in the posture of teaching the Dharma (see fig. 3.8). The Buddha's eminence is guaranteed by two devotees at his sides, a pair of bodhisattvas attending him, and garland bearers descending from heaven to honor him. The designers of the cave made a careful selection of the painting program outlined in the vinaya in order to construct their own ritual space.

Another way of contextualizing the evidence, both artistic and literary, is to place it against the background of Indian religion in the years 350–550. These years mark the latter part of what Schopen refers to as the "Middle Period" of Indian Buddhism, when local Saṃghas were organized into highly regulated, walled monasteries with extensive landholdings. The vinaya texts produced during this period, says Schopen, "are little interested in any individual religious quest, but are very concerned with the organization, administration, maintenance, and smooth operation of a complex institution that owned property and had important social obligations."[41] Finding the best way to explain karma, rebirth, and morality to laypeople was a pressing issue for the Saṃgha during the period. The Buddha's instructions on the details of the painting of the wheel of life and death, as well as the narrative about botched attempts to explain

40. See Cohen, "Setting the Three Jewels," p. 236; and my discussion of the vinaya, at the end of chapter 2.

41. Schopen, "Death, Funerals, and the Division of Property in a Monastic Code," p. 475. I follow Schopen in treating the vinaya as a clue to the concerns of the age. He writes that "the world of monastic law . . . does not appear to be a simple one of fables and fiction or half-remembered 'historical' accounts, but a complex one of carefully constructed 'cases' in which concerns of power, access and economics were being or had been negotiated" (Schopen, "Ritual Rights and Bones of Contention," p. 60). Despite his criticism of Schopen over a particular point in the Pāli vinaya, Charles Hallisey seems to suggest the same approach, namely, treating the construction of the vinaya as a clue to the *mentalité* of a specific age; see Hallisey, "Apropos the Pāli Vinaya as a Historical Document."

the wheel, suggest that as a corporation, the Saṃgha was concerned with managing its property, regularizing the support it garnered from the surrounding community, and standardizing the message its preachers gave to lay groups.

How much, if any, of this proselytizing actually took place in cave temples like Ajaṇṭā Cave 17 is another question altogether, as noted above. The painting of the wheel and the foregoing consideration of its context prove only that the Saṃgha was interested in delivering such messages and that ruling families supplied the donations for building lavish shrines. We actually know a fair amount about the elite religion of the time.[42] In the first place, it is worth repeating that the western Vākāṭaka rulers, like the Guptas in north India and many powerful families in the south, lent heavy support not only to Buddhism but also to traditional Vedic institutions and the emerging forms of Puraṇic religion. The founder of the Vākāṭaka family line was known for his devotion to Buddhism, but later generations gave equally to other religious traditions. They supported Vedic and Śrauta sacrifices, made gifts of land to support temples dedicated to Śiva and Viṣṇu, and commissioned many Buddhist sites. Their sense of religious affiliation—as well as the configuration of religion, family, and politics in Indian society—was, unlike that in the modern West, quite fluid. Secondly, for the families who supported priests of all religions and built shrines for the adoration of a vast pantheon, the high tradition of Buddhist scholasticism was important. These are precisely the centuries when the great centers of monastic learning, often housing thousands of monks, flourished at Nālandā, Pāṭaliputra, Sārnāth, and Mathurā. The coexistence of Buddhist philosophy and an opulent lifestyle among the elite is perhaps most apparent in the very paintings at Ajaṇṭā we have been discussing. Artists may have been among the most active agents in this cross-fertilization, since the same painters who decorated secular palaces also adorned the walls of *caityas* and *vihāras* at Ajaṇṭā.[43]

Finally, the fourth, fifth, and sixth centuries saw the theorization of *bhakti* (devotion) as a mode of religious practice in all Indian religions. In Buddhism it may be seen in the ritual preeminence of the Buddha image in temples, the proliferation of stūpas erected over the remains of various disciples of the Buddha, and the growing popularity of pilgrimage to places where the Buddha had preached and performed miracles. Newly emerging sites like Ajaṇṭā were an important part of this milieu. The Vākāṭaka rulers wanted their cave temples to demonstrate how to move from the evanescent perils and pleasures of life within the wheel of saṃsāra to the final goal that was achieved, and still made possible, by the Buddha. As the disciple Upagupta explains to Māra in the *Divyāvadāna*, "Only a little devotion [*bhakti*] becomes for the wise fruitful of nirvāṇa."[44]

---

42. See Bakker, *Vākāṭakas*, pp. 58–79; Dutt, *Buddhist Monks and Monasteries of India*, pp. 169–232; Gokhale, "Buddhism in the Gupta Age"; Mirashi, *Inscriptions of the Vākāṭakas*, pp. xl–xliii; Narain, "Religious Policy and Toleration in Ancient India"; and Thapar, "Patronage and Community."

43. See Sadakane, "Ajantā hekiga wa dare no tame ni kakareta ka?" esp. pp. 52–53; and idem, "Ajantā hekiga no sezokuteki seikaku."

44. Cited in Dutt, *Buddhist Monks and Monasteries of India*, p. 179.

Fig. 3.8. Main Buddha statue in rear shrine room, seen from main chamber. Ajaṇṭā Cave 17, fifth century. Photo courtesy of Leela Aditi Wood.

Chapter 4

King Rudrāyaṇa's Painting of the Twelve Conditions

The wheel of saṃsāra was simply one picture among many that depicted basic Buddhist truths about reincarnation and salvation in the medieval world. Artists, patrons, and monks had many subjects to choose from when putting cosmology into visual form, including ideas about causation, morality, the essentials of Buddhist ritual, and images of Buddhas and bodhisattvas. Paintings were not confined to murals in Buddhist temples. Executed on paper and silk, they also circulated outside of monastic control. The two major literary sources discussed so far, the Mūlasarvāstivāda vinaya and the *Divyāvadāna*, contain another story that weaves some of the elements from the canonical version of the wheel of rebirth into a long, entertaining narrative. In the tale, an *avadāna* about the king of Roruka, Rudrāyaṇa (var.: Udrāyaṇa, Ch.: Xiandao or Youtuoxian), and his descendants, the Buddha ordains a pictorial representation of himself together with the Twelve Conditions. As in the founding legend of the saṃsāracakra, the Buddha gives very precise directions about the content of the painting and how it should be explained. The Rudrāyaṇa myth also addresses the question of the power such paintings exercise over the viewer. In the tale, upon seeing the painting, the king advances on the path to nirvāṇa. The episode of the king's encounter with this important painting occurs early in the narrative. The rest of the story traces the history of his son and successor, King Sikhaṇḍi (Ch.: Dingji), who is turned to evil by two nefarious ministers. Transmitted in Sanskrit, Chinese, and Tibetan, the story of King Rudrāyaṇa demonstrates the variety and efficacious nature of didactic paintings throughout the early medieval Buddhist world.

The version of the story of King Rudrāyaṇa contained in the *Divyāvadāna* closely parallels the vinaya text preserved in Tibetan and Chinese translations of an original Sanskrit (now lost).[1] Paintings depicting the events in the story are not very common

1. John Strong translates part of the Rudrāyaṇa story from the *Divyāvadāna* in *Experience of Buddhism*, pp. 39–41; see also Huber, "Études de littérature bouddhique," pp. 12–17. For a study and translation of the version in the Tibetan vinaya, see Nobel, *Udrāyaṇa, König von Roruka*. Below

in the early period, with a few notable exceptions (at Kizil in the medieval kingdom of Kucha, as noted below). Beginning around the ninth or tenth century, however, the myth seems to have enjoyed a renaissance in both plastic and literary forms. It was recounted and expanded in later *avadāna* collections in Sanskrit and Tibetan, and it can be found chiseled in the reliefs of Barabuḍur (ninth century, Java) and painted in more recent *thangkas* from Tibet.[2]

The story of King Rudrāyaṇa is set in ancient India when the historical Buddha, Śākyamuni, is residing in the city-state of Rājagṛha, ruled by the wise Buddhist king, Bimbisāra. Rudrāyaṇa is the king of a distant, equally prosperous city-state named Roruka, and the opening of the story explains how he and Bimbisāra bestow valuable gifts upon one another. After sending letters, chests filled with rare jewels, and cartloads of beautiful clothing back and forth, it is Bimbisāra's turn to repay Rudrāyaṇa. Rudrāyaṇa's most recent gift of a set of magical, jewel-studded armor has left Bimbisāra at a disadvantage in this competition of near-potlatch proportions. Despairing of a fitting response, Bimbisāra seeks the counsel of his minister, who recommends that the ruler offer his kingdom's most prized possession, the Buddha. "That country's king merely graced us with a suit of jeweled armor," the minister tells Bimbisāra. He continues, "Within your majesty's kingdom there is the Buddha, the World-Honored One. He is a wondrous jewel among human beings. He is revered equally by all sentient beings. He is without equal in the realms of the Ten Directions."[3] The minister also recommends that, rather than dispatching such a rarity as the Buddha-Jewel himself to a foreign state, King Bimbisāra seek the Buddha's cooperation in having a painted image of him sent abroad instead.

Bimbisāra follows the minister's advice and invites the Buddha for an audience. Śākyamuni not only thinks that it is a wonderful idea for monarchs to engage in disseminating the Law and cooperates fully in posing for the artist, he also gives very precise directions about what to include in the painting. Śākyamuni's instructions to King Bimbisāra in the story of King Rudrāyaṇa can be read as a strong statement about the Saṃgha's interests at the time. As noted in the preceding chapter, the Indian Saṃgha

---

I summarize the account in the Chinese vinaya, *Genbenshuoyiqieyoubu pinaiye* (*Mūlasarvāstivāda vinaya vibhaṅga*), trans. Yijing (635–713), *T* no. 1442, 23:873b–82a, which accords closely with the Tibetan. I am fairly certain that the vinaya account does not survive in Sanskrit among the Turfan fragments; see Okano, "Chūki Avadaana bunken no kenkyū shi." An abbreviated version, beginning with the demise of Rudrāyaṇa's wife, Candraprabhā, is contained in *Za baozang jing*, trans. Kiṃkārya (Jijiaye, ca. 472) and Tanyao (ca. 453–462), *T* no. 203, 4:495a–96b; trans. Chavannes, *Cinq cents contes et apologues*, 3:127–36; and trans. Willemen, *Storehouse of Sundry Valuables*, pp. 234–40.

2. The story of Rudrāyaṇa is contained in the *Avadānakalpalatā*, written by Kṣmendra and his son, Somendra, around 1040, which was in turn translated and transcribed into Tibetan later in the eleventh century; see Tharchin, *King Udrayaṇa and the Wheel of Life*, pp. 2–81. For the reliefs at Barabuḍur, see Krom, *Barabuḍur: Archaeological Description*, pp. 282–301. For recent Tibetan examples, see the Narthang series in the von Stael-Holstein collection, in Gordon, *Iconography of Tibetan Lamaism*; and the Guimet paintings discussed in Hackin, "Les scènes figurées de la vie du Buddha," pp. 43–51, and pl. 11; and Béguin, *Les peintures du bouddhisme tibétain*, pp. 141–44 and Entry 53 (MG 16541).

3. Translation from *Genbenshuoyiqieyoubu pinaiye*, *T* 23:874a.

of the fourth through sixth centuries was a large, corporate institution. While hardly rivaling the wealth or coercive capacities that a city-state or small empire could command, large monasteries and networks of monks were deeply and apparently happily embroiled in a world of wealth, luxury, and elite privileges. In the story, the Buddha consents to have his likeness reproduced in painted form to be shared among kings. Later Tibetan paintings (see fig. 4.1) portray the Buddha posing in the middle of an assembly of monks on the left and painters on the right. An outline of the Buddha's image is produced when his shadow is cast on the painting surface. Then the Buddha very carefully spells out what else should be included in the picture. The Buddha tells the king to have written out, in linguistic rather than symbolic or pictorial form, the basics of the Buddhist path. Śākyamuni enumerates them: he instructs the king to write the Three Refuges ("I take refuge in the Buddha. . . . Dharma. . . . Saṃgha"), the Five Precepts of lay Buddhism (to refrain from killing, stealing, lying, sexual misconduct, and alcohol), and the Twelve Conditions of the cycle of dependent origination. All of these formulae are supposed to be situated below the main picture of the Buddha. Śākyamuni concludes his syllabus with the direction to copy, at the top of the painting, the same two stanzas on renunciation (translated in chapter 2) that are supposed to be included in paintings of the wheel of life and death.[4]

According to this *avadāna* tale, the leader of the Saṃgha oversees the formulation of the Buddha Dharma. Rather than leaving the articulation of the teachings to individual choice, meditative experience, or interpretation by authoritative monks, Śākyamuni details precisely what should be included in the supreme gift exchanged between the two rulers. The painting prepared by King Bimbisāra shares some of the elements that are supposed to be included in paintings of the wheel of rebirth: a Buddha image, the Twelve Conditions, and the two stanzas on renunciation. Bimbisāra's painting, however, contains more writing and fewer symbols than the canonical saṃsāracakra. The Twelve Conditions are presented in literal rather than metaphorical form; pictorial renditions of the Five Paths, Three Poisons, and nirvāṇa are missing; and other doctrinal formulations are added.

The tale of Rudrāyaṇa continues with Śākyamuni delivering further instructions about how the multimedia painting should be interpreted. The Buddha proposes that each of the components of the painting be paraphrased succinctly, often in terms of the specific path of release to which it leads:

> After completing the painting the way I have explained, give it to your messenger. You should direct him, "When you arrive in the intended country with the painted image, hang it up under a canopy in a broad, accessible space, strew incense and flowers, and present a trove of adornments before opening the image. If someone

4. A painting with essentially the same content is ordained by the Buddha in a section of the (Sanskrit version) of the Mūlasarvāstivāda vinaya, *Adhikaraṇavastu*. The Buddha directs that the painting be sent to a pious princess, who upon viewing it becomes a stream-enterer. I extend my thanks to Gregory Schopen for alerting me to the text and sharing his unpublished translation of it.

FIG. 4.1. Buddha posing for a portrait, detail of biographical painting of Buddha. Silk painting. Tibet, nineteenth century. Musée Guimet 16541. Courtesy of Réunion des Musées Nationaux/Art Resource, NY.

asks what it is, you should respond to him, 'This is an image of the form of the World-Honored One, who renounced his position as a wheel-turning king [*cakravartirājan*] and achieved true awakening.' If someone else asks what the words below mean, you should respond, 'This is the taking of refuge in the Three Jewels, which is the cause of release.' About the meaning of what is below that, respond, 'It is the teaching to uphold the Five Precepts, which lead to rebirth among humans and gods.' About the meaning of what is below that, respond, 'They are the Twelve Conditions of dependent origination, which illuminate the principles of transmigration, resuscitation and extinction, and causality within the Five Paths of the Three Realms.' If someone else asks about the meaning of the two stanzas at the top, respond, 'These two stanzas illuminate the encouragement given to all sentient beings

Fig. 4.2. Kātyāyana preaching, detail of stone relief. Barabuḍur, ninth century. Krom, *Barabuḍur: Archaeological Description*, vol. 3, series I.b., pl. xxxvi, scene 72.

to practice in accord with the teachings, to destroy the army of birth and death, to never give up, and to move quickly to *bodhi* [enlightenment].'"[5]

The Buddha's interpretation of the message of the painting seems perfectly suited to its intended audience, a king and his courtiers. According to this text, when the image is displayed, preachers should describe the figure of the Buddha as a prince who renounced his birthright. Śākyamuni tailors the presentation for a monarch, who is being told, in effect, that the World-Honored One shares with him, the intended viewer, the lot of kingship. The painting is a crystallization of lay Buddhism. The Dharma in pictorial form emphasizes adherence to morality rather than the pursuit of meditation. Although the verses at the top do mention renunciation, Śākyamuni does not advise the messenger to tout the virtues of monastic life. The goals, rather, are a higher level of rebirth and greater insight into the laws of karma, all viewed as stages on the path leading toward enlightenment.

Bimbisāra's envoys pack the holy scroll in an appropriately ornate container. Adorned with jewels and perfumed with incense, it is rolled up and placed inside a golden case, in turn set inside a silver case, in turn set within a copper case. When the procession bearing the painting arrives in Roruka, King Rudrāyaṇa reads the letter accompanying the gift from his counterpart in Rājagṛha and himself leads a retinue to receive it. When the painting is finally unrolled, the dramatic action shifts to a troupe of visiting merchants: it is they, not Rudrāyaṇa, who recognize the subject of the paint-

5. Translation from *Genbenshuoyiqieyoubu pinaiye*, *T* 23:874b.

ing. They immediately adopt the proper, reverent response and start chanting "Praise to the Buddha" (*Namo Buddha*). When Rudrāyaṇa asks them the meaning of their prayers, they explain who the Buddha is—emphasizing again his royal background and his choice to renounce worldly kingship in order to gain spiritual dominion—and what each element of the representation means. The king retires to his chambers to meditate on the lessons of the Dharma sent by Bimbisāra. Rudrāyaṇa's intensive contemplation focuses on the twelve links in the chain of causation. The text describes how he runs through them in his mind both backward and forward and is thereby able to achieve profound, clear awakening. King Rudrāyaṇa's prowess even goes beyond the benefits predicted by the Buddha: the king achieves the first fruit, that of stream-enterer (*śrotāpanna*), which means that he will progress to nirvāṇa quickly, within seven lifetimes.

Only recently introduced to Buddhism, Rudrāyaṇa has progressed very swiftly on the path, but he remains a king, and he must still, for at least a few more episodes, fulfill his royal duties. Happily for the Saṃgha, Rudrāyaṇa decides that the best way to learn more about salvation is to underwrite a large band of Buddhist monks. He sends a request for *bhikṣus* to his counterpart, Bimbisāra, who is happy to oblige him by shipping off a contingent of five hundred monks headed by one of the Buddha's favorites, (Mahā)Kātyāyana (Ch.: Jiaduoyanna). This monk is highly skilled at preaching. Relief sculpture from Barabuḍur (see fig. 4.2) places Kātyāyana on the highest seat, at left, occupying a more exalted position than that of King Rudrāyaṇa, seated on his throne at the right. The king seems to be thinking over Kātyāyana's sermon, and all the courtiers seated in the left half of the scene listen with rapt attention. The legend in the vinaya and *Divyāvadāna* explains that two sons of the court nobility, Tiṣya (Ch.: Disa) and Puṣya (Ch.: Busa), are affected so strongly by Kātyāyana's preaching that they become *arhats*, thus achieving the highest of the Four Fruits. When they die, their remains are placed inside twin stūpas for honor and worship.

King Rudrāyaṇa makes special arrangements for the edification of his wives. Since monks are not allowed into the courtesans' chambers, the king requests that a nun (*bhikṣuṇī*) be dispatched from Rājagṛha to come and instruct them in person. The nun arrives and begins preaching to the palace women. All the king's consorts are greatly moved by the new doctrines of Buddhism, and one of them, Candraprabhā (Ch.: Yueguang), exercises a particularly critical influence on King Rudrāyaṇa. According to the story, shortly after hearing the nun preach, one night when Rudrāyaṇa is playing music and watching Candraprabhā dance, the king perceives that she will be visited by death seven days later. He drops his lute in shock and rushes to her side. Candraprabhā confides that she longs to leave the world better established in the Dharma. She begs the king to let her be ordained as a nun before her death. He consents, but first makes her promise that if in her next lifetime she is still subject to rebirth, she will return to see him. She agrees, and her ordination under the *bhikṣuṇīs* visiting from Rājagṛha is quickly arranged. As predicted, she passes away seven days later and is immediately reborn in heaven as a goddess.

The narrative takes the soteriological status of the actors very seriously. In her recent life as a courtesan, Candraprabhā was simply a highly privileged human being. By renouncing the world and becoming a nun prior to her death, she theoretically moved up one step in the spiritual hierarchy. The story confirms this karmic promotion by casting her next life as that of a goddess. Although still tied to the cycle of rebirth and burdened with a female body, as a goddess she is able to travel and exercise other magical powers. Adorning herself with heavenly garlands, she flies directly to the Buddha's side in Rājagṛha. She pays her respects, listens to him preach, and thereupon becomes a stream-enterer.

Having thus achieved religious parity with the king—although she is a goddess and he a man, they are both technically stream-enterers—she now makes good on her promise to return to him. After entering the palace at night, the goddess rouses the king by plucking a string on his lute. This scene may have been portrayed in visual form as early as the fifth century in wall paintings at Kizil (see fig. 4.3).[6] He awakes in confusion, at first unable to recognize Candraprabhā. When she explains who she is, Rudrāyaṇa's immediate response is, "My good wife, you may come lie down with me." Candraprabhā then takes full advantage of Rudrāyaṇa's concupiscence. He must, she says, become a monk. If he is successful in cutting off all attachments, then he will have defeated his appetite for pleasure. She bargains with the king, arguing that if, on

6. This portion of Kizil Cave 83 was carved out, transported to Germany, and deposited in the Museum für Indische Kunst, Berlin. See the discussion in von Le Coq, *Die buddhistische Spätantike in Mittelasien*, 3:6–7; and Waldschmidt, *Gandhara, Kutscha, Turfan*, pp. 62–64. The painting is also reproduced in Xinjiang Weiwu'er zizhiqu wenwu guanli weiyuanhui et al., *Kezi'er shiku*, 3: pl. 193.

FIG. 4.3. Candraprabhā dancing for King Rudrāyaṇa, detail of wall painting. Kizil Cave 83, fifth century. Xinjiang Weiwu'er zizhiqu wenwu guanli weiyuanhui et al., *Kezi'er shiku*, 3: pl. 193.

the other hand, he still has desire for women in his next lifetime, then they can enjoy themselves together in heaven:

> Oh, great king, my body has already died and I have been reborn in the pantheon of the Four Great Heavenly Kings [Mahādevas]. Human affairs and gods' affairs are separate, and in principle they are not allowed to sleep together. If the king wishes to be able to enjoy intercourse with me, he should leave the household and cultivate the path according to the Buddha's teaching. If he permanently cuts off all of his afflictions, then his various cravings will all cease. If, however, his life comes to an end while he is still deluded, then he will be reborn among the Four Kings of Heaven and will get to see me.[7]

This interchange has the effect of seducing Rudrāyaṇa into complete renunciation. Before giving up his family to become a monk, he must first relinquish the throne. He arranges for his son, Sikhaṇḍhi, to assume power and urges him to follow the counsel of two virtuous ministers. (As we will see below, the father's advice will soon be disastrously overturned.) Having set the kingdom in order by enriching the state, introducing Buddhism, and abdicating in favor of his son, Rudrāyaṇa is finally ready to join the Saṃgha. He journeys to Rājagṛha in order to take the tonsure directly from Śākyamuni, an act that is thought to produce unusually quick, significant results. When Rudrāyaṇa hears the Buddha preach, he is transformed instantaneously into a monk: his hair falls off magically, a begging bowl pops into his hands, and his clothing is changed into monastic attire. Further fruits—becoming an *arhat*—come later in the story. In the meantime, word of Rudrāyaṇa's ordination has reached everyone in the city. Great crowds of people come to see him, and he and Bimbisāra engage in a long poetic exchange. Bimbisāra tries to convince Rudrāyaṇa to renounce his double renunciation. That is, Bimbisāra reminds Rudrāyaṇa of the pleasures of royal life and the rewards of being a Buddhist layman, but in the end Rudrāyaṇa remains steadfast in his decision to give up the kingship and the comforts of lay life.

With his father pursing nirvāṇa full time in another kingdom, Sikhaṇḍhi's rule soon turns sour. He begins to oppress the populace, and when the two wise ministers try to stop him, he replaces them with two evil ministers. Word of the son's misrule reaches Rudrāyaṇa in Rājagṛha. Hearing of the fate of his kingdom and his son's waywardness, Rudrāyaṇa exercises the privilege of a formerly righteous king and decides to return home and set things aright. The two evil ministers catch wind of the father's plan and concoct a conspiracy theory in order to convince Sikhaṇḍhi to have his father killed. They claim that Rudrāyaṇa is plotting to return home, kill Sikhaṇḍhi, and regain the throne. The two evil ministers convince the son that the only way to save his rule is to kill his father preemptively. The murder of the father is indeed carried out, but not without further karmic complications. When the assassin approaches Rudrāyaṇa, the monk-and-former-king asks for a reprieve. He seeks a postponement in order to

7. Translation from *Genbenshuoyiqieyoubu pinaiye*, 23:876b.

reach the goal of becoming an *arhat*, so that when the death sentence is eventually carried out, he will not return to the realm of life and death. The legend explains how Rudrāyaṇa acts resolutely, settling into meditation and quickly gaining diamond-like wisdom and detachment from all things. Before submitting to the executioner's sword, Rudrāyaṇa prophesies his son's fate. Rudrāyaṇa pronounces that for Sikhaṇḍhi, the act of killing his father, who has now become an *arhat*, will result in rebirth in Avīci Hell.

Sikhaṇḍhi despairs at the sight of his father's severed head, but again perverse influences appear in the narrative to assure that the son is led from remorse back to evil. His mother lies about his paternity, claiming that Rudrāyaṇa was not his biological father and thus Sikhaṇḍhi should not consider himself guilty of parricide. The two evil ministers devise a plan to convince him that he is, further, innocent of killing an *arhat*. Their strategy is to undermine the credibility of all Buddhist claims to sainthood. The two evil ministers go to the stūpas of the two famous *arhats* in the kingdom of Roruka, Tiṣya and Puṣya, and use strips of meat to train two kittens to walk in circles around the shrines. Having prepared the ruse, they lead the wayward Sikhaṇḍhi to the stūpas and clap their hands as a signal to the cats. The animals perform as they have been trained, and the evil ministers quickly advance the explanation that, far from becoming *arhats*, Tiṣya and Puṣya have instead been reborn as mere carnivorous felines, still haunting their former burial grounds. They succeed in convincing the king that the Buddha's disciples never achieve the status of saint. The whole episode is encapsulated in figure 4.4, a stone relief from Barabuḍur. The stūpas are on the left. Under them crouch the two cats, while the two evil ministers sit at the far left, gesturing toward the stūpas. In the right half of the scene, Sikhaṇḍhi, wearing an ornate crown, sits under a structure and shares the platform with his mother.

Before the story ends with an identification of the prior incarnations of the characters, the narrator explains how Sikhaṇḍhi leads his kingdom further down the road to perdition. After losing faith in Buddhist claims to holiness, Sikhaṇḍhi withdraws state support for Buddhist institutions, causing monks and nuns to flee Roruka en masse. He takes offense at the behavior of one of the last remaining *bhikṣus*, Kātyāyana, and goads his entourage into burying the old monk, nearly killing him, in a heap of sand. Rescued by the two good men who used to serve as ministers, Kātyāyana foretells the destruction of the kingdom by a sandstorm—the same substance that had nearly buried him and that, as I explain below, figured prominently in Sikhaṇḍhi's evil deeds in a previous lifetime. Kātyāyana adds that the apocalypse will be preceded by a rain of jewels for six days, and he advises the two good men to collect the precipitate for six days and then sail away before the seventh. They follow the old monk's directions and move on to establish their own small kingdoms, even as the remaining inhabitants of Roruka perish in the sandstorm. The dramatic action of the *avadāna* tale ends with a description of the later adventures of Kātyāyana, the son of one of the good ministers, and the tutelary goddess of Roruka.

The conclusion of the narrative of Rudrāyaṇa leads directly to the last section of the text, a discussion of the underlying causes of the characters' actions. The Buddhist

monks who have heard the story (as told by Kātyāyana, one of the only survivors from the kingdom of Roruka) formulate the problem succinctly to the Buddha. They ask how a man like Rudrāyaṇa, who had already achieved the highest level of spiritual perfection available to humans (*arhat*), could have suffered a violent death. They say, "World-Honored One, we pray that out of compassion you will provide us with an explanation. Having been head of state and enjoyed great happiness, and having given up that supreme position to take refuge in the Buddha and leave the family, and having cut off all afflictions and become an *arhat*, for what karmic reasons would Rudrāyaṇa the *bhikṣu* not have escaped from being killed by the sword?"[8] The Buddha responds first with the adage that Rudrāyaṇa reaped the fruit of actions whose seeds he had sown in a previous existence. No matter how virtuous his behavior and exalted his accomplishments were in his current incarnation, he was still subject to the results that he himself had caused in earlier lifetimes. The Buddha then fills in that answer by identifying who Rudrāyaṇa was and what acts he committed in the past. In a prior life, Rudrāyaṇa had been a cruel, talented hunter. He was very successful at his trade until a *pratyekabuddha* appeared on his land who by force of his presence inspired the animals to avoid the hunter's traps. Furious at the loss of his livelihood, the hunter shot the *pratyekabuddha* with a poisoned arrow. Before passing away, the *pratyekabuddha* rose into the air, a display that triggered the hunter's conversion. The hunter gathered the remains of the holy one, built a stūpa for them, and carried out rites of repentance. The hunter's actions, then, were a mixture of good and evil. Śākya-

8. Translation from ibid., 23:881b.

Fig. 4.4. Trained cats under stūpas, detail of stone relief. Barabuḍur, ninth century. Krom, *Barabuḍur: Archaeological Description*, vol. 3, series I.b., pl. xl, scene 80.

muni explains to the monks that on account of the hunter's repentance and his provision of a stūpa for honoring the *pratyekabuddha*, he reaped many benefits in his incarnation as Rudrāyaṇa: he enjoyed an indulgent life, he reigned as king, he had the rare opportunity to hear a Buddha preach, and he was able to become an *arhat*. On the other hand, the Buddha notes, having killed a *pratyekabuddha* in the past, Rudrāyaṇa was thereby destined to die a violent death.

Śākyamuni goes on to explain how the other important characters from the present story shared a causal nexus in the past. Sikhaṇḍhi in a previous lifetime was the unmarried daughter of a wealthy layman. For some time she had been seeking a husband, but without success. One day, while cleaning house, she accidentally threw dirt onto a nearby *pratyekabuddha*. By chance, later that day a suitor came to the family and arranged to marry her. Delighted with the news, the girl's brother asked what accounted for her success in finding a husband. She responded that her marriage offer was caused by having heaped dirt on a *pratyekabuddha*, a superstition that she soon popularized throughout the kingdom. Soon, as more and more young girls piled their sweepings on *pratyekabuddhas*, the local *pratyekabuddhas* and other holy men fled to other kingdoms. With no more sages left, young girls even started substituting their parents as victims of the act. Two wise elders finally managed to put an end to the noxious custom by convincing the populace that the connection between throwing dirt on *pratyekabuddhas* and securing a husband was merely a coincidence. According to Śākyamuni's explanation, the characters in the past story had all now been reborn together in Roruka. The foolish girl who had swept dirt on the *pratyekabuddha* and was responsible for spreading the custom to include people's parents was reborn as

Sikhaṇḍhi, who in one stroke killed an *arhat* and his father. The girl's brother was reborn as the honored monk Kātyāyana, while the two wise elders were reborn as Roruka's wise government ministers.

Although the legend of King Rudrāyaṇa does not explicitly mention a painting of the wheel of rebirth, it contains many of the same elements as the founding myth about the saṃsāracakra. The Rudrāyaṇa story talks about how a metaphysical painting is constructed, where it is displayed, and how people respond to it. Compared to the canonical account of the wheel of saṃsāra, the Rudrāyaṇa legend offers an alternative conceptualization of how viewing pictorial representations of the cosmos leads over many lifetimes to achieving salvation.

The paintings that figure prominently in the two stories are both concerned with basic Buddhist teachings, but their content is largely different. They have three main points of convergence. The first is the Twelve Conditions of dependent origination, which are portrayed in different media. The wheel of rebirth uses stock symbols for each of the links, while Rudrāyaṇa's painting expresses them in words. This way of talking about causality emphasizes the continuity between lifetimes and explains how the failure to vanquish ignorance leads directly to further suffering in one's next rebirth. In the Rudrāyaṇa story, the king's reflection on the twelvefold chain leads to his first enlightenment experience. The second element shared by the two paintings is a pair of stanzas discussing renunciation, saṃsāra, the Dharma and vinaya, and the end of suffering—points on which almost all Buddhists would agree. Third, in addition to these parallels, both paintings are supposed to contain an image of the Buddha, although most of the actual depictions of the wheel discussed in this book do not include a Buddha at the center of the wheel. The central Buddha image in Rudrāyaṇa's painting may have been iconic in execution—dwarfing other figures, facing the viewer frontally, carrying the requisite bodily marks, etc.—but nothing in the story suggests that Rudrāyaṇa himself treats the painting as an icon. Only a visiting group of merchants engage in the rituals appropriate for a Buddhist icon. They begin chanting prayers to the Buddha, but when Rudrāyaṇa asks about the meaning of the image, he is not instructed to worship it. Rather, he is told about the social and soteriological ranking of the person depicted in the painting.

What is most striking for our purposes is the way in which the contents of the two paintings diverge. The wheel of rebirth is composed mostly of symbols representing Buddhist doctrines, whereas Rudrāyaṇa's painting consists of important Buddhist words written below a Buddha image. The words are worth our attention since, aside from the Twelve Conditions and the two stanzas, their meaning and orientation differ from the message of the wheel of rebirth. Bimbisāra's gift to Rudrāyaṇa contains the formula of the Three Refuges. Although the doctrinal essence of the Three Refuges is, in a superficial sense, the Three Jewels, the formulation has as much to do with ritual as with belief. The key to understanding the Three Refuges is to view them as a ceremonial act; they are the program for becoming a Buddhist. The next component in Rudrāyaṇa's painting further underscores the performativity of the Three Refuges. It is the Five Precepts, to which a lay Buddhist formally commits herself or himself in the ritual entry into lay life. The core teachings of Rudrāyaṇa's painting, then, can be summarized thus: human existence is followed by an endless series of painful lives; the Buddha is a special being who renounced kingship and achieved ultimate salvation; taking refuge as a lay person in the Three Jewels is the best route to follow; and abstention from violence and following the other precepts are the duties of all laypeople.

The wider *avadāna* tale containing the story of Rudrāyaṇa's painting embellishes the lay morality enunciated in the painting. Like most Buddhist narrative, the account spins an entertaining and edifying story out of karmic webs. It shows how good deeds produce good results and how evil acts are punished. It teaches that most situations in life resemble the plight of characters in the story: they are a complicated combination of good and bad, the precise ratio of which can only be discerned afterward, with the help of an omniscient narrator or Buddha. The story makes clear that there is an underlying logic by which deeds are ranked. A large donation goes farther than a small one, a pure gift is better than a dirty one, and religious acts involving contact with the Buddha or other holy men are the most efficacious. Just as the wheel of rebirth inscribes a realm of karmically scaled suffering within a circle and places freedom from suffering outside the circle, so too does the story of Rudrāyaṇa delineate a ladder with an indefinite nirvāṇa placed above the rungs of mundane rebirth. The soteriology of the Rudrāyaṇa legend is complex, fluid, and logical. The unenlightened aspire to become practicing lay Buddhists. Poor lay Buddhists aim to become rich and happy, so that as wealthy laypeople, kings, or gods they can make even larger donations to the Saṃgha. And those especially privileged beings who have worked for many lifetimes to achieve their current state pursue a face-to-face encounter with the Buddha, which can assure them of speedily achieving nirvāṇa. The Buddhist universe constructed in the stories discussed here is a hierarchy of moral acts and levels of spirituality that takes many lifetimes to master.

Karma, morality, and lay Buddhism constitute the overt message of the narrative of Rudrāyaṇa, but its subtext is the importance of the Saṃgha and the crucial role played by kings in the life of Buddhism. After receiving the painting from Bimbisāra, Rudrāyaṇa sends for five hundred members of the Saṃgha. His conversion effected by a painting of Buddhist doctrine, Rudrāyaṇa proceeds to support the faith by enlisting monks and nuns to come teach him more. He does not take it upon himself, Aśoka-style, to inscribe the words of the Law on public pillars or to build hospitals, bridges, or other public service projects in the name of the religion. Rather, he invites a foreign Saṃgha to proselytize in his kingdom. As so often happens in the history of Buddhism, importing images leads directly to the immigration of monks. In this case the propagation of Buddhism follows a top-down rather than a bottom-up model. Buddhist symbols are exchanged first and foremost between monarchs. Buddhist influence is spread among Roruka's nobility, and soon one of Rudrāyaṇa's courtesans joins the Saṃgha as well. The Buddha's role in the story is consistent with this monarchial view of the universe. Bimbisāra's ministers treat the Buddha as a possession of the king, and the narrative answers back playfully by portraying the founder of the Saṃgha as someone who deigns to help the ruler pursue the highest goals of both statecraft and saintcraft.

What the lore about Rudrāyaṇa's painting contributes to our understanding of the saṃsāracakra is that such representations were fairly widespread in the medieval Buddhist world (or worlds). There was more than one way to explain the basic ideas of Buddhism. The truth of rebirth and karmic retribution, the paths of monk and layman, and the goals of a better rebirth and release from saṃsāra were articulated in many different ways. Visual presentations of Buddhism varied tremendously in form: some portrayed holy figures in an iconic mode, some used symbols to represent key doctrines, some depicted episodes in order to tell a story, and others were composed largely of poetry and stock formulae. Paintings of the wheel of rebirth were simply one among several such options. The mythology about the painting that inspired King Rudrāyaṇa is yet another proof that the proper way of picturing reincarnation and salvation was a matter of debate.

Another important contrast between stories about Rudrāyaṇa's painting and stories about pictures of the wheel of rebirth has to do with producers, consumers, and media. Both myths are reduplicated in the vinaya of the Mūlasarvāstivāda school and in the *Divyāvadāna*. Both myths deal with the propagation of Buddhism to laypeople. In the story of the wheel of life and death, however, the paintings are executed on monastery walls, while in the Rudrāyaṇa tale the illustration is painted on a scroll. The picture of the saṃsāracakra is stationary and overwhelmingly public; the Buddha explicitly directs his followers to paint the wheel in the outermost precincts of Buddhist temples. By contrast, in the Rudrāyaṇa story the Buddha instructs King Bimbisāra to paint the composition on silk and pack it inside three precious containers before sending it abroad. Although the whole population of Roruka seems to line the boulevards to welcome the procession bearing the image, and merchants visiting Rudrāyaṇa's court are allowed to glimpse it, there is no doubt that the gift of the scroll belongs to the king. Both stories involve the propagation of the Dharma, but the portable qualities of the painting and the dimensions of ownership are quite different in each case.

A final similarity worth noting between the two paintings is that they both stimulate the spiritual life of their principal audience. Encounters with the paintings are placed at the beginning of the two narratives in which they occur. Like Born in Poverty's (Sahasodgata's) glimpse of karmic retribution in temple paintings of the Five Paths, Rudrāyaṇa's viewing of Bimbisāra's gift is the first major episode in the king's career in Buddhism. These two pictorial encapsulations of Buddhism in the respective stories are crucial in turning the main characters toward the practice of Buddhism. Just as saṃsāracakra paintings serve a prefatory function by being placed on the outskirts of temples, so too the viewing of images in these two legends serves to initiate the protagonists into Buddhism.

Although paintings of the wheel and paintings of the Twelve Conditions are similar in that they appear at the beginning of the viewer's path to enlightenment, the two images differ in how quickly their viewers advance. The illustration of the wheel of saṃsāra is intended as a substitute for Maudgalyāyana's sermons about retribution, the original audience of which takes up the practice of Buddhist morality. Similarly, Born in Poverty reacts to a representation of the wheel of rebirth by resolving to be reborn in heaven through a rigorous program of lay donation. The goal in the legend of the wheel of life and death is undoubtedly sanctified, but it does not rank very highly in the Buddhist scheme of things. At the beginning, the Rudrāyaṇa legend also seems to attribute relatively modest powers to paintings of the Twelve Conditions, since the Buddha says that the image should incite the viewer to practice lay Buddhism. The actual consequences of seeing the image, however, are considerably greater than this. In the first place, his viewing of the painting prompts Rudrāyaṇa to call for a delegation of monks who disseminate the faith in his kingdom so successfully that even local people achieve the fruit of *arhat*. Furthermore, the eventual result of the king's vision is that he becomes a stream-enterer, one whose progress on the path is measured by its proximity to the terminus rather than (like Born in Poverty's hopes for heaven) its distance from the beginning. We must not, however, lose sight of the fact that most of the sources on medieval Buddhism agree that the Buddhist path is long and capacious. These two legends describe a journey toward salvation punctuated by a succession of statuses that are achieved by viewing paintings. Pictorial representations of Buddhist cosmology were varied, then, but the effects of seeing them were believed to lie on a single continuum stretching from lay morality and a better rebirth to the achieving of insight and release from saṃsāra.

Chapter 5

La roue imaginaire en Chine

My discussion in this chapter is hypothetical: if wheels of rebirth were painted in Tang-dynasty (618–907) China, where would such pictures have been found? Who would have seen them? How would they have been understood? My title reverts to the French, *imaginaire*, for two reasons. First, the word is a frank admission that the wheel is imaginary, in the sense that there is only intangible evidence that paintings of the saṃsāracakra existed at the time. Owing to the chance survival of paintings in cave temples and the occasionally meticulous description in literary sources of the iconographic programs at selected temples, we know some of the topics covered in Buddhist painting. The list includes hells, pure lands, gods, demons, *nāgas* (serpentlike creatures), Buddhas, and bodhisattvas, but one looks in vain for solid confirmation of any artistic representations of the saṃsāracakra. Second, the word *imaginaire* draws attention to the place that the wheel of rebirth might have occupied in the creative faculties of medieval Chinese people. I want to explore the visionary, fantastic side of painted wheels. I want to ask: How would images of the wheel have been conceptualized in temple blueprints? How would people have theorized about the significance of representations of the wheel? What would they have dreamt about the wheel? How would viewers have responded to pictures of the wheel of rebirth?

We cannot begin our story of the wheel of rebirth in China with the canonical account, as was appropriate in the case of India, because in China the canonical version of the wheel appears relatively late among surviving sources. As noted in chapter 2, Yijing (635–713) finished his translation of the *locus classicus*, the *Mūlasarvāstivāda vinaya vibhaṅga*, in 703. Yijing's vinaya, however, represented only one out of five such canons in medieval China, and the version of the vinaya followed most broadly in China, the Dharmagupta, lacked any referent to paintings of the wheel altogether. Nevertheless, Yijing's translation of the vinaya story about the wheel remained normative in a restricted sense for at least three centuries, since it is quoted in a compilation of notices on different aspects of monastic life completed in 1019. The text, *Fundamental Observations on the Śākya Clan* (*Shishi yaolan*), was written by the monk Daocheng (ca. 1017–1021) as a primer for monks and nuns entering the Saṃgha. Daocheng was from Hangzhou (Zhejiang) and lived there most of his life, first at Longhua Temple and later at Mount Yuelun (see map 5). His work includes twenty-seven entries on customs and institutions the author regarded as essential to monastic life, including names for temple personnel, types of buildings and sacred spaces, the ceremony of ordination, clothing, food, rites for laypeople, ritual deportment, the Three Jewels, cosmology, study, polite gestures, choosing friends, miscellaneous issues, treating illness, and death ritual. Throughout the text, Daocheng surveys a wide range of sources, including sūtras, the vinayas of various schools, secular texts, and histories of Buddhism compiled in China. Drawing on the Mūlasarvāstivāda vinaya, Daocheng quotes verbatim the Buddha's directions to his disciples to paint a wheel of rebirth in the Five Paths.[1] We do not know enough about Daocheng's life or the iconographic programs of early Song-dynasty Buddhist temples in Zhejiang to know with certainty whether Daocheng actually saw such a painting in the temples where he lived. His book does show, however, that he considered both the painting itself and the Buddha's directions to paint one as normative ideals in his time.

The wheel of the Five Paths shows up for the first time in the Chinese historical record long before the canonical account was even translated from Sanskrit. It appears not in a vinaya text or on the walls of a Buddhist temple, but in a layman's dream as related in a miracle tale. The story was written by a Chinese official in the late fifth century. The author, Wang Yan (ca. 454–501), who had lived in south China and in what is now Vietnam, wrote historical works and took a special interest in collecting tales of anomalous events interpreted in a Buddhist light.[2] His *Collection of Auspicious Signs from the Dark World* (*Mingxiang ji*) is the largest and widest ranging of the early books in the genre of *zhiguai*, "recording anomalies," known imperfectly in English as "miracle tales."

The protagonist of Wang Yan's story is the governor of a commandery in Sichuan. The governor, named Wang Qiu, is a devout Buddhist, but because of incompetence in performing his job he is sentenced to jail. Incarceration affords him the opportunity to develop his Buddhist virtues even further, and he wastes no time in sharing his food with other, presumably less wealthy inmates. Then, one night in jail he has a dream in which he sees a monk who hands him a text. Wang Qiu also dreams that he sees a wheel, which the apparition-monk identifies as "the wheel of the Five Paths"—these are, in fact, the only words spoken in the dream. The story says nothing else about the wheel. When the governor wakes up the next day, a miracle has occurred: his chains have been broken. According to the narrator, that unusual event leads, three days later, to a pardon for Wang. The entire tale reads:

---

1. The wheel is described in the section entitled "The Wheel of Birth and Death in the Five Paths" ("Wuqu shengsi lun"), sandwiched between discussions of wall paintings in monasteries and the ornamentation of statues; *Shishi yaolan* (1019), Daocheng (ca. 1017–1021), *T* no. 2127, 54:303c–04a. For Daocheng's biography, see Zhongguo fojiao renming dacidian bianji weiyuanhui, *Zhongguo fojiao renming dacidian*, pp. 823b–24a.

2. On Wang Yan and his work, see Campany, *Strange Writing*, pp. 82–83.

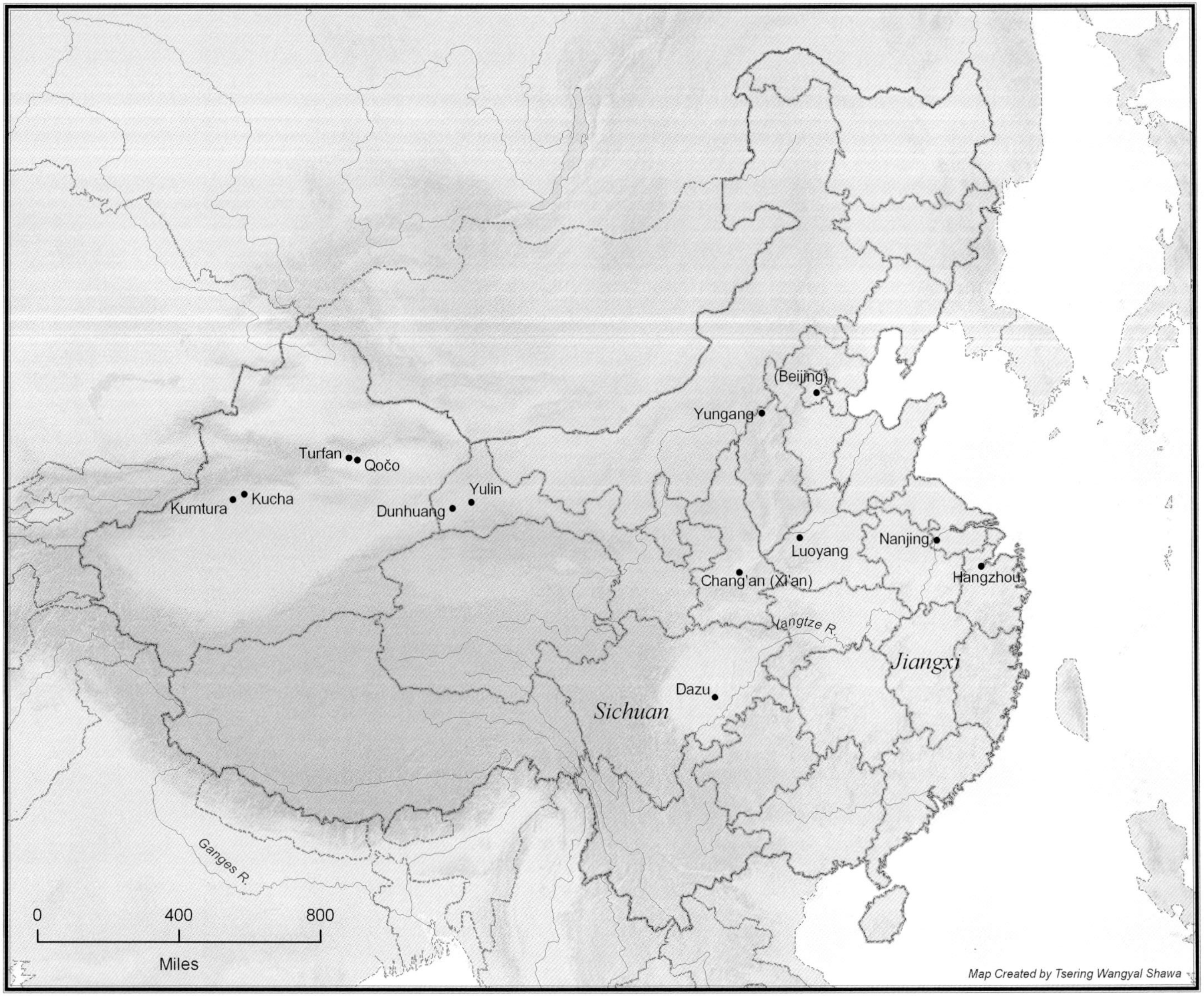

Map 5. Tang-dynasty China.

During the Song dynasty [420–479] there was Wang Qiu, courtesy name Shuda, from Taiyuan [modern Shanxi]. He was the Governor of Fuling [modern Sichuan]. Because in the ninth year of Yuanjia [452] he was derelict in his duties in the commandery, he was locked up in prison, where he was shackled in chains with strong links.

Prior to this Qiu was very vigorous in his devotion,[3] and when he landed in jail he was diligent in the extreme. In prison there were more than one hundred people, many of them hungry. Whenever Qiu ate, he would divide his food and share it.

During the day he would maintain his discipline,[4] applying his mind to invoking Avalokiteśvara [Guanshiyin]. At night he dreamt that he ascended a tall throne. He saw a *śramaṇa* [monk] who gave him a scroll of scripture. The titles on it read "Light Chapter" and "Comfortable Conduct," and it also had the names of various bodhisattvas.[5] Qiu received it and unrolled it. He missed the name of the first bodhisattva.[6] The second one's name was Avalokiteśvara, and the third one's name was Mahāsthāmaprāpta [Dashizhi]. He also saw a wheel. The *śramaṇa* said, "This is the wheel of the Five Paths."

When Qiu woke up, his chains were torn asunder.

Qiu's power of mind was vast, and his spiritual strength was concentrated. Because he unlocked his own chains, after three days he was pardoned.[7]

Taking a cue from recent studies of the genre of miracle tales, we should perhaps view this story not as a work of "fiction" or making things up, but instead as an attempt to impose a standard system of classification upon something that first appears confusing.[8] The anomalous event in the tale is the breaking of the governor's chains. Under normal circumstances, people thrown into prison, even if they have high status, are not able to escape, yet that is precisely what happens in this case. The narrator explains that the seemingly miraculous outcome is a result of the governor's pious actions. The system of classification is the Buddhist theory of causality, according to which every

3. "Vigorous in his devotion" or "vigor" (*jingjin*, Skt.: *vīrya*) is the fourth of the Six Perfections (*ṣaṭpāramitā*) in Mahāyāna thought; see Nakamura, *Bukkyōgo daijiten*, p. 1463b.

4. "Maintain his discipline" (*chizhai*) could also be rendered "uphold the fast," observing the rules of purity required of Buddhist laypeople during the fast days.

5. "And it also had the names of various bodhisattvas" renders *bing zhupusa ming*. I disagree with Lu Xun (*Gu xiaoshuo gouchen*, p. 620), who interprets the names as a single, continuous chapter title. The words in the text immediately preceding are clearly chapter titles from two different texts (see below), not one title, and I have not found chapters of any Buddhist text entitled "The Names of Various Bodhisattvas."

6. Or, "The text was missing the name of the first bodhisattva."

7. Translation from *Mingxiang ji*, as collated in Lu, *Gu xiaoshuo gouchen*, pp. 620–21. Lu relies on the citation of the tale in *Fayuan zhulin*, Daoshi (d. 683), *T* no. 2122, 53:459b–c.

8. The formulation is Robert Campany's; see *Strange Writing*, esp. pp. 199–201. See also DeWoskin, "The Six Dynasties *Chih-kuai* and the Birth of Fiction"; and Gjertson, "Early Chinese Buddhist Miracle Tale."

good deed has a good result. The hermeneutical point of the story is that we can make sense of odd events like the breaking of the governor's manacles and fetters by looking to prior acts of piety, that the present can be understood by looking for karmic causes in the past.

What is most striking about the protagonist's piety is, to use Robert Campany's term, its "ordinariness."[9] The author goes out of his way to announce that the seeds for the governor's actions in prison were planted through his practice of one of the basic virtues of the Buddhist life, "vigor." That virtue is manifested not in the extreme self-sacrifice of a bodhisattva, the reclusive antics of a hermit, or the asceticism and transcendence of Daoist holy men, but in such basic acts of piety as chanting and sharing food with others.

The author of the tale also uses the device of a dream in order to foreshadow the outcome of the story. The dream is a vehicle for revealing how the unusual result is explained by a prior deed. As Campany states, in this kind of text, "dream-encounters are not mere mental fragments, but are real."[10] We first learn that the governor is pious and that he practices Buddhist ethics while in jail. Next, we are told he has a dream in which several things are revealed to him through a complex process. In the dream the governor experiences two mysterious objects. One is a scroll containing two chapters from different texts. The narrator states the names of the two chapters, which I speculate to be extracts of two texts that circulated widely at the time.[11] This part of the story does not end with the narrator's recording of the titles, however. We are told next that after receiving the text from the monk, the protagonist proceeds to unroll the book and read it. The revelation of the meaning, however, is incomplete, since the governor somehow forgets or neglects the name of the first bodhisattva.

The haziness of the dream extends to the second object, the wheel. Here too we are told that the governor has a visual encounter with a meaning-bearing object, but the meaning of the object is not known until the monk in the dream speaks, revealing its name ("the wheel of the Five Paths"). The story leads us to infer that the monk was clarifying, rather than mystifying, the significance of the object. The governor must have had some inkling of what "the wheel of the Five Paths" meant, otherwise the monk's naming of the wheel would not have been definitive. As in the canonical account of preachers using the saṃsāracakra as a teaching device, which was translated into Chinese two hundred years after this tale was written, a Buddhist

9. Campany, *Strange Writing*, pp. 321–23.

10. Ibid., p. 265.

11. There are many chapters entitled "Light" ("Guangming") in Buddhist texts, but my guess is that the chapter in question is from *Pusa yingluo jing*, trans. Buddhasmṛti (Zhu Fonian, ca. 365), *T* no. 656. The second reference is to a chapter entitled "Comfortable Conduct" ("Anxing"), emending *anxing* (official tour) to *anxing* (comfortable conduct), following Lu (*Gu xiaoshuo gouchen*, p. 620) and the *T* editors (*T* 53:459b, n. 12). This is the title of chapter 13 in the early translation of the *Lotus Sūtra*; see *Zheng fahua jing*, trans. Dharmarakṣa (Zhu Fahu, fl. 265–313), *T* no. 263. It corresponds to chapter 14, entitled "Anle xing," in the later translation; see *Miaofa lianhua jing* (*Saddharmapuṇḍarīka*), trans. Kumārajīva (Jiumoluoshi, 350–409), *T* no. 262. Neither chapter mentions the bodhisattvas to whom the tale refers, Avalokiteśvara or Mahāsthāmaprāpta.

layman is dependent on a monk to explain the significance of the wheel of rebirth.

Ultimately, then, the breaking of the governor's locks is neither a miscarriage of justice nor an inexplicable anomaly. Instead, when it is placed in its proper context—the Buddhist scheme of causality—it appears as the karmalogical result of the governor's pious deeds. There is, in fact, a twin result, further reverberations of the governor's virtue. The narrator ends the story not with the breaking of the manacles but by adding another link to the causal chain: because he freed himself from the shackles, the governor was pardoned three days later.

If that is the narrative logic of the account, what sense can we make of the iconographic details? Wang Yan's account depicts the dreamer climbing a throne. Wang Yan does not explain whose throne it is. To figure out the possible identity of the chief deity or ruler of the throne, we should perhaps look more closely at the two bodhisattvas who appear in the dream. They are Avalokiteśvara and Mahāsthāmaprāpta, the two chief assistants to Amitābha Buddha, and they are regularly depicted in paintings and sculptures as flanking Amitābha. The location of the dream, then, could be the western pure land of Amitābha Buddha. In this reading of the tale, Wang Qiu has a foretaste of salvation: he travels in his dream to Amitābha's abode, as marked by the two saints on either side of the Buddha's throne. And, like many protagonists in Chinese miracle tales, after this oneiric encounter he returns to waking life even more dedicated to the truth of the Dharma and the practice of Buddhism.[12] Nevertheless, this interpretation is troubled by the fact that the text refrains from saying just who sits on the throne—no small issue if the event really is an epiphany of final salvation. The other strong possibility is that the incumbent of the throne is not discussed because the focus of the dream is Wang Qiu's encounter with the object of his devotion, Avalokiteśvara Bodhisattva. Wang chanted his name while awake, so it is fitting that he be rewarded by a nighttime experience of the bodhisattva himself—or, as our text construes it, the bestowal of a text containing the bodhisattva's name.

How does the wheel of rebirth fit into the scene pictured in the dream? Here too we can only make guesses. Does the wheel of rebirth—which Wang Qiu at first does not seem to recognize—stand in contrast to the throne and its location in the pure land? If so, the figure of the monk in the dream uses the wheel to emphasize that the protagonist is headed beyond the realm of the Five Paths. Pointing to the wheel of rebirth would be a way of telling Wang Qiu that he has already been reborn, in dream time, into the pure land. Alternatively, the presence of the wheel and the emphasis

12. The veracity of the dream world—not to say its opacity—is a recurring theme in medieval Chinese literature. Many stories explain how information about the afterlife is conveyed in dreams. Typically the protagonist dreams of an encounter with a monk, holy figure, or minor official in the underworld who provides pointed instruction about how to represent sites and figures seen in the dream. The protagonist often remarks on the correspondence or difference between the statues, paintings, or literary accounts above ground and the privileged information being dispensed in the dream. Sometimes after the dreamer awakes, he pursues the mission of popularizing a corrected representation of the other world. See Hegel, "Heavens and Hells in Chinese Fictional Dreams"; Lin, "Religious Taoism and Dreams"; Mair, "Records of Transformation Tableaux," esp. p. 24; Strickmann, "Dreamwork of Psycho-Sinologists"; and Teiser, "'Having Once Died and Returned to Life.'"

on describing it in words might be a way of saying that what happens in the dream is still connected to the realm of birth and death. After having the dream, Wang Qiu does, after all, return to his post in Sichuan in the year 452.

In the five centuries between the writing of the story about Wang and the first attested painting of a wheel of rebirth at Yulin (Gansu) in the tenth century (discussed in chapter 7), there are no surviving contemporaneous descriptions of any paintings of the wheel of rebirth in Chinese Buddhist temples. The indirect evidence, however, is suggestive. Illustrations of heavens, hells, pure lands, and all places in between were an important part of Chinese visual culture even before the Tang dynasty. The sites of the other world were depicted on temple walls in a genre that artists and writers of the time called "transformation scenes" (*bianxiang*). The hell regions were a particularly common subject of such wall paintings.[13] Literary sources describe "transformation scenes of the underground prisons" (*diyu bianxiang*) being painted in many different styles and places. One of the most famous painters of the mid-Tang, Wu Daozi (fl. 713–755), was known especially for his renderings of hell, inspiring many of his contemporaries to emulate his work.

The content of hell transformations varies considerably, and their significance depends on the larger ritual and iconographic programs of which they are a part. Some representations of the underworld were used to demarcate a realm of suffering in contrast to a future time of redemption. For example, a picture of hell is located in the antechamber of an early Tang cave at Dunhuang (Mogao Cave 231), the main chamber of which is focused on Maitreya, the Buddha of the future. By its placement, the picture of hell occupies the preparatory space of the cave; it defines an infernal present that will be redeemed by the coming of the next Buddha, a transformation that takes place in the inner sanctum of the cave temple. The depiction of hell emphasizes the suffering that denizens—scantily clad, with their hands bound by cangues—undergo as retribution for past deeds. There are part-human, part-bird creatures, monsters who breathe fire, guards holding pitchforks, as well as underworld sites like a mountain of knives and a forest of sword trees. A second example of a representation of hell is the early tenth-century wall painting of the journey of Maudgalyāyana depicted in the corridor of Cave 19 at Yulin (see figs. 7.7 and 7.8; the scene, found opposite a wheel of rebirth on the facing wall, is discussed in greater detail in chapter 7). In addition to driving home the points that sentient beings are punished in the afterlife and that all forms of existence are filled with pain, the painting in Yulin Cave 19 also follows the progress of Maudgalyāyana in his tour of hell. There is a clear beginning at top left, where the disciple passes through a gate and enters the city of hell, and the progression of narrative time is clearly indicated by the reappearance of the protagonist in each scene.

---

13. The name of the genre and its relation to literary accounts are much debated. See, for example, Mair, "Records of Transformation Tableaux"; and Hung Wu, "What is *Bianxiang*?" On paintings of hell, see also Du, "'Diyu bianxiang' chutan"; Hu Wenhe, "Lun diyu bianxiang tu"; Kanaoka, "Tonkōbon jigoku bunken kanki"; Naba, "Rokuchō Zui Tōdai no hekiga"; Teiser, "'Having Once Died and Returned to Life'"; and Wang Guangzhao, "Tangdai Chang'an fojiao siyuan bihua."

Some sense of how Tang Buddhists regarded pictures of hell painted on temple walls can be gleaned from a biography written in the mid-seventh century. The account concerns a monk named Jing'ai (534–578), who had precocious literary talents. His family, surnamed Zheng, from Rongyang (modern Jiangxi), opposed his early interest in Buddhism, but when he saw images of hell painted on the walls of a temple, his dedication to Buddhism became unshakeable. The account reads:

> Jing'ai went with friends to visit a temple, where they studied the illustrated transformations of hell [*diyu tubian*]. While regarding the various sentient beings, he said, "How odd—the adjudication of the law of karma. Who has the means to escape such cruelty?"
>
> From then on he firmly opposed his parents' urgent objections, and they were unable to shake his resolve. In the end, the elder Zhengs relented. Ai loved cutting off his passions and binding himself. His emotional expression was like that of a stone.
>
> Later he went to Baiguan Temple and left family life under Meditation Master He. At that time he was seventeen.[14]

Pictures of the nether regions were thought to possess great motivating power. In this biography, Jing'ai's contemplation of retribution scenes was instrumental to becoming a monk. Although it is impossible for the author of this account to have known the legend contained in the Mūlasarvāstivāda vinaya (since it would be translated into Chinese about fifty years later), nevertheless both of these texts employ the same trope: a young boy is turned to Buddhism after viewing pictures of karmic retribution painted in a temple.

In addition to representations of hell, paintings of other realms of the cosmos decorated the walls of Tang temples. A ninth-century description of temples in Chang'an and Luoyang mentions paintings of King Yama, the different forms of karmic retribution, various pure lands, Amitābha's pure land in the west, and the sixteen sights to be visualized in Amitābha's paradise.[15] The precise location of pure lands within the standard Buddhist cosmology was, and is, a matter of much debate. The plotting of the Five or Six Paths of rebirth was accomplished relatively early in the history of Buddhism. Although the notion of a pure land was probably based on the early idea of a Buddha realm (*buddhakṣetra*)—each world system being graced by one Buddha—the formalization of the concepts of the pure lands of the Ten Directions and of Amitābha's land of bliss (*sukhāvatī*) occurred later, with the growth of various Mahāyāna schools. Subsequently, medieval authors considered where such pure lands were located on the map of the Six Paths.

---

14. Translation from *Xu gaoseng zhuan*, Daoxuan (596–667), *T* no. 2060, 50:625c. For further information on Jing'ai, see Teiser, "'Having Once Died and Returned to Life,'" pp. 437–39.

15. See *Lidai minghua ji*, Zhang Yanyuan (fl. 847–874), ch. 3 (1:38–53), translated in Acker, *Some T'ang and Pre-T'ang Texts on Chinese Painting*, 1:254–377. The relevant topics are *Yanluo wang*, *shan'e chabie*, *jingtu*, *xifang*, and *shiliuguan*.

For our purposes a pictorial example like the ninth-century silk painting from Dunhuang in figure 5.1 is perhaps most relevant. The upper two-thirds of the scroll shows Amitābha Buddha enthroned in his pure land, with Avalokiteśvara Bodhisattva on the left and Mahāsthāmaprāpta Bodhisattva on the right. The picture makes clear that this realm is like a paradise: it is filled with pools of water, beautiful flowers, ornate palaces, and blessed beings like Buddhas, bodhisattvas, gods, and musicians. Its distance from the current world of saṃsāra is suggested by the clouds depicted in the top two corners. Other details draw on the medieval symbolism of rebirth to show that the land is accessible to people in their next lifetime—not so far, after all, in light of the belief in rebirth. At the bottom of the paradise segment, two large babies emerge from lotus flowers. These beings are reborn into the presence of a Buddha, not through the normal process of human birth, but through unsullied blossoming out of flowers. Their method of rebirth signifies that they have transcended the impurity of normal human birth. The horizontal panel immediately below the pure land depicts sixteen different scenes from the story of Queen Vaidehī. Her son, Ajātaśatru, had turned evil and imprisoned his mother and father. According to the story, Śākyamuni took pity on the jailed queen and personally taught her a series of visualization exercises so that she could transport herself imaginatively to a realm that was the opposite of her prison cell. This band of the painting is divided into seven scenes telling the story of the queen on the right and nine scenes on the left depicting some of the subjects for meditation in which the Buddha instructed the queen.

This pure land scroll is somewhat unusual in that it combines in one composition two subjects that are often treated in separate wall paintings: Amitābha's paradise itself plus the topics of the visualizations taught to Queen Vaidehī for the purpose of bringing her, through meditation, to that paradise. It is valuable to us because it shows in one glance the many different meanings that paintings of the cosmos could have in Tang China. The major portion of the picture glorifies its central and largest icon, Amitābha Buddha, with all of his assistants and their underlings arranged symmetrically and adoringly around him. The architecture is also significant. Rather than constituting a simple background of buildings, all of the edifices of the painting articulate the grandeur and purity of Amitābha's realm. The painting also devotes considerable space, in the middle band, to showing how one can gain access to the pure land, by following the course of visualization practices in the story of Queen Vaidehī. How people in medieval China understood such representations is an open question. The main Buddha figure faces the viewer frontally, while all the other figures seem to mime the worshipful attitudes expected of the painting's audience. The babies emerging from the lotus flowers might represent the viewer's aspiration, and the story of the queen might suggest a model for Buddhist practice. The lowest register of the piece depicts eight monks, either the actual donors of the painting or a collective representation

FIG. 5.1. Amitābha's pure land, illustration of *Visualization Sūtra*. Silk painting. Dunhuang, tenth century. Musée Guimet 17673. Courtesy of Réunion des Musées Nationaux/Art Resource, NY.

(in the trivial sense) of the institution of the Saṃgha. The painting, then, offers several ways of gaining the pure land: making donations, performing meditation, and engaging in reverence. It pictures the act of rebirth taking place there, and it describes the bliss that comes from encountering a Buddha.

Despite the complexity of the images of hells and pure lands discussed so far, they are all simple in comparison to paintings of the wheel of rebirth in the sense that they picture only one or two realms of the cosmos. Artistic representations that come closer, in this respect, to paintings of the Five or Six Paths are the depictions of the so-called cosmological Buddha in central Asia and China. Earlier generations of scholars identified this figure as a form of Vairocana Buddha and tried to assess its significance within sectarian confines as an expression of proto-Tantric Buddhism or the *Avataṃsaka sūtra*. More recently, following the pioneering work of Angela Howard, the consensus is that the main Buddha figure in these representations stems from an important artistic and cosmological tradition not confined to any one school of Buddhism.[16] What is significant for our purposes is that all Six Paths of rebirth are displayed on, or around, this Buddha.

Several examples of representations of the cosmic Buddha help shed some light on the conceptualization of metaphysical space in medieval Buddhism. Perhaps the earliest picture of a cosmological Buddha is contained in a Northern Wei (386–534) cave temple at Dunhuang, Mogao Cave 428.[17] It is a single-chamber cave with paintings on all four walls. The subject of the (east) wall through which one enters the cave is the previous lifetimes of the Buddha: it depicts three Jātaka tales. The left (south) wall contains a rendering of the cosmological Buddha (see figs. 5.2 and 5.3). The rear (west) wall shows the Buddha entering *parinirvāṇa*, and the right (north) wall illustrates the Buddha's victory over Māra. As Howard has shown, the cultic focus of the cave is Śākyamuni Buddha. After entering the cave, one can turn around (viewing the front wall) to see illustrations of his previous lifetimes. Ahead, on the main (rear) wall of the cave, is his entry into final extinction, while on the right he is shown achieving insight into the nature of existence and the certainty of nirvāṇa, symbolized by his defeat of Māra. In the context of this cave, the cosmological scenes depicted on the body of the Buddha on the left wall serve to glorify the all-encompassing power and wisdom of the Buddha, demonstrating that he is coterminous with every possible mode of existence. At the bottom of his body, on the undergarment exposed by his gown, are naked sinners being chased through hell by wardens. Above them, on the lowest horizontal portion of his robe proper, one sees animals: birds, deer, horses, and a monkey, plus a humanoid figure, perhaps carrying a lute, on the right. Above them is the realm of human beings. The people here are engaged in the work of agriculture, while to the right another figure is shown within a house. More figures are shown seated in a row of houses or structures in the row above that. Level with the Buddha's left hand (on the viewer's right) are three figures on the left side approaching a seated figure on

16. See Howard, *Imagery of the Cosmological Buddha*.
17. See ibid., pp. 33–38, whose reading I follow.

the right side. The latter is shown between two trees; perhaps he is a representation of the Buddha who incarnates himself among humans as Śākyamuni. One of the clearest iconographic identifiers of the whole painting is the large *asura* (demigod) shown in the middle of the main Buddha's chest. As in other renderings of the cosmological Buddha, he holds the sun and moon in his hands, and behind him Mount Sumeru is shown, surrounded by *nāgas*. Mount Sumeru is the center of this world system, and atop it are positioned the heavens or abodes of the gods, here depicted as a tripartite palace structure above the *asura*'s head. Considered as a subject in its own right, the painting of the cosmological Buddha in Mogao Cave 428 is a rendering of the power and pervasiveness of Śākyamuni Buddha. In relation to the broader pictorial program of the cave as a whole, the painting expresses one aspect in the holy career of the Buddha.

While the biographical and cosmological functions are allotted to different wall surfaces in the Dunhuang painting, in sculptural forms of the cosmological Buddha these two modes are sometimes combined in one three-dimensional form. A Sui-dynasty (581–618) gray marble sculpture now in the Freer Gallery, shown in figure 5.4, is one of the best examples. The front, back, and sides of the statue are incised with the structure of the cosmos and scenes from the life of the historical Buddha. The front of the robe contains a preponderance of cosmological scenes (see fig. 5.5). Mount Sumeru, which occupies the center of the world in Buddhist cosmology, is depicted in the center of the Buddha's chest, entwined by *nāgas*. Two registers below the cosmic mountain, a large horse stands out. It is probably a symbolic reference to the theme of renunciation in the Buddha's biography, since he rode a horse named Kanthaka when he left the palace and relinquished his birthright. The lowest registers of the robe depict the lowest realms of the cosmos.

These examples of the cosmological Buddha demonstrate yet another way of imagining the levels of the universe in medieval Chinese Buddhist art. Both cave paintings and free-standing statues maintain the principle of vertical order in representing the paths of rebirth. The spokes of a wheel are not used to separate the paths of rebirth, nor is there a distinction between unenlightened life within the Six Paths and nirvāṇa lying outside them. Like paintings of the saṃsāracakra, the images of the cosmological Buddha often use brief, potent symbols as metaphors for the realms of the cosmos. In all of these forms of the cosmological Buddha, the universe is, in effect, personalized or Buddhicized. That is, the cosmos is tied specifically to Śākyamuni Buddha. Unlike the wheel of rebirth, the cosmos depicted in these representations is not an independent subject of consideration. Rather, the composition ties the universe to the central figure of the Buddha. The cosmos is part of his body—a point made equally well, in different form, by the common mythological motif in which entire world systems emanate from various parts (pores, tongue, *ūrṇākeśa* [wisp of hair between the eyebrows]) of the Buddha's body. In the one mode, the whole world is projected outward from a single part of the Buddha's body. In the other mode, the world is inscribed upon the entire body of the Buddha. In both modes—unlike pictures of the wheel of rebirth—the Six Paths are tied directly to the physical body of the Buddha.

FIG. 5.2. Cosmological Buddha. Wall painting. South wall of Mogao Cave 428. Northern Zhou dynasty (557–581). Dunhuang wenwu yanjiusuo, *Dunhuang Mogaoku*, vol. 1, pl. 162.

FIG. 5.3. Sketch of cosmological Buddha. Mogao Cave 428. Courtesy of Angela Howard.

FIG. 5.4. Cosmological Buddha. Stone sculpture. Unknown provenance, Sui dynasty. Freer Gallery of Art, Smithsonian Institution, Washington, D.C.: Gift of Charles Long Freer, F1900.25.

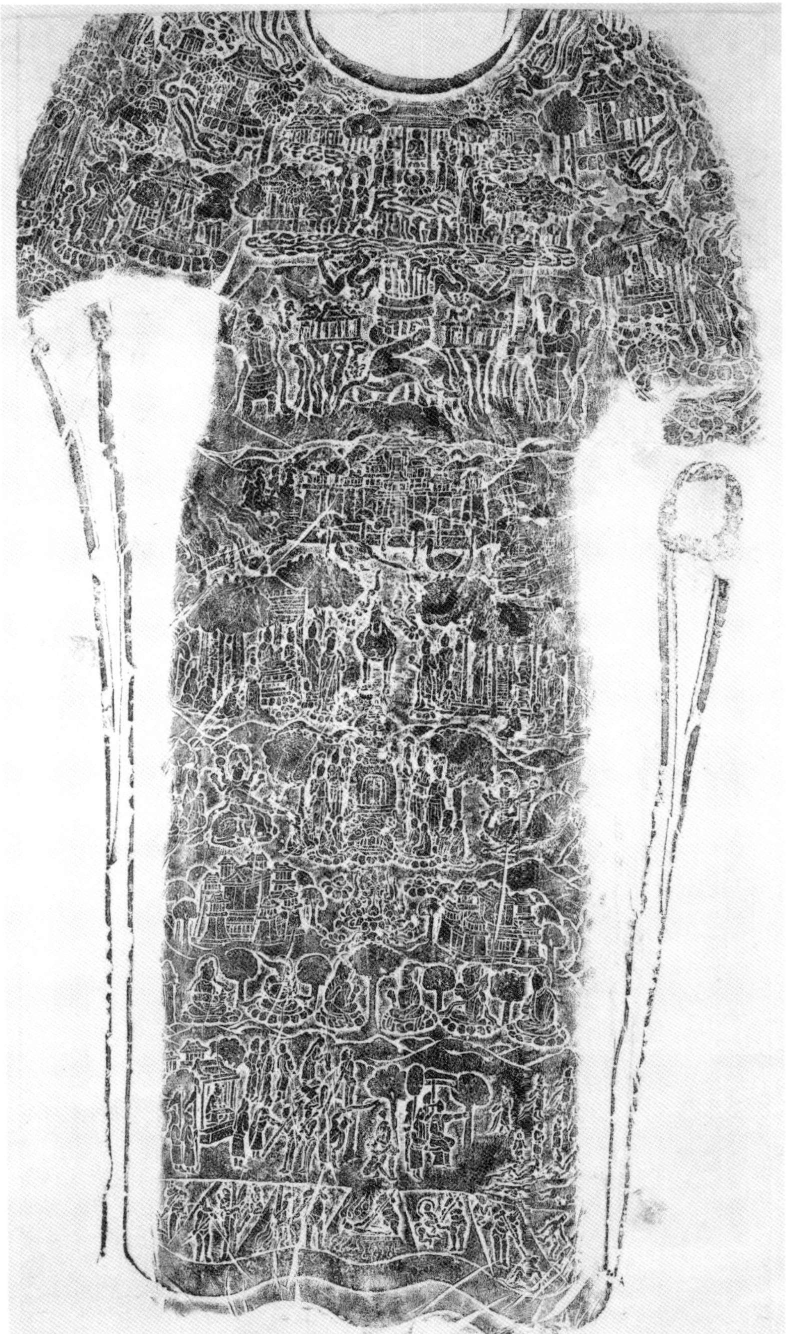

FIG. 5.5. Rubbing of front of cosmological Buddha. Freer Gallery of Art, Smithsonian Institution, Washington, D.C.: Gift of Peking University, F1980.86.1–.8.

Other clues about the possible significance of pictures of the wheel of rebirth in Tang temples can be gleaned from the structure of temple layout and the iconographic and ritual programs housed in temples. Such topics were important to monastic authorities, who were highly conscious of the symbolism of religious architecture. They often discussed the cosmological correlations of temple design, the ways in which various systems of symbolic classification (the Three Jewels, the Three Vehicles, the Twelve Conditions, etc.) could be projected onto Buddhist spaces.

Charting monastic space was one means of regulating the Buddhist path. This concern with mapping, naming, and thereby controlling institutional structures is especially apparent in the work of the eminent cleric of the early Tang, Daoxuan (596–667). Daoxuan tried to reconstruct for his Chinese readers the precise dimensions and layout of a famous Indian temple he had never seen, the Jetavana monastery in the city of Śrāvastī. Daoxuan based his project of the imagination partly on the accounts of the monastery scattered throughout Buddhist mythology and partly on stock descriptions of it written by Chinese pilgrims to India. He also proclaims to his readers that a celestial being named Zhang Yu appeared to him and instructed him about the Indian monastery. The god was the author of the true text, numbering one hundred chapters, while Daoxuan's two-chapter work was but a brief approximation of the full heavenly original.[18] In writing *The Illustrated Scripture on Jetavana Monastery in Śrāvastī in Central India*, Daoxuan was concerned "not just with the reconstruction of the monastery, which was an important stop in the Buddha's earthly sojourn, but also with the setting up of a spatial schema in which the supremacy of the Buddha's truth can be proclaimed."[19] For Daoxuan, temples provide a crucial means to escape from suffering. He writes:

> The various Buddhas display their transformations for profound reasons. They assume bodily form in the profane world, dwelling in different states. Therefore they build separate temples that stand out from the residences of common people. Their patterns and forms display what is wondrous, moving the normal mind with what is seen. They cause those who hear to be shaken up, so that they are conscious of the words and traces of their faith. Upon seeing into them, people understand their forms, comprehending how wondrous are the means of escape.[20]

Buddhist temples, in the eyes of Daoxuan, are not based on human blueprints. Rather, they are manifestations of the Buddha's compassionate urge to incarnate himself in

---

18. *Zhong Tianzhu Sheweiguo Qihuansi tujing*, Daoxuan (596–667), in 667, *T* no. 1899, 45:890a. See the study and translation by Tan, "Daoxuan's Vision of Jetavana"; see also Forte, *Mingtang and Buddhist Utopias in the History of the Astronomical Clock*, pp. 39–52; Ho, "Ideal Monastery"; and Shinohara, "Imaging the Jetavana Monastery in Medieval China."

19. Ho, "Ideal Monastery," p. 12.

20. Translation from *Zhong Tianzhu Sheweiguo Qihuansi tujing*, *T* 45:890a–b. My translation differs considerably from those in Ho, "Ideal Monastery," p. 17; and Tan, "Daoxuan's Vision of Jetavana," pp. 307–08.

forms that have an effect on people. Buddhist buildings differ from other dwellings. Something profound is discernible in their design, and those who learn to penetrate their latent meaning are able to achieve salvation.

One of the most important principles in the organization of the temple is the weighted opposition between inner and outer. The outer precincts contain structures intended for use by laypeople. These outer regions stand in contrast to the inner portions, which contain ordination platforms for monks as well as the ritual center of the temple, the main Buddha hall. The woodblock print in figure 5.6 and the legend in figure 5.7 show a close approximation to Daoxuan's description.[21] Among the buildings in the outer precincts that Daoxuan names, one particular class may be relevant to the wheel of rebirth. Although Daoxuan nowhere mentions specific scenes that are supposed to be painted in the buildings, he does refer to several structures as cloisters for teaching the twelve links in the chain of causation, which is the main subject matter of the outer ring of the wheel of rebirth. Doaxuan visualizes three different cloisters for the teaching of causality, each one corresponding to a different rank of learner. Along the southern boundary of the temple, running west to east, on the west side, is the Cloister of the Twelve Causes and Conditions for the Educated (*xueren shi'er yinyuan yuan*). Slightly closer to the center of the temple, but still outside the central precinct, are two other cloisters for teaching the twelve causes, to *pratyekabuddhas* and bodhisattvas, respectively. They are located in the second row of cloisters running south to north on the west side of the temple. The two precincts containing these three cloisters are not in the center of the temple. Teaching the Twelve Conditions is preliminary to the weightier activities, the ordination of monks and the ritual of offering to the Buddha, conducted in the main space.

Buildings in the outer precincts seem to be arranged according to two principles, clientele and curriculum. In the outermost precinct (running west to east) are cloisters patronized by persons who are not Buddhist monks. From lowest to highest, those groups are common meditation masters, non-Buddhists who wish to become monks, common people of various kingdoms who hold to the self, followers from other places of the Way of Three Vehicles and Eight Sages, and educated people who have achieved the Three Fruits. Moving closer to the center of the monastery, in the precinct running from south to north, are buildings designed for people who have progressed farther on the path: educated and uneducated people, *pratyekabuddhas*, and bodhisattvas.[22] These different classes of people are in turn subdivided according to the subject matter they are taught in the cloister. Daoxuan names three topics

21. The print in figure 5.6 (from *Guanzhong chuangli jietan tujing*, in *Z* 2a, 10:31v–33r) was composed by a later hand to accompany a different book by Daoxuan, but it largely follows the plan of *Zhong Tianzhu Sheweiguo Qihuansi tujing*; see Forte, *Mingtang and Buddhist Utopias in the History of the Astronomical Clock*, pp. 51–52 and legend to fig. 1; and Itō, "Gion shōja zu to Ankoru Watto," pp. 375–81. For architectural terms in figure 5.7, I largely follow Puay-peng Ho's partial translation in "Ideal Monastery," 2–3; cf. Tan, "Daoxuan's Vision of Jetavana," pp. 362–64.

22. The Three Vehicles (*sansheng*) here are probably not the commonly known ones of *śrāvaka*, *pratyekabuddha*, and bodhisattva, but rather those of gods, Brāhma, and sages; see Mochizuki, *Bukkyō*

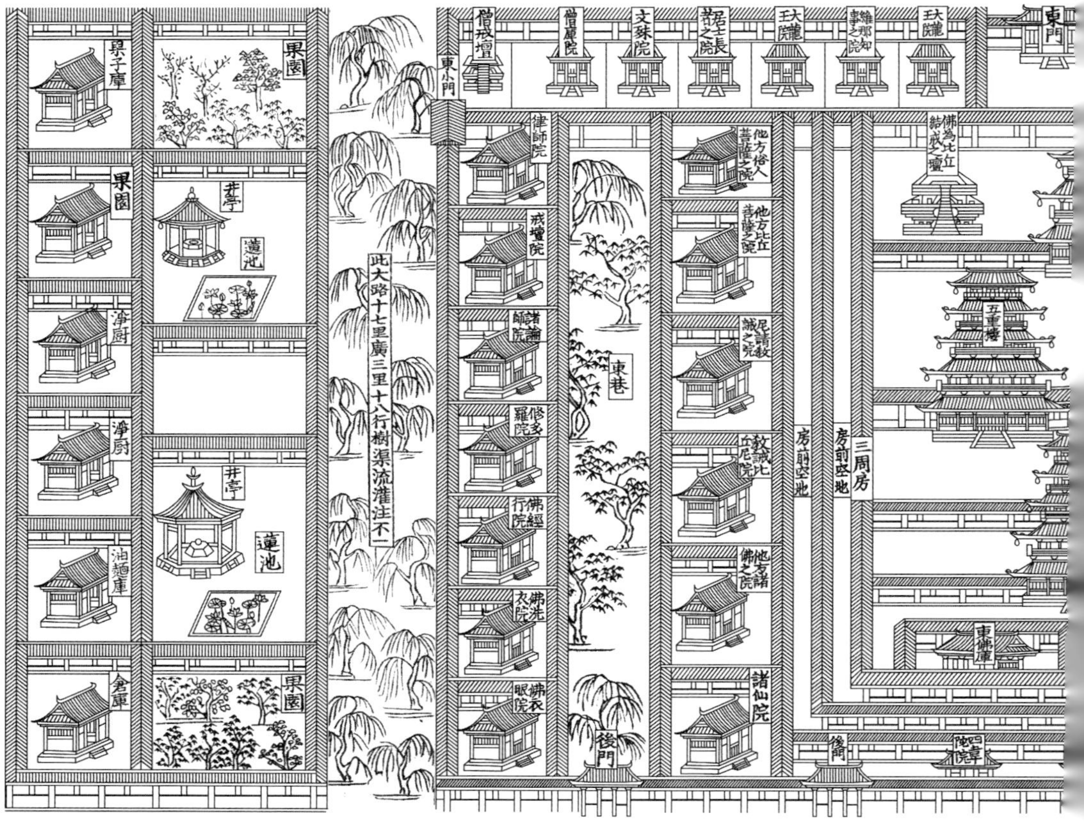

FIG. 5.6. Daoxuan's plan for Jetavana monastery. After *Guanzhong chuangli jietan tujing*, in *Z* 2a, 10:31v–33r. Drawn by Sorat Tungkasiri and Stephen F. Teiser.

of instruction: general discussion of the Dharma, the Twelve Conditions, and the Four Noble Truths. Altogether there are six cloisters dedicated to teaching the last two subjects, two cloisters apiece for educated people, *pratyekabuddhas*, and bodhisattvas.

Another hint about where the wheel of rebirth might have been located in Tang-dynasty temples is contained in a passage that Daoxuan quotes from another (now lost) source, *Instructions on Temples* (*Si gao*) by Lingyou (518–605). The author addresses the difference between inner and outer cloisters:

> The exterior cloisters are outside the main walls. They display the marks of external support for Buddhism, the reliance on the Three Refuges. The internal clois-

daijiten, pp. 1770c–72a. I interpret *xueren* (*śaikṣa*) and *wuxueren* (*aśaikṣa*) as educated and uneducated; see Nakamura, *Bukkyōgo daijiten*, pp. 178d, 1317d, and Mochizuki, *Bukkyō daijiten*, supplement pp. 90c, 1473c.

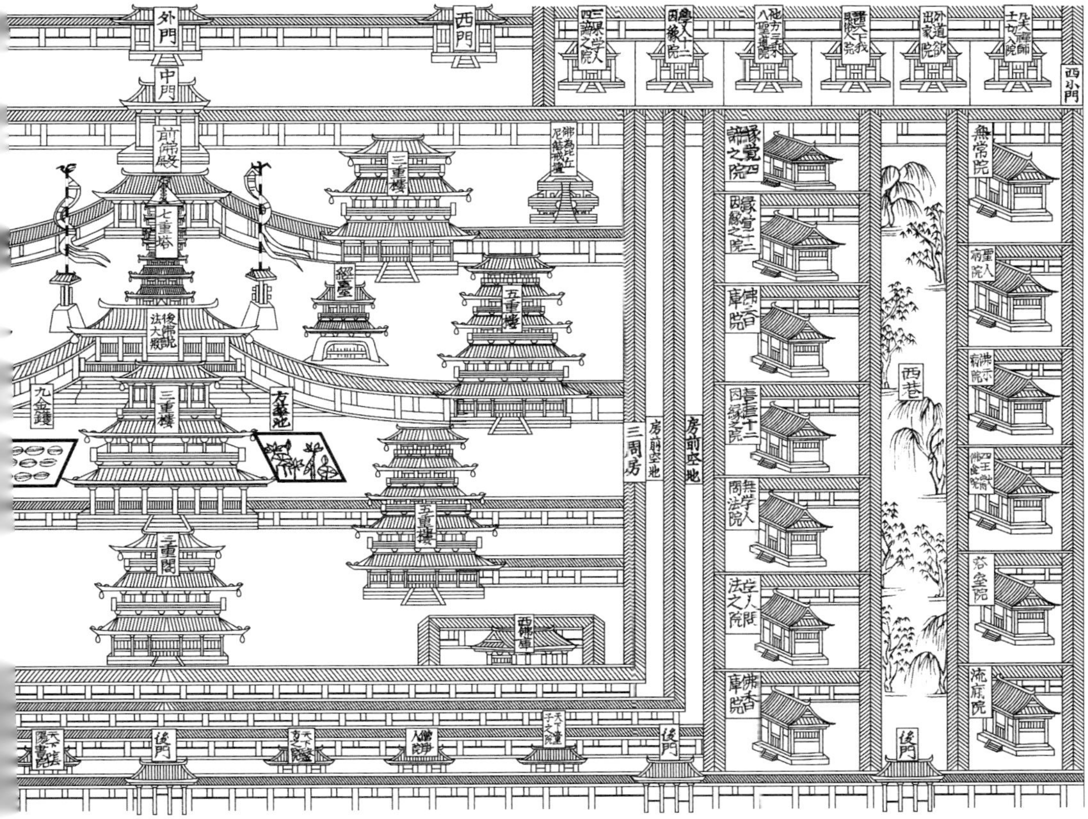

ters are inside the main walls. They display the marks of those who take refuge in the bell, the causes and conditions of the Three Jewels. The internal cloisters are taller than the external cloisters by five feet in order to demonstrate that the causes and conditions of the Three Jewels surpass the Five Paths.[23]

In this passage Daoxuan mobilizes a series of oppositions to explain why buildings in the inner cloister are taller than those in the outer cloister. The outbuildings are lower because they are exterior; they are utilized by lay donors who take refuge; and they correspond to the Five Paths of rebirth. The inner buildings are taller because they are interior; they are utilized by those who follow the monastic life; and they pertain to the Buddha, Dharma, and Saṃgha. (For a summary, see table 2.) Two points are particularly interesting for our purposes. One is that the Five Paths are positioned opposite the Three Jewels; the text places the two in separate realms. The second is that Daoxuan considers this opposition parallel to a second, the distinction between those

23. Translated from *Zhong Tianzhu Sheweiguo Qihuansi tujing*, *T* 45:883c; cf. Tan, "Daoxuan's Vision of Jetavana," p. 249.

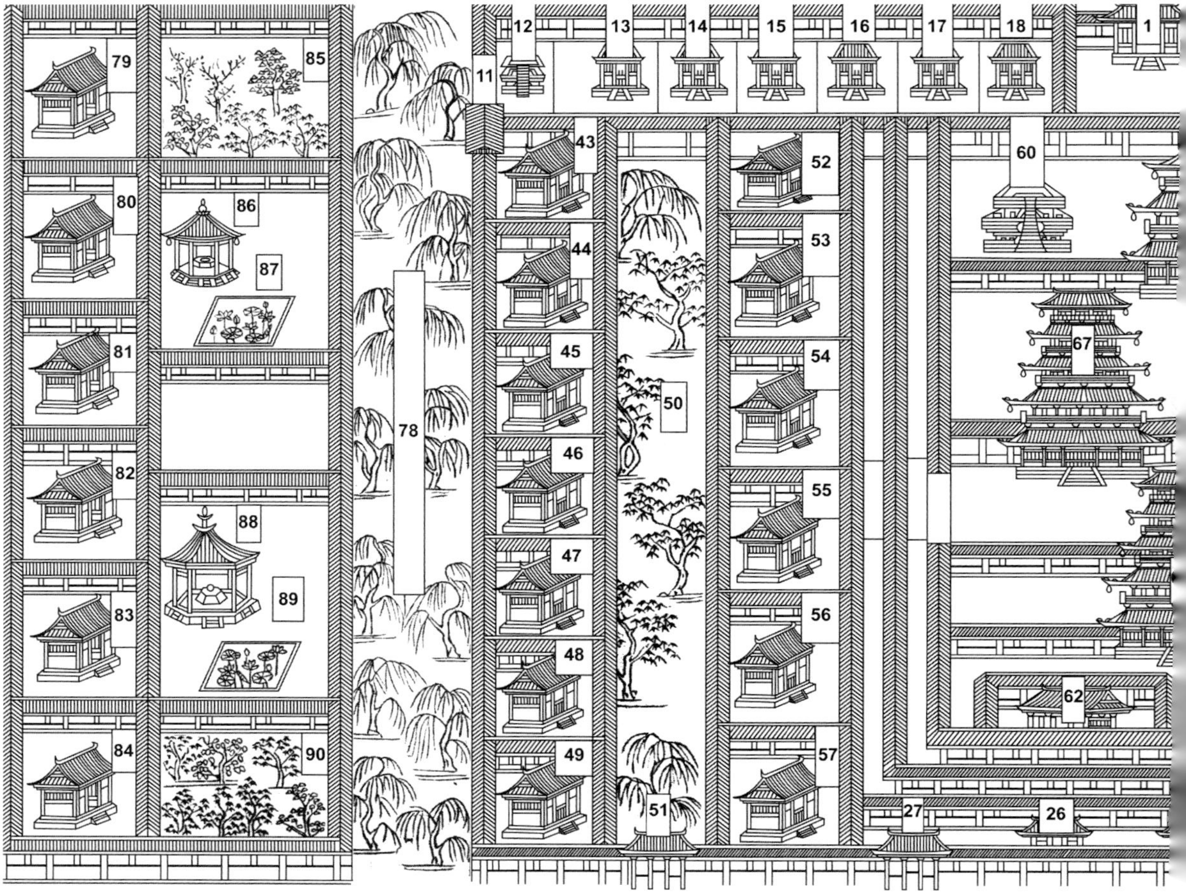

1. Eastern Gate
2. Outer Gate
3. Western Gate
4. Minor Western Gate
5. Cloister of Common Meditation Masters of the Eleven Complete Methods
6. Cloister of Non-Buddhists Who Wish to Become Monks
7. Cloister of Common People of Various Kingdoms Who Hold to the Self
8. Cloister of Followers of the Way of the Three Vehicles and Eight Sages from Other Places
9. Cloister of the Twelve Causes and Conditions for Educated People
10. Cloister of the Four Truths for Educated People Who Have Achieved the Three Fruits
11. Minor Eastern Gate
12. Saṃgha Ordination Altar
13. Cloister of the Monastic Treasury
14. Mañjuśrī Cloister
15. Cloister of Lay Elders
16. Cloister of Great Nāga Kings
17. Cloister of the Assigner of Duties
18. Cloister of the Great King Brahmā
19. Rear Gate
20. Cloister of Novices of the Empire
21. Cloister of Pure Persons of the Saṃgha
22. Cloister of Physicians of the Empire
23. Rear Gate
24. Cloister of Geomantic Books of the Empire
25. Cloister of Different Writings of the Empire
26. Cloister of the Four *Vedas*
27. Rear Gate
28. Cloister of Impermanence
29. Cloister of the Sages Who Are Sick
30. Cloister of the Buddha Manifesting Sickness
31. Cloister of the Four Kings Providing the Buddha's Food
32. Cloister of the Washing Room
33. Cloister of the Toilet
34. Western Lane
35. Rear Gate
36. Cloister of the Four Truths for Pratyekabuddhas
37. Cloister of the Twelve Causes and Conditions for Pratyekabuddhas
38. Cloister of the Four Truths for Bodhisattvas
39. Cloister of the Twelve Causes and Conditions for Bodhisattvas
40. Cloister of Asking about the Dharma for Uneducated People
41. Cloister for Asking about the Dharma for Educated People
42. Cloister of the Buddha's Incense Treasury
43. Cloister of Vinaya Masters

FIG. 5.7. Names of cloisters in Daoxuan's plan for Jetavana monastery. After *Guanzhong chuangli jietan*

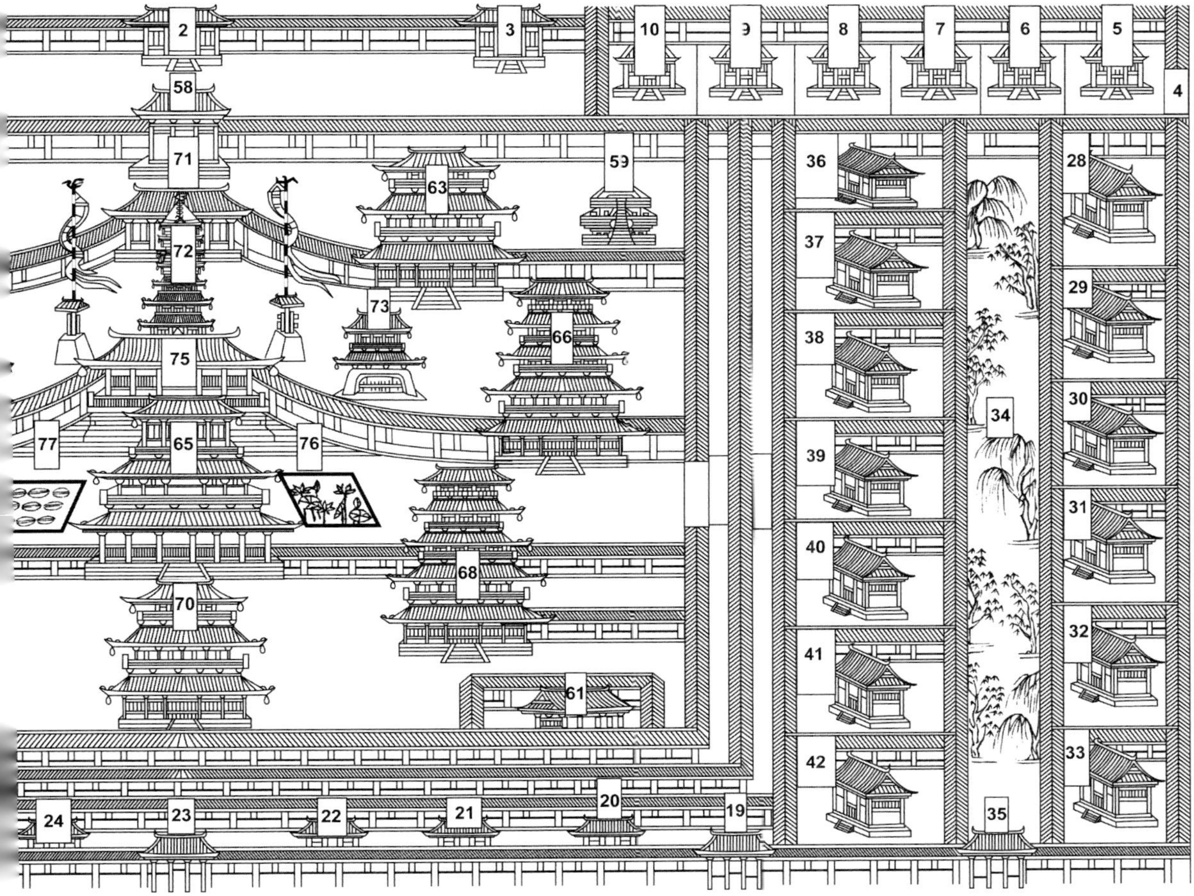

44. Cloister of the Ordination Altar
45. Cloister of the Masters of All the Treatises
46. Cloister of the Sūtras
47. Cloister of the Buddha Practicing Walking Meditation
48. Cloister of the Buddha Washing Clothes
49. Cloister of the Buddha's Clothes
50. Eastern Lane
51. Rear Gate
52. Cloister of Lay Bodhisattvas from Other Places
53. Cloister of Bhikṣu-Bodhisattvas from Other Places
54. Cloister of Bhikṣuṇīs Asking to Be Taught
55. Cloister of Bhikṣus Who Teach
56. Cloister of All Buddhas from Other Places
57. Cloister of All Immortals
58. Central Gate
59. Ordination Altar Established by the Buddha for Bhikṣuṇīs
60. Ordination Altar Established by the Buddha for Bhikṣus
61. Western Buddha Treasury
62. Eastern Buddha Treasury
63. Three-Storied Tower
64. Three-Storied Tower
65. Three-Storied Tower
66. Five-Storied Tower
67. Five-Storied Tower
68. Five-Storied Tower
69. Five-Storied Tower
70. Three-Storied Pavilion
71. Front Buddha Hall
72. Seven-Storied Pagoda
73. Scripture Platform
74. Bell Platform
75. Rear Great Hall Where the Buddha Preaches the Law
76. Square Lotus Pond
77. Nine Golden Cauldrons
78. This large road is 17 *li* in length and 3 *li* wide, with 18 rows of trees. There are many different irrigation ditches and waterways.
79. Treasury of Seeds
80. Treasury of Food
81. Monastic Kitchen
82. Monastic Kitchen
83. Treasury of Oil and Flour
84. Treasury of Provisions
85. Orchard
86. Well Pavilion
87. Lotus Pond
88 Well Pavilion
89 Lotus Pond
90. Orchard

tujing, in Z 2a, 10:31v–33r. Drawn by Sorat Tungkasiri and Stephen F. Teiser.

TABLE 2. Daoxuan's homologies. Citing *Si gao*, by Lingyou.

PRECINCT OF TEMPLE	INNER	OUTER
Location	Inside main walls	Outside main walls
Characteristics 1	Those who take refuge in the bell (monks)	External support (lay donors)
Characteristics 2	Three Jewels	Three Refuges
Height	Taller	Shorter
Domain	Three Jewels	Five Paths

who "take refuge in the bell" and those who serve as protectors of Buddhism.[24] The former category is comprised of monks, those whose lives follow a more closely regulated lifestyle. The latter consists of laypeople and rulers who offer material support for the Saṃgha. For Daoxuan, then, the contrast between the realm of Buddha, Dharma, and Saṃgha and the realm of rebirth is homologous to two other oppositions, those between inner and outer precincts of the Buddhist temple and between monastic and lay followers.

Pictorial representations of Buddhist temples abound in the wall paintings at Dunhuang depicting the pure lands of Amitābha Buddha and Bhaiṣajyaguru Bodhisattva, as well as the Tuṣita Heaven in which Maitreya resides. Like Daoxuan's vision of the Jetavana monastery (the details of which he claimed were revealed to him by a god), the anonymous murals were never intended to picture medieval Chinese temples. Nevertheless, their copious details accord remarkably well with what we know about Tang, Five Dynasties, and Song temples from other sources. Artists and artisans followed local traditions to a certain extent, and for most Dunhuang residents of the middle, professional class (like artisans, low-level officials, and most monks), a visit to the eastern part of the Hexi Corridor would have been deemed a rarity, and a trip to the Tang capitals an impossibility. Nevertheless, there is still a great deal of consistency between the design of temples in Dunhuang sources and the design of temples elsewhere. The Japanese pilgrim, Ennin, who traveled throughout central and eastern China in the 830s and 840s, believed that the temples of Chang'an were comparable in all respects except size to temples outside the capital. He wrote that "a single Buddha hall or cloister" in Chang'an "rivals a great monastery in the provinces."[25]

24. I interpret *guizhong*, "those who take refuge in the bell," as a reference to monastic life, but I have not been able to find other occurrences of the word. The term does not appear in an anthology of brief writings entitled "The Singing of the Bell" in Daoshi's encyclopedia, *Fayuan zhulin*, *T* 53:1016c–17b. The sound of the monastery bell echoes throughout medieval poetry; for a brief survey, see Xiao, *Dunhuang jianzhu yanjiu*, p. 94, n. 25. In many Tang and Song temples, a bell tower and a scripture tower flanked the main Buddha hall to its east and west; see ibid., pp. 61–63, and my figures 5.6 and 5.7. In exegetical works and apocrypha in the Sui and Tang dynasties, "external support" (*waihu*) refers to the donations of land and cash made by wealthy laypeople and important rulers; see Mochizuki, *Bukkyō daijiten*, p. 859c.

25. Reischauer, *Ennin's Diary*, p. 347. For a fuller discussion of the local and national characteristics of Dunhuang architecture, see Xiao, *Dunhuang jianzhu yanjiu*, esp. pp. 81–89, 90–92.

FIG. 5.8. Sketch of Buddha hall in Maitreya paradise. Mogao Cave 423, Sui dynasty. Xiao, *Dunhuang jianzhu yanjiu*, p. 63, fig. 24.

The evolution of temple architecture has important implications for understanding where pictures of the wheel of rebirth were located in temples and how they worked—if indeed they were painted in wooden temples during the medieval period.[26] Temples portrayed in Dunhuang murals of the late sixth century (Sui dynasty) are relatively simple in construction, focusing on the central icon in the main Buddha hall. Figure 5.8, a schematic rendering of a Sui-dynasty Maitreya paradise, depicts a five-bay Buddha hall with a large statue in the center and statues of two attendants at each side. The Buddha hall sits on a rectangular platform reached by steps. At its two sides and set back are matching three-story towers with smaller statues inside. Figure 5.9 is a tenth-century Bhaiṣajyaguru paradise from Mogao Cave 146. The temple here is built on a grander scale, and its design components are far more intricate, than the earlier example. At the center of the painting stands the main Buddha hall, with open space to its front. Its entryway is comprised of three gates, each with its own stairway, and two towers. To each side of the main Buddha hall stands a square, two-story hall, accessible by stairs on each side. The front part of the temple is encased by a long continuous corridor. Its many bays contain images. A maze of walkways connects many of the subsidiary spaces. The temple is divided into a main courtyard in front and a subsidiary one behind (to the north of) that. The subsidiary courtyard has its own entryway and a pair of hexagonal towers at each side, but its positioning behind the main hall and its smaller size clearly demonstrate its secondary status.

Despite these changes in temple design, continuities are also apparent. In both of these examples, a Buddha hall is situated at the center of the temple. (This design super-

26. My summary of the evolution of temple architecture is indebted to the more in-depth studies by Ho, "Setting for the Faith"; Li, *Zhong Yin fojiao shikusi bijiao yanjiu*, pp. 211–78; Steinhardt, "Mizong Hall of Qinglong Si"; and Xiao, *Dunhuang jianzhu yanjiu*, pp. 61–94.

FIG. 5.9. Bhaiṣajyaguru paradise. Wall painting. Mogao Cave 146, tenth century. Dunhuang wenwu yanjiusuo, *Dunhuang Mogaoku*, 5: pl. 49.

seded the earliest Buddhist temples, most of which revolved around stūpas or pagodas.) The large open space in front of the Buddha hall serves several functions. As an architectural design, the space sets off the main hall from the buildings around it; it announces that the Buddha hall is supposed to be the most imposing structure in the area. The space was also put to good use: it was perfect for accommodating the large numbers of people who gathered at temples for worship and entertainment. This is not to say that the side cloisters and other subsidiary spaces were empty of people or that they were ritually irrelevant. Rather, the layout of Sui and Tang temples lent itself to ranking people in a series of interlocking hierarchies. A similar logic probably applied to the iconographic program of the temple as well: different pictures were appropriate for different audiences, or, as noted above, different parts of the temple were intended for use by different classes of people for different ritual purposes.

Another element of temple design is the multiplicity of walkways and covered corridors. As boundaries in architectural space and as walkways in pedestrian space, they serve a dual function: they link the various parts of the temple at the same time as they demarcate different precincts. According to literary descriptions like *A Record of Famous Painters of the Tang Dynasty* (*Tangchao minghua lu*; eighth century) and *An Account of Temples and Pagodas* (*Sita ji*; ninth century), temple corridors were covered with wall paintings. Reading such accounts, one gets the feeling that every square inch of wall space was used to convey a message appropriate to the particular audience in that part of the temple. To return to the hypothetical thread in this chapter, if pictures of the wheel of rebirth were painted in Tang metropolitan temples, they were probably painted in walkways or cloisters in the outer precincts. The temple, like the Buddhist path, had many subdivisions and many stages: it claimed to be open to everyone, but not without distinction. Even the subsidiary buildings for laypeople and the connecting spaces like corridors were decorated with didactic, entertaining, and edifying images.

Chapter 6

Wheels for Meditation

Kumtura, Central Asia, Ninth Century

Two tiny paintings of the wheel of rebirth were painted on the side wall of a small meditation cave hollowed out of a cliff face in the cave-temple complex at Kumtura, probably in the second half of the ninth century. Although the paintings are only eight inches in diameter and are largely faded, the paintings are unmistakably depictions of the saṃsāracakra as I define the term. Their hubs contain the animals symbolizing the Three Poisons, the next row represents the Five Paths, and the outer circle is divided into twelve sections representing the chain of causation. Kumtura, now called Kumutula in Chinese, is located sixteen miles southwest of the modern city of Kucha (modern Ch.: Kuche), in Xinjiang Uighur Autonomous Region. Located near the capital of the medieval kingdom of Kucha, the caves at Kumtura were built over a period of six centuries, and they display all of the cultural influences that flowed through the area, including Kuchean local culture, Tibetan influence, Chinese domination, and Uighur (Turkish) control. The cave in which the wheels are located is dominated on its main wall by a larger-than-life-size painting of a monk seated in meditation. His hands hold a bowl from which the Six Paths of rebirth emanate, and the ceiling and side walls of the cave are covered with rows of meditating Buddhas, bodhisattvas, and monks, plus rows of donor portraits showing monks and laypeople. When the cave was discovered in 1979 by a research expedition from Peking University, nearly half of the cartouches and dedications, written in Chinese, were still visible, although when I visited the site in 2001 they were beyond decipherment. Despite the deterioration of the writing and the damage to the paintings, the overall design of the cave and the situational significance of the wheels of rebirth are clear. As I will argue below, the miniscule wheels on the side wall are iconic amplifications of the main meditative program of the cave. They are an artistic reminder of the kind of visualization exercise pictured on the main wall. They also prove that medieval monks in Chinese-Turkish central Asia connected paintings of the wheel of rebirth—in thought if not in practice—to monastic education.

The oasis town of Kucha is located at the northeastern edge of the Tarim Basin in the Taklamakan Desert.[1] This elliptical depression is surrounded by three mountain ranges: the Tianshan to the north and northwest, the Pamirs on the southwest, and to the south and southeast the Kunlun, Altyntagh, and Nanshan. Kucha was one of the main stops that trading caravans frequented on the so-called northern route of the Silk Road. Heading out of China, traders would have passed westward through Dunhuang and then had a choice of taking the northern or southern route around the Tarim Basin. Following the northern route, they would have passed through Hami, Turfan (modern Tulufan), and Kucha, eventually reaching Kashgar, Samarkand, Merv, Herat, Palmyra, Antioch, Tyre, and ultimately Alexandria, Constantinople, and Rome (see map 6). As an oasis, Kucha was an important watering spot, rich with fruits and vegetables, for travelers across the desert. It was also located in a strategic position, and as early as 104 B.C.E. the Chinese throne dispatched its army there. From this time onward the indigenous elite of the Kucha kingdom maintained marriage alliances and loose diplomatic relations with the Chinese government. The local rulers, whose native language was Tocharian B, a form of Indo-European, typically found themselves squeezed between the empires surrounding the Tarim Basin: the Chinese to the east; Turkish groups, including the Uighurs (and later the Khitans and Mongols), to the north; and the Tibetans to the south.

Buddhist rites and symbols circulated all along the northern silk route, and Buddhist images probably found their way to Kucha around the same time that they were transmitted to China, at least by the first century C.E. Several early figures who would become important in the dissemination of Buddhism in China were natives of Kucha, including Fotudeng (232–348?), the thaumaturge so influential in Luoyang; Śrīmitra (Bo Shilimiduoluo, ca. 307–342), a Kuchean prince to whom the translation of *The Consecration Sūtra* (*Guanding jing*) is attributed; and the most prolific translator before the seventh century, Kumārajīva (Jiumoluoshi, 350–409), whose father was Indian and mother was Kuchean. Xuanzang (602–664) visited Kucha in 630. According to his description, the city was filled with temples, pagodas, and palaces. He was particularly interested in the annual festivals that animated the whole city and in large processions of Buddhist images. He also notes that the monks there were followers of the Sarvāstivāda and observed Indian teachings and vinaya practices.[2]

If these early figures are evidence of the eastward flow of Buddhism through Kucha, other East Asian accounts demonstrate that the religion of Śākyamuni also traveled from China westward across the Taklamakan. In the early years of the Tang dynasty Chinese foreign policy became more aggressive in the area. In 640 Chinese armies pacified the area east of Kucha known as Qočo (Ch.: Gaochang) and the court instituted

1. For the early history of Kumtura, Kucha, and the Tarim Basin (encompassing most of modern Xinjiang), see Beckwith, *Tibetan Empire in Central Asia*; Han and Zhu, *Qiuci shiku*, pp. 50–84; Huang, "Lueshu Qiuci ducheng wenti"; idem, *Talimu pendi kaogu ji*; Liu, *Kutscha und seine Beziehungen zu China*; Rhie, *Early Buddhist Art of China and Central Asia*, 2:578–600; Soucek, *History of Inner Asia*, pp. 46–69; and Wu Zhuo, "Kezi'er shiku xingfei yu Weiganhe gudao jiaotong."

2. See *Datang xiyu ji*, Xuanzang (602–664), *T* no. 2087, 51:870a–b, translated in Beal, *Si-yu-ki*, 1:19–24.

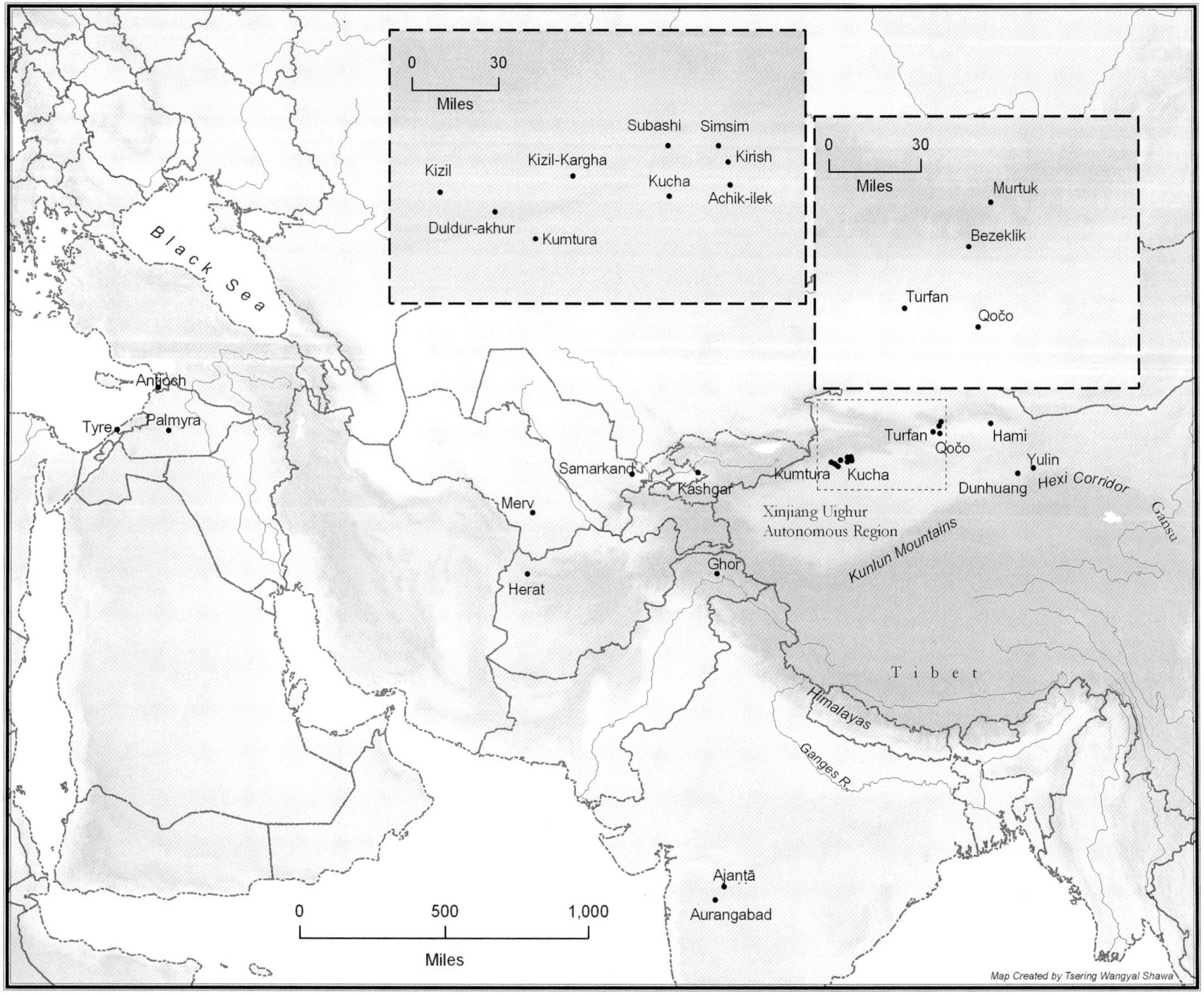

Map 6. Central Asia, ca. 850.

an administrative organ responsible for military security throughout the Tarim Basin, the Anxi Protectorate (Anxi Dudufu, literally "Protectorate of the Pacified Western Regions"), which beginning in 658 was headquartered in Kucha. By this time too Tibetan armies were beginning to strike all across central Asia, including the eastern portion of the Tarim Basin where Kucha was located. A monk from the kingdom of Silla (Korea) named Hye-č'o (704–ca. 780), who had moved to China when young, passed through Kucha on his way back to China from India. His diary describes his arrival in Kucha:

> From Kashgar I traveled farther east for one month and arrived at the country of Kucha. This is the Great Protectorate of Anxi, the great city where troops from the country of Han [i.e., China] are headquartered. In Kucha there are many temples and monks. They practice the methods of the Smaller Vehicle [Hīnayāna]; they eat meat, onions, leeks, and so forth. The Han monks practice the methods of the Greater Vehicle [Mahāyāna]. . . .
>
> There are two temples run by Han monks. . . . The head of Dayun Temple, Xiuxing, is very talented at preaching. Prior to this he was a monk at Qibaotai Temple in the capital. The *karmadāna* [assigner of duties] at Dayun Temple is named Mingchao. He is very talented at explaining the Vinaya piṭaka. Prior to this he was a monk at Zhuangyan Temple in the capital. The abbot of Dayun Temple is named Mingyun, who has many great accomplishments. He too is a monk from the capital. All these monks are eminent, capable administrators. They are endowed with penetrating minds and take pleasure in the performance of meritorious acts. The head of Longxing Temple is named Fahai. Although he was born in Anxi of Han descent, his learning and comportment are no different from those of Hua-Xia [Chinese].[3]

Hye-č'o's description says as much about his own interests as the sites he visited. Ethnicity is important to him. As a resident alien, he probably found nationality, language, and other differences to be unavoidable. He worked closely with both Vajrabodhi (662–732) and Amoghavajra (705–774) in Chang'an, and he had frequent contact with the highest echelons of the Chinese government and the Saṃgha administration. His diary invokes some of the categories that these two institutions deemed important. In the first place, Hye-č'o distinguishes between temples inhabited by Kucheans (Qiuci, the ancient Chinese transcription of Kucha) and Han (Chinese) temples, the former following Hīnayāna and the latter Mahāyāna. The monastic establishments of Kucha thus appear to have been segregated according to nationality, each group following a different vinaya. Hye-č'o makes further distinctions among the Chinese monks, subdividing them into three categories. First are the monks who were born in China and

3. Translation from *Wang Wutianzhuguo zhuan*, Hye-č'o (704–ca. 780), in *Youfang jichao, T* no. 2089, 51:979a–b; cf. Yang et al., *Hye Ch'o Diary*, pp. 57–58.

trained in the major monasteries in the capital before moving to Kucha. Second are monks whose ancestry is Chinese but who were born in Kucha. And third are those who conform to the norms of civilized behavior prevalent in China, the Hua-Xia, or literally "the Cultured Xia [Dynasty]." Hye-č'o's travelogue also makes clear that some of the institutions of the central Chinese state were still strong in Kucha when he visited. The city boasted temples constructed by order of the imperial government in 689 (Dayun Temple) and 705 (Longxing Temple). Judging from other entries of his diary that note which areas in India and central Asia were under the control of the Arabs, Turks, Tibetans, and Chinese, and which were administered by local rulers, Hye-č'o took a strong interest in the balance of political power as well as ethnicity.

In addition to local culture and Chinese influence, Tibetan and Uighur customs are evident in the area around Kumtura. The Tibetans in fact laid siege to the city of Kucha right around the time Hye-č'o visited. Chinese historical writing from the Tang and Song dynasties refers to the Tibetans controlling the city over several stretches of time, an influence largely ignored in PRC scholarship published until recently, during the latest stage of Chinese concern over Tibetan nationality. Tibetan influence in the area came to an end in the middle of the ninth century when the Uighurs took control. The Uighurs had originally forged a homeland for themselves farther north and east, in Mongolia. They were overthrown by the Kyrgyz in 840 and fled westward. One group settled in parts of Gansu, while others continued farther west and founded the Uighur kingdom of Qočo (850–1250).[4] The latter soon extended their control to the kingdom of Kucha, including Kumtura.

The cave temples at Kumtura were built in waves over a period of nearly six hundred years in the low cliffs alongside the Weigan River. It is important to remember how dependent we are on the ravages of history and modern exploration for our knowledge of the early history of the wheel of rebirth at Kumtura. Kuchean patrons probably began sponsoring the excavation of caves at the site by the early fifth century. At this time Kumtura was one of many locations in the Kuchean kingdom used for the construction of cave temples and wooden temples. Others include Kizil, Duldur-aqur, Kizil-kargha, Subashi, Simsim, Kirish, and Achik-ilek. After the heyday of these sites, the waning of Buddhism, and the ascendancy of Islam in the area, for many centuries the caves were ignored or actively ruined. Although certainly known to local people, the historical treasures of the area—including murals, statues, wooden structures, manuscripts, and silk paintings—were brought to the attention of the scholarly world through the explorations of European adventurers, including Sven Hedin (1865–1952), beginning in the nineteenth century. The entire Kucha area was the subject of the third (1905–07) and fourth (1913–14) expeditions to central Asia by the German team led by Albert Grünwedel (1856–1935), an archaeologist and historian of religion, and Albert von Le Coq (1860–1930), a businessman turned archaeologist. Their motivations were

4. See Gabain, *Das Leben im uigurischen Königreich von Qočo*, esp. pp. 175–99; Hamilton, *Les Ouïghours à l'époque des Cinq Dynasties*; Pinks, *Die Uiguren von Kan-chou in der frühen Sung-Zeit*; and Yang, *Huihu zhi fojiao*.

consistent with nineteenth-century science: to preserve, protect, record, analyze, and possess the ruins of classical civilizations they thought were being destroyed by benighted inhabitants and government neglect. In an atmosphere permeated by accounts of the decapitation of statues, the slashing of paintings, and the use of ancient murals for fertilizer, the Sinologist F. W. K. Müller would describe Xinjiang as an area "dominated by fanatic Muhammadan philistinism and iconoclastic narrow-mindedness."[5] The German expeditions, in addition to excavating and documenting the Kucha area (and the Turfan/Qočo sites farther northeast), brought back considerable booty of their own, some of it subsequently destroyed in the Allied bombing of Berlin at the end of World War II. After another fifty years of relatively benign neglect, the Chinese government granted Kumtura the status of an Important National Preserved Cultural Relic in 1961, and the conservation and study of the site is now carried out by the Kuche County Cultural Relics Preservation Institute (Kuchexian wenwu baoguansuo).

The cave temples at Kumtura are clustered along the banks of the Weigan River, in Tang times called the Baima (literally, "White Horse") River, which flows down from the Tianshan range. Their style, content, design, and patronage are generally consistent with those at Kizil, some twenty kilometers northwest along the Weigan River. Art historians typically analyze the caves according to architectural design and political periodization.[6] The most common design, evident in the earliest caves during the period of Kuchean culture, prior to strong Chinese influence, is that of a Buddha hall. Some caves have a square main chamber with a Buddha statue seated on a lion throne, attended by bodhisattvas, in the center (see fig. 6.1). Buddha hall caves have a long entry corridor with niches for smaller statues. The main pictorial programs on the walls of the main chamber are scenes from the Buddha's life, especially his battle with Māra. Donor portraits occupy the side walls. In terms of shape these caves resemble cave temples farther west in fourth- and fifth-century central Asia, such as those at Bamiyan. Gandharan and other north Indian influences are evident in the shaping of figures and decoration, while Chinese styles have been hypothesized for the ceiling design and ornamenting of palaces. Scholars portray all of these influences as coalescing into a local, Kuchean style already in the early period. Another design for caves dominated in the sixth century, that of the central pillar (see fig. 6.2). In this arrangement, a pillar containing a statue of Śākyamuni sits in the middle of the main chamber, leaving space for visitors to circumambulate the main Buddha to the left, rear, and right of the pillar. The main chamber contains wall paintings depicting Brahmā, Indra, and other gods in subservience to the Buddha. Material is also taken from *jātaka*

5. Cited in Härtel and Yaldiz, *Along the Ancient Silk Routes*, p. 27.

6. For studies of the Kumtura caves, see Chao, "Kumutula shiku chutan"; idem, "Kumutula shiku de dongku fenlei yu siyuan zuhe"; idem, "Xinjiang shiku bihua zhong de Qiuci fengge"; Han and Zhu, *Qiuci shiku*, pp. 57–64; Jia and Musha, "Lishi hualang"; Liang and Ding, "Xinjiang Kumutula xin faxian de jichu dongku"; Ma, "Kumutula de hanfeng dongku"; idem, "Xinjiang shikuzhong de hanfeng dongku he bihua"; Shinkyō Uiguru jichiku bunbutsu kanri iinkai et al., *Kumutora sekkutsu*; Wu Zhuo, "Kezi'er shiku xingfei yu Weiganhe gudao jiaotong"; idem, "Kumutula shiku bihua de fengge yanbian yu gudai Qiuci de lishi xingshuai"; and Yaldiz, *Archäologie und Kunstgeschichte chinesisch-zentralasiens*, pp. 17–98.

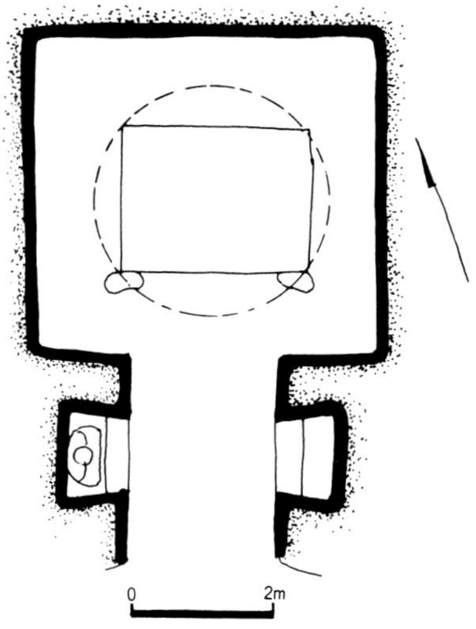

Fig. 6.1. Plan of Buddha hall cave at Kumtura. Kumtura Cave 20, fifth century. Zhongguo bihua bianji weiyuanhui, *Kumutula*, p. 4, fig. 2.

(previous lives of the Buddha) and *avadāna* tales. On the rear wall of the ambulatory, and often on the side walls as well, the pictorial program is about the Buddha's passage into final nirvāṇa. The outside rear wall typically shows him lying on his side as he passes into *parinirvāṇa*, while the internal rear wall portrays the kings of India assembling to honor his relics. Many of these central stūpa-pillar caves originally had antechambers, but they have been largely destroyed by the elements over the centuries.

These models for the construction of caves were continued during the period of Chinese influence and Tibetan sway in the Kumtura area, roughly 601–850. Many of the caves maintained a central stūpa-pillar design, with an ambulatory in the back and an antechamber in front. Paintings betray a clearer Chinese style, and the iconography of many of the major Buddhas, bodhisattvas, and gods becomes more standardized. Significant innovations were made in the content of the wall paintings and some of the main statues. Vairocana Buddha is a new and important subject in some caves, and other Tantric themes are evident for the first time.[7] Pure lands and Maitreya's descent are portrayed more frequently as well. Tibetan armies controlled the region on and off during this period, especially during the fifty or sixty years leading up to Uighur control, but Tibetan themes in the Kumtura caves have not been discussed much in scholarship to date.

Throughout the history of cave building at Kumtura there are other styles of caves. One is a generally smaller cave, square or rectangular in design, that contains a main image of a monk rather than a Buddha or bodhisattva. Some of them have multiple niches that probably contained many small statues, while others contain only a painting of one monk on the main wall. Almost all such caves are located in relatively isolated sectors of the Kumtura site, farther away from other caves or higher up the cliff

7. See Ji, "Qiuci de fojiao mizong"; and Zhu, *Qiuci shiku yanjiu*, pp. 204–17.

FIG. 6.2. Plan of typical central stūpa-pillar cave, northwest China. Xiao, *Dunhuang jianzhu yanjiu*, fig. 4.1.

face. Their precise function is a matter of some dispute. One scholar has called them "*arhat* caves" because they center on images of monks. In this view, the main purpose of such caves was to enshrine a local monk, either by including his ashes in a main statue or by painting his image on the wall, thus constituting a kind of memorial cave (*yingku*).[8] Kumtura Cave 75, the cave in which the wheel of rebirth is located, follows this design, and its meaning will be taken up in more detail below. Other designs for caves include residences for monks, the inner room of which usually contains a stove, and larger caves for collective activities like instruction and the performance of rituals.

Uighur control of the area dates from about the year 850. Under Uighur domination the patrons and artisans at Kumtura continued to utilize the central-pillar design for many caves, and they developed pure land and Tantric subjects still further. Trying to account for the addition of elements that are also evident in other parts of the Uighur kingdom, scholars refer to the "Uighurization" (*huihuhua*) of the artistic style at Kumtura.[9]

Cave 75 at Kumtura is a relatively small, isolated, rectangular, one-room cave. Its barrel-shaped ceiling is five feet eight inches high at its highest point, offering not quite enough room for the average person to stand without stooping. It faces north, and it is approximately six feet deep by five feet wide. It is located in a relatively out of the way stretch of cliff on the southern bank of the Weigan River. The largest nearby cave is Kumtura Cave 45, and several smaller caves (Kumtura Caves 73, 74, 76, 77, 78) are next to it. Its doorway, situated more than six feet above the ground, is too small to enter standing up. To get inside the cave now, one has to bring a ladder, climb to the

8. See Chao, "Kumutula shiku chutan," pp. 182–84; and idem "Kumutula shiku de dongku fenlei yu siyuan zuhe," pp. 239–40.

9. See, for example, Jia and Musha, "Lishi hualang," p. 19.

FIG. 6.3. Exterior of Kumtura Cave 75. Xinjiang Weiwu'er zizhiqu wenwu guanli weiyuanhui et al., *Kumutula shiku*, pl. 176.

top, and crawl into the cave (see fig. 6.3). It is not clear whether the ground outside the cave has eroded, nor is there any certainty that the cave's entrance was always this small, whether it possessed an antechamber, or had a wooden porch and stairs that have been washed away over the centuries. Assuming that the current topography outside the cave resembles its original condition, then the cave must have always been difficult to enter and was never able to fit more than one or two people.

Carbon-14 dating was conducted on the painted surface of the front wall in the late 1980s. The results yield a fairly wide range of possible dates, from 689 to 943.[10] However, the inscriptions inside the cave include Uighur surnames, and most donors are shown in Uighur dress (discussed below), so the cave could not have been commis-

10. See Zhongguo shehui kexueyuan kaogu yanjiusuo shiyanshi, "Xinjiang Tulufan he Nanjiang diqu bufen shiku niandai ceding baogao."

FIG. 6.4. Sketch of hungry ghosts in wall painting. Rear wall, Kumtura Cave 75, ca. ninth century. Xinjiang Weiwu'er zizhiqu wenwu guanli weiyuanhui et al., *Kumutula shiku*, p. 212, fig. 16.

sioned prior to the year 850. The few published studies of the cave date it to the period 850–900, the earliest stretch of Uighur domination over the Kucha area.[11]

The main subject of the cave takes up two-thirds of the painted surface on the main (rear, south) wall of the cave (see plate 9). It is a monk wearing a Chinese-style robe seated in meditation. Perched atop his hands is a bowl (or other round object, perhaps a large jewel) out of which stream the six realms of rebirth, each marked by a painted black line. Although the painting is seriously faded and perhaps scraped away in places, the major scenes in each of the Six Paths can still be discerned. At top left are four figures who appear to be gods. At top right is a walled city or palace, with at least two seated figures floating at the end of cloud paths. This part of the painting might be a depiction of the *asuras* (demigods), or it could be Mount Sumeru, amounting to a continuation of the realm of the gods on the top left side. The realm of humans is pictured at middle right: four human figures, two men and two women, clad in Uighur clothing, face the center of the picture. Below the gods on the left, an ox-headed figure uses a trident to stir a cauldron, with several heads poking out of the broth, presumably a depiction of hell. Below them are two animals, one of which is clearly a horse, representing the path of animals. The last path is pictured at bottom right: two figures wearing only loin cloths are bent over amid flames, probably representing the realm of hungry ghosts (see fig. 6.4). Lacking realms demarcated clearly as highest (heavens) and lowest (hells), this way of representing the Six Paths does not conform to the layout of the Six Paths in the canonical wheel of saṃsāra, nor does it match the

11. I visited the cave in July 2001 and would like to acknowledge the administrative help and scholarly advice graciously shared by my Chinese colleagues from the Xinjiang Qiuci shiku yanjiusuo, Li Li and Su Huiming. For published studies of the cave, which was not discovered until 1979, see Chao, "Kumutula shiku de dongku fenlei yu siyuan zuhe," pp. 239–40; Jia and Musha, "Lishi hualang," pp. 18–19; Liang and Ding, "Xinjiang Kumutula xin faxian de jichu dongku," pp.

latter's standard iconography. Instead, the arrangement may be related to other portrayals of the Six Paths, three on each side, emanating from Kṣitigarbha Bodhisattva (discussed in chapter 10).[12]

Above the central figure a small Buddha with halo and mandorla is visible, and below the central figure are painted five donors wearing monastic garb. Below them is a very long inscription that sheds some light on the composition. Less than half of it was legible when archaeologists first visited the cave in the late 1970s and '80s, and since then most of the characters have faded to the point of being undecipherable, so in my translation below I rely on the earliest transcriptions of the text.[13] The inscription reads:

> . . . unlimited visualization methods . . . three thousand great-thousand worlds . . . act as sages . . . the four great *bhikṣus* [?] . . . all . . . brought into being the polluted body and the dusty . . . realm of no consciousness and consciousness . . . confused . . . wheels can next be divided into . . . casting . . . bringing great salvation . . . intentions and thoughts next become . . . white-colored light rays become the wheel of water . . . consciousness travels down into the water, and gold becomes the water wheel . . . golden colored rays of yellow light become the wheel of gold . . . the thought of the golden wheel itself . . . the syllable "*an*" . . . wheel of fire burns impure sins . . . it . . .

Below that are two more rows of writing, also largely effaced, set off from the rest:

> . . . if you view your own body's bones to be the same as thought, this . . . impermanence, no-self . . .

The inscription constitutes what I believe is a liturgical text for a visualization method described in the *Mahāvairocana (Great Sun) Sūtra*. Chapter fifteen of that text describes a series of six visualizations, each one lasting one month.[14] During each month the practitioner follows a specific diet and visualizes a specific maṇḍala. The most pop-

---

3–4; Shinkyō Uiguru jichiku bunbutsu kanri iinkai et al., *Kumutora sekkutsu*, pp. 230–31, 254–56, 318; and Zhongguo bihua bianji weiyuanhui, *Kumutula*, p. 81.

12. One reading of the iconography of the cave (Shinkyō Uiguru jichiku bunbutsu kanri iinkai et al., *Kumutora sekkutsu*, p. 231) alludes to this possibility, calling the main meditating monk a form of Kṣitigarbha. Although the iconography of the Six Paths may be borrowed from pictures of Kṣitigarbha, the main monk figure does not resemble any of the known paintings of Kṣitigarbha.

13. My transcription follows that in Liang and Ding, "Xinjiang Kumutula xin faxian de jichu dongku," p. 3, occasionally emended on grounds of sense by the later transcriptions in Jia and Musha, "Lishi hualang," p. 18. Given the fragmentary nature of the surviving text, and the fact that it was so faded that I could not read any of it when I visited the site thirty years later than Liang and Ding, my translation remains highly tentative.

14. *Dapiluzhena chengfo shenbian jiachi jing* (*Mahāvairocana [abhisambodhi vikurvita ādhiṣṭhāna vaipulya] sūtra*, trans. Śubhakarasiṃha (Shanwuwei, ca. 716–735) and Yixing (673–727), *T* no. 848, 18:37b–38a. For the commentary, see *Dapiluzhena chengfo jing shu*, Yixing, *T* no. 1796, 39:751c–54a. The program of visualizations seems to be based on the *Abhidharmakośa* cosmology, in which successive discs are formed atop one another.

TABLE 3. Visualizations in the *Mahāvairocana Sūtra* and *Commentary*. From *Dapiluzhena chengfo shenbian jiachi jing* (*Mahāvairocana [abhisambodhi vikurvita ādhiṣṭhāna vaipulya] sūtra*), trans. Śubhakarasiṃha (Shanwuwei, ca. 716–735) and Yixing (683–727), *T* no. 848, 18:37b-38a; and *Dapiluzhena chengfo jing shu*, Yixing, *T* no. 1796, 39:751c-54a.

MONTH	WHEEL	SHAPE	COLOR	MUDRĀ	MANTRA	CLASS OF FOOD
1	Gold	Square	Yellow	Diamond	E	Milk
2	Water	Round	White	Lotus	Fu	Pure Water
3	Fire	Triangular	Red	Wisdom Knife	Luo	Not Begged for
4	Wind	Crescent	Black	Dharma Wheel	He	Wind
5	Gold and Water					
6	Fire and Wind					

ular medieval commentary on the text, by Yixing (673–727), explains the color and shape of each maṇḍala and notes which corresponding seed syllable one is supposed to concentrate on (table 3). The first month is the visualization of a golden wheel, the second month of a water wheel, the third month of a fire wheel, the fourth month of a wind wheel, the fifth month of the golden and water wheels combined, and the six month of the wind and fire wheels combined. The sūtra's description of the third month reads:

> Then in the third month
> Practice the supremely wondrous visualization of the fire wheel
> And eat food that is not begged for.
> Then use the power of your wisdom
> To burn up all sins
> And give birth to body, mind, and word.[15]

The language of "burning up all sins" (*shaomie yiqie zui*) in the sūtra is closely paraphrased by the cave inscription ("burns up impure sins," *fenshao bujing zui*). If my interpretation is correct, the cave inscription refers to three of the four wheels (gold, water, and fire) included in the visualization, and it describes in detail how the wheels of gold and water are to be eidetically conjoined in the meditation of the fifth month. The colors cited in the inscription all match the visualization text as well.

The visualizations described in the *Mahāvairocana sūtra* are only one possible form of meditation that could be the subject of the main wall at Kumtura. Central Asia, and the Kuchean kingdom in particular, was home to many different forms of visualization practice. One text, an untitled Sanskrit manuscript found at nearby Kizil, also bears close resemblance to the technique outlined in the Kumtura cave. The text,

15. *Dapiluzhena chengfo shenbian jiachi jing*, *T* 18:37c.

which its modern editor and translator, Dieter Schlingloff, has called a "Yogalehrbuch," contains a section detailing the method for visualizing the Four Elements of earth, water, fire, and wind. It directs the *yogin* to produce mental images of a circle or disk (maṇḍala) of wind, earth, gold, and water.[16]

The *Mahāvairocana Sūtra* and related visualization texts, then, describe techniques similar to the practice enjoined in the Kumtura cave, and they are all clustered in a reasonably well-defined space and time. Despite these connections, however, we still need to acknowledge the distance between the visualization methods described in the inscription and the pictorial content of the cave itself. The circles or disks mentioned in the inscription do not appear anywhere in the cave, and there is nothing else to indicate a maṇḍala-like arrangement of deities or their residences in the cave paintings. However, the invocation of these visualizations in this particular cave suggests that the designers of the cave thought that the production of the Six Paths of rebirth out of the monk's bowl in the pictures was related to specific practices of visualization.

Before turning to the miniature wheels of rebirth painted on the side wall, it is worth discussing what light the other paintings in the cave might shed on the significance of the cave. The rest of the wall surface (on the right and left walls) is covered with figures in two poses: either meditators (Buddhas, bodhisattvas, or monks) or standing donor figures. The right (west) wall of the cave contains eight horizontal rows of figures. The top seven rows depict people sitting in meditation: three Buddhas at the top, eight bodhisattvas below them, then seventeen or eighteen meditating monks in each of the next five rows (rows three through seven). The bottom (eighth) row contains fourteen donor portraits. A fragmentary donor inscription remains. It reads, "Offered with a sincere mind by Daoxiu, of Brahmā . . . Temple."[17]

The pattern of meditating figures with donor portraits below is repeated on the left wall of the cave. From the top of the ceiling downward, there are seven rows: (1) two Buddhas seated with legs crossed; (2) nine seated bodhisattvas, the first eight of whom hold bowls in their hands like the monk in the main painting in the cave, some of them accompanied by a Buddha and paired bodhisattvas; (3) five monks seated in meditation; (4) five monks seated under a tree meditating, with a small wheel of rebirth painted to the right; (5) five more monks meditating, the middle one seated on a chair, with a second small wheel of rebirth painted to the right; (6) six monks meditating; and (7) seventeen donors, one wearing monk's clothing, one wearing Chinese clothing, the rest wearing Uighur dress. Several donor inscriptions are still legible beneath some of the figures. Written in Chinese, they appear to name members of a Uighur

16. See Schlingloff, *Ein buddhistisches Yogalehrbuch*, esp. pp. 85–95. For general discussions of the same text, see also Ruegg, "On a Yoga Treatise in Sanskrit from Qïzïl"; and Yamabe, "The Significance of the 'Yogalehrbuch.'" For a broader study of visualization practice in central Asia, see Yamabe, "Practice of Visualization and the *Visualization Sūtra*"; and idem, "*Sūtra on the Ocean-Like Samādhi of the Visualization of the Buddha.*"

17. My translation of the donor inscriptions is based on the transcriptions given in Liang and Ding, "Xinjiang Kumutula xin faxian de jichu dongku," pp. 3–4, occasionally emended on grounds of sense by the later transcriptions in Jia and Musha, "Lishi hualang," p. 18.

family and specify the donor's kinship relation (to whom?—my guess, explained below, is to the monk pictured in the major painting). They read: "Older sister [Gu?]lusi," "Older brother Gulu[si?] . . . ," " . . . son's mother Si," " . . . Gulusi. . . ," "Younger sister Gulusi Li," and "Offered with a sincere mind by the disciple. . . ." One other donor inscription was visible in the cave in 1979. Written on the front wall of the cave, it reads, "The Buddha's disciple of pure faith, Mao. . . ."

How do we make sense of all of this data: the remaining inscriptions, the family relationships and names they mention, the pictures of the donors, the profusion of meditating figures, and their relationship to the subject painted on the main wall of the cave? The names of the donors provide a starting point. They are evidently a Uighur surname transcribed in Chinese as Gulusi. They are listed in order of age, and apparently sisters of the main subject are included; that is, the sisters' natal as opposed to exogamous ties are acknowledged. The fact that most of them are portrayed in Uighur fashion (especially apparent in their hairstyles and collars, and perhaps in the shape of their faces) confirms this ethnic hypothesis. But the donors are not all Uighur laypeople. On the right wall one of the inscriptions names a monk, Daoxiu, who is also listed as a donor for other caves.[18] On the left wall one of the donors wears monk's clothing and four are pictured in Chinese-style dress. The donors of this small, out-of-the-way cave, then, were a largely Uighur family. They had probably intermarried with Chinese residents (or Kuchean residents who had adopted Chinese customs), and the artist made a point of marking ethnic difference in the donor portraits. Some members of the family were monks; although they may have "left the family," adopted the surname of Śākyamuni, and taken vows of celibacy, they were still included as members of their natal family when it came to performing important religious services like the donation of cave temples. It is also possible that members of a prominent Uighur family joined together with Chinese monks in a cooperative effort to build the cave. Such voluntary associations of laypeople, usually led by monks, are well attested in Chinese circles in western Gansu and Turfan (Xinjiang), but evidence for them has not been found in the Kucha kingdom.[19]

If we now know who sponsored the cave, it remains to consider why they built it and what kind of temple it was. The answers have to do, I think, with whom they commissioned the cave for. I believe that the main subject of the cave is straightforwardly pictured on the main wall: a Chinese monk in meditation. Probably related to the donor family, he was a local monk well known in his day for the practice of meditation. The vast majority of subjects on the two side walls of the cave depict the rest of the Buddhist world—from Buddhas and bodhisattvas down to other monks—engaging in exactly the same activity. The remains of the inscription specify the precise form of meditation he taught: the practice of visualization, perhaps as outlined in the

18. Daoxiu's name appears in the inscription of Kumtura Cave 78; see Liang and Ding, "Xinjiang Kumutula xin faxian de jichu dongku," p. 4.

19. See Hao, *Tanghouqi Wudai Songchu Dunhuang sengni de shehui shenghuo*; Jiang, *Tang Wudai Dunhuang sihu zhidu*; and Ning and Hao, *Dunhuang sheyi wenshu jijiao*.

Mahāvairocana Sūtra. And, if the object in the main subject's hands is indeed a bowl, this would provide further symbolic reinforcement of the focus on the role of the monk. Three possessions above all others were associated with members of the Saṃgha in Buddhist mythology: the robe, the staff, and the bowl. The bowl, in particular, is a reminder of the allegedly daily connection between renouncers and householders, because the bowl is the receptacle for food offerings given to the Saṃgha by the laity.

The visual dynamics of the cave also support the argument that the cave was constructed in order to memorialize the main subject in meditation. The donor figures on the side walls are all profiled, row after row, in three-quarter pose, facing the dominating figure on the main wall. Their focus is not a Buddha statue in the center of the floor, nor do they engage with the visitor to the cave. Instead, they direct their gaze—and encourage the audience to do the same—to the subject on the main wall. The painter's palette reinforces the centrality of the meditating monk. He is portrayed in red and other warm earth-colors, while his adoring audience on the side walls is painted in green and other dull colors against a plain white background. The architecture of the cave is also important. It has a rounded ceiling, like the inside of a stūpa. The shape of the cave at Kumtura contrasts with the coffered ceilings of caves built as Buddha halls or the drapery suspended from ceilings in freestanding temples, architectural forms that support the ritual of worshiping a Buddha image placed in the center of the room. By contrast, the rounded ceiling in Kumtura Cave 75 suggests the stūpafication of the monk for whom the cave was built.

The meditation cave was never a public cave open to all visitors. It was designed to benefit one specific family and the memory of one particular, probably highly placed monk. It was located in an isolated spot, it was hard to reach, and it could not have accommodated more than one or two people at a time. We have no photographs or records of monks engaging in meditation in the cave, but the design of the cave overwhelmingly suggests that use. Its primary subject is a meditating monk, it is lined with almost one hundred subsidiary figures seated in meditation, and its main dedication invokes a visualization exercise. Furthermore, its low, rounded ceiling virtually requires the visitor to sit or kneel. Once seated, one finds oneself gazing directly, at eye level, at a monk who is engaged in the activity of meditating. What, then, is the function of the two small paintings of the wheel of rebirth in this private cave given by one family and focused on the practice of meditation?

The two wheels are located on the lower right quadrant of the left wall in the fourth and fifth rows of seated, meditating monks (see plate 10). The wheels are each about eight inches in diameter. They are nearly identical, both constructed of three concentric circles. In the top wheel a snake is visible in the inner circle, and in the bottom wheel a bird and snake can be seen, thus confirming two of the canonical Three Poisons. The second circle in each wheel is divided into five segments. In both wheels, buildings representing the palaces of the gods are visible in the topmost segment. Two other realms of rebirth are discernible in the upper wheel: human beings at right and hell, with a person splayed out for torture, at bottom. In the bottom wheel the specific symbols in the outer ring of the wheel are obliterated, but in the upper wheel three of the symbols for the Twelve Conditions can be guessed. At the two o'clock position is a monkey painted in red, at the three o'clock position a human figure is on or in a structure of some kind, the next position is totally effaced, and at five o'clock there are two figures. In my reading, these follow the canonical enumeration of a monkey representing consciousness, a person in a boat for name and form, and people embracing as a representation of contact.[20]

The paintings of the two small wheels of rebirth thus seem to conform in their design and iconography to portions of the vinaya account. My invocation of the vinaya, a textual source, to make sense of iconography is reasonably well supported by the historical evidence. As was noted in chapter 3, on western India, an undated Sanskrit fragment closely paralleling the Mūlasarvāstivāda was discovered nearby, in the area of ancient Kucha, and we know from Xuanzang's diary that several centuries before this cave was built, monasteries in the area followed the Sarvāstivāda rules. Unfortunately we do not know of other artistic traditions dealing with the wheel of rebirth in the area. But the painting in the cave does provide important evidence about how paintings of the wheel of rebirth were thought to have been used by residents of the Kucha kingdom in the ninth or tenth century. The wall painting clearly depicts groups of monks, seated in meditation, next to the wheel of rebirth. The mural does not provide enough detail in its current state to decide if the wheels in question were mounted on scrolls or painted in an outdoor pavilion, but it does prove that people in Kumtura associated paintings of the wheel of rebirth with monks meditating. Monks meditated in groups with pictures, and the wheel of rebirth was the subject of one such picture, perhaps (or perhaps not) taught by the main subject of the cave, an influential local monk. Paintings of the saṃsāracakra, in short, functioned as visual aids in monastic practice.

The small paintings of the wheel can also be read in relation to the cave as a whole. In terms of content, the theme of reincarnation on the side wall resonates with the cosmic visualization performed by the monk on the main wall. Of course the two walls each represent the paths of rebirth in different ways. The wheel of rebirth on the side wall utilizes the segments of a circle to lay out the Five Paths, while the picture of the meditating monk on the main wall uses a black cord to link the six destinies, three on each side, to the center of the circle. In good Buddhist fashion, that center may be conceived in multiple terms: as the center of the impermanent world, as the driving force of egocentrism, as the mind/heart of the practitioner, or as the begging bowl—a symbol of the interconnection of Saṃgha and lay community—held in the monk's hands. On the side wall no single monk stands out from the rest as teacher or abbot. These pictures of the cycle of rebirth are authorized by the assembled monks; they are a standardized curriculum. By contrast, the emanation of the Six Paths on the main

20. Liang Zhixiang and Ding Mingyi ("Xinjiang Kumutula xin faxian de jichu dongku," p. 4) correctly identify the two wheels as wheels of rebirth connected to the account in the Mūlasarvāstivāda vinaya, but they believe the visible figures in the outer circle of the upper wheel represent twelve animals.

wall suggests the influence of one monk and the shaping power of the mind, from which all realms of saṃsāra are produced. Both compositions, however, are in the shape of a circle. In this sense, then, the wheels of rebirth on the side walls augment the circular form of the main painting, which depicts the monk's shoulders as rounded and accentuates the round, billowing cassock around his knees. The different forms of the circle on both walls suggest both completion and orderliness.

Did the actual subject of Kumtura Cave 75, the monk himself, use the cave for practicing meditation? Did the Uighur family build it for him while he was alive? Was he in fact a member of their family? Is it an ancestral shrine, built to commemorate the elder brother of the family? Did they conceive of it as a funerary cave, the main painting functioning as an ancestor portrait of the monk? Did they commission it after he died, choosing the specialized form of visualization for which he was best known in the monastic community? Did they inter his ashes inside the cave? Did later monks use the cave for the practice of visualization? Absolute certainty about the answers is out of our reach, but it is clear that the commissioners sponsored the cave in order to memorialize the monk and his specialty of meditation. The cave also announces the merging of Uighur and Han ethnicities as well as the close connection between the family and the Saṃgha.

We can also draw some conclusions about the significance of paintings of the wheel of rebirth at Kumtura. In the other settings analyzed in this book (porches of grandiose temples, hallways of private cave temples, antechambers of Tantric temples, pilgrimage sites), the wheel of rebirth serves a prefatory function. A symbolic program situated at the margins of architectural space, it introduces the visitor and prepares him or her for a higher, more fundamental—literally inner—truth. By contrast, the paintings of the wheel of rebirth at Kumtura serve to reinforce the practice of visualization by monks. Situated inside a private, one-room shrine, the paintings hint at the power of the meditating monk. The wheels are a "vision" in several senses: the monks meditating in rows are looking at them, their circular form contributes to what the monk on the main wall visualizes, they shape the artist's presentation of the main subject, and they help to define the observer's understanding of the monk's meditation. Within the setting of the side wall, the wheels of rebirth are situated among ranks of meditating monks, suggesting that such paintings may have been used in monastic education. Considered in relation to the subject of the whole cave, their cosmological import adds to the majesty of the vision of the monk pictured on the main wall.

Chapter 7

Wheels in Cave Temples

Yulin, Gansu, Tenth Century

The cave temples carved into the cliffs at Yulin (near Anxi in Gansu) preserve the earliest indisputable painting of the wheel of rebirth within the bounds of the medieval Chinese polity. Commissioned in the early tenth century, the program of paintings in Yulin Cave 19 offers a unique interpretation of the vinaya account: the saṃsāracakra is positioned opposite a tableau depicting Maudgalyāyana's tour of hell. The designers of the temple thus seem to be invoking the canon, in which the Buddha directs monks to paint a wheel of rebirth in place of Maudgalyāyana delivering lectures. Although the Yulin cave temple was not designed to mimic a public temple or residence for monks (*vihāra*), the placement of the wheel in an outer hallway adheres to the Buddha's prescription that such teaching devices be painted near the outskirts of monasteries. The rest of the cave contains an antechamber with protector deities and a main inner chamber depicting pure lands. The picture of the wheel introduces the visitor to the varieties of life within the realm of saṃsāra, while the innermost sanctuary recreates a paradise beyond suffering.

The wheel is painted on the south wall of a corridor leading to the antechamber of Yulin Cave 19 (see plate 11). Fully half of the surviving picture was destroyed by the cutting of a passageway through the corridor in modern times. Nevertheless, enough of the standard iconography is preserved to show that the subject of the composition is beyond dispute: a hub in the center of the wheel, the Six Paths around that, the normative symbols for the chain of causation, and the demon holding the entire wheel in his mouth. In addition to these canonical citations, local readings are also apparent: two more rings are added outside the rim of causation, and hell scenes are painted outside the wheel. Opposite the wheel, on the north wall of the corridor, is the Maudgalyāyana story (fig. 7.1). The corridor leads into an antechamber containing depictions of various deities who serve as protectors of the Buddhist Law. The antechamber is connected to the main chamber by a second, shorter corridor. In and around this short passageway are located the inscriptions and some of the portraits depicting the donors of the cave. A group of laypeople commissioned the cave in 926. Nearly forty

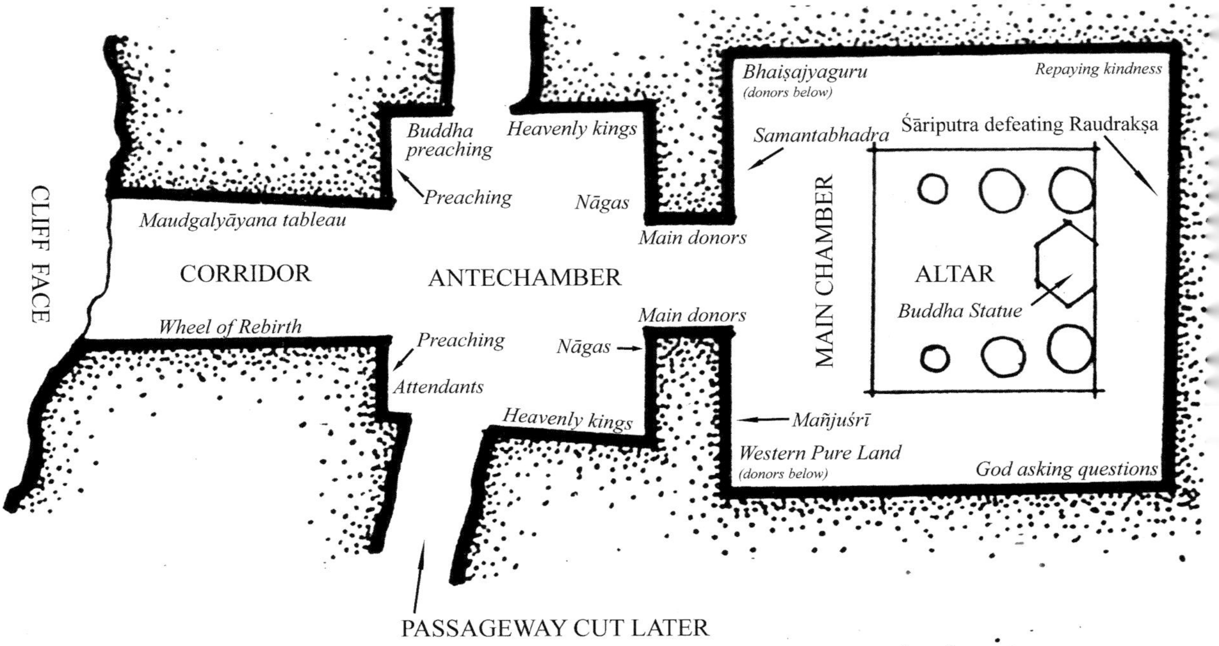

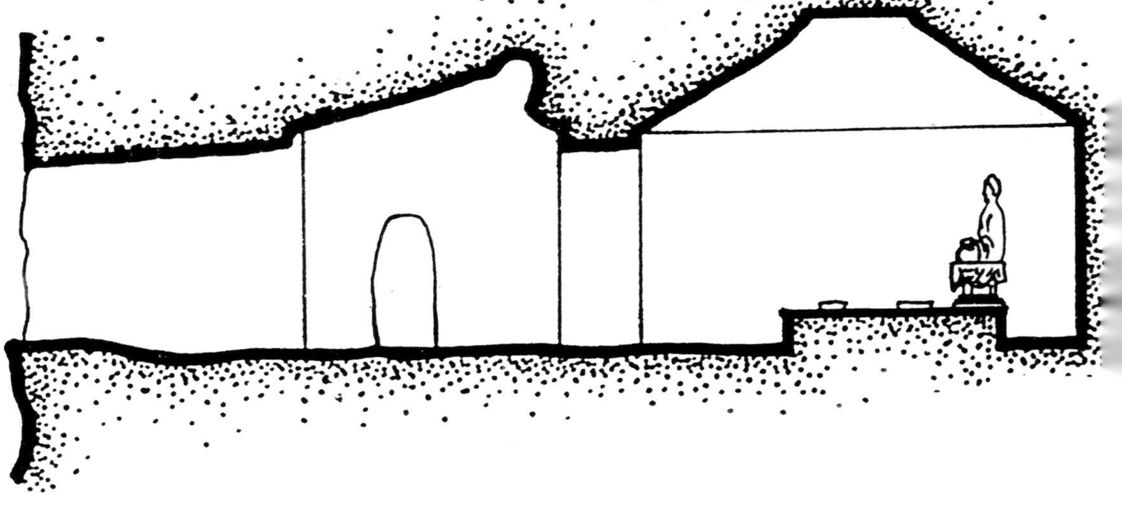

Fig. 7.1. Iconographic program of Yulin Cave 19. After Dunhuang yanjiuyuan, *Anxi Yulinku*, fig. 1. Drawn by Sorat Tungkasiri and Stephen F. Teiser.

years later, between 962 and 964, the cave was rededicated by the local ruler, Cao Yuanzhong, whose portrait occupies the position of honor in the corridor leading to the main chamber. Judging from the remains of a square altar, the main chamber of the cave originally housed several statues. Its walls were decorated with scenes of various paradises as well as a narrative that may have likened Śāriputra's defeat of non-Buddhist magicians to the support of Buddhism offered by the Cao family.

Below I survey the most important facets of Yulin's local history in order to assess the significance of the wheel of rebirth. Yulin Cave 19 is in relatively good repair. Many of the inscriptions made by donors are still partly legible, and, despite the ravages of time, many of the paintings in the cave are well preserved. The riches of Dunhuang—wall paintings, cave design, manuscript sources—are also relevant, since the two areas are not only geographically close but were ruled by the same prominent families, under the same branch of the government, during the period under discussion. They were both part of the popular Buddhist culture of tenth-century northwest China.

Yulin is located near the northwestern tip of the Hexi (literally, "West of the [Yellow] River]") Corridor, the narrow strip of arable land fed by the western reaches of the Yellow River (Huang He; see map 7). It runs the length of modern Gansu, from Gulang northwestward to Dunhuang, for some one thousand kilometers. The geographical and agricultural significance of the Hexi Corridor was augmented by its economic and political value. It was the route connecting the metropolitan centers of the medieval Chinese empire to the empire's westernmost garrison town of Dunhuang. For caravans exporting silk and other Chinese products, Dunhuang was the last town under direct Chinese rule. After leaving Dunhuang they trekked west across the Taklamakan Desert. Central Asian merchants with jewels, precious metals, musical instruments, statues, and Buddhist monks entered the Chinese empire at Dunhuang and continued, via Yulin and other stops in the Hexi Corridor, into the Chinese heartland. Sticking out like a thumb from the Chinese empire (when viewing the back of one's right hand), the Hexi Corridor was a military and cultural battleground. Conquered by the Tibetan empire in 786, it was restored to Chinese rule only in 864. Either as rulers in their own right or as tribute-bearing foreigners, other peoples to the west and north of China, especially the Tibetans, Uighurs, and Khotanese, played prominent roles in the life of the Hexi Corridor. The Yulin caves are situated in a relatively remote site that takes advantage of the cliffs carved by the Yulin River, located seventy-five kilometers south of the modern town of Anxi. During the period under discussion, Yulin was part of the administrative region known as Guazhou (Gua Prefecture) and the Mogao caves near the town of Dunhuang were part of Shazhou (Sha Prefecture).

Currently at Yulin forty-two caves have been excavated.[1] The earliest caves probably date from the beginning of the Tang dynasty, since they utilize a central stūpa-pillar design that fell into disuse soon after that. On the basis of painting style, they range from the Tang dynasty (four caves), the Five Dynasties period (eight caves), the Song

1. For overviews of the Yulin caves, see Duan, "Yulinku de bihua yishu"; Fan, "Yulinku"; Dunhuang yanjiuyuan, *Anxi Yulinku*; and Zhang Boyuan, *Anxi Yulinku*.

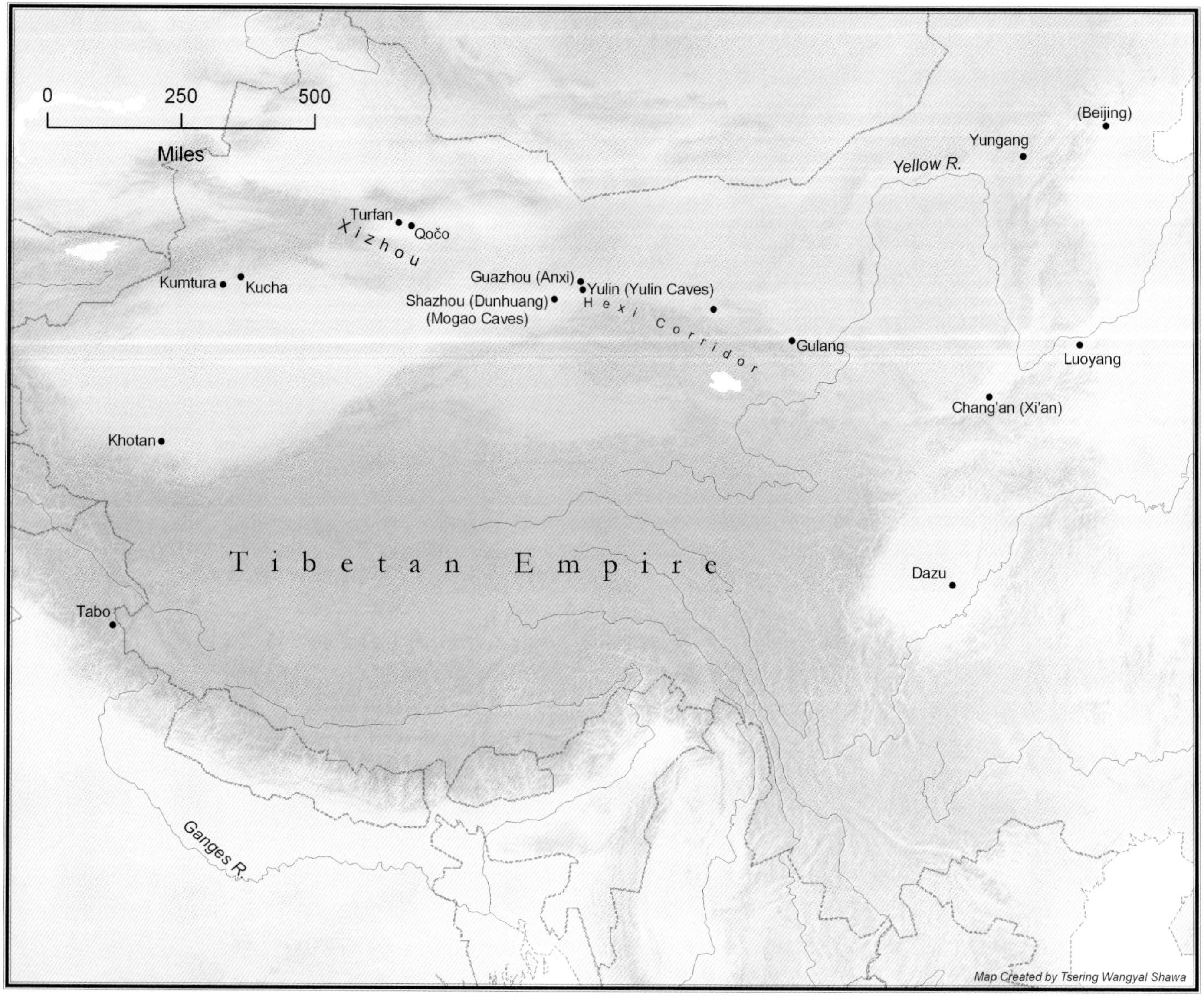

MAP 7. Northwestern China, late tenth century.

dynasty (thirteen caves), Uighur rule (one cave), Tangut rule (four caves), the Yuan dynasty (three caves), and the Qing dynasty (nine caves). Smaller in scale and more remote than the Mogao caves near Dunhuang, the site was placed under government protection in 1961. Conservation efforts and research have proceeded apace, and it was officially opened to foreigners in 1994.

For much of the medieval period, the history of Guazhou (containing Yulin) and Shazhou (containing Dunhuang) were intertwined.[2] Since the end of the third century, Buddhism was a significant cultural factor in Hexi. The great translator Dharmarakṣa (Zhu Fahu, ca. 265–313), known as the "Bodhisattva of Dunhuang" (Dunhuang pusa), studied and taught there. The unification of China under the Sui and Tang dynasties brought the area into close touch with central China. Official temples, erected in each province and maintained at state expense, were located in the region. Manuscript copies of Buddhist texts were sent to monastery libraries in Dunhuang from the government sūtra-copying offices in Chang'an. After the An Lushan rebellion (755–763) weakened the central government, the Tibetan empire moved quickly to take control of the Hexi Corridor. Their campaign began in the southeastern part of the corridor and moved northwest, with Shazhou falling to Tibetan rule in 786. During the period of Tibetan domination (786–864) the entire Hexi Corridor had very little contact with central China. Having themselves recently converted to Buddhism, the Tibetan rulers were heavy patrons of Buddhism in Guazhou and Shazhou. They erected and supported temples, they sponsored the translation and expounding of texts in both Tibetan and Chinese, and they underwrote the activities of Buddhist monks. Buddhist institutions in the area thus flourished during precisely the period, brief but furious, when Buddhism was suppressed by the Chinese state in 845 and 846.

Chinese rule over the area was reestablished through the military victory of Zhang Yichao in 848, leading to the establishment of the administrative post known as the Military Commissioner of the Returning to Righteousness Army (Guiyijun jiedushi). Between 851 and roughly 1037, the person occupying this office was, in effect, the autonomous regional governor of the entire Hexi Corridor, comprising some eleven prefectures (*zhou*). The title was nominally granted by the Chinese emperor, first of the Tang dynasty, then of the various short-lived regimes of the Five Dynasties, then of the Song dynasty. But the weakened condition of the Chinese economy and the decimation of the central army meant that real power lay in the hands of the various Military Commissioners. Zhang Yichao was instrumental in building Buddhist institutions in the area. He did so by reviving some Chinese practices, maintaining many Tibetan forms, and crafting local arrangements. He imported texts from central China to fill in gaps in monastic libraries. He continued to support the eminent Tibetan cleric Čhos-grub (Facheng, 832–865), with whom he had studied as a layman. He under-

2. My overview of Hexi, concentrating on the tenth century, is based on Rong, *Guiyijun shi yanjiu*, pp. 1–147, 266–97, 298–398. See also Duan, "Mogaoku wanqi de yishu"; Fujieda, "Shashū kigigun setsudō shi shimatsu"; Enoki, *Tonkō no rekishi*, pp. 233–96; Tang, "Cao Rengui jiedu Shazhou guiyijun shimo"; and Yang, "On the Sha-chou Uighur Kingdom."

took surveys of temple holdings, sponsored a new census of monks and nuns, and made lavish donations for temples, caves, and the upkeep of the clergy. His son, Zhang Huaishen, held the post of Military Commissioner after him. He too lent strong support to the Buddhist church, commissioning the colossal Buddha statue at Mogao Cave 96 and rebuilding his own family cave temple, Mogao Cave 94.

After an interregnum declared by a later Zhang-family ruler, the Cao family gained control of the area and reestablished the post of Military Commissioner of the Returning to Righteousness Army in 914. The Cao family maintained control of western Hexi (Guazhou and Shazhou) and exerted a strong influence on the region's Buddhism for the next eighty-eight years. It was during this period that the wheel of rebirth in Yulin Cave 19 was executed. The timeline in table 4 is intended to illustrate some of the interconnections between the Buddhist cave shrines at Yulin and Mogao, the commissioning of Buddhist texts, the involvement of lay societies in Buddhist activities, patronage by the Cao family, and the network of governmental and marriage relations that made the area around Yulin a fertile meeting ground of Chinese and central Asian influences.

The picture of tenth-century Buddhist culture in Hexi that emerges from this survey is important for understanding the wheel of rebirth at Yulin. The Cao family was involved in many of the large-scale projects engineered in Guazhou and Shazhou in the tenth century. They were responsible for the commissioning of over seventy caves: forty-two at Mogao (Dunhuang) and twenty-eight at Yulin.[3] Their power as local governors depended on military might as well as a careful orchestration of relations with the successive ruling houses of the Chinese state and with foreign peoples. They maintained a Chinese administrative system and received nearly unbroken support from the weakened Chinese state. The Cao family was related by marriage to the rulers of Khotan and maintained close military ties with them. Cao Yuanzhong, whose rule over Hexi was strongest and longest, followed the lead of Khotan in breaking with the Song court. The Caos also entered marriage alliances with the Uighur kingdom in Ganzhou, to the east of Guazhou. They established friendly relations with the Uighurs of Xizhou and with the Liao and Jin peoples. Cao Yuanzhong was a heavy supporter of the copying and dissemination of Buddhist texts, and he built and renovated cave temples in both Mogao and Yulin. The Caos instituted an academy in Shazhou for the training of artists who worked at the local cave temples; it was similar to the professional academies in the capital supported by the Chinese court.[4] The Caos were not alone in these endeavors. Lay Buddhists in the area banded together to commission their own caves as a group. Other lay Buddhists acted as individuals to pay for the copying of scriptures. A recently compiled tally of all texts known to have been copied in Dunhuang between 918 and 985 provides an interesting picture of tenth-century interests.[5] Out of forty-eight physical copies of texts recorded during that period, thirty

3. See Duan, "Yulinku de bihua yishu," pp. 167–70.

4. Ibid., p. 162.

5. See the listing in Rong, *Guiyijun shi yanjiu*, pp. 277–78, based largely on Ikeda, *Chūgoku kodai shahon shikigo shūroku.*

were not contained in the official canon of the time as defined by Zhisheng's (669–740) *Catalogue of the Buddhist Teachings during the Kaiyuan Era* (*Kaiyuan shijiao lu*). Some of the texts are copies of the *Heart* and *Diamond* sūtras. Others are the chapter of the *Lotus Sūtra* detailing the compassion of Avalokiteśvara, while others deal with the goddess Marīci. Some are copies of monastic lectures on standard Buddhist sūtras or texts extolling filial piety and general morality. The vast majority of texts on the list, however, are concerned with the practice of basic Buddhist rituals: confession and chanting, curing, averting evil, funerals, memorial rites, casting spells, attaining long life, celebrating festivals, and the lay Buddhist practice of fasting.

Yulin Cave 19 is consistent with the picture of Buddhism sketched above. Inscriptions in the cave indicate two major periods of activity. The cave was originally commissioned in 926 by a group of lay donors, many of them lower-ranking members of the local administration, led by a monk named Daoshou. Their dedication, now partly effaced, was inscribed above the doorway of the corridor leading to the main chamber of the cave.[6] It is dated "the fifteenth day of the first month of the fourth year of Tongguang of the Great Tang" (1 March 926). It includes the vow, "May our parents be reborn together . . . " and mentions Avalokiteśvara and Maitreya. Twice it refers to "thirty people." Donor portraits are painted inside the main chamber on the south and west walls; they total thirty males and fourteen females. They wear Five Dynasties–style clothing, similar to the portraits in Yulin Cave 12. Thus, in all likelihood the cave was begun by a group of thirty Buddhist laymen and their families in the year 926.

The second major period of activity at the cave was 962–964. In the corridor leading to the main chamber are two large donor portraits, with inscriptions. The one on the south (right) wall pictures Cao Yuanzhong and his son (see fig. 7.2). The cartouche reads, "Offered with a single mind by Cao Yuanzhong, Investigatory Supporter of the State, Protector of the Garrison, Meritorious Minister, Appointed as Military Commissioner of the Returning to Righteousness Army, Lord Especially Advanced, Acting Grand Preceptor, Concurrently Secretariat Director, Dynasty-Founding Duke of Qiao Commandery." The cartouche beside his son reads, "His son, Yanlu, Court Gentleman for Ceremonial Service." On the north (left) wall of the corridor is a portrait of Cao Yuanzhong's wife, née Zhai, and their oldest daughter. The official and honorific titles for Cao Yuanzhong are consistent with those claimed for him in other dedications dating between 962 and 964.[7] Hence I date the rededication of the cave by Cao to this three-year period. The relationship between the Caos and the earlier donors is not explicit. The portraits of the Cao family occupy the position of honor in the

6. For transcriptions of the inscriptions discussed below, see Xie, *Dunhuang yishu xulu*, pp. 457–62; and Zhang Boyuan, *Anxi Yulinku*, pp. 214–19. A third period of activity at Yulin Cave 19 can be inferred from inscriptions in the corridors and antechamber. They contain dates in the 1340s and 1360s, when Hexi was under the control of the Yuan dynasty. They are probably the jottings of pilgrims who visited the caves briefly. Only Zhang Boyuan (ibid., pp. 218–19) deals with the Yuan inscriptions.

7. See Rong, *Guiyijun shi yanjiu*, pp. 113–22; and Ji, *Dunhuangxue dacidian*, s.v. Cao Yuanzhong, pp. 364–65.

TABLE 4. Selective chronology of the Cao family in northwestern China, 914–974. For documentation, see Rong, *Guiyijun shi yanjiu*, pp. 1–43; supplemented where necessary by Shi, "Dunhuang Mogaoku dashi nianbiao."

907	Chinese Later Liang (Houliang) dynasty founded
914	Cao Yijin assumes control of Guazhou and Shazhou from Zhang Chengfeng, appointed Deputy Military Commissioner (Jiedu liuhou shi)
916	Cao Yijin marries Uighur royalty from Ganzhou
918	Cao Yijin authorized to rule by Liang dynasty, appointed Military Commissioner (Jiedushi)
	Cao Yijin commissions Mogao Cave 98
923	Chinese Later Tang (Houtang) dynasty founded
924	Cao Yijin receives titles from Later Tang dynasty
	Two monks from central China, Zhiyan and Guiwen, stop in Shazhou en route to western regions
925	Khotanese ambassador performs Buddhist ceremonies in Dunhuang
	Cao Yijin commissions Mogao Cave 98
	Zhai Fengda refurbishes Mogao Cave 220
926	Uighur ruler from Ganzhou marries Cao Yijin's daughter
	Yulin Cave 19 commissioned by thirty lay donors
931	Cao Yijin appointed Secretariat Director (Zhongshu ling)
933	Khotanese Prime Minister visits Mogao caves
934	Mogao Cave 387 refurbished
935	Cao Yijin dies
	His son, Cao Yuande, succeeds him, entitled Minister of Works (Sikong)
	Lay society commissions Mogao Cave 38
936	Chinese Later Jin (Houjin) dynasty founded
939	Cao Yuande dies
	His brother, Cao Yuanshen, succeeds him, entitled Minister of Works (Sikong)
940	Mogao Cave 100 completed
943	Mogao Cave 412 refurbished
944	Cao Yuanshen dies
	His brother, Cao Yuanzhong, succeeds him, entitled Vice Director of the Department of State Affairs (Puye)
945	Cao Yuanzhong commissions Mogao Cave 256
946	Cao Yuanzhong appointed Deputy Commander (Liuhou)

947 Chinese Later Han (Houhan) dynasty founded

Khotanese ambassador visits Shazhou

949 Cao Yuanzhong propagates printed images of Avalokiteśvara (Guanshiyin) and Vaiśravana (Bishamen)

950 Cao Yuanzhong propagates printed versions of *Diamond Sūtra*

Cao Yuanzhong commissions Mañjuśrī hall, Mogao Cave 61

951 Chinese Later Zhou (Houzhou) dynasty founded

Khotanese ambassador visits Shazhou

953 Cao Yuanzhong sponsors large feast at Mogao Cave 469, commissions Mogao Cave 53

Cao Yanzhong commissions *Scripture on Prolonging Life (Yanshouming jing)*

Mogao Caves 123, 124, 125 refurbished

955 Khotanese ambassador visits Dunhuang

Uighur delegations from Xizhou and Ganzhou visit Dunhuang

Cao Yuanzhong appointed Military Commissioner of the Returning to Righteousness Army (Guiyijun jiedushi) and Acting Grand Guardian (Jianjiao taibao)

Cao Yuanzhong commissions Moao Cave 51

957 Mogao Cave 5 completed

958 Monk Fazong passes through Shazhou, returning from western regions

960 Chinese Song dynasty founded

Khotanese princess establishes gardens in Shazhou

962 Cao Yuanzhong commissions Mogao Cave 55

Cao Yuanzhong commissions Yulin Cave 19

964 Khotanese princes visit Shazhou

Expedition of three hundred monks, led by Xuye, passes through Shazhou and Guazhou en route to Khotan and India

966 Cao Yuanzhong visits Mogao caves, propagates *Scripture of the Buddhas' Names (Foming jing)*

Cao Yuanzhong and wife refurbish Northern Great Buddha (Maitreya) at Mogao Cave 96

969 Cao Yuanzhong breaks relations with Song court

970 Khotan asks Cao Yuanzhong for military help

Monk Fuhui and others commission Mogao Cave 427

974 Cao Yuanzhong commissions Mogao Cave 25

Cao Yuanzhong dies

His son, Cao Yangong, succeeds him

FIG. 7.2. Donor portrait, Cao Yuanzhong and his son. Wall painting. Corridor of Yulin Cave 19, tenth century. Dunhuang yanjiuyuan, *Anxi Yulinku*, pl. 63.

cave, as far as donor portraits are concerned, and their images are larger than the rest (with Cao's slightly larger than his wife's). This would suggest the Caos' preeminence as donors. The portraits of the earlier donors were left undisturbed in the main chamber, and there are no obvious signs of repainting or redesign of the iconographical program. Thus, in all likelihood the cave was largely completed in 926 by the earlier group—many of whom served as minor officials under Cao Yijin—and rededicated between 962 and 964 under the patronage of Cao Yijin's son, Cao Yuanzhong.

Now I turn to an analysis of the iconographic program and architectural design of the cave. The main chamber of Yulin Cave 19 is large and square, with a nearly square, raised platform in its center (see fig. 7.1). The platform originally was the base for a set of statues now lost. Most likely they were a set of three, five, or seven figures, with Śākyamuni Buddha in the center. The ceiling above the statues is in the shape of a dome. This coffered style of ceiling is thought to be a method of mimicking the way in which canopies were hung over Buddha statues in medieval Chinese temples.[8] The details of cloth canopies and wooden posts and beams were often painted onto the stone surface of caves, all in an effort to lend grandeur to the statues enthroned underneath. The size and location of the altar imply that one of the major religious activities that took place there involved the worship of the main Buddha image. Offerings could be presented at an altar in front of the dais, and participants could circumambulate the image in a clockwise direction (that is, keeping the right side, the honored side, toward the Buddha).

The north wall of the cave contains the first set of images a person would see after making offerings, bowing, and beginning to circumambulate, hence its content can be read as preparation for the paradise scenes depicted on the south wall. The north wall is composed of two basic programs. The first depicts scenes from the various sūtras describing the activities of Bhaiṣajyaguru Bodhisattva (Yaoshiwang pusa; see a similar painting at the Mogao caves, fig. 5.9). Bhaiṣajyaguru is best known for granting long life to his devotees, saving them from misfortune, and curing sickness. Paintings typically portray the ritual activities of his cult: the lighting of sets of seven seven-tiered lamps and the unfurling of banners. Although only some of the painting at Yulin Cave 19 is legible, it appears to depict Bhaiṣajyaguru's paradise. The matching of an Amitābha scene with a Bhaiṣajyaguru paradise is a common theme in medieval Chinese cave temples. As Ning Qiang has suggested for the late Tang dynasty, both scenes were ways of representing pure realms, and this mirroring effect reinforced the impression of idealized comfort.[9] The second program on the north wall is a set of scenes from *The Scripture on Repaying Kindness* (*Bao'en jing*). This Chinese apocryphon weaves together basic Buddhist teachings in the format of a sūtra narrative focused on the traditional Chinese concerns of filial piety and the duties owed to one's superiors and rulers. It emphasizes ethical values and the fulfillment of social roles. As a whole, then, the north wall can be regarded as a way of filling out the transcendent realm depicted on the south wall. Performing rituals that invoke the help of Bhaiṣajyaguru Bodhisattva and following the ethical precepts appropriate to lay life are part of achieving rebirth in paradise.

The paintings on the south wall of Yulin Cave 19 set the tone for the entire cave. The wall is divided in two, the front side depicting scenes of Amitābha Buddha's paradise, the rear side depicting scenes from *The Scripture of the God Asking Questions* (*Tian qingwen jing*). Amitābha's paradise is one of the most popular scenes in medi-

8. See Xiao, *Dunhuang jianzhu yanjiu*, pp. 44–50, and figs. 12-1, 12-2, and 12-3.
9. See Ning, *Art, Religion, and Politics in Medieval China*, chap. 1.

eval Chinese art; at Dunhuang alone, over 215 caves are dominated by it (for a related painting on silk, see fig. 5.1). Although the current state of Yulin Cave 19 does not allow a scene-by-scene analysis, enough of the painting is visible to identify it as a depiction of the pure land of Amitābha in the west. This land of happiness is filled with cooling ponds, lush trees, lotus flowers, and soothing music. It is portrayed as a kind of palace or temple, with Amitābha Buddha (Emituo fo) reigning and two bodhisattvas, Avalokiteśvara (Guanshiyin) and Mahāsthāmaprāpta (Dashizhi), assisting him. As a pure land, it stands in contrast to all of the woes and impurities of sentient existence. It is transcendent and free from suffering. Once reborn there, according to the daily prayers and canonical texts of medieval Buddhism, one is assured a speedy entrance into final deliverance. Amitābha's paradise is thus as far along the path as many practitioners could hope to get, or as close to the ultimate as artists could hope to depict. The rear portion of the south wall contains scenes in which a god visits the Buddha, worships him, asks questions and receives answers, and departs. The questions and the answers outline some of the key teachings of Buddhism: the Four Truths, the Six Perfections, the precepts for lay life, and so on. The surroundings of the Buddha in many such paintings often look like the palaces in pure land paintings, with thrones, halls, towers, and ponds. One could thus argue that the painting of *The Scripture of the God Asking Questions* resonates pictorially with the scenes of Amitābha's paradise beside it. Its doctrinal message is also congruent with that of its neighbor: in the face of suffering caused by desire and ignorance, one should seek rebirth in a realm that transcends impurity.

The east (rear) wall of the main chamber is different in tone from the main walls, but its content no less interesting. It is a scene of Śāriputra doing battle with the heterodox teacher, Raudrakṣa (see fig. 7.3 for a similar painting). The story, which also circulated in the form of a popular entertainment involving singing, reciting, and pictures, may well be related to the sponsorship of the cave.[10] The narrative is set at the time of Śākyamuni. It begins with the disciple of the Buddha, Śāriputra, convincing Sudatta (aka Anāthapiṇḍika), a minister to the king of Śrāvastī (King Prasenajit), to donate a large park for the use of Śākyamuni and his disciples. Hearing that the Buddha is about to receive a grant from such a powerful patron, six other non-Brahmanical teachers, led by Raudrakṣa, raise objections. It is decided that the conflict will be settled by a battle of magical abilities, with Śāriputra representing the Buddhists and Raudrakṣa representing the other heterodox traditions. The match lasts for six rounds, in each of which Śāriputra's conjurings vanquish those of Raudrakṣa. Raudrakṣa's magical mountain is reduced to rubble by Śāriputra's diamond deity; his fierce buffalo is defeated by Śāriputra's lion; his ornately decorated pond is sucked dry by Śāriputra's white elephant; his poisonous dragon is gobbled up by Śāriputra's king of birds; his fire-breathing monsters lose to Śāriputra's Vaiśravana; and his huge tree is blown over by the god of wind invoked by Śāriputra. With Raudrakṣa's final defeat, all six hereti-

10. For a translation of the *bianwen* (transformation text) on Śāriputra defeating the demons, see Mair, *Tun-huang Popular Narratives*, pp. 30–84.

cal leaders become followers of the Buddha, and Sudatta proceeds with the donation of land to the Buddhists. The concerns of the story are manifold. The most striking visual characteristics have to do with magical abilities, battles of prowess, the marshalling of cosmic forces, the control of huge and hideous beasts, and the deeds of gods and heroes. The winner is defined not by brute physical strength, but rather by the overpowering nature of the minions whom he can invoke. The painting depicts the victory of Buddhism over other religions; it justifies the support of Buddhism by the state and, more specifically, by the wealthy minister to the ruler. Śāriputra's battle is depicted on the rear walls of many caves at Mogao and Yulin. Placed at the back of the cave, the painting may allude to behind-the-scenes support for Buddhism by preeminent local officials.

The west wall of the main chamber is bisected by a corridor. On one side is a scene of Samantabhadra Bodhisattva (Puxian pusa), on the other a scene of Mañjuśrī Bodhisattva (Wenshu pusa), a common pairing for the west wall of caves at Yulin.[11]

As noted above, portraits of the original group of donors are contained in the front half of the main chamber, that is, on the west half of both the south and north walls, and on the west wall. Donor portraits of Cao Yuanzhong and his wife, and of their son and daughter, are painted in the corridor that connects the main chamber to the antechamber.

The iconographic program in the antechamber is less complicated and more generic than that of the main chamber. The south and north walls contain paintings of the Four Heavenly Kings (*catvāsraḥ mahārājikāḥ*, Ch.: *sitianwang*) and of a Buddha preaching. In Buddhist mythology the Four Heavenly Kings reside on Mount Sumeru, each guarding one of the four directions. They are assigned the responsibility of protecting the Buddha's teaching after the demise of Śākyamuni. They are majestic and more powerful than human beings, and hence they serve as effective protectors of Buddhism. Nevertheless, they have not yet entered the path of renunciation or found a way to conquer rebirth, hence their placement outside of paradise. The east wall of the antechamber contains pictures of *nāgas*, mirrored by more scenes of preaching on the west wall. As a species, *nāgas* rank slightly below heavenly kings but play a similar role: enlisted by the Buddha, these powerful serpentlike creatures help to advance the cause of Buddhism.

The long corridor leading from the entrance of the cave to the antechamber contains the wheel of rebirth on the south side (the right side as one enters) and scenes from the story of Maudgalyāyana on the north side. Both walls have suffered much from decay, and only one-half of the painting of the wheel now survives. As noted above, the wheel contains several of the canonical elements (see plate 11).[12] The center of the wheel is badly damaged, but seems to contain a lone figure, perhaps a female. In the second ring around that, three paths out of an original six are visible. In the

11. The pairing of Samantabhadra and Mañjuśrī also occurs in Yulin Cave 25, for instance.

12. My reading of the wheel differs from that in the only article on the wheel at Yulin that I know of, Zhang Boyuan, "Anxi Yulinku 'liudao lunhui tu' kaoshi."

(a) Fig. 7.3. Śāriputra (a) and Raudrakṣa (b), detail of wall painting. Rear wall of Mogao Cave 196, tenth century. Dunhuang yanjiusuo, *Dunhuang Mogaoku*, 5: pls. 184, 185.

(b)

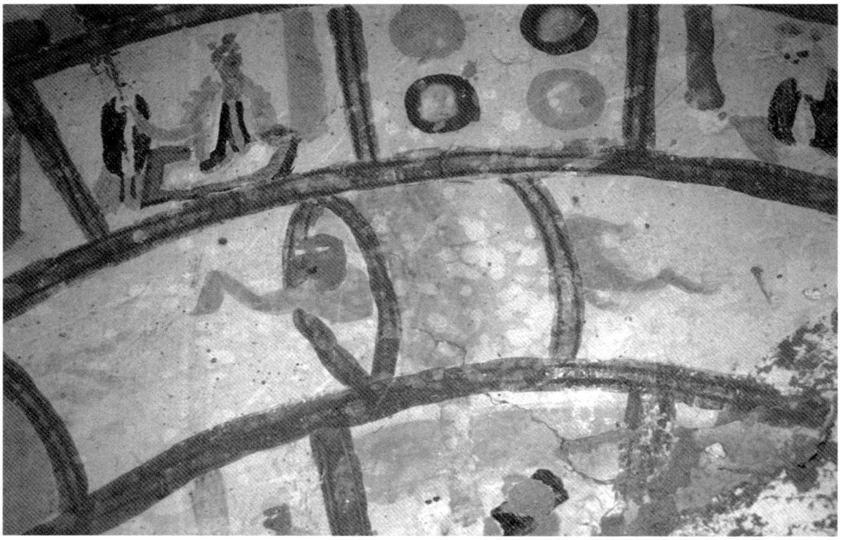

FIG. 7.4. Detail, top of wheel of rebirth. Wall painting. Right wall of corridor, Yulin Cave 19, tenth century. Photography: Stephen F. Teiser.

top path one can see the sun and a person. Based on its position as the uppermost of the Six Paths, this must have been the realm of the gods. On the right side of the middle path are visible a dwelling and two figures, probably a seated Buddha and a disciple. This path probably represents the realm of humans. In the remaining path, at bottom left, the outline of a horse can be made out, indicating the path of animals.

The links in the chain of causation are represented in the next ring of the wheel, although the current state of the painting makes it difficult to be very precise. In the eight visible segments (presumably out of an original ring composed of eighteen), I propose the following identifications, starting at the top and moving counterclockwise: (1) person in cangue; (2) old person with cane; (3) woman holding child (= desire); (4) old woman and young person; (5) corpse on platform (= death); (6) three people sitting on ground; (7) old man and young person; and (8) woman. What I am calling segments three and five appear to follow the canonical symbols for representing desire and death, respectively. However, there are two problems with this interpretation. One is that the segments do not follow the prescribed order for the Twelve or Eighteen Conditions. The other is that they run counterclockwise, which would be unusual but which parallels the direction of movement in the next ring. Alternative interpretations, however, do not hold up any better.[13]

13. Zhang Boyuan ("Anxi Yulinku 'liudao lunhui tu' kaoshi," p. 21) proposes that the segments of this ring correspond to each of the Six Paths in the next inner ring. According to him, the cycle of causation is pictured in the outermost circle. His individual identifications sometimes make sense in visual terms (man throwing rope around woman = touch), but many of them are unconvincing or without precedent.

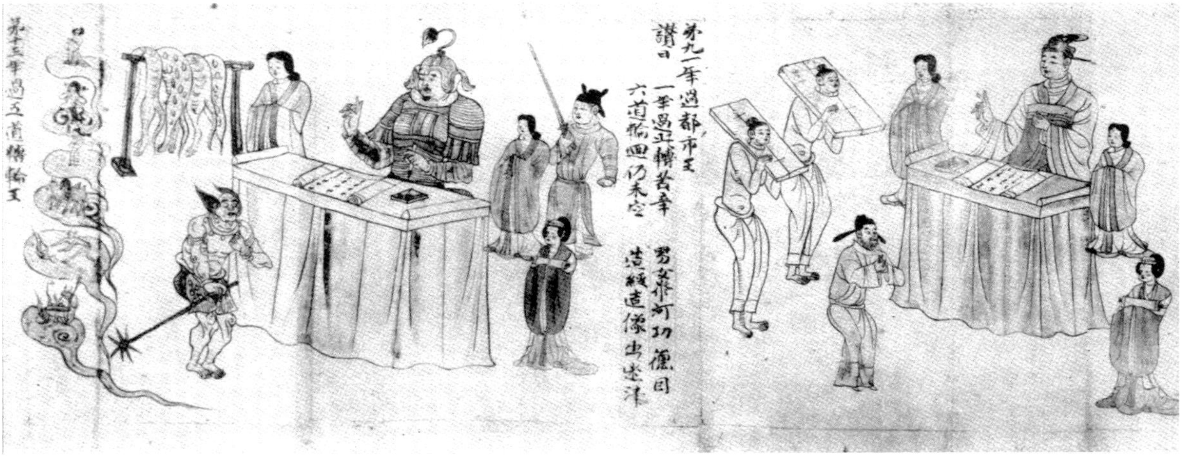

FIG. 7.5. Ninth and tenth courts of hell, *Scripture on the Ten Kings*. Modern collotype reproduction (in author's collection) of illustrated manuscript, tenth century, Satō collection. Photography: John Blazejewski.

The next ring in the wheel contains a representation without any apparent precedent in the history of Buddhism. We see at the top of this ring, running counterclockwise, a horizontal figure moving through what looks like a barrel (see fig. 7.4). The barrel obscures the trunk of the body, leaving exposed the figure's head and arms on one side and legs on the other. The head is that of a human, the legs those of a deer. Similarly, near the ten o'clock position, we see another figure with human head and animal tail. The vinaya text on the wheel of rebirth contains directions to paint humans with either their heads or their feet sticking out of buckets, indicating their progress (upward) or failure (downward) in their next rebirth. This ring in the wheel may be an interpretation of that directive. In any event, the painting here reinforces the notion of repetition, since the circle has no beginning or end. It draws particular attention to the idea of interspecies migration, the tenet that one will be reborn into a different form of life in one's next rebirth. The general idea was, of course, well known. In tenth-century illustration versions of *The Scripture on the Ten Kings*, for instance, animal skins are draped over a rack that stands in the final court of purgatory, presumably to be thrown over sinners assigned to rebirth as an animal (see fig. 7.5). In the cases pictured in the wheel of rebirth at Yulin, however, animals are being reborn as human beings, and the process is represented as one of continual passage, moving through one tunnel after another. (The same motif reappears later in western Tibet and Sichuan, discussed in chapters 8 and 9.)

The outer ring of the wheel is more resistant to interpretation. Some thirteen out of an original twenty-four segments still remain, although all have faded or suffered damage. All but one of them contains a female figure, some of whom wear caps and are flanked by an attendant. They all clasp their hands together in a gesture of respect, and they all face the center of the composition. These visual details suggest that the entire composition might be iconic in design, that is, centered on the presence of a holy figure, now only faintly visible, in the center of the wall painting.

Like the canonical saṃsāracakra, the wheel at Yulin is grasped by a large demon whose eyes and claws are visible at the top of the wheel. Around the outside of the wheel are several scenes (six by my count), some of which deal specifically with hell and rebirth.[14] To the right of the demon's head is a monk in meditation, seated in front of a more majestic figure. To the far left of the demon's head in the corner is a group of three figures, seated and facing a larger figure. Below them is a standard depiction of hell as a walled city. In front of the wall is a cart, pulled by an ox and trailing banners. The iconography of the banners and the walled city suggest that this scene depicts the arrival of a recently deceased person at the underground prisons. Below them is the fourth scene. It begins with a small bridge at the circumference of the wheel and leads to a figure standing before a mirror and a seated figure with a halo. Such bridges typically appear in pictures of purgatory, and the mirror shown outside the wheel is undoubtedly the Mirror of Deeds (or karma mirror, *yejing*), which always appears in the fifth court of purgatory, ruled by King Yama (Yanluo wang). The mirror is usually located in the same court as Kṣitigarbha Bodhisattva (Dizang pusa), who specializes in saving people from painful retribution (see fig. 7.6). At Yulin, these scenes outside the wheel of rebirth narrate the arrival of the deceased spirit in the city of hell, the passage across the river of the underworld, judgment in front of King Yama's karma mirror, and the hope of deliverance by Kṣitigarbha. It is also possible that all of these scenes are connected to the story of Maudgalyāyana shown on the opposite wall. The first scene might picture Maudgalyāyana as a disciple of the Buddha, the second scene could be Maudgalyāyana perfecting his meditative abilities, the third scene could be his arrival in hell, and the fourth scene his encounter with King Yama. The fifth scene shows a large, seated monk with two smaller figures, and the sixth scene depicts a figure seated on a platform, but both scenes are too faded to identify precisely. The scenes to the right of the wheel (now destroyed) might have portrayed other events in the afterlife, adding grisly and entertaining details about the lower paths of rebirth, elaborating on rebirth in the heavens, or spelling out the process of judgment between lifetimes.

Facing the wheel of rebirth, on the north wall of the corridor, is a painting of the story of Maudgalyāyana. Until recently the painting was considered simply a generic hell program, but Fan Jinshi and Mei Lin showed conclusively in 1996 that the scenes narrate the exploits of Maudgalyāyana.[15] The specific tale told in this painting is not the story about Maudgalyāyana attracting crowds with his tours of the underworld, as related in the charter myth for the wheel of rebirth in the Mūlasarvāstivāda vinaya.

---

14. Zhang Boyuan ("Anxi Yulinku 'liudao lunhui tu' kaoshi," p. 21) reads these scenes as the four kinds of sacred beings: *śrāvakas*, *pratyekabuddhas*, bodhisattvas, and Buddhas.

15. Fan and Mei, "Yulinku dishijiuku Mulian bianxiang kaoshi." See also the partial translation with more photos and plans in Fan and Mei, "An Interpretation of the Maudgalyayana Murals in Cave 19 at Yulin."

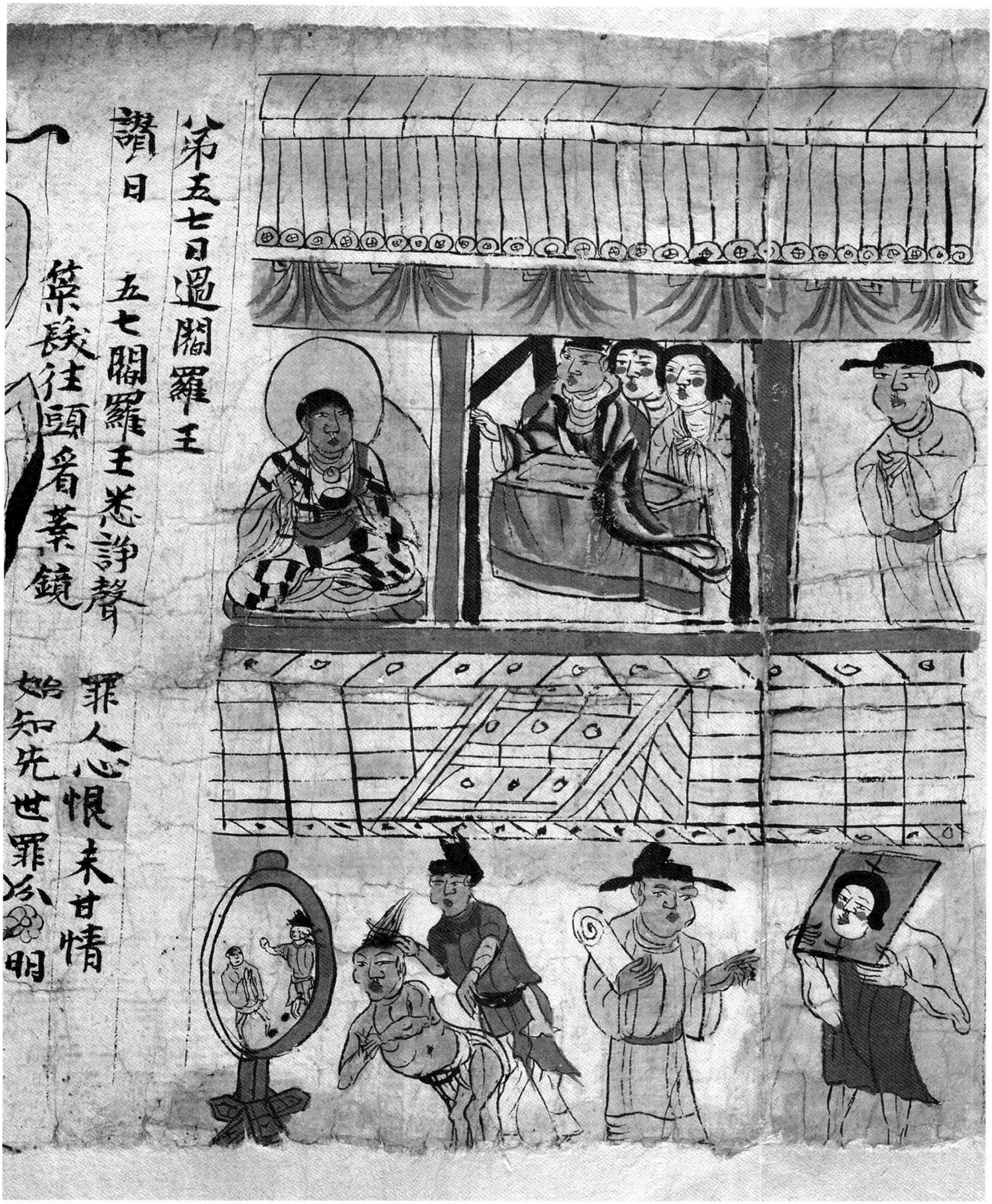

Fig. 7.6. Fifth court of hell, *Scripture on the Ten Kings.* Illustrated manuscript, tenth century. Stein Dunhuang no. 3961, by permission of the British Library.

Nor is it the story of Maudgalyāyana's discipleship under the Buddha, nor the narrative of his meditative powers. Instead, the scenes tell the story about Maudgalyāyana best known in China during the medieval period: the legend of how he endured the worst chambers of hell in order to release his mother from the tortures of karmic retribution. While based on some Indian elements, this version of the Maudgalyāyana legend was constructed in China in conjunction with the celebration of the Ghost Festival of the seventh month. According to legend, the Buddha established the Ghost Festival so that laypeople could bring salvation to their parents by making offerings to monks, following the model enacted by Maudgalyāyana. The mythology of the Ghost Festival circulated among all social classes and in many different media, including apocryphal sūtras, commentaries, transformation texts, and images. Fan and Mei tie the scenes in Yulin Cave 19 to the version of the Maudgalyāyana story contained in transformation texts. They specify ten distinct scenes in the cave painting (see fig. 7.7). It begins with Maudgalyāyana in a cemetery mourning his parents' death. It follows Maudgalyāyana as he encounters various figures in the underworld, including groups of sinners in cangues (see fig. 7.8), King Yama, the Boys of Good and Evil, Kṣitigarbha Bodhisattva, and the General Who Turns the Wheel of Rebirth in the Five Paths. It ends with Maudgalyāyana finding his mother in Avīci Hell and securing her salvation through the intervention of the Buddha. Fan and Mei demonstrate that the picture is composed in the shape of a backward letter S: the top panel proceeds from left to right, the middle panel from right to left, and the bottom panel left to right. They argue that the pictorial narrative in Cave 19 places particular weight on Maudgalyāyana's journey through hell. According to them, the mural, rather than emphasizing Maudgalyāyana's filial piety, focuses instead on his difficulties in the underground prisons.[16]

The pairing of the wheel of rebirth and scenes of Maudgalyāyana's adventures in hell in Yulin Cave 19 is remarkable and, to the best of my knowledge, unique in the history of Buddhist art. It is interesting for our purposes because of the peculiar relation it suggests between the pictorial program of the cave and the plot of the vinaya text. The designers of the cave seem to be invoking the canonical account, quoting it in pictures rather than words. The vinaya story describes how Maudgalyāyana attracts large crowds by telling of his travels in other realms, yet the cave painting makes no mention of Maudgalyāyana's audience or of the Buddhist Saṃgha, both of whom figure prominently in the vinaya. Rather, the painting depicts what the average resident of the Hexi Corridor in the tenth century might have known about Maudgalyāyana, his exploits in hell on behalf of his mother.

Another problem of interpretation concerns the placement of the wheel at Yulin: why is the wheel of rebirth painted in the corridor leading to an antechamber of a cave temple? To claim that artists simply sought recourse to a textual precedent is to obscure the problems that artists and their patrons faced. The vinaya account is unambiguous about where the saṃsāracakra should be painted: on the porches of monasteries. At

16. Fan and Mei, "Yulinku dishijiuku Mulian bianxiang kaoshi," esp. pp. 53–54.

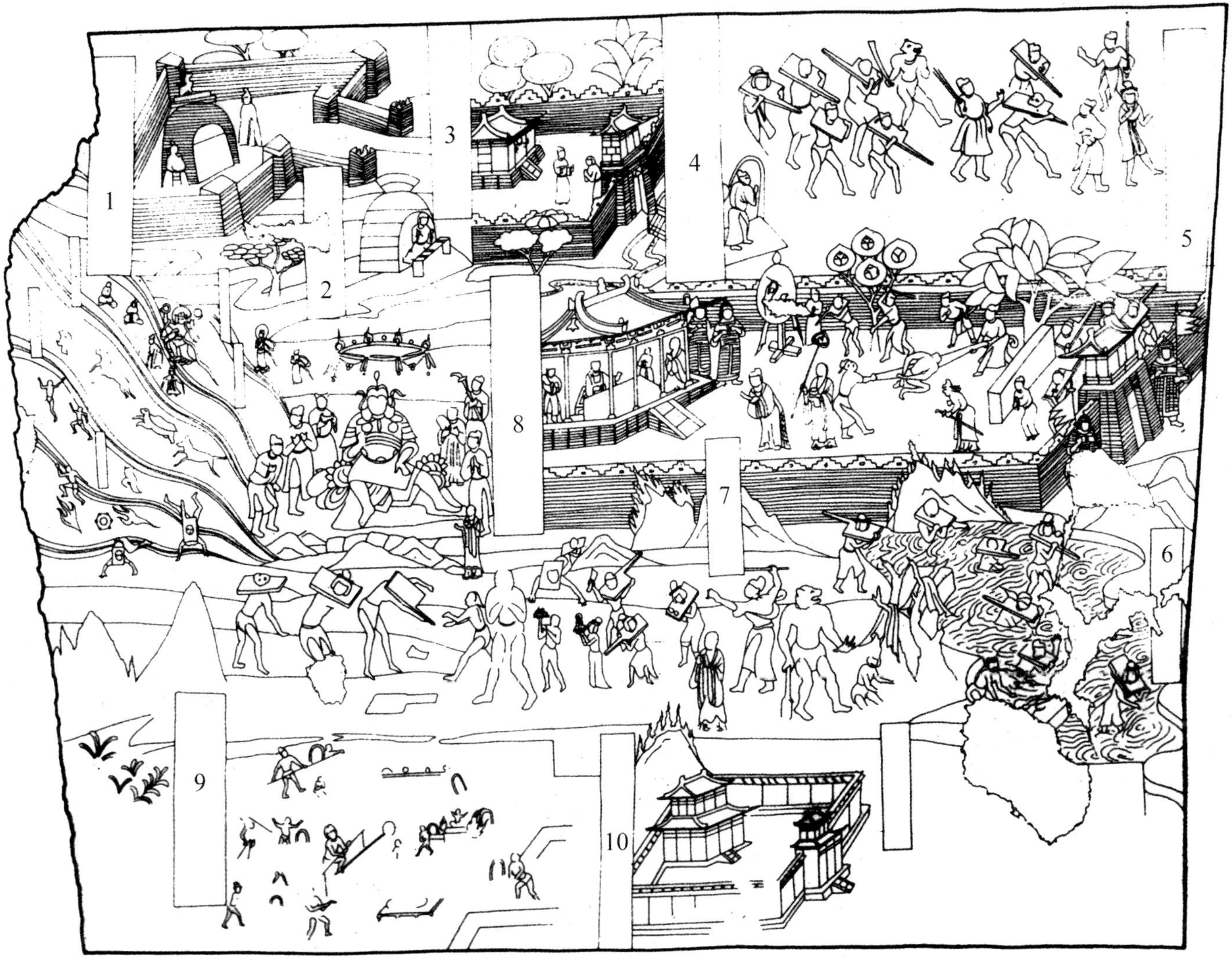

Fig. 7.7. Diagram of Maudgalyāyana tableau. After Fan and Mei, "Interpretation of the Maudgalyayana Murals in Cave 19 at Yulin," fig. 2.

FIG. 7.8. Maudgalyāyana and sinners in cangues, detail of wall painting. Corridor to Yulin Cave 19, tenth century. Photography: Stephen F. Teiser.

Ajaṇṭā (Maharashtra, India), that was a relatively easy command to obey, at least for caves built in the *vihāra* style, which imitated the layout of a monastery. And as I have speculated (in chapter 5), when wooden monasteries were created in Chinese cities, the porch of an Indian monastery could be translated into the outer halls of a Chinese temple. But the model of translation from a source language to a target language is too simple, because in the process of translation the target language itself—the architecture of Chinese Buddhist cave temples—was undergoing change.

Some of the earliest temples carved out of rock in China followed a style that architectural historians call the "central stūpa-pillar style" (*zhongxin tazhu shi*).[17] As seen in figure 6.2, this form left a relatively large space, with a higher ceiling, at the front of the chamber. In the rear of the chamber stood a stūpa-like structure, which enshrined a sculpted image of the Buddha and sometimes ran from floor to ceiling like a pillar. This design allowed people to gather as a group in the front of the cave and then individually to perform the act of circumambulating the stūpa at the back. It was ideally suited to public, relatively small-scale ritual events.

Another early form of cave-temple construction, seen in central Asia at Kizil and in China at Dunhuang, appears to be modeled on the *vihāra* (see fig. 7.9).[18] Small square

17. See Xiao, *Dunhuang jianzhu yanjiu*, pp. 35–42; Su, "Liangzhou shiku yiji yu 'Liangzhou moshi'"; and Soper, "Northern Liang and Northern Wei in Kansu."

18. See Xiao, *Dunhuang jianzhu yanjiu*, pp. 42–44.

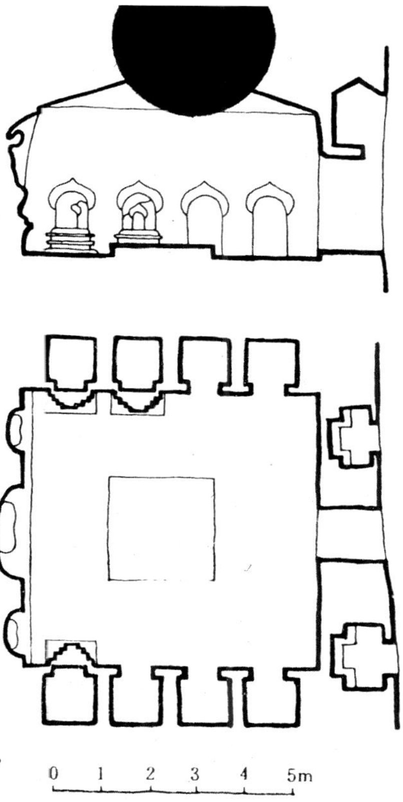

FIG. 7.9. Diagram of *vihāra* cave temples in medieval China. Mogao Cave 285, Western Wei dynasty. Xiao, *Dunhuang jianzhu yanjiu*, fig. 9-2.

rooms were arranged around the sides of a large square hall, in the center of which stood a raised platform with statues. Although such caves followed the form of the *vihāra*—originally used as a residence for monks—the small size of the rooms in Chinese *vihāra*-style caves (one meter square in most cases) indicates that no one actually lived in the side rooms. These first two styles of cave-temple design fell into disuse in China after the sixth century. They provided neither living quarters for monks nor sufficient space for the performance of large public rituals.

Two other styles took prominence in the cave temples of Hexi beginning in the Sui and Tang dynasties. The first is composed of a large room with a coffered ceiling in the shape of an inverted basket, with a raised niche on the back wall containing statues, as seen in figure 7.10.[19] The niche at the back may have been based on the positioning of Buddha halls, which in Chinese temples housed the principal images of the temple and were located near the rear of the temple compound. Similarly, the ceiling in such caves may have been an imitation of the canopies suspended above statues in temples; in some caves the wooden posts supporting actual canopies in temples are painted onto the walls of the cave. The coffered ceiling design of caves can thus be

19. See ibid., pp. 44–50.

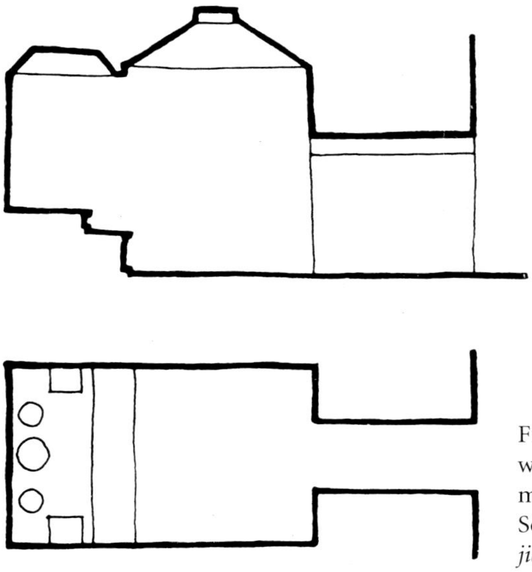

FIG. 7.10. Diagram of cave temples with coffered ceiling and niche in medieval China. Mogao Cave 326, Song dynasty. Xiao, *Dunhuang jianzhu yanjiu*, fig. 10-6.

viewed as a selective miniaturization of temples: the structure of the entire cave mimics one particular structure within the temple complex.

The other style popular beginning in the Tang was the two-chamber design. It is seen occasionally at the Mogao caves in the early Tang, and it is very important at Yulin.[20] As seen in the design of Yulin Cave 19 in figure 7.1, the main chamber is a large square with a coffered ceiling. A raised platform stands in the middle of the main chamber. Worshippers could provide offerings to the statues seated on the platform. The antechamber is typically smaller than the main chamber. The implicit ranking of the two rooms is apparent in the pictorial program as well: the main chamber usually contains paradise scenes (Amitābha's, Maitreya's, and/or Bhaiṣajyaguru's) and preaching scenes, while antechambers are decorated with guardian figures and protectors of Buddhism. Double-chambered caves at Yulin frequently have long corridors leading from the doorway into the antechamber.

At the Mogao caves the architectural equivalent of the long entry corridor may have been made of wood rather than constructed out of stone. Careful excavation of the ground in front of the cliffs at Dunhuang proves that many caves had large wooden structures functioning as entry halls, positioned in front of the cliff face, prior to the

20. Standard treatments tend to slight this style: they don't give it a separate name, and they treat it as a combination of other, more integral styles. Xiao (*Dunhuang jianzhu yanjiu*, pp. 33–55, 44–50) views it as a cross between the "antechamber" form and the "coffered-ceiling style." See also Ho, "Setting for the Faith"; idem, "The Symbolism of the Central Pillars in Cave-Temples of Northwest China"; and Steinhardt, "Early Chinese Buddhist Architecture and Its Indian Origins." Current typologies seem to be based on the idea of India as a source, central Asian sites as a conduit, and the Mogao caves as the ending point. Perhaps as sites with examples different from the Sui and Tang caves at Mogao become better known, the typology of cave temples will change too.

corridor that was cut into the cliff and that led into the stone temple. Figure 7.11 reconstructs the stone underlayment and the bases for the various pillars that supported a wooden entry hall to Mogao Cave 98, constructed during the Five Dynasties under Cao Yijin's patronage. Such wooden buildings, according to Pan Yushan and Ma Shichang, "formed an integral whole with the caves themselves. Connected front and back to the caves, the vast majority of them were equivalent to the cave's antechamber. With the rear chamber (also called the main chamber) carved out of the inside of the cliff face, the antechamber extended to the exterior of the cliff face, and wooden structures were employed in their construction. Thus, most of them took the shape of an architectural structure composed of a front hall and a rear cave."[21] Pan and Ma add that the majority of wooden antechambers at Mogaoku were constructed during the hegemony of the Cao family in Hexi, which is precisely the time when the wheel at Yulin was painted. Thus, if any of the Mogao cave temples ever did contain a painting of the wheel of rebirth, it most likely would have been located in the wooden structure serving as an antechamber to the main cave. This architectural hypothesis would also explain why so few medieval specimens of the wheel of rebirth have survived: they were positioned on the walls of wooden structures that have decayed, unlike the murals painted inside the inner chambers made of stone.

At any rate, architectural historians are quite explicit about the significance of the two-chamber design: the antechamber serves as a profane prelude to the sacred realm of the main chamber. As Xiao Mo remarks, "The cave antechamber is the transition from exterior space to the space of the cave. When people enter the realm of the Buddhas from the realm of humans, an emotional transformation occurs here."[22]

Statements made by donors of double-chambered caves lend further weight to the claim that such structures were systematically divided into two distinct realms. As noted above, the inscriptions to Yulin Cave 19 are fragmentary and do not address the architectural structure of the cave. A full statement is contained, however, in the dedication for a two-chamber cave constructed at Dunhuang in the second half of the ninth century. The dedication was written by or for the highest-ranking official in the area, Zhang Huaishen, the nephew of Zhang Yichao, who served as Military Commissioner from 872 to 892. Zhang Huaishen was the principal donor for Mogao Cave 94, constructed between 867 and 872. Like Yulin Cave 19, the Mogao cave has an antechamber and a main chamber with a coffered ceiling. Five portraits of members of the donor's family survive, but presently there are only fragments of the other original paintings and none of the medieval statues in the cave. The historical circumstances surrounding the creation of the cave can be reconstructed, however, from Dunhuang manuscripts.[23] The dedication for Mogao Cave 94 is a multivalent piece of writing. After extolling the Zhang family for bringing peace and stability to the region,

21. Translation from Pan and Ma, *Mogaoku kuqian diantang yizhi*, p. 114; see also pp. 116–20.

22. Xiao, *Dunhuang jianzhu yanjiu*, p. 35.

23. The best study is by Fujieda, "Tonkō zenbutsudō no chūkō," pp. 60–87. See also He, "Cong gongyangren tiji kan Mogaoku bufen dongku de yingjian niandai," pp. 212–13; and Tang Changru, "Guanyu guiyijun jiedu de jizhong ziliao ba."

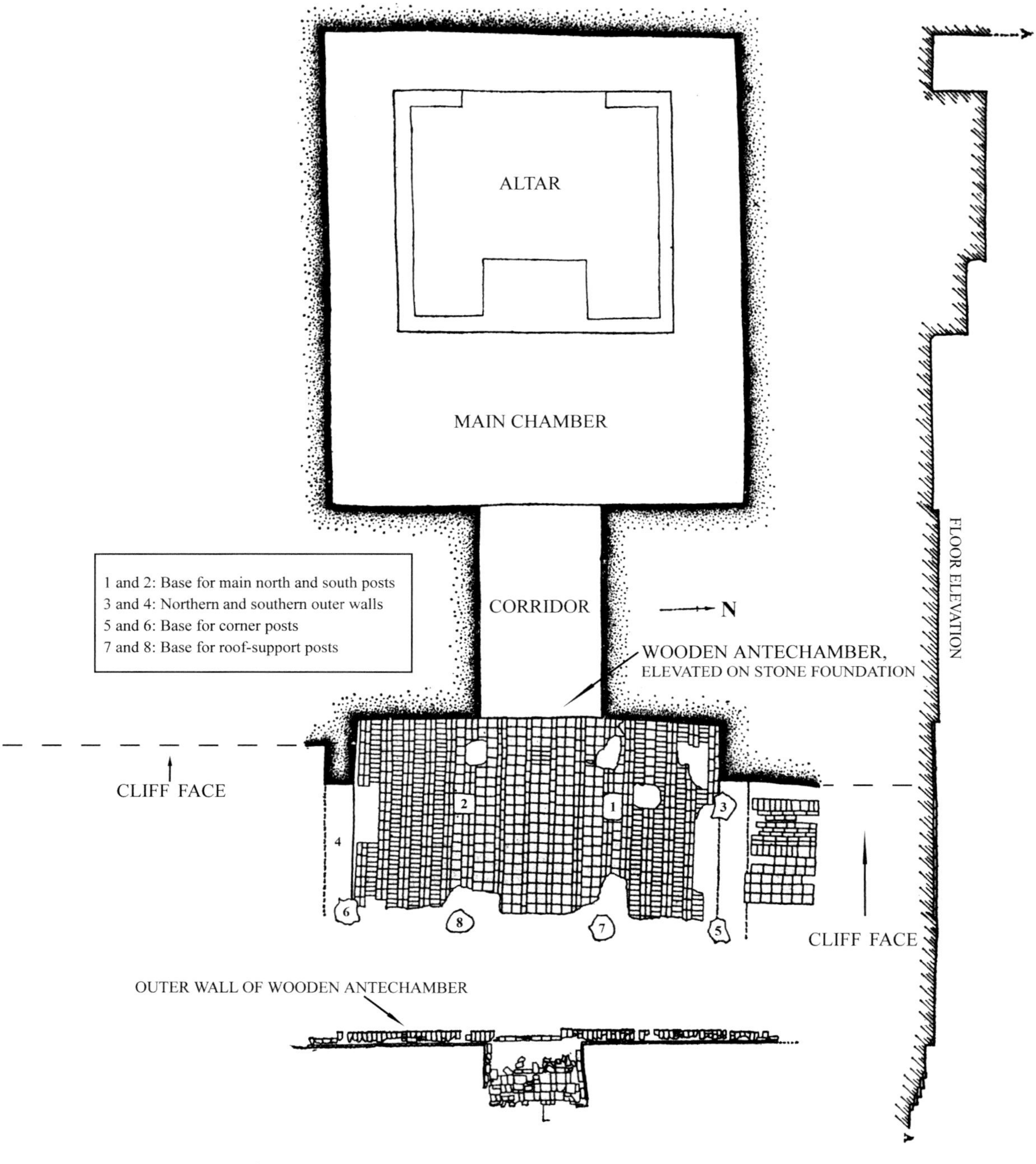

FIG. 7.11. Plan of wooden entry hall, corridor, and main chamber. Excavation plan of Mogao Cave 98, tenth century. After Pan and Ma, *Mogaoku kuqian diantang yizhi*, fig. 8.

the piece considers the repair of statues and the building of Cave 94. It mentions the cave's art, discusses the cosmological assumptions underlying the design of the cave, and invokes well-known phrases describing Chinese religious sites:[24]

> In the [main] niche are fashioned[25] an image of Śākyamuni together with a set of his disciples.[26] The four walls illustrate sixteen sets of sūtra-transformation tableaux.
>
> The Ten Thousand Images[27] are magnificently displayed, manifesting the numerous entryways provided by the traces left by the [Buddha's] transformations. The assembled phenomena return to what is truly real, uniting the Three Bodies [of the Buddha] without differentiation. Within a small square room, the transformations fill the Ten Directions. Inside one cave, the Three Realms are accommodated.
>
> The Five Colors fly along the eaves,
> The moving doors welcome the wind.
> Azure torrents flow clearly,
> Forest groves have trees of enlightenment.
>
> Elms and willows are decorated for the occasion,
> The fast has no limit.
> Monks and nuns take the tonsure,
> Lamps are carried from the Deer Park.
>
> The Seven Rare Jewels are given as donations,
> Resulting in preservation of the Three Certainties.
> The Ten Virtues are vigorously cultivated,
> Bringing the Five Blessings to completion.

This dedication begins by describing the contents of the main chamber of the cave: statues of Śākyamuni with his disciples, plus sixteen wall paintings depicting transformations of various Buddhist scriptures.[28]

In the second paragraph the dedication explains the principles used in decorating the cave. The cosmology is based on the pattern of expansion followed by contraction. The first sentence describes the multiplicity of images and the many routes to salvation depicted in the cave. The author of this dedication chooses language from

24. The dedication can be pieced together from four manuscripts, all partial: Stein nos. 6161, 3329, and 6973 and Pelliot no. 2762. For an excellent edition and Japanese translation, see Fujieda, "Tonkō zenbutsudō no chūkō," pp. 64–70, 70–73. The portion I translate is from the end of Pelliot no. 2762, transcribed in ibid., p. 69.

25. Reading *su* (simplify) as *su* (fashion), following Fujieda, "Tonkō zenbutsudō no chūkō," p. 73.

26. Reading *shicong* (events follow) as *shicong* (disciples), following ibid.

27. On Ten Thousand Images (*wanxiang*), see Morohashi, *Dai kan wa jiten*, no. 31,399.207.

28. For a tentative, complete reconstruction of the sixteen transformation tableaux and their arrangement in the cave, see Fujieda, "Tonkō zenbutsudō no chūkō," pp. 84–86.

both Buddhist and pre-Buddhist traditions to portray the process of diffusion. The Ten Thousand Images (*wanxiang*) are related to the notion of the Ten Thousand Things (*wanwu*), while "the traces left by [the Buddha's] transformations" (*huaji*) and "numerous entryways" (*duomen*) evoke Buddhist ideas of the enlightened being's willingness to incarnate himself in various bodies and to adapt his teachings to his audience. In the second sentence of this paragraph the author uses a similar mixture of vocabularies to explain that the diffusion of images is ultimately based on a more elementary, unifying principle. Here too the pattern of dispersal and congealment, the latter expressed as "returning to what is truly real" (*guizhen*), meshes perfectly with the overtly Mahāyāna notion of the nonduality or nondifference (*wuyi*) of the Three Bodies of the Buddha.[29] The third sentence could be read as making a crucial statement about the difference between the images in the main chamber and those in the antechamber. Some modern interpreters, for instance, believe that "within a small square room" (*fangzhang shinei*) is a reference to the main chamber, which contains images of pure lands and Buddha realms, while "inside one cave" (*yiku zhi zhong*) means the antechamber, filled with images of the Three Realms of no form, form, and desire.[30]

The last portion of the dedication of the Mogao cave consists of twelve short lines of four words apiece. By speaking of colors applied to the architectural elements of the cave, the first stanza seems to be about the paintings depicted on the walls of the cave. The subject seems to fit such a straightforward reading as well: scenes of water and forests are painted on the walls. On closer inspection, however, another influence appears to be working in the piece, since the author is very careful to choose words from some of the best-known poets of Chinese sacred sites. "Azure torrents" (*bijian*), for instance, was first used in a poem by Xie Lingyun (385–433), and its echoes reverberate throughout Tang poetry.[31] Through its diction, the dedication thus uses landscape poetry to link this cave to other hallowed terrain. The second stanza describes large-scale feasts and the ordination of monks and nuns, speaking as if such observances are taking place in the paintings depicting the Buddha's first sermon in the Deer Park in India. Yet here too there is another effacing of distance, since similar ceremonies would also have been performed at the inauguration of the Mogao cave. This part of the dedication connects the celebrations during the Buddha's life, pictured on the walls of the cave, to celebrations marking the creation of the cave. The third stanza

---

29. "Returning to what is truly real" (*guizhen*) as a philosophical concept predates the entry of Buddhism into China. Afterward it is used to indicate the achieving of nirvāṇa. See the entries in Zhang Qiyun, *Zhongwen dacidian*, no. 16714.136. The Three Bodies of the Buddha are the body of law (*dharmakāya*, Ch.: *fashen*), the body of response or enjoyment (*sambhogakāya*, Ch.: *baoshen*), and the body of transformation (*nirmāṇakāya*, Ch.: *huashen*).

30. See Mei, "Sibailiushijiuku yu Mogaoku shishi jingzang de fangwei tezheng"; and Fan and Mei, "Yulinku dishijiuku Mulian bianxiang kaoshi," p. 53, the latter of which states, "The antechamber symbolizes the Three Realms, and the rear chamber symbolizes the realms of the Buddhas of the Ten Directions."

31. For the use of the expression in poems by Chu Guangxi, Wang Wei, Du Fu, and others, see Zhang Yushu, *Peiwen yunfu*, p. 3021b.

invokes four different numerical categories, all as a way of explaining the idea of donation. Seven Rare Jewels (*qizhen*) are presumably the Seven Jewels (Skt.: *saptaratna*, Ch.: *qibao*), gifts that only wealthy donors and kings can afford: gold, silver, lapis lazuli, crystal, agate, ruby, and cornelian. The Three Certainties (*sanjian*), having to do with health, longevity, and wealth,[32] are the benefits derived from making gifts of such value. The Ten Virtues are the keeping of the Ten Precepts for advanced lay practitioners of Buddhism: abstention from killing, stealing, adultery, lying, double-tongue, coarse language, filthy language, covetousness, anger, and perverted views. Cultivation of the virtues leads to the Five Blessings of longevity, wealth, high position, good health, and many progeny.[33] The language of merit making is the substratum of Chinese Buddhist practice and pervades much of Buddhist liturgical writing. By ending on such a note, the dedication brings closure to the charitable act noted at the beginning of the piece. The fashioning of images is an act requiring piety and resources. The cave spreads the message of Buddhism, and creating a cave redounds to the benefit of its commissioner. As a whole, then, the lines at the end of the dedication suggest that the cave is worthy of poetic allusion, that it deserves to be placed in the tradition of refined writing about holy places, and that its construction is a sign of both great distinction and, in the Buddhist scheme of things, calculable merit

I would like to turn from the significance of two-chambered caves at Mogao to a fuller interpretation of the wheel of rebirth in a two-chambered cave at Yulin. Patrons of double-chamber caves viewed them as marking off a dualism: the main room contains scenes of purity and paradise, while the antechamber portrays the unclean space of birth, death, and rebirth. One is beyond impurity, transformed by the Buddhas, while the other is positioned within the desire-filled realm of form. This structuralist reading of cave design works well for Yulin Cave 19, which has a main chamber depicting paradise and transcendence and an antechamber containing lower-ranking guardians who help prepare the way.

How do we make sense, then, of the placement of the wheel of rebirth, not in the antechamber, but in the corridor *before* the antechamber? Following the logic above, what is important about the structure of the cave is the way that it mediates an opposition between rebirth and paradise, between a world close to hand and a world beyond. The wheel of rebirth in the corridor teaches about desire, rebirth, suffering, and salvation as a prelude to the realms of purity that lay farther within the cave. To put it in terms of an analogy, corridor:entire cave::antechamber:main chamber::rebirth:paradise. The relationship between the corridor and the entire cave is the same as the relationship between the antechamber and the main chamber, which is again equivalent to the relationship between rebirth and paradise. The same homology exists in the design of wooden temples, in which front halls stand in opposition to Buddha halls.

32. *Sanjianfa* are mentioned in the *Vimalakīrti Sūtra*; see *Weimojie suoshuo jing* (*Vimalakīrti nirdeśa*), trans. Kumārajīva (Jiumoluoshi, 350–409), *T* no. 475, 14:543c.

33. For the Five Blessings (*wufu*), I follow the listing in the *Tongsu bian*; see Zhang Qiyun, *Zhongwen dacidian*, 262.943.

At Yulin, then, the wheel of rebirth is located in the passageway leading to paradise, a perfect realm at once pictured on the walls and invoked for the visitor. Placed physically on the outside of the sacred space, the wheel is nevertheless connected to that space. The wheel of rebirth and the pictures of Maudgalyāyana are a way of loosely paraphrasing the canonical account of the creation of the wheel. They are a narrative prelude to the act of worshipping the Buddha and encountering his pure realm in the center of the cave.

Chapter 8

Wheels in Esoteric Temples

Tabo, Western Tibet, Eleventh Century

Beginning in the late tenth century and continuing into the eleventh, the ruling family in the ancient kingdom of western Tibet commissioned a large temple made of wood and sundried brick whose entry hall contains a wall painting of the wheel of rebirth. Their state spanned the region now controlled by Pakistan to the far west, the Indian principalities of Kashmir, Ladakh, and Himachal Pradesh to the south, and the Tibetan People's Autonomous Region of China to the east. The painting at the main temple (*gtsug-lag-khang*, pron.: *tsuklak khang*) in the town of Tabo (also called Ta-po, Ta-pho, and rTa-pho in early Tibetan sources) is the earliest known example of the saṃsāracakra serving as a preface to a maṇḍala. Like the wheel of rebirth at Yulin, the painting at Tabo is positioned in an introductory space, an entry hall, external and prior to a larger, more sacred space where the ritual is consummated. The specific ritual followed at Tabo is defined by the maṇḍala, a complex palace-cum-cosmos containing all the deities of the Vajradhātu (Diamond Realm), in the assembly hall. The practitioner progresses through the various subchambers of the palace in order to merge with the primary deity inhabiting its center, Vairocana Buddha. At Tabo, the painting of the wheel of birth and death prepares the believer for the performance of Tantric ritual. Further clues to the meaning of the pictorial program of the temple are contained in the story of its founding by kings, highly placed monks, and prominent local families, as well as in art, architecture, inscriptions, and later Tibetan chronicles.

Although the geography of western Tibet has not changed much over the past one thousand years, the political and cultural contours of the area then were somewhat different than they are now (map 8).[1] Defined largely by the valley carved by the Spiti

1. For the early history of western Tibet, I rely especially on Petech, "Western Tibet: Historical Introduction." Some of the primary sources are available in Snellgrove and Skorupski, *Cultural Heritage of Ladakh*, 2:83–116; Obermiller, *History of Buddhism (Chos-hbyung) by Bu-ston*, 2:201–14; Sørensen, *Tibetan Buddhist Historiography*, pp. 451–58; Roerich, *Blue Annals*, pp. 68–74; Stein, *Une chronique ancienne de bSam-yas*; Samten Karmay, "The Ordinance of lHa Bla-ma Ye-shes-'od"; and Vitali, *Kingdoms of Gu.ge Pu.hrang*, pp. 143–49. For secondary studies, see also Beckwith, *Tibetan*

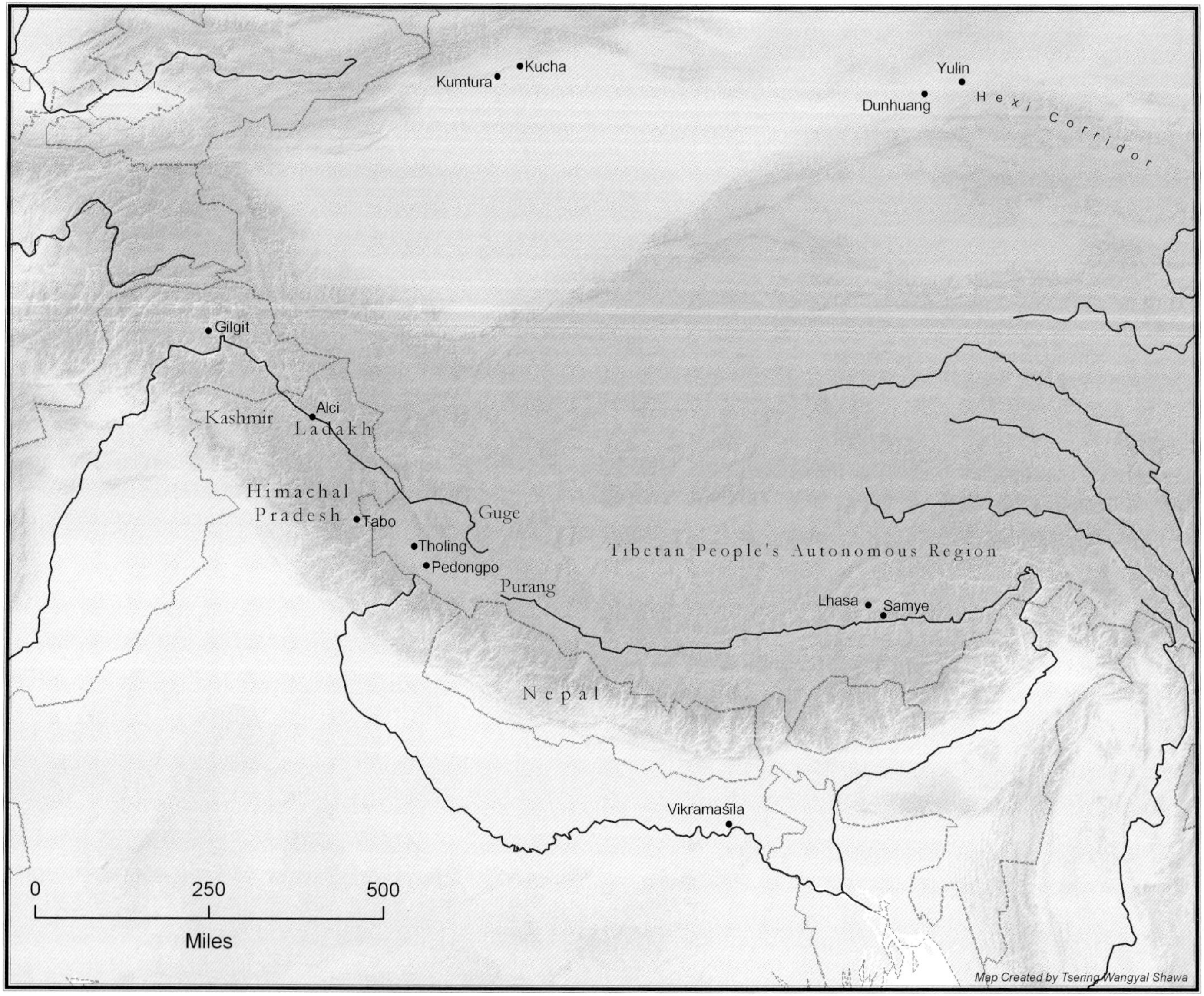

MAP 8. Western Tibet, eleventh century.

River, the general area of Tabo is situated near the northwestern tip of the Himalayan range, which was formed some fifty million years ago after what is now the Indian subcontinent broke free of Australia, Antarctica, and Africa, drifted north, and rammed against the southern edge of Eurasia. At an altitude of roughly 10,600 feet, the Spiti and surrounding river valleys support subsistence agriculture (mostly barley) and nomadic pastoralism. The Spiti Valley had originally been home to an indigenous, probably non-Tibetan group of people later known as the Zhang-zhung. They maintained political ties with the courts of both China and central Tibet, and they were essentially annexed by the latter by the beginning of the seventh century. Some forms of Buddhism, as yet unknown, were trickling into the area by the middle of the seventh century, funneling through China and central Asia. The famous legend of the conversion of the Tibetan king Srong-btsan-sgam-po (pron.: Songtsen Gampo, d. 649) to Buddhism is no doubt a later fabrication, but some of its themes do reflect seventh-century trends. According to the story, two wives were given to the king to further political alliances: one was Nepali, the other Chinese. The devotion of his Chinese wife (or, in other accounts, his Nepalese wife) to Buddhism made such an impression on him that he took refuge in the Three Jewels and initiated a broad program of state support for Buddhism, much amplified in later sources. The pro-Buddhist policies of one of his successors, Khri Srong-lde'u-btsan (pron.: Trisong Detsen, 756–797?), are better documented. The latter king founded the famous bSam-yas (pron.: Samye) monastery (central Tibet) in the 770s and established Buddhism as the state religion in 779. He organized many teams of translators, sponsored visits by the monk Śāntarakṣita (Zhi-ba-'tsho) and the translator Padmasambhava (Padma-'byung-gnas), and presided over the debate between Kamalaśīla and the Chinese monk Moheyan. The eighth century and the first part of the ninth century marked the height of the Tibetan empire, as Tibetan armies rode victoriously across all of central Asia, stretching as far east as Gansu in China and as far west as Samarkand. Buddhism provided not only an all-encompassing worldview but also a well-trained literate elite, a system of scholarship, and a ritual technology that played an integral role in empire building. In western Tibet the Buddhism of the period was based on the veneration

---

Empire in Central Asia; Francke, *Antiquities of Indian Tibet*, 2:167–71; Heller, "Eighth- and Ninth-Century Temples and Rock-Carvings of Eastern Tibet"; Kapstein, *Tibetan Assimilation of Buddhism*, esp. pp. 23–65; Heather Karmay, *Early Sino-Tibetan Art*, pp. 1–34; Samten Karmay, "A Discussion on the Doctrinal Position of rDzogs-chen"; Klimburg-Salter, *Silk Route and the Diamond Path*, esp. pp. 152–68; Luczanits, "Another Rin chen bzan po Temple?"; Pal, *A Buddhist Paradise*; idem, *On the Path to the Void*; Rhie, "Tibetan Painting: Styles, Sources, and Schools," esp. pp. 45–51; Richardson, "Monuments of the Yarlung Dynasty"; Scherrer-Schaub, "Was Byang chub sems dpa' a Posthumous Title of King Ye śes 'od?"; Singer, "Painting in Central Tibet, ca. 950–1400"; Snellgrove, "Buddhism in North India and the Western Himalayas"; Snellgrove and Skorupski, *Cultural Heritage of Ladakh*, 1:1–18, 2:9–14, 37–43; Stoddard, "Early Tibetan Paintings"; Thakur, *Buddhism in the Western Himalaya*, pp. 20–58; idem, "Earliest Tibetan Inscription from Tabo"; idem, "Nako Monastery"; Tucci, *Religions of Tibet*, pp. 16–23; idem, *Rin c'en bzan po e la rinascita del Buddhismo nel Tibet*; idem, *Temples of Western Tibet and Their Artistic Symbolism*, pp. 5–20; Vitali, *Early Temples of Central Tibet*, pp. 37–68; idem, *Kingdoms of Gu.ge Pu.hrang*, pp. 171–333; and idem, *Records of Tho.Ling*.

of Buddhas, bodhisattvas, and gods; belief in karmic retribution and merit making; doctrines ranging from the Four Noble Truths to the teachings of the Mādhyamika philosopher Nāgārjuna and early Tantric texts; state-mandated support for monasteries by neighboring farms; and the possession of large tracts of land by Buddhist institutions. The formation of a Buddhism local to western Tibet took place through contact with Buddhist cultures coming from what is now India and Nepal, from farther west in Gilgit (Pakistan), from the various oasis cities of the Silk Road, and from China.

The decline of the higher-profile forms of Buddhism began with the destruction of Buddhist institutions under King Glang Dar-ma (pron.: Lang Darma, d. 842), coinciding with the breakup of the larger Tibetan empire. Although Buddhism in many communities certainly survived over the next few centuries, Tibetan political theology portrays the period as a dark age. In this view, the growth of a new line of kings in western Tibet at the end of the tenth century constituted the foundation for a renaissance of Buddhism as a whole, known as the "later spread of the teaching" (*bstan-pa phyi-dar*, pron.: *tenpa chidar*). It is at this point in the history of western Tibet that the temple at Tabo enters the story. The plot, explained below, involves the pairing of royal brothers as rulers and renouncers, the construction of temple complexes, the translation of texts from Sanskrit into Tibetan, and the constant reclaiming of connections, via art, texts, and monks, to what was perceived as the normative Buddhist traditions of India.

The capital of the new dynasty in western Tibet was first located in Purang, at the eastern edge of the region (with Tabo, in the Spiti Valley, at the western end—see map 8); in later centuries it was shifted westward to Guge. The first king of Purang, bKra-shis-mgon (pron.: Tashi Gön), probably reigned from 950 to 975 (see table 5). The founding of the temple at Tabo is associated with his two sons, 'Khor-re (pron.: Khoré, ca. 959–1036?, r. 975–985?) and Srong-nge (pron.: Song Ngé, r. 985–1000?). The elder son ruled first and had two sons, Na-ga ra-tsa (Nāgarāja) and Dhe-ba ra-tsa (Devarāja). After holding the throne for some ten years, around 985 'Khor-re abdicated in favor of his younger brother and joined the Buddhist Saṃgha. He retired only partly, taking the Dharma name of Ye-shes-'od (pron.: Yeshé Ö; Skt.: Jñānaprabha), by which he is known in later Buddhist sources, and concentrating his efforts on the support of institutionalized Buddhism. He supervised monasteries, regulated Buddhist activities, and sponsored the building of many temples and smaller shrines throughout the empire. One such temple was the complex at Tabo, first erected in the year 996. The earliest building in the main temple at Tabo is the entry hall, which, in addition to the painting of the saṃsāracakra, contains portraits of the founder/ex-king/monk, Ye-shes-'od, plus his two sons (see fig. 8.1), discussed in more detail below.

As part of their efforts to rebuild Buddhism in the area, Ye-shes-'od and his brother sought to reinforce their connections to Buddhist traditions then practiced in Kashmir and the other kingdoms of northern India. One method was to sponsor the visit of Indian Buddhist authorities. They tried this at first, but the effort allegedly failed because there lacked translators capable of understanding Indian dialects. To redress

Table 5. Early kings of western Tibet, tenth through twelfth centuries. Data from Petech, "Western Tibet: Historical Introduction." D.n. = Dharma name.

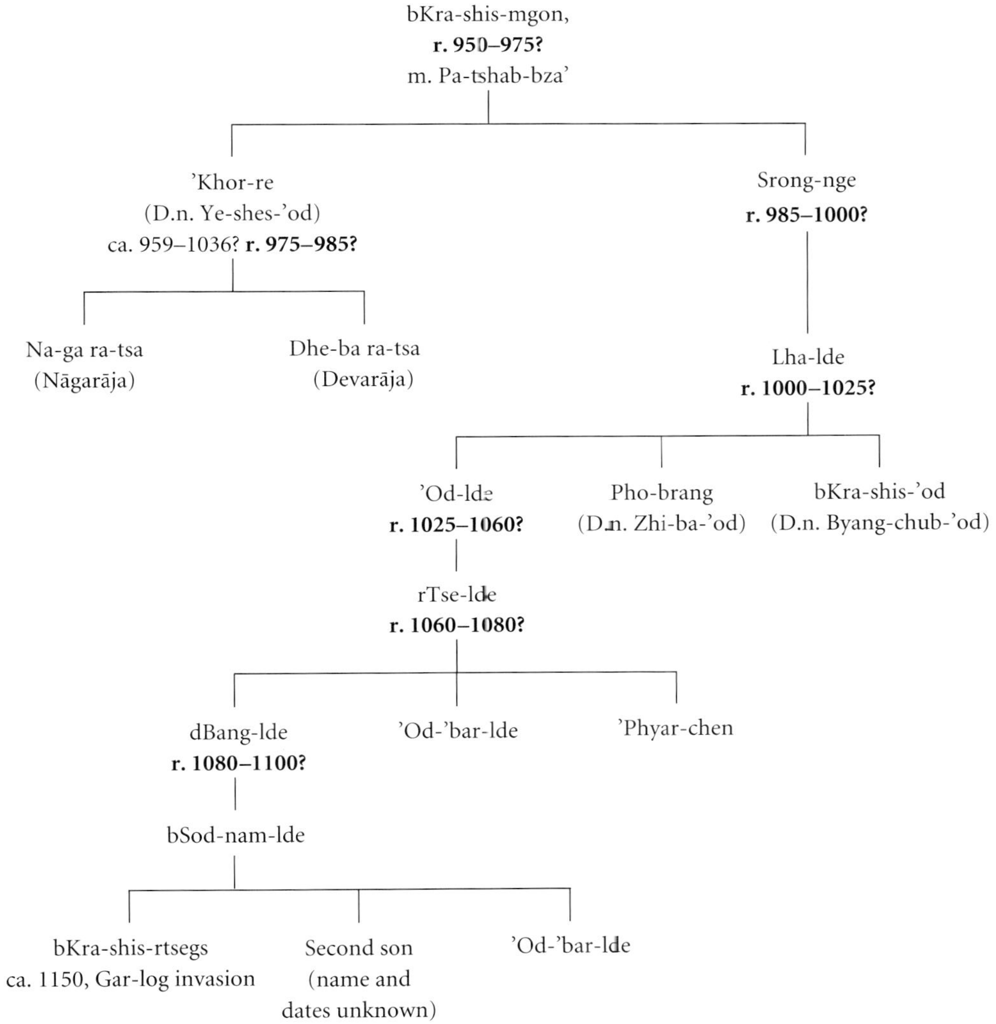

the problems of intercultural exchange, Ye-shes-'od and his brother dispatched a group of twenty-one local men to Kashmir to be trained as translators (*lo-tsā-ba*, pron.: *lotsāwa*). Only two were successful; one of them, Rin-chen-bzang-po (pron.: Rinchen Zangpo, 958–1055?) from Guge, would become one of the most important figures in western Tibetan Buddhism.

Rin-chen-bzang-po's biography invests him with preternatural abilities in foreign languages: at the age of two he was moved to chant the Sanskrit alphabet, write Sanskrit letters on the ground, and ask for instruction. At the age of seventeen, according to the same account, he dreamt of a woman who spoke to him:

Fig. 8.1. Ye-shes-'od and his son Devarāja. Wall painting. Entry hall, Tabo main temple, eleventh century. Courtesy of Christian Luczanits, 1991, Western Himalaya Archive Vienna.

Whoever wants bliss and salvation goes to the northern lands of Kashmir,
Obtaining joy in translating into Tibetan the oceans of holy scripture,
Which spread like a flood over India from east to west.[2]

Rin-chen-bzang-po trained in monasteries in Kashmir and eastern India for thirteen years, returning to Purang via Guge. By this time the throne had passed from Ye-shes-'od's brother to his brother's son, Lha-lde (pron.: Lhadé, r. 1000–1025?). Lha-lde and Ye-shes-'od gave tremendous support to Rin-chen-bzang-po's activities and granted him high status in the monastic order. Rin-chen-bzang-po oversaw the construction of many new Buddhist complexes, allegedly numbering 108. These included the royal shrine in Purang, the main temple at Khar-char (pron.: Kharchar; Khojarnath in the Purang region), the main temple of mTho-lding (pron.: Thoding; Tholing in the Guge region), and Nyar-ma (pron.: Nyarma) in Mar-yul (pron.: Maryül; Ladakh). After ranging across the entire western half of the Himalayan plateau, Rin-chen-bzang-po returned to Kashmir. The purpose of this second mission was to obtain Indian texts and bring back artists and craftsmen. Judging by the number of Indian originals he later rendered into Tibetan (161 separate works), his retrieval and transmission of texts were a grand success.[3] Together with his venerable Kashmiri teacher, Śraddhākar-

2. Translated in Snellgrove and Skorupski, *Cultural Heritage of Ladakh*, 2:87.

3. See the list in Tucci, *Rin c'en bzan po e la rinascita del Buddhismo nel Tibet*, pp. 40–45; rearranged in Handa, *Tabo Monastery and Buddhism in the Trans-Himalaya*, pp. 134–41.

avarman, he translated a variety of Buddhist texts, including key tantras (ritual texts) prescribing rites and maṇḍalas dedicated to Vairocana Buddha, Akṣobhya Buddha, and others; sūtras and commentaries on the perfection of wisdom (*prajñāpāramitā*); later Indian Mahāyāna sūtras and commentaries; and meditation texts. He took part in a wide range of religious activities, including an Amitāyus maṇḍala to cure his mother's illness, memorial rites for his father, exorcisms, and various Tantric rites intended to vanquish local gods and goddesses. On the artistic front Rin-chen-bzang-po made great progress as well, establishing a host of smaller chapels near Tabo. He was probably closely involved in the renovation of the assembly hall of the main temple at Tabo, which occurred in 1042 (described in detail, below).

The other major actor in the renovation of the assembly hall of the main temple at Tabo was one of the sons of King Lha-lde. Lha-lde had three sons, grandnephews of Ye-shes-'od, who had died around the year 1036. The oldest, 'Od-lde (pron.: Odé), reigned after his father, from about 1025 to 1060. The youngest, bKra-shis-'od (pron.: Tashi Ö), entered the monkhood and took the Dharma name of Byang-chub-'od (pron.: Changchup Ö). The inscription written to commemorate the Assembly Hall names this third son (three times) as the donor of the renovation work. It also cites Ye-shes-'od as the original founder of the whole temple.[4]

One other important historical personage who might be linked to the early years of Tabo is Atiśa (Jo-bo-rje, 982–1054), otherwise known as Dīpaṃkara Śrījñāna. Atiśa studied in Java (Indonesia) and later gained fame as a teacher at the monastic center in Vikramaśīla (Bengal in eastern India). Invited by Byang-chub-'od, he traveled to Purang by way of Nepal and beginning in 1042 stayed in western Tibet for three years, mostly at mTho-lding. Some scholars speculate that his visit to the area was the occasion for the renovation of part of the Tabo temple in 1042.[5] Atiśa's influence over the development of Indian and Tibetan Buddhism was undoubtedly strong. He supplied the impetus and the know-how for a massive translation effort. His emphasis on the priority of the teacher's interpretation over the literal meaning of the scriptures would have a lasting impact on later Tibetan religion. Nevertheless, many of the major trends in the Buddhism of western Tibet during this period had been established in the preceding centuries. Most of the important temple complexes in western Tibet were founded during the reign of this line of kings. The dynasty included at least eight generations, beginning with bKra-shis-mgon and ending with bKra-shis-rtsegs (pron.: Tashi Tsek), who was probably king when the area was invaded by the powerful Gar-log (pron.: Garlok) around 1150. This era saw the maturation of a new administrative system marked by a symbiosis of secular and sacred power. Kings abdicated the throne in favor of their brothers, received ordination as monks, and then continued as even stronger patrons, perhaps, of the empirewide rebuilding of Buddhist establishments. In any one royal generation, the eldest son held the position of king and his younger brothers were ordained as monks. Tantric models of ritual were combined with earlier

4. See Steinkellner and Luczanits, "New Translation of the Renovation Inscription," p. 258, parts of which are discussed later in this chapter.

5. Klimburg-Salter, *Tabo: A Lamp for the Kingdom*, p. 18.

forms of Buddhist practice. And accommodations were sought at the local level between the religious beliefs of the native place and those of outlying areas, a process in which traditions rooted in India were accorded the highest prestige.

The painting of the wheel of rebirth at Tabo needs to be understood also within the context of Tantric ritual. The wheel is located in the entry hall (*sgo-khang*, pron.: *gokhang*) that precedes the major assembly hall (*'du-khang*, pron.: *dukhang*), cella (*dri-gtsang-khang*, pron.: *dritsang khang*), and ambulatory (*skor-lam*, pron.: *korlam*), as seen in figure 8.2. (My analysis is confined to the earlier buildings, ignoring the additions to the complex erected after the eleventh century.) Below I interpret the painting of the wheel of life and death as a multivalent preface to the Tantric practices in the other rooms of the temple. Hence, I begin in the center and work outward, discussing the artwork in the center and rear of the temple before analyzing the wheel of rebirth located at the front of the temple.[6]

At Tabo, religious significance follows size: the assembly hall is the largest room in the main temple, and its art constitutes the ritual center of the complex as a whole. In fact, the hall possesses not one but five (or more) liturgical programs. The most important ritual was based on the placement of thirty-three painted statues of Buddhas and bodhisattvas around the perimeter of the hall (see fig. 8.3). Thirty-two nearly life-size painted statues are affixed to the wall, hovering in space just above eye level. The thirty-third statue is the true center of the hall (see fig. 8.4). Situated near the back of the hall, this statue of Mahāvairocana Buddha is four-bodied, so that the viewer always faces one entire deity and vice versa. The Great Vairocana is larger than the other statues. In this context Vairocana is the supreme Buddha, ensconced in his palace at the center of the world. Surrounding him in the four corners of the room are four groups, in each of which seven bodhisattvas revolve around a key Buddha: Akṣobhya, Ratnasambhava, Amitābha, and Amoghasiddhi (see fig. 8.2). As sculptural forms, the images of the deities are alike in having smooth faces and torsos, rounded cheeks, dimpled chins, broad shoulders, and narrow waists. Yet each can also be distinguished on the basis of its placement, size, color, *mudrā*, and vehicle.

Who are the thirty-three deities, and what is their significance? Following Giuseppe Tucci's early suggestion and its recent refinement by Deborah Klimburg-Salter and others, these thirty-three figures constitute a version of one of the most important cosmic maps (maṇḍalas) in the ritual repertoire of early Tantric Buddhism, the Vajradhātu maṇḍala (Diamond Realm maṇḍala), with Vairocana Buddha at its center. As Tucci remarks:

---

6. For most of my description and analysis of the art and architecture of Tabo, even when I disagree with her on minor points of interpretation, I rely on the masterpiece by Klimburg-Salter, *Tabo: A Lamp for the Kingdom*. I am much indebted to her and to Christian Luczanits for generous help and advice. For other treatments of the Tabo main temple, see Deshpande, "Buddhist Art of Ajanta and Tabo," pp. 37–39; Khosla, *Buddhist Monasteries in the Western Himalaya*, pp. 37–48; Francke, *Antiquites of Indian Tibet*, 1:36–43; Luczanits, *Buddhist Sculpture in Clay*, pp. 35–56; Pritzker, "Tabo Monastery"; idem, "The Wall Paintings in the Dukhang of Tabo"; Singhal, "Identification of Sculptures in the Central Hall of the Tabo Monastery"; Thakur, *Buddhism in the Western Himalaya*; Tucci, *Temples of Western Tibet*, pp. 21–90.

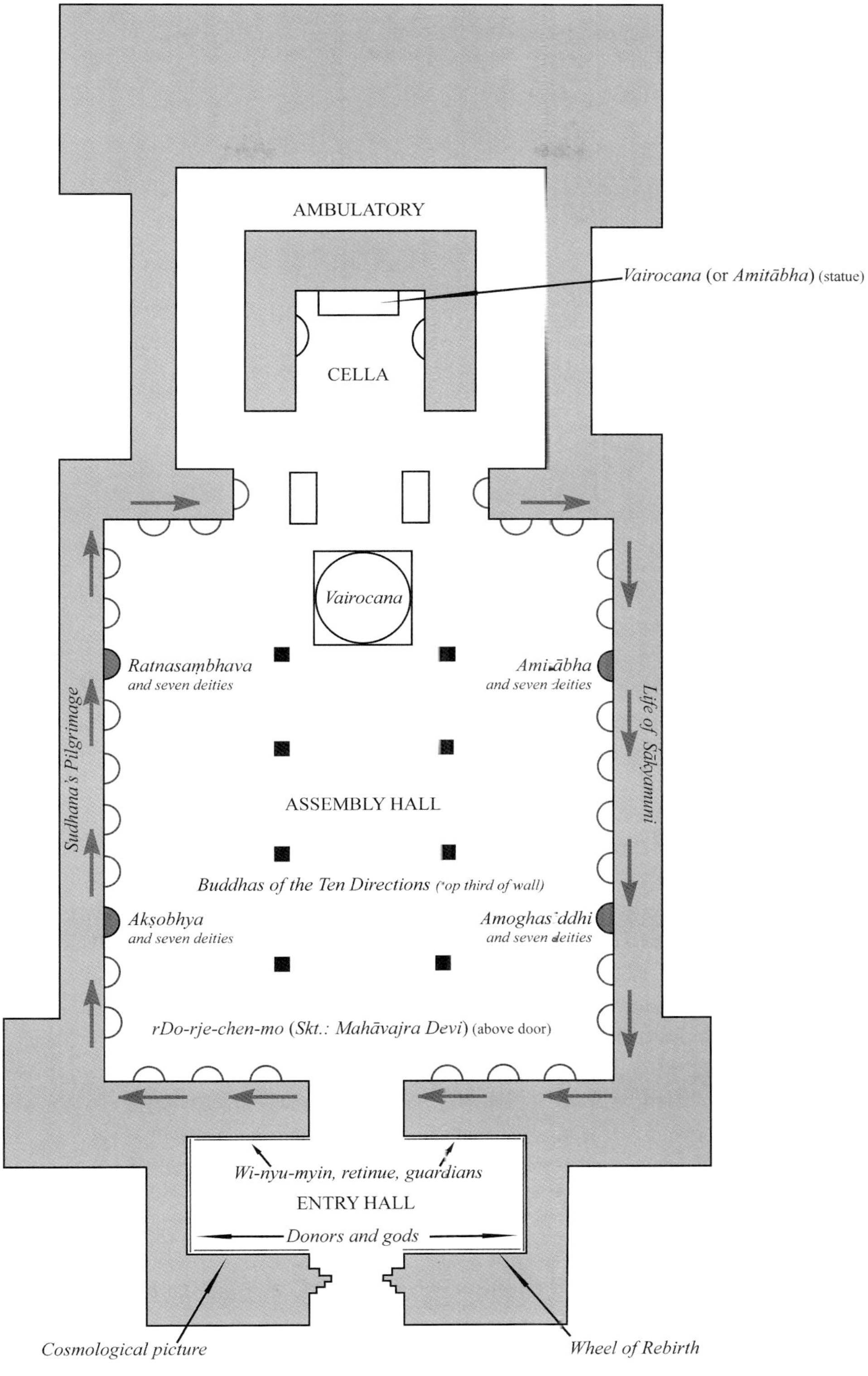

FIG. 8.2. Iconographic program of main temple, Tabo. After Thakur, *Buddhism in the Western Himalaya*, p. 66, fig. 6.

FIG. 8.3. Deities of the Vajradhātu maṇḍala. Wall painting. Assembly hall, Tabo main temple, eleventh century. Photo courtesy of Jaroslav Poncar, 1984.

> In the temple of Tabo we see thus, the plastic reflection, so to speak, of the mystical experiences predominant in Western Tibet at the time of Rin-chen-bzang-po; the *gtsug-lag-khang* [main temple] was almost the architectonic correlation of the translation of the sacred texts which the Lotsāba [translator, i.e., Rin-chen-bzang-po] had led to completion by transplanting in his own country and amongst his people some of the methods of realization of the deepest spiritual experiences of India; in other words the ideal and religious motive which inspired the foundation of the temple must be sought within the doctrines for initiation expressed and symbolized in the *Tattva-saṃgraha* and in the Tantric literature related to it.[7]

I aim to show that Tucci's reading is correct. The source he cites is the early Indian text known as *Sarvatathāgata-tattva-saṃgraha*.[8] According to Tucci, the major

7. Tucci, *Temples of Western Tibet*, p. 39.

8. On the Sanskrit and Tibetan versions of the text, see Chandra, *Sarva-Tathāgata-Tattva-Sangraha*; Snellgrove, introduction to Snellgrove and Chandra, *Sarva-Tathāgata-Tattva-Saṅgraha*; and, with caution, Shashibala, *Comparative Iconography of the Vajradhātu-Mandala*, pp. 50–102. On the Chinese translations, see Iyanagi, "Récits de la soumission de Maheśvara," pp. 656–57.

FIG. 8.4. Mahāvairocana. Statue. Assembly hall, Tabo main temple, eleventh century. Photo courtesy of Jaroslav Poncar, 1984.

maṇḍala in this text, which Rin-chen-bzang-po translated into Tibetan, is the model for the layout of the thirty-three deities in the assembly hall. The same maṇḍala is also represented four times in the gSum-brtsegs (pron.: Sum Tsek) temple at A-lci (pron.: Achi) and in painted and sculpted forms throughout the region in temples built between the eleventh and thirteenth centuries. Tucci's broader point is that the assembly hall is itself the maṇḍala, in architectural form. A maṇḍala is a three-dimensional cosmic palace with deities residing in its various compartments. And the purpose of any maṇḍala, as Tucci insists throughout his work, is to conduct the practitioner in a structured fashion through the realms of the cosmos to achieve, ultimately, mystical identification with the major deity, in this case Vairocana Buddha.[9] As a liturgical space, the assembly hall organizes a dazzling array of painted sculpture that leads the visitor through the houses of the various deities before arriving at the center of the world.

Tucci may have tended to wrap his interpretation of Tantric meditation and the practice of the maṇḍala too much in the language of Jungian psychoanalysis. There can be no doubt, however, that the maṇḍala practiced at Tabo was a ritual and artistic program culminating in union with the deity. When Ye-shes-'od's grandnephew undertook the renovation of the temple and rebuilt the assembly hall in 1042, he had a long prayer inscribed in the cella. The dedication is a formal genre that has an important ritual function in Buddhism. It names the original commissioner of the temple (Ye-shes-'od) as well as its renovators, glorifying their actions. The words of the vow also act to transfer the merit created by the renovation of the temple. Like many dedications in the world of Buddhist texts, artwork, and architecture, the piece grants three wishes—three boons or results the donors hoped would be achieved through their contributions. The first is that the principal donor be set on the bodhisattva path and eventually achieve highest enlightenment. The second benefit is supposed to accrue to anyone who visits the temple. By viewing or coming into contact with the Buddhas and bodhisattvas in the maṇḍala and hearing them preach the Dharma, such a person is ultimately supposed to be able to merge herself or himself with them. As the dedication states, "May also all the visitors who see or touch all these many painted images of the Lords of [the five kinds of] Existence, the Sugatas [those who have gone the right way, i.e., Buddhas] together with their sons . . . after seeing in person the Sugatas of the good age and their sons, and hearing the best teaching identify [their] minds with . . . the guides who rescue all living beings from the ocean of saṃsāra!"[10] The third wish is designed to harness the merit created by the second wish (giving benefits to all who visit the temple) and bestow it upon anyone connected to the restoration of the temple. In the language of the dedication, the beneficiaries should be transported from a house filled with woe to "the excellent house, the house of the thought of truth."

9. According to Tucci (*Theory and Practice of the Mandala*, p. vii), the purpose of the maṇḍala, as a "psycho-cosmogram," is to "lead the neophyte, by revealing to him the secret play of the forces which operate in the universe and in us, on the way to the reintegration of consciousness."

10. Steinkellner and Luczanits, "New Translation of the Renovation Inscription," p. 258. Ernst Steinkellner and Christian Luczanits propose the word "identify" in their translation as uncertain and put it in italics. The ellipses represent effaced portions of the inscription.

Unlike the sculptures of the thirty-two deities, the second and third liturgical programs are two-dimensional paintings on the walls of the assembly hall. They are scenes of the pilgrimage of Sudhana (Tib.: Nor-bzang) and episodes from the life of the Buddha, respectively. The former follow the basic plot of Sudhana's journey toward enlightenment as recounted in the *Gaṇḍavyūha Sūtra*, which constitutes the last, longest portion of *The Flower Garland Scripture* (*Avataṃsaka Sūtra*). During his quest, Sudhana encounters fifty-four mentors (*kalyāṇamitras*), most of whom offer lessons and demonstrate wonders to the spiritual seeker. As Jan Fontein has suggested, Sudhana's teachers play a variety of roles:

> The *kalyāṇamitras* sometimes lift a corner of the veil and allow Sudhana a glimpse of these Buddha-*kṣetras* [Buddha-fields] and the resplendent holy figures residing in them. They also explain how they accumulated wisdom and virtue by paying homage to innumerable Tathāgata in their precedent births and how the working of the karmic law in their own chain of successive rebirths as virtuous and pious men and women resulted in their present stage of advanced spiritual attainments. . . . The *kalyāṇamitras* are not only there for the specific purpose of instructing the pilgrim Sudhana, they too are cogs in the wheels of the immense and inexorable machinery of the karmic law.[11]

As shown in figure 8.2, the scenes begin after one enters the assembly hall on the left (east) wall, continue clockwise along the south wall, and end just before the doorway in the west wall leading into the cella. By following this semicircumambulation, the viewer traverses the same path as Sudhana, beginning with his encounter with Mañjuśrī and ending with the completion of the bodhisattva career in the presence of Samantabhadra. These scenes are accompanied by extracts from the Tibetan version of the *Gaṇḍavyūha Sūtra*, which are painted in large blocks next to the corresponding scenes. According to Ernst Steinkellner, the selection of written texts inscribed on the wall is significant. Just as the painter chose a particular style and specific portions of the pilgrimage to portray visually, the designer of the cave also made a conscious choice to shorten but not otherwise change the cited passages.[12] By clothing most of the characters in eleventh-century Tibetan garb, the painter seems to be saying that you—that is, the eleventh-century western Himalayan pilgrim—can become a bodhisattva too, just like Sudhana. In Steinkellner's analysis, the inscriber of the textual story attempts to prove the authenticity of the painting's claim by quoting the words of the Buddha. For Steinkellner, the "authenticating wall text" is evidence that the accompanying pictorial program carries canonical authority.

The third pictorial program commences on the first open wall space after the preceding program ends. The first picture depicts the soon-to-be Buddha in Tuṣita Heaven,

---

11. Fontein, *Pilgrimage of Sudhana*, p. 22, capitalization modified.

12. See Steinkellner, "Notes on the Function of Two 11th Century Inscriptional Sūtra Texts in Tabo"; and idem, *Sudhana's Miraculous Journey in the Temple of Ta pho*.

the perch from which the bodhisattva enters rebirth on the continent of Jambudvīpa to begin his final incarnation as a Buddha. The majority of the scenes, continuing back toward the entrance on the north wall, deal with Śākyamuni's birth and early years. The final scenes, painted on the east wall just before the entry, depict the *parinirvāṇa* of the Buddha and the distribution and honoring of his relics by the kings of India. It is entirely fitting that the Śākyamuni cycle picks up where the Sudhana cycle ends. The visitor to Tabo first follows the quest of Sudhana, ending with his entry into bodhisattvahood. Then the visitor follows the progress of the most recent bodhisattva in history, Śākyamuni, who moves from the status of bodhisattva to that of a fully enlightened being.

The fourth and fifth ritual programs, in my reading of the assembly hall, amount to two different ways of orienting the temple as a whole. The fourth program is painted along the top third of the two long, uninterrupted walls (north and south). It depicts the Buddhas of the Ten Directions, each attended by two bodhisattvas.[13] In Mahāyāna thought, every Buddha presides over his own Buddha-field or pure land. Although in theory Buddhas are infinite in number, their omnipresence throughout the conceivable world is often symbolized in finite terms by placing them in the ten directions: north, east, south, and west, plus northeast, northwest, southeast, and southwest, plus the zenith and nadir.[14] Locating the Buddhas of the Ten Directions in the same architectural space as the Diamond Realm maṇḍala can be interpreted from two different perspectives. From one angle, the ten Buddhas intrude into the Diamond Realm; they have been called down to inhabit and thus sanctify the major ritual arena of the temple. From another angle, the deities of the Diamond Realm are projected outward toward the named margins of the known world. Whichever perspective we adopt—and perhaps ultimately, with or without Jung, they dissolve into each other—the same point holds: the maṇḍala is positioned according to the Ten Directions, and vice versa. The sculpted deities of the Diamond Realm are oriented in relation to all Buddhas.

The fifth item on the agenda of the assembly hall also has to do with ritual space. It is a painting above the east doorway leading back into the entry hall (see fig. 8.5). The painting depicts a large goddess in the center. She has a halo, red face, long black hair, and a crown of blue stones, and she wears a large cape. She is attended by nine female attendants to each side, wearing garb similar to hers, and is accompanied by various animals. Based on modern folklore and the positioning of the same goddess over the doorways of later chapels at Tabo, Klimburg-Salter identifies her as the Buddhicized version of the protective deity of the Tabo area and of the temple in particular.[15] In Buddhist form she is named rDo-rje-chen-mo (pron.: Dorjé Chenmo, Skt.: Mahāvajra Devi), who may have overlaid an earlier, pre-Buddhist female deity named Wi-nyu-myin (pron.: Wi Nyu Nyin). Wi-nyu-myin, identified as such in a cartouche,

---

13. Thakur, *Buddhism in the Western Himalaya*, pp. 165–71, collates the cartouches and likely textual sources for the Ten Buddhas and twenty bodhisattvas.

14. See Nakamura, *Bukkyōgo daijiten*, p. 596a.

15. Klimburg-Salter, *Tabo: A Lamp for the Kingdom*, pp. 79, 94–95. See also Nebesky-Wojkowitz, *Oracles and Demons of Tibet*, pp. 36–37.

FIG. 8.5. rDo-rje-chen-mo, protectress. Wall painting. East wall, assembly hall, Tabo main temple, eleventh century. Photo courtesy of Deborah Klimburg-Salter, 1991, Western Himalaya Archive Vienna.

is in fact represented in a wall painting, now largely destroyed, on the opposite side of the same doorway, that is, above the doorway on the west wall of the entry hall. If Klimburg-Salter's hypothesis is correct, then when the paintings in the entry hall were made in 996, the protector god represented therein was considered a pre-Buddhist goddess indigenous to the area. By the time the assembly hall was repainted nearly fifty years later, the rebuilders of the temple wished to portray themselves, their temple, and their entire religious world in conformity to the more thoroughly Buddhicized pantheon then being disseminated by the powerful families of the day. Later folk tradition, in fact, says that the Buddhist form of the deity was the personal guardian of Rin-chen-bzang-po. A Buddha flanked by two bodhisattvas plus a triad of bodhisattvas round out the panel in which rDo-rje-chen-mo is painted. The religious significance of the painting is that the goddess ensures the safety and sanctity of the entire ritual space of the assembly hall. As a local goddess, she roots the maṇḍala, the narratives, and the higher cosmos in the hallowed ground of Tibet, and as a Buddhist deity she protects those who practice the Dharma.

If, as I have suggested above, the art of the assembly hall constitutes the ritual center of the temple as a whole (and hence of the wheel of rebirth in the entry hall that precedes it), I still need to explain how the five liturgical programs are related to each other. In my interpretation, the rituals of the Diamond Realm maṇḍala are the focus of the entire main temple, and the other four artistic agendas serve to ground it and augment it.[16] The most clearly defined ritual program in the assembly hall is the rite of identification with the primary deity of the Diamond Realm maṇḍala, Vairocana. The corresponding text details all of the procedures such as cleansing the space, making offerings, chanting syllables, and visualizing deities, and it is unequivocal in describing the climax of the ritual as the merging of the practitioner with Vairocana Buddha (and through him, identification with the other deities of the maṇḍala). The climax is, in a sense, prolonged, since once conjoined, the practitioner/deity moves on to achieve other results, be they curing, acquiring merit, gaining worldly success, or other mundane ends, or achieving supreme, perfect enlightenment.

The Tantric ritual is not only the center point of the religious program in the assembly hall, it is also located at the visitor's focal point. The bases of the thirty-three statues stand five and one-half feet above the floor, roughly one-third of the way up the wall, which is almost fifteen feet tall.[17] The deities of the Diamond Realm face the viewer

---

16. Deborah Klimburg-Salter attaches religious significance to the vertical arrangement of the hall. She treats the location of the art as a direct reflection of its mystical meaning: the narrative paintings of Sudhana and Śākyamuni are literally lowest, symbolizing the "form-body" (*nirmāṇakāya*) of the Buddha; the statues of the maṇḍala are placed in the middle, representing the body of response (*sambhogakāya*); and the Buddha-fields in the Ten Directions occupy the highest space on the wall, emblematic of the body of law (*dharmakāya*). See Klimburg-Salter, *Tabo: A Lamp for the Kingdom*, p. 108, where she also describes the ritual process as one of ascension: "Thus through meditation and ritual circumambulation he performs a symbolic pilgrimage which also leads to successively higher levels of consciousness." See also Linrothe, "Mapping the Iconographic Program of the Sumtsek."

17. The thirty-two statues are 1.65 meters above the floor, Vairocana is 1.68 meters above the floor, and the ceiling is 4.52 meters tall; see Thakur, *Buddhism in the Western Himalaya*, p. 64.

essentially at eye-level and command his or her attention. The other four artistic programs in the assembly hall serve as support, some below and some above, for the primary ritual, which takes place in the cosmic palace ruled by Vairocana Buddha. The two painting cycles, dealing with Sudhana and Śākyamuni, are not artifacts of a participatory ritual in the way the thirty-three deities of the Diamond Realm are. Rather, these paintings tell a story: as narrative art, they allow the observer to follow the protagonist—not to ritually merge with him—as he negotiates a series of crises and adventures. Unlike the maṇḍala and its ritual, which are completed only when the viewer fully inserts himself or herself into the palace, the paintings tell a complete story from beginning to end. One can empathize with Sudhana, but that form of audience identification is different from the unification of the Tantric *yogi* or *yogini* with the deities of the Diamond Realm. The stories of Sudhana and Śākyamuni form a temporal sequence. As I suggested above, the former narrative shows how a normal human being can follow a path that leads to becoming a bodhisattva, someone fully dedicated to achieving enlightenment and guiding others to the same goal. The story of Śākyamuni continues from that point onward, detailing the progress of the bodhisattva through miraculous birth, early life as a prince, renunciation of his kingly heritage, finding a middle path between indulgence and asceticism, achieving enlightenment, preaching the Dharma, achieving a peaceful death, and being honored by assembled royalty. While the narrative art emphasizes a temporal flow, the portrayals of the Buddhas of the Ten Directions and the goddess serve locative functions. The Ten Buddhas constitute a cosmic frame of reference for the palace of Vairocana; they provide the bearings for the realization that Vairocana resides at the center of the universe. They are too high above the viewer to be visualized in great detail; their emplacement provides the navigational points of reference for the maṇḍala, which stands at their center. The painting of rDo-rje-chen-mo performs a different but not necessarily antagonistic service of alignment. Her portrait at the entrance to the assembly hall suggests that whatever realm the meditator may enter in the maṇḍala, his or her ritual practice remains grounded in the sacred and secure precincts of Tabo.

Before discussing the wheel of rebirth in the entry hall, it is helpful to analyze the ritual art contained in the room behind the assembly hall. The rear hall is a square room, about half the size of the assembly hall, with a smaller, three-sided wall built in the middle of it (see fig. 8.2). If one leaves the assembly hall and proceeds directly west toward the back of the temple, one enters the smaller inner sanctum defined by the three internal walls. The rear hall is, in effect, subdivided into this smaller area, which some scholars call a cella by analogy to Greek and Roman models, and a larger corridor surrounding it on all four sides. The latter is usually called the ambulatory, since it allows circumambulation around the inner sanctum.

The architectural model of inner and outer rooms conforms to the religious ordering of the space. The inner sanctum is perhaps a pure land, specifically Amitābha Buddha's land of bliss located in the west. A large statue of Amitābha in *samādhi mudrā* sits on the back wall of the cella, facing the viewer who has entered from the assembly hall. Statues of his attendant bodhisattvas, Avalokiteśvara and Mahāsthāmaprāpta, sit perpendicular to him on the left and right. (Another possibility is that the main statue in the cella depicts Vairocana, the rear space serving as a complement to the Vairocana-centered maṇḍala in the assembly hall.)[18]

The space of the sanctum seems to follow, ritually and temporally, the main religious events in the assembly hall. In this reading, once the practitioner has achieved identification with the deity in the maṇḍala, he or she proceeds to the pure land constructed in the innermost realm of the whole temple. He or she worships the Buddha presiding over the pure land and can then pass into the area of circumambulation. The walls of the ambulatory are filled with paintings of hundreds of Buddhas, whose presence attests to Amitābha's power. Similar paintings of the One Thousand Buddhas are also present at the main temple at mTho-lding, founded by Ye-shes-'od in the Guge region.[19] The north and south walls of the Tabo ambulatory include other paintings as well: eight Buddhas, sixteen bodhisattvas, sixteen mahāsattvas, and other narrative cycles that scholars have not yet fully deciphered. As one moves into the cella from the assembly hall, one walks between statues of two other bodhisattvas who demarcate the passage into the pure land, Kṣitigarbha on the left and Ākāśagarbha on the right.

The cella also contains portraits and inscriptions portraying the wishes of those who renovated the temple in 1042, as noted above. The main portrait (fig. 8.6), painted on the south wall of the ambulatory just outside the cella, depicts Ye-shes-'od's grand-nephew, Byang-chub-'od, in the center. At the time of the renovation he had already entered the monkhood. On the right side are assembled members of the Saṃgha of Tabo. On the left important monks are at the top and laymen are seated at the bottom. Below the painting is the inscription, an important piece of writing in its own right.[20] (Parts have already been discussed above, and here I offer only a summary.) The inscription begins by dating the present renovation by Byang-chub-'od in relation to the history of the temple, begun by Ye-shes-'od, referred to as "the ancestor, the bodhisattva," forty-six years earlier. It notes the conditions under which it was written: "Therefore, when the painting of the cella [*dri-gtsang-khang*, Skt.: *gandhakuṭī*] was completed, the wish to make a record [of this] and a transfer [of merit] arose. . . ."

18. I follow Giuseppe Tucci (*Temples of Western Tibet*, pp. 78–86), Romi Khosla (*Buddhist Monasteries in the Western Himalaya*, p. 45), and Laxman Thakur (*Buddhism in the Western Himalaya*, pp. 115–20) in my reading of the main figures in the cella. Deborah Klimburg-Salter (*Tabo: A Lamp for the Kingdom*, pp. 140–49) and Christian Luczanits (*Buddhist Sculpture in Clay*, pp. 35–43) argue instead that the Buddha icon is Vairocana and that his two attendants are Avalokiteśvara and Vajrasattva Bodhisattvas. The issue is complex, and I do not claim to offer a definitive solution. Sudarshana Singhal ("Identification of Sculptures in the Central Hall of the Tabo Monastery," esp. pp. 26–27) interprets the main Buddha icon in the cella as the Abhisambodhi Vairocana and argues that the cella program reproduces the Garbhadhātu (Womb Realm) maṇḍala, so that in the end the main temple at Tabo combines, in the style of Japanese esoteric Buddhism, the Vajradhātu and Garbhadhātu maṇḍalas.

19. See Henss, "Wall-Paintings in Western Tibet," p. 204.

20. I rely on the translation in Steinkellner and Luczanits, "New Translation of the Renovation Inscription," with occasional changes in the capitalization of Sanskrit words and the addition of glosses in brackets. See also Thakur, *Buddhism in the Western Himalaya*, pp. 252–57.

Fig. 8.6. Sponsors of the renovation and inscription. Wall painting. South wall of ambulatory, Tabo main temple, eleventh century. Photo courtesy of Jaroslav Poncar, 2001, Western Himalaya Archive Vienna.

It describes in greater detail the glorious acts of Ye-shes-'od, amplifying his insight and the corresponding virtues of the temple:

> This king [i.e., Ye-shes-'od], personification of a god, born of divine race, of the lineage of bodhisattvas, lord over all black-headed [people], who by [his] perfect, innate insight brought the "light of wisdom" [*ye-shes-'od*, Skt.: *jñānaprabha*] to the darkness of ignorance, abandoned [his] reign, which is connected with saṃsāra, like a withered garland of flowers because he regarded [it] as an illusion. [He] then offered the whole [kingdom?] for the sake of the Dharma. When the lay people of the realm had become white, [he] erected here the temple Dpal-ldan bkra-shis bde-gnas [pron.: Penden Tashi Dené, literally, Glorious, Auspicious, Happy Place] as a lamp for his kingdom.

The inscription moves on to discuss Byang-chub-'od's orders to local artists to renovate the temple. It states, "When the sovereign, the *lha-btsun* [pron.: *lhatsün*, monk] Byang-chub-'od, regarded the work of the ancestor as old, he gathered many masters and craftsmen, and provided the materials. When we, then, were commissioned by [his] profound order, we purified [the place] well and [the work] was done." Next the inscription includes the dedication of merit. As noted above, the benefits are assigned three times, first to the commissioner's (Byang-chub-'od's) achieving of enlightenment, second to the meditative union with Vairocana Buddha of all visitors to the temple, and third to the enlightenment of all those engaged in restoring the temple. The inscription closes with the hope that the commissioners succeed in raising "the banner of the *bodhimaṇḍala* ["maṇḍala of enlightenment," sacred space in general or the Diamond Realm maṇḍala in particular] in this monastery . . . in which nirvāṇa and tranquility are beginning to bloom." The cella also contains what some scholars call "The Admonitory Inscription," which refers obliquely to a persecution of Buddhist establishments and includes the warning not to punish monks.[21]

Having portrayed the assembly hall's ritual program as a carefully constructed climax and the art of the cella as a dénouement, it is now possible to appreciate the significance of the prefatory mise-en-scène supplied by the wheel of rebirth and other art in the entry hall. The entry hall is shaped like a rectangle, approximately twenty-four feet wide by eight feet deep. One enters on the long side of the rectangle, the east wall, and proceeds into the assembly hall by passing through a passageway marked by what used to be two statues on either side of the door. All four walls contain pictorial programs, although many of them are very hard to identify with certainty due to water damage.

The wheel of saṃsāra is on the east wall, on its north half. In other words, if one turns around 180 degrees after walking into the entry hall, the saṃsāracakra is located in front of the viewer, to the left (see fig. 8.2). The painting itself is in very poor condition, and less than half of it remains. Nevertheless, the surviving portions provide significant evidence about how the symbol of the wheel of rebirth was understood in western Tibet. Above the wheel, in the center, sits a Buddha in *varāda mudrā*, seated on a lotus throne (see fig. 8.7). To the left and beneath the Buddha, but still outside the wheel, are the stanzas on renunciation prescribed in the vinaya, written in Tibetan.[22] Traces of the demon are also faintly visible at the top of the wheel. To these elements drawn from the canonical account, the Tabo artists have added other figures outside the wheel. Four gods were originally placed around the wheel at top left, top right, bottom right, and bottom left. Plate 12 shows the best preserved god, a red-faced deity at top left. He wears a crown, earrings, and a necklace, and his long, delicate fingers stretch down around the wheel.

According to the Buddha's directions in the origin legend, the outer rim of the wheel is supposed to contain symbols for the Twelve Conditions in the chain of causation.

21. See Klimburg-Salter, *Tabo: A Lamp for the Kingdom*, p. 137.
22. For a study and translation, see Luczanits, "Minor Inscriptions and Captions," pp. 114–17.

FIG. 8.7. Buddha and verses outside wheel of rebirth. Wall painting. East wall, entry hall, Tabo main temple, eleventh century. Photo courtesy of Christian Luczanits, 1991, Western Himalaya Archive Vienna.

The wheel at Tabo offers an interesting variation on this element as well. A human figure wearing a cap and drinking from some kind of vessel is partly visible at the ten o'clock position, but I do not understand his significance. What is clear in this outer band, however, is that some of the Twelve Conditions were portrayed in writing rather than being represented by their canonical symbols. The words for "old age and death," for instance, can be made out on the right side of the outer rim.[23] It is not possible to decide whether these functioned as complete depictions, in writing, of the links in the chain of causation, whether they were cartouches accompanying pictures of the symbols, or whether they were preparatory labels that were supposed to be painted over. Nevertheless, coupled with the writing of the canonical verses in their own text box

23. Ibid., p. 116.

outside the wheel, they highlight the importance of writing in this version of the saṃsāracakra.

Moving inward, the part of the wheel just inside the outer ring contains an interesting representation of beings undergoing change. The pattern of wavy lines in the background symbolizes water, perhaps a stream. Within that band are depicted beings passing through barrels. A human figure is visible in plate 12, while figure 8.8 shows the next lower section, containing first a dog and then two humans in succession passing through barrels. It is possible that this band is related to the description of the pails of the water wheel contained in the Buddha's instructions in the vinaya. It is also noteworthy that the figures move through the barrels but do not, like the figures in the wheel seen at Yulin (see chapter 7), undergo a change in species.

The Six Paths of rebirth are shown next. The segment of the wheel depicting the gods was probably placed at the top. The largest surviving segment is at the top left of the wheel (fig. 8.8), which probably depicts the realm of the *asuras* (demigods). A male and female figure are seated together in the middle, while in the frame above them and to the right sits another figure. The significance of the pond and two trees below them is unclear. The lowest part of the wheel depicts hell beings, barely clothed and fleeing from torment.

Images on the rest of the wall containing the wheel of life and death are even more fragmentary. On the other side of the doorway, to the right if one is facing the wall, is what Klimburg-Salter calls a "cosmological picture." She argues that it parallels the placement of similar paintings in the porches of assembly halls at mTho-lding and bSam-yas and that, together with the wheel of rebirth, it demarcates "the boundary between the profane, outside world, and the sacred world, the world of the maṇḍala."[24] It seems to be a schematic rendering of the cosmos arranged vertically, with the highest heavens represented by colored horizontal bands at the top and ponds, trees, and palaces shown in the levels underneath. Above the doorway, above the space between the two paintings, is another scene difficult to make out. The clearest portions depict figures divided by a horizontal rope. The figures below are suspended from the rope, while those standing on the rope seem to be making love.

Opposite the wheel of rebirth, on the long west wall of the entry hall, are the protectors of the temple. As noted above, the main goddess is painted above the doorway. Although the central figure herself is effaced, other details mark her unmistakably as the local deity. First, the head of her vehicle, a reindeer, is visible in the painting. Second, her attendants (eighteen women, nine on each side) match similar depictions elsewhere. Third, below the painting is an inscription which explicitly states: "The protectress of the main temple [*gtsug-lag-khang*], Wi-nyu-myin [together with] her retinue."[25] As we have seen (fig. 8.5), the deity is depicted elsewhere in the temple in her Buddhicized form as rDo-rje-chen-mo (Skt.: Mahāvajra Devi). Above the goddess is a series of ten or eleven guardians, all deriving from the Hindu pantheon and

24. Klimburg-Salter, *Tabo: A Lamp for the Kingdom*, p. 82.
25. Translation from Thakur, *Buddhism in the Western Himalaya*, p. 242.

FIG. 8.8. Top left section of wheel of rebirth. Wall painting East wall, entry hall, Tabo main temple, eleventh century. Photo courtesy of Christian Luczanits, 1994, Western Himalaya Archive Vienna.

assimilated into Buddhist cosmology.[26] Rounding out this phalanx of protection are two statues originally standing on either side of the door. The statues themselves have been destroyed, but their halos, painted on the wall behind where they would have stood, do survive.[27]

The two side walls of the entry hall contain pictures of the people involved in the original founding of the temple in 996. The south wall, to the left as one enters, is in excellent condition and allows identification of most of its figures. The bottom half of the wall depicts what were originally eight rows of donor figures, most of whom were identified in cartouches. At the very center of the top row sits Ye-shes-'od, flanked by his two sons. The positioning makes clear that Ye-shes-'od is the major founder of the temple. At the time of the temple's establishment in 996 he had presumably abdicated in favor of his brother and entered the monkhood. Nevertheless, the painting depicts only one of his sons, Dhe-ba ra-tsa, not Ye-shes-'od, in monastic garb (see fig. 8.1). The picturing of a retired king/monk in secular clothing, however, is perfectly consistent with the concerns of ancient Tibetan Buddhism: the portrait shows in visual form how royal and monastic power were thought to coalesce. The picture also conceives of the donors' glory in dynastic terms, placing the two sons right next to their father. The other figures are various monks, nuns, and laypeople from the area.

The top half of the south wall depicts three horizontal rows of eight deities apiece. The top row contains eight major Indian gods (*mahādevas*). The middle row depicts eight great *nāgas* (*mahānāgas*). The third row shows the deities who control the eight planets.

The paintings on the north wall are almost completely destroyed, but their layout and content seem to match those of the south wall. The north wall contains rows of gods at the top and rows of human figures at the bottom. The latter are probably the local aristocracy: there are cartouches for their names, and some are called by the title of "prince" (*lha-sras*, pron.: *lhasé*).

How do the paintings and statues in the entry hall hang together, so to speak? And what is their relationship to the rest of the temple? My answer to these questions can be summed up as preface, protection, and patronage.[28]

The prefatory function of the entry hall derives from its special relationship to the

26. For different identifications, see Klimburg-Salter, *Tabo: A Lamp for the Kingdom*, pp. 79–80; and Thakur, *Buddhism in the Western Himalaya*, pp. 145–46.

27. Thakur (*Buddhism in the Western Himalaya*, pp. 120–21) hypothesizes that they were Vajrapāni and Hayagrīva.

28. Using a similar model from which I have learned much, Christian Luczanits (personal communication, Nov. 2004) explains, "We may thus read the increasing sacredness of the temple in terms of the Buddhist path as it is expressed frequently, namely in terms of ground, path, and result. The ground of the path is right understanding of the cycle of suffering as it is represented by the Wheel of Life. . . . The Assembly Hall expresses different stages of the path: the initial Bodhisattva practice leading to the ultimate stage of Bodhisattvahood (Sudhana), the initiation into esoteric practice, the ultimate consecration by the Buddhas of the Ten Directions as precondition of Buddhahood, and the ultimate display of Buddhahood by showing the life of the Buddha. . . . Ambulatory and Cella then represent the result: the highest stage of Bodhisattvahood that enables one to work for the benefit of all sentient beings, and Buddhahood itself."

central ritual program of the assembly hall, which I have analyzed above as the Diamond Realm maṇḍala. In this respect my interpretation follows Philip Denwood's analysis of Tibetan temple architecture. "At the level of the single building," writes Denwood, "the maṇḍala concept leads to a square or cruciform chamber containing three-dimensional images of divinities arranged in a symmetrical array around a central figure or object, sometimes with a circumambulation corridor around the outside. However, a worshipper can only approach the chamber from one direction at a time and it is tempting to leave a space for an entryway and to rearrange the images so as to increase the internal room."[29] If the main chamber of the temple is defined as a maṇḍala, then the room leading to it is, in spatial terms, external to the maṇḍala. The entry hall occurs prior, chronologically, to the ritual of identification that is performed in the palace of Vairocana. The cosmological principles embodied in the wheel of rebirth and other paintings in the entry hall encapsulate the central maṇḍala; they prepare the practitioner for what lies ahead in sacred space. The text written above the saṃsāracakra quotes from and thus enacts the canonical account, according to which paintings of the wheel are supposed to be positioned in the outer precincts of the temple. The painting is next to the door; it marks the initial passage from outside the temple to inside the sacred area.

The second doorway through which one passes runs through the west wall of the entry hall. The deities depicted there are guardians, and Wi-nyu-myin is identified as such in her cartouche. She, her retinue, the gods drawn above her, and the two statues stationed beside the door guarantee the safety of the maṇḍala located on the other side of the door. They secure the perimeter of the ritual space and bless the practitioner as he or she passes through it. The mix of indigenous and foreign troops in this divine phalanx reinforces the protective function of the entry hall. Some of the deities are Indian in origin and were absorbed into the Buddhist pantheon. As gods, they are more powerful than human beings, but are still subject to suffering and doomed to a succession of rebirths in saṃsāra. They have, however, converted to Buddhism: under the sway of Buddhas, they marshal their forces on behalf of the Dharma, and they stand guard over Buddhist ritual space. Wi-nyu-myin, on the other hand, is a chthonic goddess. As a tutelary deity, she extends her protective power over the Buddhist complex located within her territory.

Local figures are also invoked on the side walls (south and north) of the entry hall. Paintings there depict the members of the community involved in founding the temple: the retired king of western Tibet and now-monk, Ye-shes-'od; his two sons; male and female members of the Saṃgha; male and female lay followers; and other local notables. In formal terms they are represented hieratically: the most important donors occupy the center and top of any given pictorial space, and they are arranged in rows that define their members by rank. On the other hand, they are also individualized, since some of them are portrayed with distinctive features or clothing, and most of them are named in cartouches. As patrons, they played an important role in found-

29. Denwood, "Tibetan Architecture," p. 60.

ing the temple. Their representation in this room ensures that their actions in the past are made present again whenever a practitioner enters the temple.

The wheel of rebirth at Tabo was probably not the only such painting in western Tibet at the time; the temples at A-lci and mTho-lding probably also contained similar representations. A painting of the saṃsāracakra that has withstood the ravages of time better than Tabo's is contained in a cave temple at Pad-ma'i-sdong-po (pron.: Pemé Dongpo; or shortened to Pad-sdong-po, pron.: Pedongpo), also in western Tibet, dating from about one hundred years after the construction of Tabo. Helmut Neumann hypothesizes, on stylistic grounds and on the supposition that it must have been built prior to the Gar-log invasion around 1150, that the cave temple was constructed in the late eleventh or early twelfth century.[30]

The wheel of rebirth is painted on the left wall of the entrance corridor (see plate 13). Like the canonical version, the Pad-ma'i-sdong-po saṃsāracakra contains the Three Poisons in the inner circle, represented by the three animals. Around that is a fairly standard rendering of the Six Paths: gods at the top, with *asuras* on their right and humans on their left, and hell beings at the bottom, with hungry ghosts to their right and animals to their left. Like the composition at Tabo, the Pad-ma'i-sdong-po wheel contains an additional band of beings passing through barrels, but at Pad-ma'i-sdong-po they are undergoing visible change from one species to the next. In the outer ring are the Twelve Conditions depicted not in words but with their conventional symbols. Figure 8.9 shows a woman giving birth. As at Tabo, four beings are arrayed around the wheel, but at Pad-ma'i-sdong-po they are goddesses, not gods. Above the wheel is a wide band depicting a procession of what may be protective deities and other figures. Below that is a small panel showing devotees, perhaps the commissioners of the painting.

Like most paintings of the saṃsāracakra, the wheel of reincarnation at Pad-ma'i-sdong-po is introductory: it is located in a vaulted entrance corridor. The inner part of the cave contains paintings of the One Thousand Buddha motif, and the survival of a pedestal in the center of the small chamber indicates that a Buddha statue was originally enshrined at the heart of the temple. The focus of the temple, then, seems to be the worship of a Buddha whose statue is now missing.

Another interesting point of comparison would be the painting on the wall opposite the wheel of rebirth. Unfortunately I have not visited the site and know it only secondhand, so further research must be left for others to pursue.[31]

The wheel of rebirth at Tabo has both similarities to and differences from the wheel of rebirth painted elsewhere in the Buddhist world. Its current decayed condition discloses unambiguously only some of the canonical elements: a circular or elliptical shape,

---

30. See Neumann, "Wheel of Life in the Twelfth Century Western Tibetan Cave Temple of Pedongpo," esp. pp. 82–83.

31. Neumann focuses on the representation of the Six-Armed Avalokiteśvara on the wall facing the wheel (ibid., p. 82 and pl. 81), but his photo makes clear that it is but one small part of a rather complex composition. Could the wall depict a version of the Maudgalyāyana legend, opposite the painting of the wheel, as at Yulin?

FIG. 8.9. Top right section of wheel of rebirth. Wall painting. Entrance corridor, Pedongpo cave temple, twelfth century. Photo courtesy of Lionel Fournier.

distinct sectors within the wheel, a Buddha stationed outside the wheel, and the poems on renunciation beside the painting. Like almost all the other wheels discussed in this book, the one at Tabo is positioned in the introductory space of the temple. At Tabo the wheel of rebirth is portrayed in the same hall as are paintings of protective deities, an arrangement similar to that at Yulin. Although in formal terms the wheel serves as a preface to a more important ritual program, the content of that ritual program at Tabo differs from that of other sites where the wheel is located. The wheel of rebirth at Tabo introduces a Tantric ritual in which the practitioner merges his or her identity with Vairocana Buddha. The ritual is articulated through a maṇḍala representing the various compartments of the Diamond Realm. (Or, to translate back into Sanskrit: the saṃsāracakra introduces the Vajradhātu maṇḍala.) In spatial terms, the visitor to the temple must pass beyond the wheel of rebirth before being able to perform the rite of unification.

There appear to be some parallels between the religious function of the wheels painted at Tabo and the function of the wheel in the small chamber at Kumtura (Xinjiang, China; discussed in chapter 6). In both places the main religious activity in the cave falls under the modern western category of "meditation." But the forms of meditation and ritual action at each location are quite different. At Kumtura the meditation program, to the extent that it can be reconstructed, is about the act of meditation itself, and the connection between the sketch of the wheel and the larger paintings is inexplicit. The wheel of rebirth and other sketches on the side wall at Kumtura do stand in contrast to the dominating composition of the meditating monk on the back wall, but otherwise the relation between the two remains unsystematized. At Tabo, on the other hand, the painting of the wheel is a component of the smaller space that is logically external to the main sanctuary, in which the primary ritual is conducted. The spatial and ritual organization of the temple makes very clear the relationship between the painting of the saṃsāracakra and the rest of the art.

In very general terms the structural position of the wheel at Tabo is similar to that of the illustrations of stories of karmic retribution at the ninth-century temple of Barabuḍur (Java, Indonesia), which might well have shared many sets of Tantric programs with Kashmir. Although the paintings on the ground floor of Barabuḍur do not explicitly picture the wheel of rebirth, they do focus on the workings of causality and rebirth in general, and, as seen in chapter 4, they do contain a sequence on King Rudrāyaṇa's vision of the painting of the Buddha with the Twelve Conditions. At Barabuḍur one first views the karmic narratives and then proceeds to the next two levels, which deal with events in the life of the historical Buddha and the episodes in the pilgrimage of Sudhana.[32] The parallel to the sequence of programs at Tabo continues in the highest floor at Barabuḍur, which is dedicated to a maṇḍala of Vairocana Buddha. At both sites, scenes depicting the process of rebirth are the first stage, the journey of Sudhana and the quest of Śākyamuni are the second stage, and the ritualized merging with Vairocana in the center of the world is the final stage. This is not, of course, to deny the obvious and important differences between the two sites. One is a stone maṇḍala constructed out-of-doors, the other a wooden and brick temple with restricted access. The workings of karma are not expressed in the form of a wheel in the southeast Asian site, whereas they are at Tabo.

In any event, the art in the assembly hall at Tabo defines a symbolically ordered cosmos for the initiate. As a Tantric practice, the maṇḍala ritual is accessible to those who are formally under the guidance of a teacher. The esoteric nature of the rituals performed within the maṇḍala thus stands in contrast to the exterior placement of the painting of the wheel of rebirth, which serves to initiate the practitioner and define the outer perimeter of the ritual field.

---

32. For some astute comments on the coordination of the various iconographic programs at Barabuḍur, see Fontein, *Pilgrimage of Sudhana*, chap. 5, esp. p. 172.

Chapter 9

Wheels for Pilgrims

Baodingshan, Sichuan, Thirteenth Century

The wheel of rebirth at the thirteenth-century pilgrimage site of Baodingshan in Sichuan (see plate 14) seems to be the architectural opposite of the wheels at Ajaṇṭā (Maharashtra, India), Yulin (Gansu), and Tabo (medieval western Tibet). Rather than lining a corridor accessible only after entering a cave or temple, the wheel at Baodingshan is not a painting but a relief carving, over twenty-five feet high, that stands open to any pilgrim visiting the site. Some ten thousand individual relief carvings at Baodingshan, situated eleven miles from the town of Dazu (Sichuan, now officially part of the Chongqing Special Administrative Region), were completed around the year 1250 under the direction of a local religious impresario whose secular name was Zhao Zhifeng (1159–1249). Although the area had been home to a Buddhist temple during the Tang dynasty, Zhao completely remade and expanded it. Beginning in 1177 he administered the construction of the first niches, continuing steadily over the next seventy years. The fact that one man was largely responsible for the development of the center over such a long period of time accounts for a certain amount of consistency in both content and style. Indeed Zhao seems to have memorialized his own contributions by having himself sculpted into many of the scenes there. He is present at the Buddha's entry into nirvāṇa pictured in one of the largest niches, occupying the very first position under the eyes of Śākyamuni (see figs. 9.1 and 9.2).[1] Of course it is every pious Buddhist's wish to see a Buddha in person; and hence it is entirely fitting that the man who was so instrumental in the articulation of the Dharma in this part of Sichuan should be placed in the Buddha's presence. His position right next to the Buddha also helps to vouch for the authenticity, the veracity of the site as a whole. The niche in which the saṃsāracakra is located also quotes the standard passages from the vinaya, but in other ways it engineers its own local variations. Chanted hymns are

1. The archaeological report states that a statue of Kāśyapa originally stood in front of Zhao's, but is now lost. That would make Zhao the second disciple in the first generation after the founder. See Sichuansheng shehui kexueyuan et al., *Dazu shike neirong zonglu*, p. 472.

FIG. 9.1. *Parinirvāṇa* scene. Relief carving. Dafowan Niche 11, Baodingshan, Sichuan, thirteenth century. Zhongguo meishu quanji bianji weiyuanhui, *Sichuan shiku diaosu*, pl. 181.

added to the canonical poems, for instance, and the Three Buddhas of past (Dīpaṃkara), present (Śākyamuni), and future (Maitreya) appear authoritatively at the very top of the scene. Perhaps the most daring of Zhao's innovations is placed at the axis of the wheel. In the center sits a meditating figure, probably a depiction of Zhao himself, from whose chest emanate the six spokes defining the subrealms of saṃsāra.

Zhao designed the site as a narrative compendium of basic Buddhist teachings and as a testament to the miraculous deeds of a holy man from Sichuan, Liu Benzun (844–907).[2] Liu's ancestry is unclear; later accounts explain his surname (Liu, liter-

2. My rough biography of Liu Benzun is based on one of the earliest surviving accounts of his life, the biography inscribed on a stele now standing in the main hall in the Smaller Buddha Bay (Xiaofowan) at Baodingshan. The text, entitled "Biography of Layman Liu of the Tang" ("Tang Liu jushi zhuan"), was written by a Song-dynasty monk named Zujue (1087–1150), edited by Zhang Min, and inscribed by Wang Bing. It was probably erected between 1131 and 1163, and may have been based on the stele erected at Liu's grave at Mimou. It is in poor condition. I follow the transcription in Chen Xishan, *Dazu shike zhilue jiaozhu*, pp. 294–97; and in Chongqing Dazu shike yishu

FIG. 9.2. Detail of *parinirvāṇa* scene. Relief carving. Dafowan Niche 11, Baodingshan, Sichuan, thirteenth century. Photography: Stephen F. Teiser.

ally "Willow") by telling the story that he was born from a large growth on a willow tree. Liu was originally from Jiazhou in the westernmost part of Sichuan, home of Mount Emei (Emeishan). He journeyed eastward to central Sichuan, spending time at Mimou (or Mimeng) in Chengdufu and at Guanghan in Zizhou (see map 9). He was known for using spells (*dhāraṇīs* and *mantras*) to banish evil spirits, cure illnesses, and accompany extreme displays of asceticism. He gouged out one of his eyes in 903, an act later codified as the fourth in a series of ten self-mutilations. During his lifetime he received support from both local gentry and the ruler of Sichuan. After his death in 907 his followers continued to build up his cult. Mingzong (r. 926–934), emperor of the Later Tang, bestowed a plaque on one of his temples, granting him an honorific title. In 1068 his home temple was further honored by the court with a name plaque calling it "Cloister of the Sagely and Long-Lived" (Shengshou yuan). His fame spread throughout Sichuan, and his cult was still thriving when Zhao visited the home temple in the second half of the twelfth century.

---

bowuguan et al., *Dazu shike mingwen lu*, pp. 207–10. I rely heavily on the critical study of the inscription by Chen Mingguang, "Song ke 'Tang Liu Benzun zhuan' bei jiaobu"; and Hu Zhaoxi, "Dazu Baodingshan shike qianlun," pp. 68–72. For other studies of Liu Benzun, see Chen Mingguang, "Sichuan moyan zaoxiang Liu Benzun huadao 'shilian tu' youlai ji niandai tansuo"; Howard, *Summit of Treasures*, pp. 100–108, 170–77; Hu Wenhe, "Anyue Dazu 'Liu Benzun shilian tu' tike he Song li 'Tang Liu jushi zhuan' bei de yanjiu"; Kucera, "Cliff Notes," pp. 167–82, 395–400; and Wang Jiayou, "Liu Benzun yu mijiao."

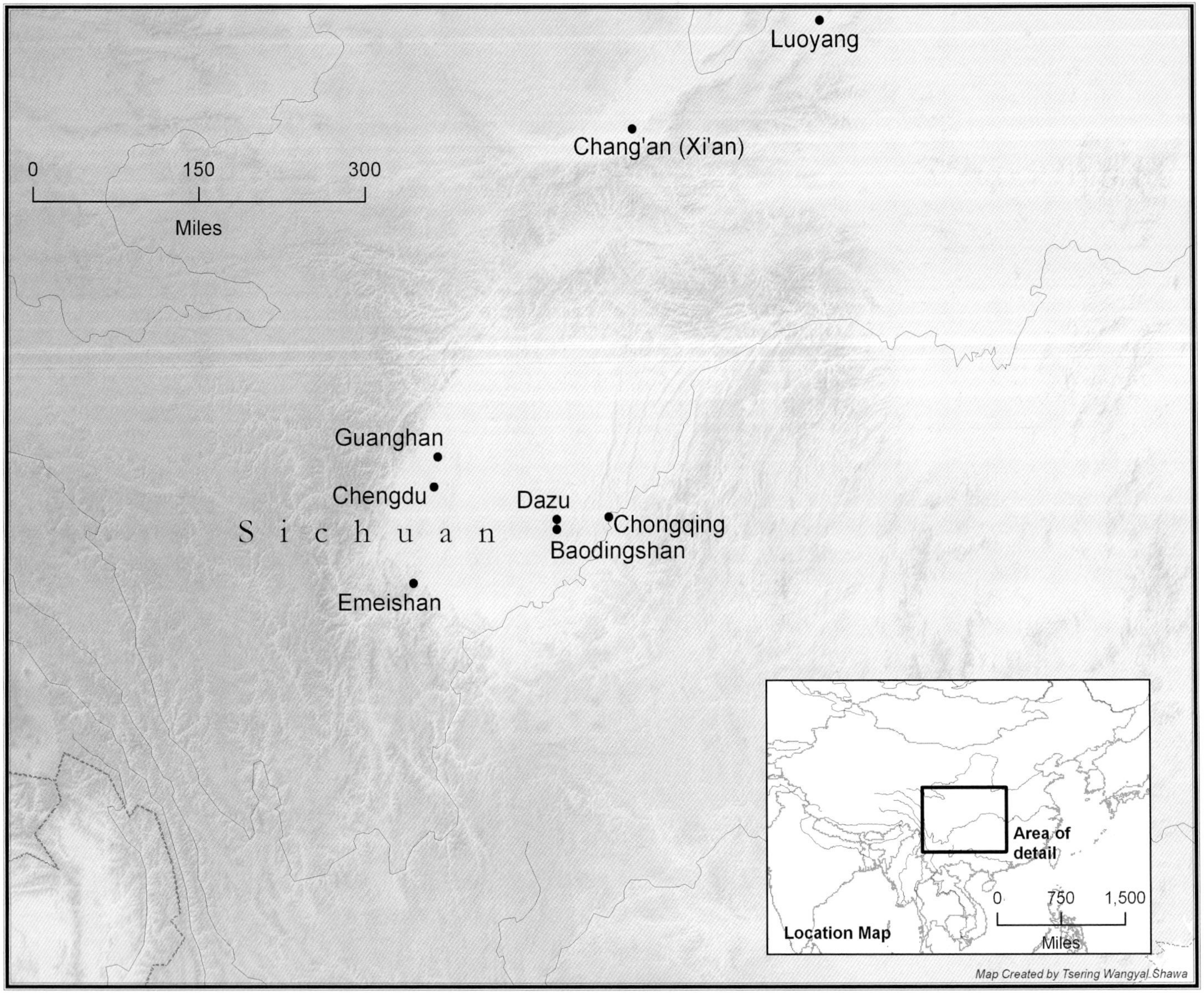

MAP 9. Sichuan, ca. 1250.

The visual material at Baodingshan provides a good idea of how Liu was understood in thirteenth-century Sichuan. He is the main subject of two niches. The smaller one (Daofowan Niche 27) has a central statue of Vairocana Buddha. An image of Liu is contained in a ray of light emanating from Vairocana's flowered cap, suggesting that Liu is a manifestation of the cosmic Buddha himself. The larger niche (Dafowan Niche 22) is one of the central scenes at Baodingshan (see fig 9.3). It depicts the ten ascetic feats for which Liu was famous: (1) cutting off a finger, (2) standing in the snow, (3) burning his ankle, (4) gouging out an eye, (5) cutting off an ear, (6) burning incense next to his heart, (7) burning incense on the crown of his head, (8) cutting his shoulder, (9) burning his penis, and (10) burning incense on his knees. The niche is dominated by a seated image of Liu. Each of the ten acts is pictured in a row of illustrations to the left and right of the main figure's head. The ten austerities, dubbed "The Ten Acts of Refining" (*shilian*), were undertaken to bring enlightenment to other beings, to serve as proof of his detachment, and to match the devotions shown by Buddhas and bodhisattvas. His eighth form of self-mutilation, for instance, involved chopping forty-eight pieces of flesh from his left shoulder. With each slice he repeated one of the forty-eight vows that Amitābha Buddha had taken as a bodhisattva. His tenth austerity, burning incense on his knees, is described in an inscription that reads:

> The tenth ascetic act is burning the knees. Benzun was a worthy and a sage. The Prince of Shu had respected and worshipped him for a long time. He decreed that he [come for an audience] and inquired, "Sir, what Way do you cultivate in order to call yourself 'Benzun' [literally, 'Original Honored One,' an epithet of Vairocana]?[3] Sir, what numinous power has been bestowed on you that you can save the common people?" Liu responded, "I cultivate the essence and practice asceticism every day. I vow to seek the fruit of no outflows and non-action. I concentrate on upholding the five-part spirit spells of the great wheel, bringing salvation to sentient beings." On the eighteenth day of the first month in the sixth year of Tianfu [Feb. 16, 906] he made a seal over incense and burned it on his knees, offering it to all the Buddhas. He made a vow that all sentient beings be able to meet each other in the three assemblies under [Maitreya's] dragon-flower tree.[4]

Judging from this text, in the popular mind Liu achieved fame as a wonder worker and ascetic. He garnered respect from Wang Jian (847–918), the Sichuan leader who came to the aid of the Tang ruling house and was named Prince of Shu (Shuwang) by Zhaozong (r. 889–904), becoming de facto ruler of Sichuan after the fall of the Tang in 907. Liu's techniques were, according to the inscription, based on the mastery of

---

3. The epithet "Benzun" has many other possible meanings, including the original principle underlying different manifestations of a deity. See Mochizuki, *Bukkyō daijiten*, pp. 4697b–98a.

4. Translation of inscription at Baodingshan, Dafowan Niche 22, transcribed in Sichuansheng shehui kexueyuan et al., *Dazu shike neirong zonglu*, p. 492; Chongqing Dazu shike yishu bowuguan et al., *Dazu shike mingwen lu*, pp. 160–61; cf. translation in Howard, *Summit of Treasures*, p. 177.

FIG. 9.3. Liu Benzun's austerities. Relief carving. Dafowan Niche 22, Baodingshan, Sichuan, thirteenth century. Bai Ziran, *Zhongguo Dazu shiku*, pl. 84.

Tantric spells, especially a five-word *dhāraṇī* that had been transmitted by Śubhakarasiṃha (ca. 716–735).[5] Liu's austerities marked him as a unique holy man and a saint accessible to all. On the one hand, they were manifestations of his resolve and his spiritual standing, which was articulated in the terms of popular Chinese Buddhism. Such terms were both specifically Buddhist ("no outflows" [*wulou*], "fruit" [*guo*]) as well as generic to Chinese religion ("cultivate the essence" [*jingxiu*], "non-action" [*wuwei*], "practice asceticism" [*lian*]). His actions were proof of his elevation above the average person. On the other hand, his self-abnegation brought benefits to others, since he accompanied each act of mutilation with a formal vow dedicating

5. The five-part spirit spells of the great wheel (*dalun wubu shenzhou*) are most likely a five-syllable *dhāraṇī* associated with the Vajradhātu maṇḍala (*Jingangjie mantuoluo*). The transmission

specific benefits, such as rebirth in the presence of the future Buddha, to other beings.

Although separated by over 250 years, Zhao Zhifeng regarded himself as a direct successor to Liu Benzun.[6] Zhao grew up very close to Baodingshan, where Buddhist carvings into the cliffs may have already been executed. He took an early interest in Buddhism, adopting a monastic lifestyle, though probably without benefit of training under other monks. The remaining inscriptions at the site omit any reference to an ecclesiastical organization or the ordination of disciples by masters. Zhao's biography claims that he reached a turning point in his life when he traveled to Liu's cultic center. From then on, Zhao devoted himself to popularizing Liu's methods and constructing a series of cliffs and caves at Baodingshan. His success in preaching, curing, and administering the precepts of lay Buddhism apparently provided enough support for him to develop Baodingshan into a thriving pilgrimage center. A stele erected at Baodingshan nearly two hundred years after Zhao's death explains how the site developed. Entitled "A Record of the Repair of the Cloister of the Sagely and Long-Lived at Baodingshan" ("Chongxiu Baodingshan Shengshou yuan ji"), it was written in 1425 by a local official named Liu Tianren. It reads:

> Baodingshan is situated about one *she* [thirty *li*] east of the District Hall of Dazu. Its cliffs and valleys are deep and imposing, its wooded ravines enticingly beautiful. Its bamboo thickets and old wood are elegant and luxurious, alternately bright and shady. It is truly a region that is a sacred ground of Buddhist purity and peace.
>
> According to tradition, someone named Zhao Zhifeng was born on Sha Creek in Miliang Village[7] on the fourteenth day of the seventh month, the twenty-ninth year of Shaoxing [August 28, 1159], under Gaozong of the Song. Even at the age of five he was not fond of adornment. There had long been Buddhist cliffs where he lived,[8] so he cut off his hair, trimmed his nails, and lived there as a monk. At the age of

---

of the *dhāraṇī* has traditionally been ascribed to Śubhakarasiṃha (Shanwuwei, ca. 716–735); see Ono, *Bussho kaisetsu daijiten*, 9:322a–d. If this tradition is correct, then the five syllables of the *dhāraṇī* are *e-wan-lan-han-qian*. See *Sanzhong xidi podiyu zhuanyezhang chusanjie mimi tuoluoni fa*, trans. Śubhakarasiṃha (Shanwuwei, ca. 716–735), *T* no. 905, 18:910c; *Foding zunshengxin podiyu zhuanyezhang chusanjie mimi sanshen foguo sanzhongxidi zhenyan yigui*, idem, *T* no. 906, 18:912b; and *Foding zunshengxin podiyu zhuanyezhang chusanjie mimi tuoluoni*, idem, *T* no. 907, 18:915a. Jinhua Chen, however, argues that all three texts were later Japanese creations, in which case Liu could not have learned the *dhāraṇī* from these particular texts. See Jinhua Chen, "Formation of Esoteric Buddhism in Japan," pp. 122–234; and idem, "Construction of Early Tendai Esoteric Buddhism," pp. 47–74.

6. My account of Zhao's life is based on Hu Zhaoxi, "Dazu Baodingshan shike qianlun," pp. 65–68; Howard, *Summit of Treasures*, pp. 108–18; Kucera, "Cliff Notes," pp. 6–10, 401–03; and the inscription discussed below.

7. Present-day Miliang Township (Miliangxiang) is five miles south of Baodingshan. Hu Zhaoxi ("Dazu Baodingshan shike qianlun," pp. 65–66) suggests that Sha Creek (Shaxi), not currently identifiable, was a tributary of Yong Creek (Yongxi).

8. A later source claims that before Zhao's lifetime there were Buddhist statuary carved into the cliffs at Baodingshan, some depicting hell scenes and some attributed to the sculptor Lu Ban. See *Dazu xianzhi*, chap. 8, in *Zhongguo difangzhi zongmu tiyao*, sec. 21, pp. 87–88, cited in Hu Zhaoxi, "Dazu Baodingshan shike qianlun," p. 66.

sixteen he traveled west to Mimou, where he wandered for three days.[9] When he returned, he ordered work to begin on the construction of the Hall of Benzun, Sagely and Long-Lived,[10] and he named his mountain "Summit of Jewels" [Baoding]. He propagated the Buddhist vows, disseminated the water of the Dharma, warded off calamities, and cured sickness. His virtue spread near and far, and there were none who did not take refuge. Buddha images were carved in cliffs and caves all over the mountain, creating unlimited merit.

Benzun, Sagely and Long-Lived, was born on the fifth day of the sixth month, the ninth year of Dazhong [July 23, 855], under Xuanzong of the Tang. According to legend, to the north of the city of Jiazhou, there was a willow tree [*liushu*] that had a large growth [*ying*]. One day the growth ruptured and out came a child [*ying'er*]. The Local Inspector of the prefecture[11] regarded this as auspicious, and he brought up the child as his son. As he grew up he practiced many austerities and rolled the great wheel of Dharma, his influence becoming very strong. Mingzong [emperor of the Later Tang, r. 926–934] bestowed the name plaque of "Great Wheel" [Dalun] on his cloister. During the Xining era [1068–1078] of the Song, under Shenzong, the name "Benzun, Sagely and Long-Lived" [Shengshou Benzun] was bestowed.

Later [Zhao] Zhifeng upheld his teachings, so he used this as the name for the temple [at Baodingshan]. Originally the temple was founded by Zhifeng, and nothing was left incomplete.[12]

The text of the stele continues with the later history of Baodingshan, including a pause in activity during the Yuan dynasty and its repair and expansion several times under various caretakers during the Ming.

Liu himself probably never visited Baodingshan; if he had, the inscriptions in the niches or the steles erected at the mountain certainly would have remarked upon the honor. Instead, the epigraphical evidence suggests that Zhao and later generations were responsible for turning the area into a premier pilgrimage site.[13] Liu's cult was already widespread throughout Sichuan. Zhao in part transplanted the legend of Liu at Bao-

9. Mimou is probably the same as Mimeng, the site of Liu's home temple. Most scholarship (e.g., Hu Zhaoxi, ibid., p. 66) interprets "three days" (*sanzhou*) as three years, without explanation.

10. According to Hu Zhaoxi (ibid.), the Hall of Benzun, Sagely and Long-Lived (Shengshou Benzun dian) constitutes what is now called the Smaller Buddha Bay (Xiaofowan) at Baodingshan and was used as a prototype for the construction of the Larger Buddha Bay (Dafowan), in which the wheel of rebirth is located.

11. The details are anachronistic. The position of Local Inspector (Duli, used for Duyou) did not exist after the sixth century; see Zhang Qiyun, *Zhongwen dacidian*, no. 40,388.45; and Hucker, *Dictionary of Official Titles*, pp. 545–46.

12. The text of the stele is transcribed in Chen Xishan, *Dazu shike zhilue jiaozhu*, pp. 265–66.

13. I am indebted to Angela Howard, who for over fifteen years has unstintingly shared her firsthand knowledge of the site, pointed me to important sources, and offered advice. Her *Summit of Treasures* sheds important new light on the artistic and religious significance of the entire site. In it she speculates that Baodingshan was the culminating stop on a pilgrimage route in central Sichuan. For other studies of the site, see Howard's bibliography; Hu Zhaoxi, "Dazu Baoding-

dingshan and helped it thrive, and in part he built the center in accordance with his own vision of Buddhist piety. As noted above, the positioning of the figures in the niche at Baodingshan depicting Śākyamuni's *parinirvāṇa* suggests that Zhao was willing to acknowledge publicly his role in designing the site (see fig. 9.2). After the Buddha, Zhao comes first, followed by Liu, the latter wearing a conical hat and carrying a melon.

Before examining the niche with the wheel of rebirth in more detail, it is worth considering the content of the site as a whole. The wheel of rebirth at Baodingshan is situated near the Song-dynasty entrance to the site. Pilgrims would enter via a stairway leading down into a U-shaped park. First they pass a stone tiger and then a large niche of protector gods—powerful beings who, after being converted by the Buddha, promised to ensure the survival of the religion. Next comes the niche with the wheel of rebirth. The saṃsāracakra at Baodingshan thus seems to perform a role similar to those it plays in other locales: it serves as an introduction to Buddhist teachings. It prepares the visitor by providing basic knowledge of morality and cosmology, after which the pilgrim is ready to absorb other scenes and teachings.

Deities in their Tantric form were extremely important at Baodingshan and other Song-dynasty centers in Sichuan. Avalokiteśvara with one thousand arms was well known in western Sichuan. Vairocana Buddha is the subject of several important niches at Baodingshan, and the ten Vidyārājas (Mingwang) have their own niche as well. The themes of transmigration and rebirth are repeated in many scenes. One large niche depicts the various tortures of hell, while another portrays the paradise of Amitābha. Śākyamuni is an extremely important figure at Baodingshan. In addition to the Buddha's death (noted above), his birth and his devotion to his parents are also themes of specific niches. The whole circuit ended with niches depicting perfect enlightenment and the taming of the ox, the latter serving as both entertainment and as a metaphor for the calming of the mind.

One of the most arresting features of the wheel of rebirth at Baodingshan is its axis (see fig. 9.4). In the hub of the wheel is a semirobed figure with curly hair seated in a posture of meditation. From the center of his chest emanate six rays containing a number of smaller figures. The lower two ribbons each contain five figures wearing crowns, perhaps denoting bodhisattvas. The upper four ribbons all contain Buddha images, totaling twenty-seven. I have not been able to determine the significance of ten bodhisattvas or twenty-seven Buddhas.[14] Considering only a visual analysis, the six ribbons are striking. In addition to defining the sections of the circle, the ribbons move beyond the wheel in two dimensions. In terms of depth, they stand out from the wheel; they have greater depth and appear closer than the rest of the wheel to the

---

shan shike qianlun"; Kucera, "Cliff Notes," esp. pp. 1–15; Zhang Hua, "Songdai Dazu shike jueqi neiyin tantao"; and the studies collected in Liu et al., *Dazu shike yanjiu wenxuan*.

14. One reading, from a Theravāda perspective, is suggested by John Strong (personal communication, Sept. 2004). The twenty-seven Buddhas could represent those in the list of twenty-eight (minus Śākyamuni), e.g., in the *Buddhavaṃsa Commentary*, while the ten bodhisattvas could represent the ten Buddhas of the future, a tradition that was popular in northern Southeast Asia.

FIG. 9.4. Axis of wheel of rebirth. Relief carving. Dafowan Niche 3, Baodingshan, Sichuan, thirteenth century. Photography: Stephen F. Teiser.

viewer. The Buddhas and bodhisattvas inscribed inside them add further depth. The second dimension is length: the six rays extend well beyond the outer rim of the wheel and join the outer edges (the three-dimensional frame) of the niche. The ribbons of Buddhas and bodhisattvas are projected even beyond the great demon who holds the wheel of rebirth in his mouth. If the Buddhas and bodhisattvas can be read as figures who, in Mahāyāna fashion, have escaped the grip of birth and death but have decided to remain within the realm of saṃsāra, then this element of the composition is saying something important. While freely intermingled with impurities and available to all sentient beings in need, these figures of salvation also transcend the world of suffering.

The head, shoulders, and chest of the central figure are all clearly defined in the carving of the wheel at Baodingshan, emphasizing that the six rays originate from his chest. The source is not the meditator's *ūrṇākeśa*, the wisp of white hair between his eyebrows. Chinese Buddhism was acquainted with this spot as a source of other worlds: rays of light were known to emanate from the *ūrṇākeśa* of various Buddhas, and many of the Buddhas at Baodingshan (especially Vairocana) are depicted with cloud paths flowing from their heads. What, then, is the significance of the chest as the point of origin?

The Six Paths emerge from the heart of the meditator. As is well known, in the traditional Chinese understanding, the heart is the location of the mental function or mind. If this line of reasoning is correct, then the scene of the wheel of rebirth is a fitting illustration of one of the slogans of the Yogācāra school, that the entire world is "mind only" (*weixin*). This claim is not equivalent to European notions of idealism. In the Buddhist case, there is not a fundamental disparity between the consciousness of the individual and the external world. The shaping power of the mind is not absolute, in that it does not bring the world into existence out of a previous state of non-being. To say that all varieties of birth and death are mentally constructed is not to say that they lack reality. It is to claim, rather, that all forms of existence are just as real as the mind: both are impermanent and provisionally real. The Buddhist credo emphasizes the predominance, not the immutability, of the mind.

The idealistic reading of the wheel of rebirth is further justified by the even more explicit statements made in a niche that stands diagonally across from the wheel of rebirth at Baodingshan. It is Dafowan Niche 19, entitled "Illustration of the Binding of the Monkey of the Mind and Locking up the Six Sources of Waste" ("Fu xinyuan suo liuhao tu"). The inscriptions in the niche equate the Six Sources of Waste with the Six Bandits (*liuzei*), the six senses in Buddhist thought. One central inscription reads:

> The eyes, ears, nose, tongue, body, and mind
> Through darkness enslave the spirit of the mind.
> To lock up the Six Sources of Waste
> Is to practice the great awakening of spirits and immortals.[15]

The inscription continues, in shorter lines, to explain how salvation can be achieved once the senses are mastered. Rather than transcending saṃsāra, the paradises (as well as the hells) of the other world are immanent:

> The land of utter happiness in the west
> Isn't very far from here.
> Putuoshan in the Southern Sea
> In fact is not distant.
>
> The halls of heaven and the prisons underground
> Are right in front of your eyes.
> All the Buddhas and bodhisattvas
> Are no different from me.

15. The inscription is transcribed in Chen Xishan, *Dazu shike zhilue jiaozhu*, p. 286; and Chongqing Dazu shike yishu bowuguan et al., *Dazu shike mingwen lu*, pp. 131–32.

Other inscriptions in the niche quote from the work of Fu Xi (497–569), a layman well known for his various writings, for engaging in ascetic acts, for sponsoring large, popular feasts, and for gaining support from Liang Wudi (r. 502–550). At the center of the niche sits a figure that appears to be the same as the central figure in the wheel of rebirth. From the top of his head emanates a Buddha identified in a cartouche as a transformation of Maitreya. To the sides of his head are inscribed the lines, "The halls of heaven as well as the prisons underground / All are produced from the mind" (*yiqie you xin zao* [second line]).[16] Other lines quote copiously from Fu Xi's "Inscription on the Mind as Ruler" ("Xinwang ming"). Thus, the pictures and texts in the niche focus on the power of the mind to fabricate the cosmos. They lend further weight to the claim that the niche of the wheel of life and death portrays the mind as the source of saṃsāra and nirvāṇa, as the origin of beings both within and beyond the realm of rebirth.

The similarities between these two niches lead me to claim that the depiction of the meditating figure at the center of the wheel of rebirth is a way of making a statement about the creation of the pilgrimage site as a whole. The same meditating figure with curly hair, a full, round jaw, sitting on a lotus throne, and lacking a halo occurs in fourteen scenes in the Larger Buddha Bay (Dafowan) alone. Scholarly opinion over the years has offered a number of different readings of him. He has been identified as Bodhidharma, Liu Benzun, Zhao Zhifeng, a generic monk, or a Buddha. Following the argument of Deng Zhijin, I believe that the figure is modeled after the organizer of the site, Zhao Zhifeng.[17] If we read the scene as a self-reflective commentary on the activity of representation, this scene suggests that in designing the sculptural program at Baodingshan, Zhao was responsible for defining the Six Paths and the Buddhas who operate within them and beyond them. In this sense, Zhao is not simply the author of Baodingshan or its version of the wheel. Rather, his mastery of the esoteric arts grants him access to knowledge about the cosmos, a world that contains the seeds of both ignorance and enlightenment. The creator of the site is no different than pilgrims to the site, in that both are endowed with the capacity to achieve salvation.

Also depicted in the center of the wheel are the Three Poisons in animal form, in keeping with the canonical version. Then come three rings outside the center. In the first ring are the Six Paths of rebirth. The palaces of the gods are at the top, with *asuras* (demigods) to the left and humans to the right. A torture chamber in hell is shown at the bottom, while to the right a demon is shown eating a person in the realm of ghosts, and animals are shown to the left. The second and third rings are each divided into eighteen segments. They offer different readings of the notion of change. The second ring contains the eighteen stages in the cycle of causation. Almost all of the images match the descriptions in the canonical account, which allows for Eighteen Conditions (see table 1 in chapter 1).

---

16. The lines are transposed in the transcription in Sichuansheng shehui kexueyuan et al., *Dazu shike neirong zonglu*, p. 484.

17. See Deng, "Dazu Baodingshan Dafowan 'liuhao tu' kan diaocha."

FIG. 9.5. Lower portion of wheel of rebirth. Relief carving. Dafowan Niche 3, Baodingshan, Sichuan, thirteenth century. Photography: Stephen F. Teiser.

The third ring focuses on another aspect of impermanence, the transition from one form of life to the next. Each of the eighteen segments in this ring portrays a being moving through a tube, with the head sticking out the front and the feet visible behind, a motif seen in the wheel of rebirth at Yulin. Movement proceeds in a counterclockwise direction. At the bottom of the wheel, in the six o'clock position, for instance, is a figure with the head of a fish and the tail of a snake (see fig. 9.5). At the next station (to the right), the same being has transmogrified one more step, its head turning into a horse and its tail remaining that of a fish. The circle continues around in a similar way (see table 6). Like the chain of causation, the individual stations in this ring are connected to each other in an irreversible sequence. They drive home not simply the truth of impermanence, but the point that change follows a recurring pattern.

The area outside the wheel seems to have particularly encouraged variations, visual and textual, on the stock themes seen elsewhere. The wheel is grasped by the great demon of impermanence, which is quite canonical. But the demon's power is indexed by his standing on a dragon, a figure new to the iconography of the saṃsāracakra (and now only partly visible). Four other figures stand below the wheel, two on each side

Table 6. Species in the outer (third) ring of the wheel of rebirth, Baodingshan, Sichuan, thirteenth century.

Position (1 = top center, proceeding counterclockwise)	Head	Tail
1.	woman	man
2.	man (official)	woman
3.	tiger	man (official)
4.	ox	tiger
5.	?	ox
6.	reptile	?
7.	pig	reptile
8.	dragon	pig
9.	snake	dragon
10.	fish	snake
11.	horse	fish
12.	goat?	horse
13.	monkey	goat?
14.	?	monkey
15.	duck	?
16.	rat?	duck
17.	dog	rat?
18.	man	dog

(see fig. 9.6). At bottom right is a woman and a monkey engaged in rubbing its genitals, perhaps a way of representing greed or lust. At the left are two government officials, one dressed as a civilian and the other in military attire.

Tokens of transcendence are sculpted above the wheel of rebirth (see fig. 9.7). Directly over the wheel are seated three Buddha figures, probably representing the Buddhas of the past (Dīpaṃkara), present (Śākyamuni), and future (Maitreya). They may or may not be symbols for the cessation of suffering that occurs in nirvāṇa. In any event, their presence at the top of a tall sculpture serves as a stamp of approval, a validation of the entire scene by the Buddhas of all times.

The written elements in the scene at Baodingshan also emphasize the possibility of salvation from the turning of the wheel. The two stanzas of the canonical account encouraging renunciation are inscribed at the top, to the left and right of the wheel. A new element is added too, a hymn in four lines of seven syllables each:

FIG. 9.6. Figures below wheel of rebirth. Relief carving. Dafowan Niche 3, Baodingshan, Sichuan, thirteenth century. Photography: Stephen F. Teiser.

FIG. 9.7. Figures above wheel of rebirth. Relief carving. Dafowan Niche 3, Baodingshan, Sichuan, thirteenth century. Bai Ziran, *Zhongguo Dazu shiku*, pl. 62.

> The myriad forms of life within the wheel of the Three Realms
> Originate in passion and will end in drowning.
> Please observe all the Buddhas, like sands of the Ganges, outside the wheel,
> Are all old companions inside the wheel.[18]

Rather than hewing to the canonical stanzas and stressing the difference between inside and outside, suffering and non-attachment, this stanza emphasizes the accessibility of enlightenment and those who exemplify enlightenment. Buddhas are not limited to a world beyond saṃsāra; they provide support to beings within the realm of birth and death as well.

The content of the wheel at Baodingshan is heavily localized, and the site as a whole testifies to the regional character of Buddhism. Much of the material at Baodingshan is consistent with the forms of Buddhism found all across Sichuan during the late Tang

18. Hymn transcribed in Chen Xishan, *Dazu shike zhilue jiaozhu*, p. 279, except that the editors mistakenly transcribe the beginning of the third line. The characters were easily legible when I visited Baodingshan in 1999, and they are transcribed correctly in Chongqing Dazu shike yishu bowuguan et al., *Dazu shike mingwen lu*, p. 94.

dynasty, the Five Dynasties period, and the Northern and Southern Song dynasties.[19] With increasing trade and soaring growth in population, the economy of the whole region flourished during this long period, during the first half of which China's political center was either weak or nonexistent. Traditions originating in central China are clear in Sichuan, which served as home-in-exile to two Tang emperors, Xuanzong (r. 712–756) and Xizong (r. 873–888). They both moved their courts and established academies there, and the marks left by these literati, artisans, and monks from central China are indisputable. Wang Jian (847–918) rose from being a thief, to serving as a general in the Tang army, to founding his own state based in Chengdu in 907. According to Robert Somers, under him Chengdu "became a great refuge for artists and poets, not to mention members of the Tang official class who were able to escape the brutal fighting taking place in the north. His regime was one of the most stable and peaceful of these years."[20] Sichuan also received cultural influences from the southwest (the Nanzhao kingdom of Dali) and the west (Tibet). The result was a vibrant synthesis of local traditions and themes from a variety of sources. Sichuan Buddhism appears to have pioneered in placing images of Mañjuśrī and Samantabhadra at the sides of Vairocana, a representation dubbed "The Three Sages of Huayan" (Huayan Sansheng). Liu Benzun's cult was distributed widely across central and eastern Sichuan. In addition to emphasizing Vairocana and using mantras and maṇḍalas, the Buddhism of Sichuan maintained a strong interest in ascetic acts, filial piety, rebirth in the paradises of Amitābha and other figures, the tortures of hell, the codified virtues of lay life, and the story of Śākyamuni's life. Artisans took advantage of cliff faces to carve a variety of architectural forms: the recessed niche is most common, but other styles also appear, such as deeper grottoes in imitation of Buddha halls. Many sites incorporated citations from texts, ranging from canonical sūtras to apocrypha, traditional poems, and local hymns. Texts were incorporated into shrines in a variety of formats. In some places they were subsidiary accompaniment to colossal statuary, while in other places they covered three or four walls of a small shrine or constituted an entire niche of their own. Sponsors of all such sites seem to range from individual lay Buddhists and local monks to large organizations of donors.

Unlike temples at Ajaṇṭā, Kumtura, Yulin, and Tabo, Baodingshan was neither constructed by a small group of donors nor limited to a particular family or social class. It was open to all pilgrims, and its founder sought to popularize the teachings of Buddhism. The context itself, then, was exoteric, and by placing the niche of the wheel of rebirth near the beginning of the site, the designers intended for it to function as a preparatory lesson to the scenes that followed. The main organizer even appears to have had himself portrayed in the center of the wheel, turning the site, in effect, into

19. For an excellent overview of art and religion during this period, see Ding, "Sichuan shiku zashi." See also Howard, *Summit of Treasures*, pp. 121–46; idem, "Tang Buddhist Sculpture of Sichuan"; Hu Wenhe, *Sichuan daojiao fojiao shiku yishu*; Sorenson, *Survey of the Religious Sculptures of Anyue*; Ueno, "Shisen ni okeru Tō Sō jiki no sekkoku zōzō sekkyō jigyō," esp. pp. 297–303; and Zou and Hu, "Qianshu Houshu yu zhongyuan zhengquan de guanxi."

20. Somers, "End of the T'ang," p. 789.

Zhao Zhifeng's view of the world. Nevertheless, it would be a mistake to overlook the canonical meanings at Baodingshan. Most architects and designers of the wheel of rebirth in Asia situated the wheel in the most accessible, most exterior position, even when (at Yulin, for instance) one had to enter a narrow passageway to see it. Accessibility could always be turned into a local virtue, no matter how public or private the site was as a whole. The apocryphal hymn inscribed at Baodingshan shows that local preferences in liturgy were being respected. But rather than dispensing with the canon, the creators dutifully quoted the vinaya account before adding their own words. The wheel of life and death at Baodingshan thus formulates its own interpretation of the truths prescribed in the monastic regulations. Baodingshan reiterates the message that hints of nirvāṇa can be found within the cycle of suffering. The site as a whole is home to several Buddhas, including Vairocana as cosmic lord, Amitābha residing in paradise, Maitreya, and Śākyamuni as the closest, most recent, and most filial of all enlightened beings. Buddhas and bodhisattvas make their appearance within the wheel of rebirth itself, meditating calmly in the spokes of the Six Paths. The collapsing of the distinction between suffering and release is perhaps most apparent in the positioning of Zhao in the center of the wheel, with Buddhas and bodhisattvas streaming from his chest. For the creator of the site, as well as for the implied pilgrim, the path to transcendence begins in the heart of saṃsāra.

Chapter 10

Conclusions

In the introduction I invoked the bivalent notion of discursive practice in order to justify a dual focus in this book. In the first place, a discourse is a way of conceptualizing, talking or writing about, or picturing. Although all people eventually die, it would be misleading to treat death as a universal experience, a singular precultural touchstone that is then viewed differently in a variety of pictures and words. Instead, in this book I emphasize the ways in which specific representations give rise to different understandings of life and death, how discourse shapes experience. Rather than reading images as simple reflections of preexisting meaning, I ask how images engender values. In this concluding chapter I want to speculate further on the possibilities for imagining rebirth that are opened up by the formal properties of the wheel. In the second place, discourse is a social practice. Discourse is a conventional act of speaking (or writing or painting), bound loosely by rules, governed by institutions, and negotiated differently by individual actors. Discourses of rebirth empower some people to draw while asking others to observe. In this chapter I want to return, on and off, to these two senses of discursive practice.

Circles and Lines

The canonical account of the Buddha's instructions to paint a wheel of life and death institutes a contrast between two discursive situations. In the first, a charismatic disciple of the Buddha, Maudgalyāyana, tells a large audience about his travels in the other world. In the second practice, a picture of a wheel is painted on the porch of a large temple and a preacher is appointed to explain its symbols. Boiled down to their geometric essences, Maudgalyāyana's journey takes the shape of a line, while the discourse of the painting describes a circle. These two Euclidean concepts do not completely encapsulate the materials discussed here, but their abstract quality helps to clarify the two discursive paradigms.

As a line, Maudgalyāyana's journey is defined by two points, a beginning and an end. Movement takes place in one direction only. Repetition is not possible; there is no backtracking. In this sense the line is the basic organizing principle for both time and space: the journey commences at the first point, proceeds along the line, and concludes at the last point. To make our geometric figure correspond more closely to the narrative possibilities, it is probably best to conceive of a segmented line, with each point defining a particular encounter in the journey or explaining how to overcome obstacles. This line corresponds to what medieval Chinese audiences probably saw when they attended a performance of transformations. We need to remember that the genre of transformation text (*bianwen*) was not *ab origine* a textual phenomenon, but a spectacle. Working from memory, storytellers would alternate between poetry put to song and the colloquial language spoken without metrical limitation, relating the story of Maudgalyāyana's pilgrimage through the dark regions in search of his mother. While speaking and singing, they would point to paintings of particular scenes. The paintings were executed on scrolls, and a full performance might involve fifteen to twenty scrolls. This kind of partly visual, partly auditory entertainment is like a modern slide show or PowerPoint presentation. None of the scroll paintings used in a performance of the Maudgalyāyana drama survives. But their format was undoubtedly sequential, depicting Maudgalyāyana first in one scene and then in another.

As discussed in chapter 7, a picture of Maudgalyāyana's journey that does survive is painted in Yulin Cave 19 (Gansu, China), on the wall of the corridor opposite that on which the wheel of rebirth is painted (see figs. 7.7 and 7.8). The Maudgalyāyana painting has a linear composition. The scenes are laid out in the shape of a backwards letter S. To follow Maudgalyāyana's progress, the viewer starts at top left and reads to the right, moves down to the second row and reads right to the left, then drops to the lowest tier and reads left to right. Although one needs to shift one's gaze and shuffle a few steps left and right, the narrative is clearly laid out as a progression from one scene to the next.

Another approximation to a linear journey appears in a late narrative of Maudgalyāyana's quest, a Japanese printed text based on a Chinese original dated 1251 and bound in scroll format (see fig. 10.1).[1] The entire scroll narrates Maudgalyāyana's tour of the underworld, from right to left, with text at bottom and pictures on top. The section of the scroll shown in figure 10.1 depicts two scenes, the hell of hungry ghosts and the hell of the flaming river. The two scenes are separated in the middle by a cloud, which demarcates two frames and suggests movement. In the first scene Maudgalyāyana speaks with hungry ghosts whose condition is exemplified by their swollen bellies, emaciated necks, and flames emanating from their mouths. Whenever they try to slake their thirst or satisfy their hunger, the food they are about to eat bursts into flames before reaching their mouths. Their bodies display all the signs of advanced starvation: their stomachs are distended, their arms, legs, and chests are

1. The text is entitled *Mokuren kyūbo kyō* (*Scripture on Maudgalyāyana Saving His Mother*) and dates from the fourteenth century. See Miya, "Mokuren kyūbo setsuwa to sono kaiga."

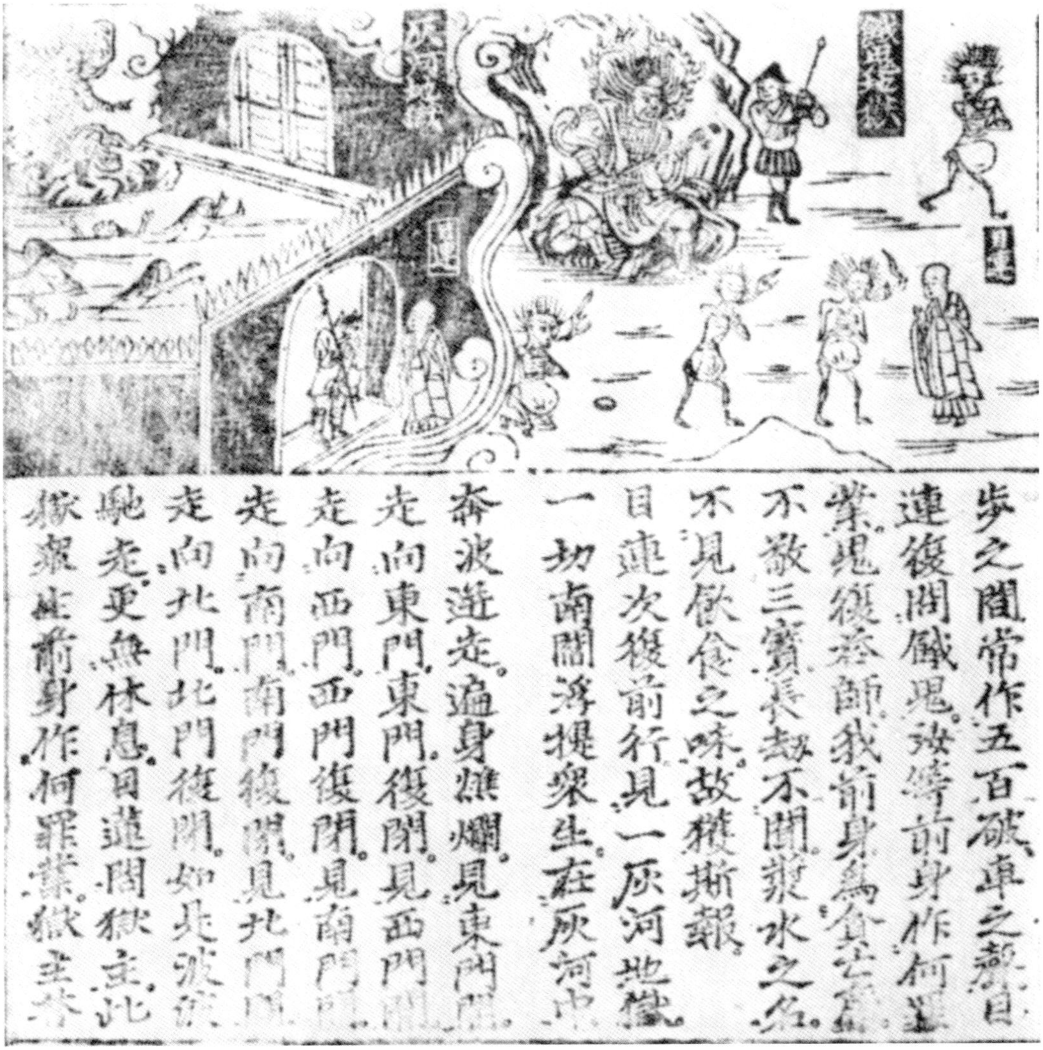

Fig. 10.1. Hungry ghosts and flaming river, scene from *Scripture on Maudgalyāyana Saving His Mother*. Fourteenth-century Japanese woodblock printed text. Courtesy of Konkōji, Kyōtō, and Tokyo National Research Institute of Cultural Properties.

reduced to skin and bones, and their thinning hair stands on end. In the next scene Maudgalyāyana's linear progression is highlighted by the use of a wall surrounding his next stop, the river of embers. The figure of Maudgalyāyana reappears in each scene, conforming to one of the classic modes of narrative representation, the cyclic method in which the main character is shown in successive scenes.[2]

2. See Weitzmann, *Illustration in Roll and Codex*, pp. 12–46.

A related kind of illustrated text, *The Scripture on the Ten Kings* (*Shiwang jing*), also pictures the process of birth and death as a line.[3] The earliest copies date from the tenth century and were found in Dunhuang. This text narrates the journey of the soul after death. Each deceased person passes through a series of ten courts, laid out from right to left along the length of the scroll (see fig. 7.5). Each court is administered by a stern judge who has access to the person's life history and recourse to various forms of torture to encourage honesty. At the very moment when the deceased is standing before a magistrate, the family of mourners is supposed to perform ceremonies dispatching offerings to the magistrate. The rituals are held at seven-day intervals during the pan-Buddhist intermediary period of forty-nine days after death, and then at one hundred days, one year, and three years after death. This purgatory comes to an end when the deceased is assigned rebirth in one of the Five Paths by the tenth magistrate and passes into the clouds leading up to the left. Like the course traced by Maudgalyāyana's travels, the progressive arrangement of *The Scripture on the Ten Kings* emphasizes regularity, sequence, and closure. The end is not final, since the deceased is born again as a sentient being, but it does mark the conclusion of one journey and the commencement of another.

In contrast to Maudgalyāyana's line, the circle defined by the discourse of the wheel of rebirth has no beginning and no end. The figure of the wheel is well suited to represent an unending process. As a humanly constructed object in circular form, the wheel offers a wealth of possibilities. Rebirth in the Five or Six Paths, marked out as segments of the wheel, can in principle go on forever. The outer ring or felloe, consisting of the Twelve Conditions in the chain of causation, suggests that death is simply one stage in the life cycle of the individual, since old age and death are inevitably followed by a new life marked by ignorance. This is not to say, however, that progress is impossible. The wheel does indicate positionality: the two paths of rebirth at the top (gods and humans) are preferable to the lower three paths, and in some versions (the vinaya account and paintings in modern Tibet) some people are portrayed heading upward, others downward.

The spatial properties of the figure of the circle have a significant effect upon how ideas about life and death are expressed. Plotting the Five Paths within a circle presents a problem. Since the top half of the circle is divided between gods and humans, how can the artist both maintain spatial symmetry and find a way to propound the idea that gods are situated above humans? As we have seen, different traditions responded to this problem in different ways. The two tiny wheels at Kumtura (Xinjiang, China) simply divide the top semicircle in half, whereas the painters at Ajaṇṭā (Maharashtra, India) relied on the canonical notion of Four Continents in their exegesis of the doctrine of the Five Paths. They subdivided the human world into four subrealms, two displayed on each side of the realm of the gods. They created a pic-

---

3. See Du, *Dunhuangben foshuo shiwang jing jiaolu yanjiu*; Teiser, "*Scripture on the Ten Kings*" *and the Making of Purgatory in Medieval Chinese Buddhism*; idem, "Growth of Purgatory"; and Tokushi and Ogawa, "*Jūō shōshichi kyō* sanzuken no kōzō."

torial arrangement in which gods reside above humans and in which both gods and humans stand higher in the realm of saṃsāra than the three lower paths of rebirth. In this respect, the Ajaṇṭā painters offered an elegant solution to a dilemma that not all artists had to face. Specifically, those artists who inherited the concept of Six Paths (rather than five) had no need to subdivide realms, since the mansions of the gods could always be shown at the top, flanked by humans and *asuras* (demigods). And even those artists whose vinaya traditions did mandate Five Paths, such as those at Yulin, Tabo (medieval western Tibet), and Baodingshan (Sichuan, China), did not feel bound by the canonical account: they pictured six instead of five. The concept of the Five Paths (*pañcagati*) was closely associated with the Sarvāstivāda school, but even in medieval India the Buddhist tradition offered a variety of ways of enumerating the paths of rebirth.[4]

A consideration of geometrical forms related to the wheel sheds further light on the logical possibilities afforded by using the symbol of the wheel to conceive of life and death. These circular shapes, considered in conjunction with the linear depictions analyzed above, bring the significance of the wheel of rebirth into sharper focus. A loose definition of the wheel family would include spokes emanating from a center as well as rims circumscribing a series of radii.

One of the earliest representations of the paths of rebirth resembling the spokes of a wheel is the ninth-century wall painting of a meditating monk at Kumtura, discussed in chapter 6 (see plate 9). In its center sits a monk in meditation posture, holding a bowl in his hands. Lines representing the Five Paths emerge from his bowl and flow to his two sides. To the right of the monk, at the top, is the realm of gods, indicated by Mount Sumeru, pavilions, and a statue of a Buddha, beneath whom kneel four gods. The path at bottom right is probably the hell regions, denoted by a cauldron. On the left side of the bowl, the middle path is that of human beings, with four people dressed as officials facing a monk. Below them are represented animals.

The outward projection of the paths of rebirth from a single locus in the Kumtura painting highlights several features of the spoke pattern in the wheel of rebirth. The design at Kumtura is both centrifugal and arrayed. All realms of rebirth emerge from one source: they flow out of the monk's bowl, just as all forms of life are produced by greed, hatred, and delusion, symbolized by animals in the center of the wheel. At Kumtura the paths of rebirth are centrifugal, not in the physical sense of moving away from an axis or in the political sense as fleeing central authority, but rather in the botanical sense of developing outward from a center. In pictorial terms, the use of five vectors or spokes sharing an origin also allows for systematic placement of the endpoints around the central figure.

Another spokelike format for representing the paths of rebirth occurs in the iconography of Kṣitigarbha Bodhisattva (Dizang pusa), the saintlike figure who special-

4. On the Five and Six Paths, see Mochizuki, *Bukkyō daijiten*, pp. 1206b–07c, 5071c–72a; Lamotte, *Le traité de la grande vertu de sagesse*, pp. 612–14, n. 1; and Mibu, "Rokudōsetsu ni kan suru nisan no mondai ni tsuite."

izes in rescuing those reborn in the hell regions. Recent scholarship has documented that Kṣitigarbha's association with the underworld began relatively late, in the eighth or ninth century.[5] Chinese scriptures compiled around that time weave together three themes. First, they delineate Kṣitigarbha's career as a bodhisattva, explaining his dedication over many lifetimes to bringing salvation to sentient beings. They emphasize his connection to Śākyamuni Buddha and the importance of his positioning in time, which is between the most recent Buddha (Śākyamuni) and the one in the future (Maitreya). Second, according to the scriptures, Kṣitigarbha makes a special point of saving beings who reside in the underworld, whether that realm is conceived as the hells underground or as the shadowy state of purgatory through which all souls pass on the way to their next rebirth. The third component of Kṣitigarbha belief that emerged in the eighth and ninth centuries is his role in guaranteeing safe passage to rebirth in the pure land, a Buddha realm free of impurity from which one can achieve final release.

Six Paths emanating from Kṣitigarbha's mandorla are depicted in paintings on silk dating from the ninth century, like the two-tiered composition in figure 10.2. Kṣitigarbha sits on a lotus throne, attended by two groups of figures below him, including the Ten Kings of Hell, the monk Daoming and his lion, and (at the bottom two corners) the Boys of Good and Evil, who keep track of peoples' deeds. The rays of the Six Paths are marked by wavy cloud paths leading upward from Kṣitigarbha's mandorla. At top right is the realm of the gods with three figures seated in meditation: a male, a female, and a Buddha. Below them are a man and a woman, and below them is the realm of animals. The top left path is that of the *asuras*; the one pictured here has three heads and four arms. Below him are hungry ghosts, running through flames. Hell is depicted at the bottom, with demons wielding long pokers to help stir the inmate cooking in the pot. The top half of the painting stands in contradistinction to the Six Paths at bottom. It follows the general conventions for pure lands, without making overt reference to any specific paradise (that of Amitābha, Maitreya, or Bhaiṣajyaguru). The Buddha in the center is accompanied by two crowned bodhisattvas on each side, behind whom stand two monastic disciples with shaven heads. Beside the bodhisattvas are two guardian kings, underneath whom are seated two smaller bodhisattva figures. Four musicians at the Buddha's feet complete the assembly. They are all ensconced on a platform with a balustrade, and the whole upper scene, as befits a pure land, is graced by two ponds. Access to this paradise from the realm of saṃsāra is provided by three bridges. Kṣitigarbha's soteriological function is similar to that of the three bridges: he is an intermediary between this world and the pure land. Beings in the Six Paths may use their devotion to him as a way of ascending to paradise.

The use of spokelike rays in representing the Six Paths around Kṣitigarbha offers an interesting variation on the theme of emanation. Rather than producing the Six

5. I rely especially on Ng, "The Formation and Development of the Dizang Cult," esp. pp. 108–296; and Wang-Toutain, *Le Bodhisattva Kṣitigarbha*. The apocryphal scriptures I refer to are the *Dizang pusa jing* (various Dunhuang versions conveniently listed in ibid., pp. 309–10); and the *Dizang pusa benyuan jing*, attributed to Śikṣānanda (652–712), *T* no. 412.

FIG. 10.2. Kṣitigarbha and the pure land. Silk painting. Dunhuang, ninth century. Musée Guimet, EO 3580. Courtesy of Réunion des Musées Nationaux/Art Resource, NY.

Paths, Kṣitigarbha rules over them. He is the central figure who mediates between the Six Paths and the realm of the transcendent Buddha pictured above him.

The theme of production from a center is enunciated even more clearly in other representations of the Six Paths utilizing a spoke design. The wheel of life carved at Baodingshan in the thirteenth century (plate 14 and fig. 9.4), examined in chapter 9, is a good example. The ribbons separating the Six Paths emerge from the chest of the meditator. The Buddhas and bodhisattvas visible within the ribbons are generated from the heart/mind as well. Illustrations of the Ten Realms painted in Japan in the early modern period pursue this psychological reading of the Six Paths.[6] The pilgrimage to Kumano (Wakayama Prefecture, south-central Honshu) had been a widespread feature of Japanese religion for centuries by the time the screen painting in figure 10.3 was executed in the early seventeenth century. The painting depicts a female storyteller at the Sumiyoshi Shrine using a feather to point out scenes in a painting she is narrating to her audience, composed entirely of women. Her subject appears to be the word for "mind" (*shin*), written at the top center in the painting. The painting she is using belongs to a genre entitled "Illustration of the Ten Realms of Mind Contemplation" ("Kanshin jūkai zu"), which makes the point that all realms are created by the mind, that all forms can be discerned through contemplation. Such paintings add four more stations to the canonical Six Paths: Buddhas, bodhisattvas, *śrāvakas* (voice-hearers), and *pratyekabuddhas*. It is interesting to note that paintings of the wheel of rebirth in the form of a proper wheel are relatively uncommon in Japan; when the Six Paths are displayed in circular format, they are usually portrayed as part of the Ten Realms. The Buddha figure in the center is usually Amitābha. The hell regions and the realm of hungry ghosts are typically staffed by King Yama or other judges. The word for heart or mind is actually painted into the cosmography, just under the main Buddha.

This idealistic bias in the interpretation of Buddhist cosmology is clear in the portrayal of the Six Paths emanating from the meditator in the center of the wheel at Baodingshan. The psychological reading is even more pronounced in later Japanese representations in which the word for mind (or heart) is drawn in the shape of a pearl, containing within it all Ten Realms.[7] By contrast, the nineteenth-century woodblock print in figure 10.4 portrays the relation between mind and world not as one of encapsulation, but as projection: the Ten Realms emanate from the mind, the very center of the picture. In this reading, both the other world and this world, the transcendent states achieved by Buddhas and bodhisattvas as well as the six worldly states of suffering, are tied to human experience through the power of meditation.

The other wheellike form used to represent the Six Paths consists of concentric

6. For the history of this storytelling tradition, see Hagiwara, *Miko to bukkyō shi*; and Moerman, *Localizing Paradise*.

7. See, for example, the painting of the Ten Realms entitled *Shōzō en'yū sandai zusetsu*, from Kokawadera, reproduced in Ōsaka shiritsu hakubutsukan, *Shaji sankei mandara*, p. 111. Humans occupy the center, with the other nine paths arranged clockwise from the top, beginning with Buddhas.

FIG. 10.3. Storyteller at the Sumiyoshi Shrine explaining "Illustration of the Ten Realms of Mind Contemplation," detail of screen painting. Japan, early seventeenth century. Freer Gallery of Art, Smithsonian Institution, Washington, D.C.: Purchase, F1900.26.

觀心十方界圖

華嚴經云若人欲了知三世一切佛應觀法界性
一切唯心造ト云ル文ハ佛法ノ極妙ノ旨ヲ説セ給フ大宋
國ノ慈雲大師此文ニ依リテ觀心十界ノ圖ヲ顯シ
丞相王欽若序ヲ作リテ流通シ給ヘリ誠ニ我カ一念
惡心ヲ起セハ忽チ地獄餓鬼等界ニ落チ善心ヲ起
セハ忽チ佛菩薩等ノ界トナル一旦佛心ヲ起ストモ又惡
ヲ起セハ佛界変シテ地獄トナル縦令地獄ノ念ヲ起スト
モ心ヲ翻セハ地獄モ変シテ佛界トナル方ノ界皆各十界
ヲ起スハ十界互ニ具シテ本來一念三千即空假中ナルニ
由ル此妙理ヲ觀スレハ念々佛心トナルサレハ地獄ノ猛火ニ
燒ルノモ佛果ノ微妙ノ樂ミヲ受ルモ唯タ我カ心ノ
善惡ニ在リ時々刻々心ヲ省テ心ノ駒ニ手綱許スヘカ
ラス然ルニ六道界ノ苦果ヲ離レ一佛界ノ淨樂ヲ
得ルコハ極樂往生ヲ願フヨリ直捷ナルハナシ極樂往
生ニ遂ルコハ此十界ノ圖ノ道理ヲ信スルヨリ至
要ナルハナシ既ニソレ吾一心ニ十界三千ノ法ヲ具スト信
スレハ十萬億土ノ外ノ安養モ吾カ心内ノ淨土ナレハ
誓願ハ此ノ唯心ノ淨土ニ生センコヲ願ヒ信願已ニ
導キテ行スル所ノ念佛ハ我カ本性ノ彌陀如來
ナレハ圖ノ道理ヲ信セハ是眞ノ融通念佛ニシテ
其功德甚タ深ク其利益至ツテ廣シ願クハ有縁
同志此圖ニ依テ唯心ノ淨土ヲ信シ此理ヲ以テ往生ノ
誓願ヲ深フシ信願已ニ固ケレハ行スル所ハ念佛ニ
於テ信願行ノ三ツ備リテ十方三世佛祖ノ大道
モ茲ニ在ルコヲ知ルヘシ若然ラハ唱ル所ノ念佛
千遍萬遍乃至十萬ト云ヘトモ圖スル所ノ圈
點ヲ消シテ其數ヲ記シ方ニ百萬遍ニ滿タハ
決定往生豈疑フベケン哉

寛文己酉印施

若人欲了知

應觀法界性

三世一切佛

一切唯心造

檜前斐成畫

FIG. 10.5. Cosmological Buddha. Wall painting. Kizil Cave 175, Xinjiang, sixth century. Zhongguo bihua quanji bianji weiyuanhui, *Kezi'er*, pl. 146.

circles. A good example is located at Kizil (Xinjiang, China), in the ancient kingdom of Kucha near Kumtura on the northern Silk Road, in Cave 175, which dates from the sixth century. As shown in figure 10.5, the wall painting has a seated Buddha at the center with halo and mandorla. Above him are seven meditating figures, perhaps the Seven Buddhas of the Past. The central Buddha is surrounded by a large cast of characters arranged in three concentric circles. Beginning closest to the Buddha at bottom left, we see a funeral procession. The details are hazy, but it is possible to discern mourners carrying a coffin with a corpse on top, trailed by a mourner. In the second circle, also starting on the left, a potter is visible. He uses a long stick to turn his wheel, on which he is shaping a large pot. Proceeding counterclockwise to the next station in the circle, there is a man plowing with two oxen. Farther around that circle, at the top right of the painting, is a farming scene, with two men using hoes to till. At two points in the inner circle we can make out scenes of pleasure: at the ten o'clock and two o'clock positions, pavilions contain dancers and musicians. The third circle on the left side

Facing page: FIG. 10.4. Illustration of the Realms of the Ten Directions of Mind Contemplation. Hand-colored woodblock print. Japan, 1669. The Trustees of the British Museum.

contains a number of beings belonging to different paths of rebirth, including ghosts, criminals or sinners, tigers, birds, elephants, and rabbits, and perhaps a cauldron.

Previous scholarship on this cave claims that this Buddha scene is a wheel of rebirth in the Five Paths.[8] Although its circular form constitutes an interesting parallel to the wheel of rebirth, I believe instead that it is a mandorlic representation of Śākyamuni as the cosmological Buddha, of the sort analyzed by Angela Howard and discussed in chapter 5.[9] The larger agenda of the cave's iconographic program as well as the visual details of the painting itself all point to the grandeur and power of the central figure of the cave, Śākyamuni. The architecture of the cave is a central stūpa pillar (see fig. 10.6). The cave probably originally possessed a full antechamber, now missing. As a central stūpa-pillar cave, its ritual focus is the main Buddha statue that used to stand in front of the main (north) wall of the main chamber, which is the surface of the stūpa one faces upon entering the cave. The walls of the main chamber contain scenes from various stories of the Buddha's previous lifetimes, including the prophecy of his birth, the miracles he performed as a child, and his defeat of Māra. As one proceeds clockwise around the stūpa through the corridor on the left, one encounters further evidence of the Buddha's holiness. The rear wall of the rear corridor is a *parinirvāṇa* scene: Śākyamuni reclines on a couch, surrounded by disciples as he passes into final extinction. The wall opposite the *parinirvāṇa* scene depicts the way in which the Buddha, having already achieved liberation, was later made accessible to followers of Buddhism. The paintings show his cremation and then the distribution of his relics between the eight kings of ancient India. At least six other caves at Kizil dating from the sixth and seventh centuries utilize the same architectural design and portray the same three scenes of *parinirvāṇa*, cremation, and relic distribution in their passageways.[10] In Kizil Cave 175, the placement of the cosmological Buddha in the corridor leading away from the *parinirvāṇa* is significant. As a stūpa, the entire cave brings the visitor into the presence of the Buddha and allows him or her to engage in the ritual of circumambulation. The paintings on the walls depict the progression of Śākyamuni's career: his previous lifetimes, his birth as a prince, his enlightenment, his death, and his dissemination into the world. The cosmological Buddha is located on the last wall surface one passes before returning to the main chamber. It shows that the Buddha has not passed away into oblivion, but rather has been revealed as the center of life. Assuming his position under the Seven Buddhas of the Past, he is present everywhere. As

8. The major study is by Ma Shichang, "Kezi'er zhongxinzhuku zhushi quanding yu houshi de bihua," pp. 217–19. The same identification ("illustration of rebirth in the Five Paths") is given in Xinjiang Qiuci shiku yanjiusuo, *Kezi'er shiku neirong zonglu*, p. 196. Although I disagree with Ma's reading of this particular painting, I am much indebted to him for alerting me to its existence and generously sharing his unparalleled knowledge of the site. For general studies, see also Howard, "In Support of a New Chronology for the Kizil Mural Paintings"; Su, "Xinjiang Baicheng Kezi'er shiku bufen dongku de leixing yu niandai"; and Yuan, "Qiucifeng bihua de xingcheng yu fazhan."

9. See Howard, *Imagery of the Cosmological Buddha*. Her more recent research on sites in Kucha, which she has graciously shared in public lectures and personal correspondence, returns to this theme.

10. The other caves are Kizil Caves 4, 27, 98, 163, 179, and 224.

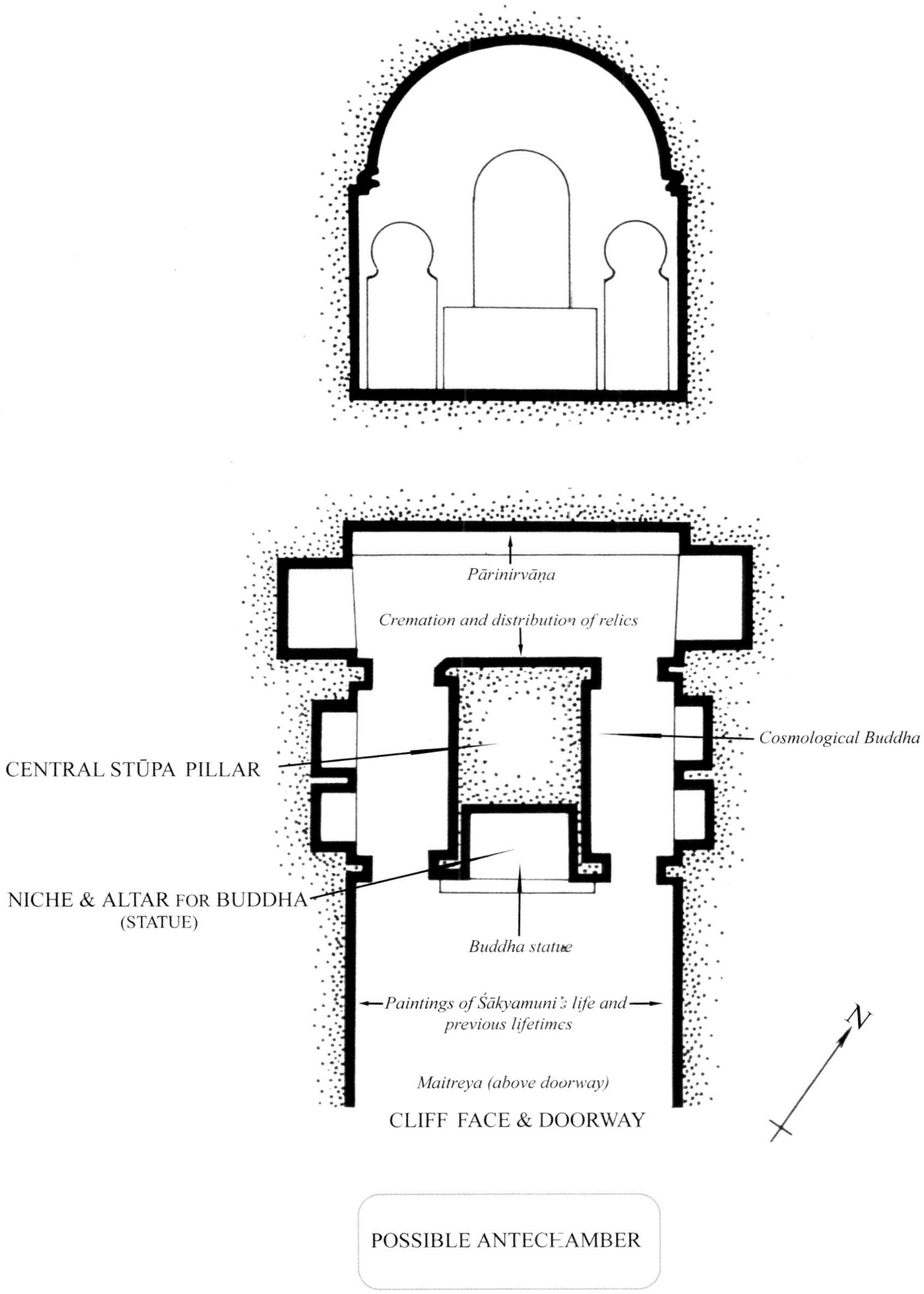

FIG. 10.6. Iconographic program of Kizil Cave 175. After Xinjiang Weiwu'er zizhiqu wenwu guanli weiyuanhui et al., *Kezi'er shiku*, 3:241. Drawn by Sorat Tungkasiri and Stephen F. Teiser.

one leaves the cave, a painting of Maitreya Buddha is located above the door, constituting an assurance that the all-powerful Buddha exercises dominion over the future.

The visual details of the painting in Kizil Cave 175 support this reading of the cave's overall religious significance. The composition is unlike the wheel of rebirth in several respects. It does contain figures from different realms of rebirth, and some of its symbols (e.g., the potter) overlap with those for the Twelve Conditions. However, the composition is not, properly speaking, a wheel, since it does not contain any spokes. The artist displays no interest in visually discussing, via the spokes of a wheel, the demarcation between paths of rebirth. Nor does the composition possess any true felloes. At both top and bottom, the three concentric rings around the Buddhas are broken rims; they are not complete, nor were they ever intended to be, since the finished composition is sized well to the existing wall space. The painting is dominated by the large icon of the Buddha at its center, and the arrangement of realms, though not entirely clear, seems to follow the principle of vertical ranking. There is no hint of a final nirvāṇa lurking outside the wheel, as there is in paintings of the saṃsāracakra. Rather, the ontological principle of Buddhahood manifests itself in the circles radiating outward from the center, in the form of seated and standing Buddhas in each of the concentric rings. Unlike the wheels of rebirth portrayed on the outskirts of temples, the painting of the cosmological Buddha in Kizil Cave 175 serves as a conclusion to the story of Śākyamuni's perfection. It confirms the presence of enlightenment within the cave and the possibility of salvation throughout the universe.

What is the payoff to these speculations about the wheel family? The formal properties of circles and wheels, as opposed to those of a line, exercise some influence over what ideas about saṃsāra can be expressed. I would isolate four distinct compositional elements that are developed, to differing degrees, in the various versions of the wheel of rebirth considered in earlier chapters. First, all wheels have hubs. In part this is a cultural elaboration of the mathematical postulate that every circle has a focus. The hub is what drives the wheel, what makes it go around. The hub supplies the motivation for the wheel; situated at the axis of the wheel, its influence is pivotal. In Buddhist terms, the wheel of rebirth is driven by whatever forces are pictured in the hub of the wheel. However, the content of the hub, and hence the emotional or existential quality of the wheel, vary tremendously from one representation to the next. Some wheels are driven by hatred, greed, and delusion; the sorrows of the Six Paths derive from the Three Poisons. The moral of this representation seems to be that one should flee from the center and all that it entails. Other wheels are visualized as originating in the mind, an iconography that stresses the power of the individual to generate every kind of worldly possibility through the exercise of meditation. This kind of hub is more neutral, both ontologically and morally, since the training of the mind strives for neutrality and the acceptance of impermanence. If the center contains the mind, which is ultimately equivalent to all things, then it is senseless to seek escape from the mental wheel. In other paintings a Buddha is placed at the center of the wheel, profoundly influencing the quality of life in saṃsāra. Each segment of the circle is blessed by his compassion, as he manifests himself in the guise appropriate to each form of life.

The second component of the wheel is the spokes. Whereas all radii are equal in length, spokes serve to demarcate qualitatively different modes of life within each segment of the wheel. Even those who desire a quick exit from the cycle of existence cannot ignore the inequalities determined by their level of rebirth. In traditional Buddhist cosmology, access to Buddhahood or enlightenment—movement out of the circle—is limited to human beings. Creatures born into other paths of rebirth are not damned, however. They are simply required to wait until their intentions are pure enough to achieve rebirth as a human being. Differences between, say, a god and a hell being are both important and impermanent. Gods lead a delightful existence marked by dancing and music, but at the end of their very long lives, they will inevitably be reborn lower down in the hierarchy. The denizens of hell are tortured, but not for an eternity; eventually they will work their way up the Six Paths. The spokes of the wheel are thus placed in some sense arbitrarily, since all of saṃsāra is marked by suffering. At the same time, the provisional distinctions between different species are unavoidable and, while not eternal, are no less real.

The third part of the wheel is the rim or felloe. Whereas most wooden wheels would be weakened by the multiplication of felloes (and strengthened through the addition of spokes), the wheel of rebirth gains in meaning by possessing more than one felloe. In a vehicular wheel, the rim distributes the force of movement around the circumference. In the wheel of rebirth the rim also functions as a boundary, distinguishing one logic from another. The Six Paths, for instance, represent the different species of life within Buddhist evolution, corresponding to phylogeny. The Six Paths are separated by a rim from the next circle, the Twelve Conditions, which epitomize the distinct stages of life through which a person passes within one lifetime. In this sense, then, this rim of the wheel of rebirth distinguishes phylogeny from ontogeny. Some wheels of rebirth have three or four rims, adding the unending cycle of transformation from human to animal to human and so on, or they have circles (defined by rims) indicating the direction in which beings are moving, up or down. Constructing wheels with more than one rim thus allows this Buddhist image to speak with more than one voice, to focus on different aspects of change, and to move in different directions.

The arrangement of inner and outer rims of the wheel may also be related to traditional accounts of the Buddha's enlightenment experience underneath the Bodhi tree at Bodhgaya.[11] In the first watch of the night, Śākyamuni recalled all of his previous lives, during which one could say that he was still subject to the Three Poisons pictured in the hub of the wheel. During the second watch, he used his enhanced power of vision to observe beings undergoing transmigration, from the heavens down to the

11. I owe this line of thinking to a suggestion from John Strong (personal communication, Sept. 2004). For accounts of the enlightenment experience of the Buddha, see Bareau, *Recherches sur la biographie du Bouddha*, 1:75–91.

hells, pictured in the main segments of the wheel. The third watch is when, according to some accounts, the Buddha realized the truth of dependent origination (*pratītyasamutpāda*), symbolized in the outer rim of the canonical Wheel of Rebirth. If these speculations are correct, then the soteriology of the wheel, moving from its center to its margin, accords well with the tradition's understanding of the founder's experience of awakening.

The fourth property of the wheel is that it marks off an inside from an outside. This attribute is nearly absent in the extreme form of the wheel noted above, the illustration of the Ten Realms in a circular pearl-heart. Even in this representation, however, something stands outside the circle: the square margin to the painting. Wheels of rebirth are always surrounded by a square frame, if only because without a frame they would be difficult to hang, mount, or carve. This practical limitation has interesting soteriological implications. It may be a structuralist excess to link the enclosure of the wheel of rebirth by a square to other cosmic and architectural formulations, such as the bounding of the cosmic mountain by a square or the square railing built around stūpas. Nevertheless, one of the important geometric functions of a circle is that it inscribes a distinction between inside and outside, an interpretation advanced long ago by Paul Mus.[12] According to Mus, it was in the interest of Buddhist authors, artists, and preachers to maintain ambiguity about the relative ranking of the beings pictured *within* the wheel of rebirth. Some representations contain the early canonical number of paths of rebirth (five), while others add the *asuras* to form six. The *asuras* had always been viewed as a problematic species in India, constantly fighting with the gods over the right to enjoy ambrosia and reside in heaven. In Mus's reading, the purpose of using a circle to symbolize the process of life and death is to show that all paths of rebirth, including heavens and hells, humans and *asuras*, are filled with suffering. The wheel is drawn, says Mus, not to mark a firm line between the paths of rebirth within the wheel, but rather to show that the only worthwhile distinction is that between the realm of saṃsāra inside the wheel and release from the cycle of rebirth indicated outside the wheel. The Buddha who achieved nirvāṇa, the white altar symbolizing nirvāṇa, and the poems advocating renunciation as the means to nirvāṇa are all exterior to the wheel of life and death. The wheel of rebirth, then, provides a nonlinear method for indicating transcendence, for suggesting an alternative beyond the realm of birth and death. The point of the wheel, so to speak, is to move outside it.

Architecture and Audience

The second sense of discursive practice involves not the formal properties of representations of rebirth but rather the social arrangements for learning about rebirth. As we have seen, patrons mobilized vast resources to construct temples. Some temples mimicked the layout of a monastic assembly hall but were in fact limited to members

12. See Mus, *La lumière sur les six voies*, pp. 153–83.

of the elite, while other sites were more easily accessible. Commissioners and viewers often had divergent interests, and monks also played a role in the social nexus. Two rather different kinds of social institution—and their associated mechanisms of interpretation—are implicated in the canonical account of the wheel of rebirth.

In the first discursive situation related in the vinaya, that of Maudgalyāyana telling tales, an entertainer spins a story about his adventures. Maudgalyāyana commands the attention of his audience not because he is appointed to the office of preacher or he wears a cassock. Rather, his authority derives from his firsthand experience in the other world. The audience's knowledge of life and death is mediated not by an ecclesiastical organization or by a curriculum, but by one talented individual. In the literary accounts in the vinaya and the *Divyāvadāna*, Maudgalyāyana is a guide who relates his own experiences to listeners who neither see the journey nor embark on one themselves. He is engaged in representing his own visions to a group. The narration consists of a retelling of events, the believability of which is founded on the unusual powers of the narrator.

The social dynamics of the second discourse, that of paintings of the wheel of rebirth, are quite different. According to the vinaya, the Buddha tells the monks not—to use the vernacular—to share their experience, but to deliver a prepackaged visual aid. He instructs the makers of the chart exactly what to include in the diagram, and he mandates what each element means. The components of the standardized curriculum are not words or experiences, but visual symbols. As the title of Robert Pinsky's poem suggests, it is a "Figured Wheel," each figure of which prompts reflection on the part of the viewers/listeners and explanation by the teacher. In other words, the teaching method the Buddha prescribes is the explaining of an allegory, rather than the recounting of an experience.

Furthermore, preachers must undergo a process of selection and training. Chosen from the ranks of the Saṃgha by monastic authorities, they are certified as teachers only after they are trained in the interpretation of the symbols. In the canonical account of the wheel, the Buddha and the Saṃgha seem a little stodgy, as if they are grappling with the problems of administering a complex social institution comprising monks, nuns, and laypeople, property and possessions, and a lively calendar of feasts and celebrations sponsored by the laity. In the text the Buddha says that people like Maudgalyāyana are rare, but we are left wondering whether that claim is more normative—the early medieval Indian Saṃgha managing its corporate affairs by stifling potential irregularities—than descriptive. In establishing the office of lecturer, whose duty is to explain the wheel of life and death, the Buddha is also supplanting the authority of lone virtuosos like Maudgalyāyana.

Treating paintings of the wheel of rebirth as a discursive practice helps to answer the kind of questions typically raised by social historians. Who makes art: who excavates caves, who prepares walls, who chisels reliefs and statues, where are they trained, what models do they use, how do they become artistically literate, what visual canons do they follow? Who sees art: commissioners, monks, laypeople, local officials, everybody in the neighborhood, pilgrims from far away? The canonical story of the wheel is a good place to start looking for answers to these questions. The vinaya account makes it clear that monks are supposed to do the explaining and laypeople the listening. It also establishes the rule that no matter what kind of space it is located in, the wheel is exoteric: it should be drawn on the outside, it should be the first scene encountered. According to the Buddha, the layout of the temple in which the wheel is painted is a major determinant of the painting's audience.

The paradigm for the painting of the wheel of saṃsāra established in the vinaya account needs supplementing by other kinds of evidence, however. Like any representation, this account leaves some things out of the picture. Specifically, the canon hides the role of the producers; it elides the question of who actually pays for the temple, who builds it, and who paints the pictures. The paintings of the wheel of rebirth that survive in the temples discussed in this book do not tell us very much about what their viewers thought about them. They are reflections, in the first place, of their patrons' interests. This fact is both overwhelming, because of the grandeur of the early temples that do survive, and limiting, since it means that the social group to which we have the best access in historical hindsight is in actuality quite tiny. As Romi Khosla, discussing the importance of wealthy donors for both Indian and Tibetan monasteries, writes, "This fundamental relationship between the dependent Buddhist monastery and the patron merchant or ruling class remained with every institution that developed in the course of the history of the religion. The grandeur of its art and architecture was only able to reach such heights because of the tremendous resources that were utilized in giving these institutions a grand and permanent form."[13]

Our evidence is misleading for another reason as well. Whereas the normative account would lead us to believe that paintings of the wheel are public institutions, offering free access to the Dharma for all people, the actual temples show otherwise. Ajaṇṭā Cave 17 was one man's *vihāra*, intended to support at most a small group of monks. The small cave at Kumtura could fit one or two people inside, and its principal intended viewer might have been the deceased monk pictured on the main wall. The cave temple at Yulin was the family shrine of the local potentate. The paintings of the wheel of rebirth that I have hypothesized in the Tang-dynasty metropolitan temples and the relief carving of the wheel at Baodingshan in Sichuan are clear and important exceptions to the rule of private wheels. The other medium in which the saṃsāracakra was transmitted, the painted scroll, also afforded only restricted access. In the miracle tale relating Wang Yan's dream, the painting of the wheel is exchanged between two people, and no one else sees it. In the story of King Rudrāyaṇa, the painting of the Buddha and the Twelve Conditions is created by one hereditary ruler as a gift to another. Members of the court, merchants, and other nobility are allowed to glimpse the king's property and to take part in honoring it, but in the end the painting—as well as the Buddha—remains the possession of kings.

One other factor has to be considered in trying to understand the relationship between the organization of space and the organization of people in the various tem-

13. Khosla, *Buddhist Monasteries in the Western Himalaya*, p. 8.

ples that house paintings of the wheel of rebirth. Each site in which the wheel is placed has its own ritual program or logic of practice. Scholars working at the intersection of art, architecture, and Buddhist studies have long grappled with questions of representation, ritual, and meaning. To make sense of the symbolic space in cave temples, Eugene Wang quite aptly invokes Mikhail Bhaktin's notion of chronotope, since structures like temples and stūpas are totalizing environments that attempt to create distinctive arrangements of time and space.[14] Each temple organizes its wall paintings, statues, and architectural layout in a specific configuration linked to ritual. Some temples guide the visitor to the worship of a central Buddha figure. Others lead the commissioner and/or his ancestors through a narrative that climaxes with rebirth in the pure land. Still other temples constitute a cosmic mansion in which the practitioner eventually consummates union with the resident deity. It makes a difference precisely what kind of religious goal the wheel of rebirth is linked to. As a prefatory painting, the wheel of life and death takes its meaning from the specific ritual program that it precedes. A reading of temple architecture, then, does not lead straightforwardly to the discovery of an empirical audience. Rather, the layout of sacred space tells us as much about the implied ritual participant as it does about actual visitors to the site.

The cave temple in which the wheel of rebirth is painted at Ajaṇṭā was commissioned by a ruler of the Vākāṭaka dynasty in the second half of the fifth century. The cave was excavated and decorated at the height of that dynasty's sway over central and western India, and the reasons for making such a lavish monument were surely multiple. Its purposes were, at the very least, to generate a great store of merit for the commissioner and his family, to display his munificence in regal fashion, to proclaim his bodhisattva-like qualities, and to propagate the Dharma. But the question remains: to whom? Who was the audience for such ornate, sensuous, all-encompassing enactments of faith? Like most of the temples examined in this book, Cave 17 at Ajaṇṭā is largely a private space, not a public one. Nevertheless, it mimics the layout of a public temple. It contains a porch that is exoteric, open in front. It includes small residence cells for monks around the sides of the main chamber. Its central area is a large square space suitable for communal rituals. In its rear, innermost chamber visitors are supposed to encounter the Buddha preaching the Dharma. What role does the wheel of rebirth play in this architectural plan? The painting of the wheel on the porch constitutes a preface to the space as a whole, the paintings of the previous lives of the Buddha in the main hall reiterate the spiraling perfection of the being destined to become the Buddha, and the rear of the temple houses his sacred presence. During the founder's lifetime the temple was probably frequented only by his family mem-

14. See Eugene Wang, "Grotto-Shrine as Chronotope," pp. 286–90. A small sampling of representative scholarship on this vast topic would include Li, *Zhong Yin fojiao shikusi bijiao yanjiu*; Ning Qiang, *Art, Religion, and Politics in Medieval China*; Raie, *Fo-kuang ssu*; Soper, "Northern Liang and Northern Wei in Kansu"; Su, "Liangzhou shiku yiji yu 'Liangzhou moshi'"; and Xiao, *Dunhuang jianzhu yanjiu*, pp. 33–94.

bers, a few monks he supported who lived at and helped maintain the cave, and perhaps visiting dignitaries. Despite the actual closure to the general public, then, the design of the temple maintains the illusion of access. The architecture designates the brighter, outer precincts as introductory and attaches the values of mystery and sacrality to the inner space. In keeping with the claims of the vinaya account, the painting of the wheel of rebirth at Ajaṇṭā performs an exoteric and prefatory function.

If my speculations are correct and there were indeed paintings of the saṃsāracakra in the metropolitan temples of the Tang dynasty, they too were external and introductory. Built by the state and by prominent landed families, large Chinese temples propagated the Dharma, constituted important festive spaces in the urban landscape, and displayed and created merit for their commissioners. Some of them were public institutions, accessible to many residents of the city. As Buddhist as opposed to secular spaces, they created an alternative social world that laypeople could visit and in which monks could live. There were complex, multichambered structures covering many acres, yet their principles, as Daoxuan explained, were clear: the Dharma took precedence over the secular, and monks were holier than laypeople. Temples were marked by balance, symmetry, and hierarchy. If wheels of rebirth were there, they were painted in the outer precincts. The same hypothesis can be extended to cave temples like the ones at Dunhuang, except that access to them was more restricted, and the theoretical wheels there were probably located in wooden entryways and porches attached to the cliff face.

The small wheels of rebirth painted in the meditation cave at Kumtura were located in a small, isolated cave commissioned by a Uighur family that aligned itself closely and consciously with Chinese monks and central Asian forms of visualization. The cave at Kumtura not only made merit for the family, it also memorialized a local monk and meditation teacher whose prowess was the primary subject of the main wall. The cave was private in many senses. It was intended for one family's benefit, and access to it was probably restricted. It was also protected from the public by virtue of its size: it could comfortably accommodate one seated person. It may well have been used for the individual practice of meditation, perhaps involving the visualizations mentioned in the cave inscription. At the same time, the paintings of the wheel of rebirth in this Sino-Turkish cave also reflect the public use of such paintings. The side wall of the cave depicts wheels of rebirth situated in the midst of assemblies of meditating monks. These paintings are the clearest indication that representations of the wheel of life and death were used as a communal teaching device.

Farther east, near the western tip of the Hexi Corridor at the complex of cave temples at Yulin, a tenth-century painting of the wheel of rebirth was also commissioned by and for a prominent local family. Access to it too was probably restricted to family members (the local rulers of the Cao clan), their legatees, and members of their monastic estates. In keeping with the discursive practice proposed by the Buddha in the vinaya account, the painting of the wheel of rebirth at Yulin is located external to the main portion of the cave temple. It is on the right-hand wall of the hallway leading to the antechamber of the cave. It lines the visitor's passage into the two-chambered interior of the cave. It is followed in the antechamber by a pictorial program of various gods and spirits converted to the Buddhist path and a set of donor portraits. The main, innermost chamber of the cave is dominated by paintings of paradise. At Yulin, then, the wheel of rebirth serves a liminal function, marking the crossing of a threshold, first into a Buddhist space protected by deities, and then into a pure realm in the main chamber of the cave. Although there are no words inscribed around the painting of the wheel of rebirth at Yulin, nevertheless the cave invokes the other form of discursive practice described by the vinaya account, the telling of a story by a lone adventurer. On the wall opposite the wheel there is a transformation tableau of Maudgalyāyana touring the regions of hell. The painting of the wheel at Yulin is unique for the way in which it references the canonical account in pictures but not in words, and for the validation it gives to Maudgalyāyana's powers, so vividly depicted in his adventures in the walled cities and torture chambers of hell.

The temple at Tabo in medieval western Tibet was founded by Ye-shes-'od, a local ruler who retired from the government so that he could devote his attention full-time as a monk to building up the Saṃgha. About fifty years later his grandnephew refurbished the temple and had a long prayer chiseled into the rear hall. The inscription honors Ye-shes-'od as the founder of the temple, thus cementing the family's tie to the flourishing of Buddhism. It also regards the function of the temple as the propagation of the Dharma in the kingdom of western Tibet. But we still need to ask the critical question: among whom was Buddhism thereby disseminated? There is no evidence that anybody except the donor family and the monastic elite—the only humans pictured on the walls—attended the temple or took part in the rituals performed there. The audience in this sense was limited to the elite. In both spatial and ritual terms, however, the painting of the wheel of rebirth at Tabo may be considered more exoteric than esoteric. Together with the local goddess and some cosmological scenes, it is located in the entry hall of the temple. The saṃsāracakra thus serves to ground the Buddhist edifice in local holy space. The painting of the wheel is external to the major room of the temple, the assembly hall, which houses the Vajradhātu maṇḍala. The maṇḍala constitutes a liturgy in which the practitioner, once initiated under the guidance of a teacher, proceeds through a series of purifications, invocations, and visualizations, to achieve union with the deity residing in the cosmic palace. That merging of identities is then harnessed to a number of goals, ranging from magical powers to complete enlightenment. The wheel of life and death stands as a preface to this esoteric ritual.

The sociospatial properties of the pilgrimage center at Baodingshan are different from those at other temples. It was engineered in the thirteenth century through the efforts of one main planner, Zhao Zhifeng, whose role as author is clear in various scenes at the site. Members of the gentry were no doubt involved as donors, but so too were individuals of lesser means. People from south-central China frequently made pilgrimages to Baodingshan. They typically traveled as groups, and local people at Baodingshan probably served as guides.[15] Visitors to the site may have depended not on a charismatic figure like Maudgalyāyana, but rather on a tour leader, who delivered prepackaged comments and functioned like the branch representative of a tour agency. For pilgrims, going to Baodingshan, located in hilly terrain a day's walk from the nearest town, was the culmination of a period of spiritual cultivation and material preparation. More than any other site discussed in this book, Baodingshan allows for visitation by *le grand public*. The shallow niches there have no inside and no outside, no front or back. There are a few roomlike niches, but generally the art at Baodingshan is relief sculpture. That is, it all stands out, and neither the artistic medium nor the layout of the site offers much basis for a distinction between exoteric and esoteric. In keeping with the precedent established in the canonical account, the scene of the wheel of rebirth there plays a largely prefatory function. Positioned near the beginning of the complex, it introduces the pilgrim to the whole range of subjects that follow: scenes of suffering and paradise, demons and Buddhas, and local holy men, including the creator of the site.

The Local and the Canonical

The theme of the local and the canonical has resurfaced throughout this book. One of the reasons for the wide dissemination of the wheel of rebirth across Buddhist Asia is that it is canonical. It is prescribed in a vinaya text that was deemed authoritative for Buddhist communities in India, central Asia, China, and Tibet. But we have to remember what "canonical" means. Recent scholarship is beginning to show how Buddhist canons were made and unmade and to suggest that what was deemed canonical at any one time and place was a function of the privileging of one group of texts over another.[16] Beginning in India, where the first canons consisted of institutionalized oral traditions, each community of monks defined its own authoritative scriptural collection. As schisms proliferated, so did canons. When Vasumitra, writing in the fourth century, describes the doctrines of sixteen different sects or schools (*nikāya*, a group of persons subscribing to the same rule), it is likely that each of the sixteen social groups maintained its own distinctive canon, subdivided into three baskets (*tripiṭaka*) of vinaya, sūtra, and *śāstra* (treatise).[17] Of those earlier sixteen vinaya, only six have survived in near entirety into modern times, and only one out of those six, the vinaya of the Mūlasarvāstivādins, contains the story of the Buddha directing his followers to paint the wheel of rebirth.

15. See Hu Zhaoxi, "Dazu Baodingshan shike qianlun." Angela Howard (*Summit of Treasures*) sees the site as part of a broader, more populist movement, while Karil Kucera ("Cliff Notes," esp. pp. 1–15) is more circumspect about attendance by the lower classes.

16. See Collins, "On the Very Idea of a Pāli Canon"; Fang, *Fojiao dazangjing shi*; Makita, *Gikyō kenkyū*; and Tokuno, "The Evaluation of Indigenous Scriptures in Chinese Buddhist Bibliographical Catalogues."

17. See Bareau, *Les sectes bouddhiques du petit véhicule*, pp. 16–17.

In the case of China, the formation of Buddhist canons was even more complicated, since the authoritative collection of all approved Buddhist texts was redefined, sometimes as frequently as once every decade, by monastic authorities responding to government pressure. Among the shifting corpus of Buddhist texts, those books selected for translation from Indic languages into Chinese were not chosen according to a consistent rule. Not one of the canons of any Indian Buddhist school was translated in its entirety into Chinese.[18] Rather, translators decided which texts to render into Chinese according to tradition, following the relatively small body of texts they had memorized or carried back to China. The question of size is of course relative. Xuanzang (602–664) translated 73 works in 1,330 chapters, and Yijing (635–713) translated 56 works in 230 chapters—literally volumes Nevertheless, compared to the total number of books in the Chinese canon of the time—1,076 works in 5,048 chapters—the number of texts rendered into Chinese by any single translation team was relatively small.[19] Sometimes concerns about practice determined whether texts about breath meditation, visualization, the making of images, rebirth in pure lands, or the ritual of confession were translated Other times decisions about which books to translate were driven by debates over the Buddhahood of all beings, nondualistic wisdom, nirvāṇa, or the nature of consciousness.

For the first four centuries of its existence in China, the Buddhist community lacked a full set of vinaya rules.[20] The earliest vinaya texts in China dealt with general Buddhist morality and the ordination of monks. The fifth century witnessed an explosion of interest in securing canonical footing for the more extensive regulation of monastic life. Between 404 and 424 four relatively complete vinaya canons were translated into Chinese: the Sarvāstivāda, Dharmagupta, Mahāsāṃghika, and Mahīśāsaka. Of these four vinaya canons, the first two seem to have been distributed across China most broadly, the Sarvāstivāda vinaya (Ch: *Sifen lü*) prevalent in the south and the Dharmagupta vinaya (Ch.: *Shisong lü*) popular in the capitals and in the north. Despite this broad dissemination, it would be an exaggeration to claim without qualification that either one of these vinayas was "popular" in China in the early part of the fifth century. There was never empirewide agreement about which vinaya was authoritative. And even when monks or specific monasteries studied one particular vinaya, the rules were not always applied *in toto*, and the mythological core of the vinaya was so vast that any one canon allowed for multiple interpretations.

The specific vinaya canon containing the Buddha's instructions to depict the wheel of rebirth on monastery walls was translated only later. It was part of the corpus of

18. See, for example, the discussion in Tang Yongtong, *Han Wei Liangjin Nanbeichao fojiao shi*, pp. 374–414.

19. Totals are from *Kaiyuan shijiao lu*, Zhisheng (669–740), *T* no. 2154, 55:714c, 723a.

20. The study of the vinaya in China is still in its infancy. Hirakawa, *Ritsuzō no kenkyū*, remains the standard work on the Indian schools and the translation of various vinaya texts into Chinese. The most important analysis of how the vinaya actually functioned in China is the groundbreaking study by Tso [Cao], "Transformation of Buddhist Vinaya in China," on which I draw below. See also Yifa, *Origins of Buddhist Monastic Codes in China*, pp. 3–98.

the Mūlasarvāstivāda vinaya (Ch.: *Genbenshuoyiqieyoubu pinaiye*) that Yijing (635–713) retrieved from India, brought back to China, and translated in the first decade of the eighth century. Understood in context, Yijing's vinaya was not only later than the four earlier translations, but it was, like most of them, not very authoritative. That is, it was never adopted in its entirety as the standard for monastic life in China, and it was only inconsistently invoked to adjudicate conflicts over proper monastic behavior. As Tso Sze-bong has argued, although Yijing translated the Mūlasarvāstivāda vinaya and wrote extensively on it, he also remained a follower of the Dharmagupta vinaya.[21] The first time any vinaya was adopted as a national standard in China was in the year 709, and it was not Yijing's Mūlasarvāstivāda vinaya, but rather the Dharmagupta vinaya, as understood through the commentaries of Daoxuan (596–667) and his disciples. Even that vinaya maintained a tenuous and short-lived claim to authority, since about one hundred years later Buddhist monasteries began the shift toward a radically different, much shorter set of collective regulations associated with the figure of Baizhang Huaihai (720–814).

What, then, does it mean to say that the wheel of rebirth in China (or, by implication, elsewhere) was "canonical"? Did Śākyamuni himself or the ancient vinaya mandate a new iconography for the wheel of rebirth, as the vinaya story itself suggests? Or was it rather the case that the canon was invoked more as an excuse, to rationalize a long-established discursive practice? Based on the social history of the vinaya sketched above, the answer is closer to the latter than the former. Yijing's nearly complete translation of the Mūlasarvāstivāda vinaya stands in contrast to the fact that it was not, on the whole, put into practice. It is true, as noted in chapter 5, that the story of the painting of the saṃsāracakra contained in the vinaya was quoted later by Daocheng (ca. 1017–1021), who treated it as authorization for the painting of the wheel of rebirth in Song-dynasty monasteries. But in this case the vinaya served as charter *ex post facto*. The vinaya account was important in China, then, because across the stretches of Buddhist history it pointed backward in time, toward the founder in India, rather than forward. It functioned as citation, as textual verification for action. Just as the Mūlasarvāstivāda vinaya in India was created as justification for Indian Buddhist monastic institutions, so too the same canon in Chinese translation was quoted in order to authenticate practices already underway in China.

The contrast of the Chinese case with the canonical status of the wheel of rebirth in Tibet is particularly interesting. From the fifth through the eighth centuries, a total of five separate vinaya canons were translated into Chinese. The vinaya containing the account of the wheel of life and death was the last of the vinayas to be translated. In describing the wheel of rebirth as "canonical" in China, then, it is important to remember that it was only one-fifth canonical. Tibet, on the other hand, followed only one vinaya, that of the Mūlasarvāstivāda, and pictures of the wheel were ubiquitous in late medieval and modern Tibet. In China, where the Mūlasarvāstivāda vinaya was

21. See Tso [Cao], "Transformation of Buddhist Vinaya in China," pp. 4–117.

merely the latest and ultimately minor addition to four prior vinaya collections, representations of the wheel of rebirth appear to have been much less widespread.

As an institutionally approved standard of authenticity, the canon in the case of the wheel of rebirth was more than simply a literary account with status—it was also a pictorial tradition. The wheel was canonical not only because it was related to a literary canon, but also to an artistic canon. This in turn raises the question of the transmission of knowledge in artistic canons: what sources did artists draw on in order to draw? Until recently the standard answer in the field of iconography was that artists knew what was in texts, and so to understand an element in a painting, an analyst needs to cite a textual precedent. More recently art historians have argued convincingly that paintings are interpictorial. From this perspective, rather than following a textual tradition, artists—many of whom were illiterate or barely literate—followed pictorial conventions that governed content, composition, and style.[22] The case of the wheel of rebirth at Yulin suggests that both interpretations have validity. In pairing Maudgalyāyana and the wheel of rebirth, the cave is alluding to the legend contained in the vinaya account. Other elements seem to be direct quotations and paraphrases of the teaching in the vinaya, as seen in the use of stock symbols for the chain of causation. On the other hand, knowledge of the standard symbolism and the conventions of the wheel may well have derived not from an acquaintance with texts but from the practice of other artists and the constraints of artistic tradition.

In literary studies we are accustomed to a complicated notion of "citation." To cite a text is always a way of creating, not simply a means of reworking or deferring to authority. The same holds true in the case of the different versions of the wheel of rebirth, except that we have the added dimension of pictures. The canonical story of the wheel contains a multitude of symbolic systems and media: it is a text (the vinaya) about a person (the historical Buddha) prescribing a picture (the wheel of rebirth) that contains images (animals, gods, symbols of causation) as well as words (the poems on renunciation). The concept of intertextuality fails to capture the variety of media and the many subtle forms of reference in this literary account. The pictures of the wheel of rebirth are even more complicated. At Ajaṇṭā the picture of the wheel may not have included the lines of poetry. We do know that the picture prescribed in the canon is positioned on the porch and serves as a preface to the scenes inside—which were, in fact, noncanonical, since they are mostly related to *jātaka* tales, which long circulated outside the canon. At Kumtura the wheel of rebirth is pictured among rows of monks, as if it were used for formal instruction as the vinaya demands. On the other hand, the painting at Kumtura depicts the wheel as a portable object, not as a painting decorating the walls of a monastery. In the Tabo monastery the painting of the wheel of rebirth contains the mandated lines of poetry, and the main chamber of the

22. The case for the artist's practice has been made most convincingly in Fraser, "Manuals and Drawings of Artists, Calligraphers, and Other Specialists from Dunhuang"; and idem, *Performing the Visual*. For a methodological analysis of the field of iconography, see Yan, "Fojiao yishu fangfaxue de zai jiantao." On compositional logic, see Hung Wu, "What is *Bianxiang*?"

monastic complex cites other canonical texts as well. At Yulin there is no text at all, just a picture, and there are new elements in the painting like the passage from one species to the next. Yet this version of the wheel may also be judged more canonical than all the rest, because the pictorial program of the cave invokes the vinaya account by portraying Maudgalyāyana's tour of hell on the wall opposite the wheel. The canonical antagonism between the charismatic monk and the Saṃgha is rendered into architectural terms as the opposition between left and right walls. At first sight the wheel of rebirth at Baodingshan seems closest to the local and most distant from the canonical. It is the most overtly popular of all the sites, since it was defined for a broad, regional audience. It was farthest from the vinaya in that the saint to whom it is dedicated was probably not even a monk. It adds its own hymns to the scene, and it inserts the creator of the site into the center of the wheel. All of these characteristics are expressions of its local appeal. Nevertheless, the wheel at Baodingshan cites the verses stipulated in the vinaya and invokes the Buddhas of past, present, and future as authorities for the scene. It constructs its own framework for balancing an understanding of the pan-Asian requirements of the wheel of rebirth with the kind of Buddhism prevalent in Sichuan.

So far the thrust of my analysis has been to break down and historicize our conception of the canonical. I have suggested that canons are social institutions that change over time, that canons include both literary and artistic conventions, and that what is considered canonical stands in a complex relation to the local. It is important to note, however, that the concept of "the local" does not constitute empirical bedrock either. Taking medieval Chinese sources as an example, I would argue that Buddhists throughout Asia took a complex attitude toward the meaning of "the local." One of the best examples of how informants on the ground viewed the interplay of local and, in effect, transnational forces is contained in a popular entertainment dealing with the exploits of the ruler of the Dunhuang (Shazhou) area, Zhang Huaishen (831–890). Zhang defeated Uighur armies, twice, beginning in 883, and reinstituted the mantle of the central Tang government over the area. Lacking both a title and any attribution of authorship, the transformation text extolling Zhang represents local folklore put into the form of a prosimetric narration (now fragmentary) and picture scrolls (now lost). The text explains how an emissary from the Tang court was led into the official temple established during the Kaiyuan era (713–742) under the reign of Emperor Xuanzong (r. 712–756). The official from Chang'an was shown a portrait of the emperor and was delighted to see that it preserved the emperor's likeness in a lively and convincing manner. Since the emissary could not have been alive during Emperor Xuanzong's lifetime, his criterion for verisimilitude must have been representations of the emperor that he would have seen at court in Chang'an. The text reads:

> After the minister [Zhang Huaishen] received the imperial orders for his appointment, he led the emissary of Heaven to the Kaiyuan Temple, where he personally paid obeisance to the Sagely Visage of our Xuanzong [whose name means literally, "Mysterious Progenitor"]. Observing that the imperial throne of past years [in the

portrait] was just as dignified as if it were in front of him now, the emissary exclaimed, "Although for one hundred years the Dunhuang area has been opposed to the Han and fell into the hands of the western tribes (*xirong*), still it manages to pay respect to its true ruling dynasty and maintain our emperor's image, whereas none of the other four commanderies in the area is able to preserve it. I also see that in the other four commanderies of Liang, Gua, Su, and Zhi, the parapets have been defaced, and the [Han] residents and the smelly barbarians stand shoulder to shoulder. How could they fail to button their clothing to the left? Only in the lone commandery of Shazhou are the styles and ornamentation of the people the same as those in the inner region."[23]

This fascinating legend attempts to valorize a local hero whose military exploits and political power were extremely important in northwest China. Yet the text construes his value as transcending the local and conforming to central Chinese values. The myth deploys the terms of Chinese political hegemony ("true ruling dynasty," *benchao*) and Han ethnic superiority, drawing on centuries of prejudiced vocabulary to refer to local tribes, malodorous foreigners, non-Chinese clothing, and decrepit building practices. The story of Zhang Huaishen offers the modern reader a rare chance to consider how residents of medieval Gansu reflected on the interplay between the regional and the national. What makes Zhang Huaishen a hero is the way in which he preserves translocal practices like Chinese clothing and the regalia of the central government. This kind of folklore suggests that some regions in the northwest were better than other surrounding districts because they conformed to Chinese (that is to say, Han) conventions and displayed their fealty to the imperium.

The explanatory value of the local (like that of "history," "context," etc.) lies in how it helps to clarify the dynamics involved in paintings of the wheel of rebirth in China. The concept of the local is valuable if it forces our attention, as historians, to the possibility of agency and creative reinterpretation by medieval Buddhists, whether they were monks or laypeople, painters or viewers, storytellers, preachers, or listeners. My account stresses the political consequences of local architectural form. A high-ranking minister's chapel at Ajaṇṭā drew a viewing audience quite different from that of a public pilgrimage site like Baodingshan. Local variations also involve differences in ritual. At Yulin the wheel of rebirth marks a preliminary stage in the rite of entering into paradise and worshipping the Buddha, while at Baodingshan the visitor encounters the sculpture of the wheel as a preface to a long narrative about filial piety, asceticism, and the power of cosmic deities and holy men from Sichuan. I emphasize the narrative, ritual, and architectural aspects of the canonical and the local, then, in order to explain how meaning is constructed at particular sites through the interplay of local forces and pan-Buddhist symbols.

---

23. Translation from untitled text, Pelliot Dunhuang ms. no. 3451, in Wang Zhongmin, *Dunhuang bianwen ji*, p. 124; see also Rong, *Guiyijun shi yanjiu*, p. 268.

Art and Mor(t)ality

I want to return one last time to the two discourses of rebirth established in the vinaya in order to raise some questions about temporality. The painting of the wheel of saṃsāra and the story of its creation are in many ways bound up with problems of time: impermanence, death, rebirth, suffering, and salvation.

As noted above, the first discursive situation, Maudgalyāyana retelling his journey, takes the form of a line. A line is the geometrical figure best suited to narration, since the story itself develops over time and the narrator tells one event after another. Artistic representations of Maudgalyāyana's tour, as we have seen, present one frame at a time, in sequence. The linear form of representation also implies a specific temporality of the viewing experience. Just as Maudgalyāyana cannot explain his journey in an instant, the observer of the painting depicting Maudgalyāyana's travels does not see the whole painting at once. Rather, the viewer looks at one scene at a time, moving from one occurrence to the next. To learn something about the composition, one measures later events against earlier events. One might note, for instance, how Maudgalyāyana's tour is a progression, its beginning and ending points clearly differentiated. Or, in the linear presentation of the soul's journey through purgatory after death, one comes to see that life begins anew where it ends, with the experience of the infernal bureaucracy.

The discourse of the wheel entails a rather different form of temporality, having to do with circular time. Actually, as Edmund Leach has shown, there are two distinct forms of circular time, one involving repetition, the other nonrecurrence.[24] Both are operative in the story of the wheel of rebirth. The death of an unenlightened being highlights the repetitive nature of time. Death brings a movement from one segment of the circle to another, not a shift outside of the circle. Each death is followed by rebirth, another lifetime, which in turn ends in another death, and so on. Profane death is not a conclusion but a transition to another form of life; it does not remove the person from the realm of suffering. Its temporality is that of repetition. There is an interesting congruence here between Buddhist claims about death and the analysis of *rites de passage* in the anthropological literature. Arnold van Gennep's and Robert Hertz's theories are well known: like other rites of passage, the rituals surrounding death help to bring about a change in status, a movement of the deceased from one group to another.[25] In this line of reasoning, rather than defining an ending point, funerals mark a transition of the deceased from the group composed of living family members to that made up of ancestors. Monks appointed to explain the wheel of saṃsāra would not in principle disagree, I think, with this essentially Durkheimian reading of death. They would specify, however, that the new community joined by the deceased is not the simple, formless category of "ancestors," but rather one of the five or six species

24. See Leach, "Two Essays Concerning the Symbolic Representation of Time."

25. Van Gennep, *Rites of Passage*; Hertz, *Death and the Right Hand*; and Turner, "Transformation, Hierarchy and Transcendence."

of sentient beings. Mortuary ritual surrounding this form of death ameliorates grief by nurturing the hope that the deceased have achieved a happy state of existence: they will be reborn as a god in one of the heavens, there to enjoy the pleasures commensurate with their enhanced physical form, or else they will become human again, which offers another chance to achieve liberation.

The second form of death represented by the wheel is, in a sense, unique. The death of an enlightened being marks a conclusive ending: the person does not return—at least not in the same unenlightened way—to experience the realm of suffering. Under the category of enlightened being would be included the Buddha (or a Buddha—any "awakened one") and those who have achieved any of the Four Fruits that sooner or later assure nirvāṇa. This kind of death is not a repetition of the past or the manifestation of a recurring pattern. It is exceptional and unrepeatable—which is not to say that the saint becomes totally inaccessible after death. Quite the contrary: in some depictions of the wheel of existence, the Buddha is enshrined outside the rim of the wheel, while in other versions the Buddha or a saint sits in the center of the wheel. His intervention demonstrates that the release from repetition achieved by the Buddha is still somehow available to others.

Whether repetitive or exceptional, the temporality of the wheel also implies a distinctive aesthetic experience. Paintings of the wheel of rebirth are nonnarrative art: they have no beginning or ending, and one does not follow the progress of a character from one scene to the next. The logic of arrangement is not linear. There are other ways to make sense of the wheel. Rather than being composed of a succession of scenes, the wheel is made up of its constituent parts: the hub, the spokes, the felloes, and the basic distinction between inside and outside the wheel. All Six Paths exist at once. To make sense of this simultaneous composition, one stands back and analyzes it, breaking it down into its components and then putting it back together again. The viewing experience involves discriminating between the different parts of the composition and learning their symbolic value, not following a story.

We gain a fuller understanding of the wheel of rebirth by comparing it to forms of Buddhist art and modalities of the viewing experience that it does not resemble. The topic is vast, and the following list of five examples is meant to be illustrative rather than exhaustive.[26]

Paintings of the wheel of rebirth are unlike, first, representations of the Buddha image. Painted icons of the Buddha usually face the viewer frontally, inviting him or her to imagine himself or herself in the presence of the Buddha. Sculpted images of the Buddha are placed in a ritualized setting, typically on an altar, which allows the viewer to worship the Buddha. Both painted and three-dimensional programs depict the Buddha accompanied by other deities and marked by a halo and other attributes,

26. For related studies of the forms of Buddhist art, see, for example, Dehejia, *Discourse in Early Buddhist Art*; Huntington, "Aniconism and the Multivalence of Emblems"; Kinnard, *Imaging Wisdom*, esp. pp. 25–44; Murray, "Buddhism and Early Narrative Illustration in China"; Mus, *Barabuḍur: Sketch of a History of Buddhism*; and Sharf and Sharf, *Living Images*.

all of which assure the viewer of his holiness. In Buddhist art, the image in many ways is the Buddha, and the artistic conventions draw the viewer into the scene, convincing the viewer of the presence of the Buddha, and ultimately turning the viewer into a worshipper.

Paradise scenes are a second form of Buddhist art; they include pure lands of Buddhas as well as godlike realms blessed by a Buddha or bodhisattva. From an aesthetic perspective, what is crucial about them is not so much the central Buddha figure as the surrounding scenery. The ponds, the luxuriant vegetation, the attendant dancers and musicians, the walkways and courtyards of the palace all help to create the impression that one has actually entered paradise, not simply looked at a two-dimensional painting. When executed in cave temples, these illusionistic pictures are usually placed in the innermost sanctum of the temple. The transformation of space is supposed to draw the visitor into another world and provide a foretaste of paradise.

A third form of Buddhist art is the maṇḍala. The main Buddha inhabiting a maṇḍala is typically shown frontally in an iconic pose. The aesthetically convincing part of such representations is the edifice, the structural features of the chief deity's palace. The architectural details combine to demonstrate the centrality of the deity and the orderly arrangement of his world. The ground plan also furthers the viewer's involvement in the scene: one enters the sacred precincts, invokes the deity, shares a ritual meal, and thereby merges with him.

A fourth kind of Buddhist art is a representation of a patriarch or bodhisattva. The masters' statues in Chan (Zen) ancestral halls, for instance, are embodiments of enlightenment. Similarly, paintings of bodhisattvas depict models of compassion. As representations of exemplary holiness, such pictures are symbols of selected virtues (enlightenment, wisdom, compassion, etc.) that are supposed to be emulated. The viewer sees them and tries to be like them.

The fifth form of Buddhist art is narrative: it tells a story. Buddhist narrative art uses a variety of compositional arrangements: some trace a linear journey from one scene to the next, as noted in the discussion of Maudgalyāyana's tour of hell, above, while others arrange paradigmatic scenes or symbols of scenes in a nonlinear, iconically organized composition. Rather than inserting oneself into the painting, the viewer learns a story about the Buddha or other figure that teaches an inspiration lesson, warns of punishment, or provides entertainment.

The point of this selective survey of Buddhist aesthetics is to highlight the dissimilarities between the didactic nature of paintings of the wheel of rebirth and the modes of visual experience in other forms of Buddhist art. Buddha figures usually are included in the wheel of rebirth, but, unlike viewing most Buddha icons, the viewer is not really supposed to worship them. The Buddha or bodhisattva figures in the saṃsāracakra appear in the form appropriate to each path of rebirth, ministering to that path's sentient beings. The residents of each represented path, rather than the viewers of the painting, are the ones who are supposed to experience the presence of the Buddha. Nor is it a question, as in some readings of Mahāyāna aesthetics, of encountering the Buddha's absence. Moreover, nothing about the form or content of the paintings of the wheel of rebirth allows the viewer to unite with the Buddha, as in a maṇḍala. Looking at a painting of the wheel of rebirth, one is certainly supposed to experience something, but not by projecting oneself into the scenes depicted. Sacred figures often appear in paintings of the wheel, but the first purpose of the painting is not to encourage the copying of saints' lives. Nor does the painting tell a story or offer up a model of progress.

As didactic art, the discourse of the wheel of rebirth fosters distance between the viewer and the painting. Rather than effacing the individuality or egocentrism of the observer by absorbing him or her into the magnificence of the Buddha, paintings of the wheel of rebirth militate against direct personal involvement in the pictorial subject. Buddhas are present in the painting, we might say, but their holy presence is not thematized. Instead, the painting pushes the viewer away; it encourages the viewer to step back and think. To appreciate the painting, one is supposed to maintain control and exercise thought.

The painting of the wheel of rebirth fosters intellection through its form, which is that of a complex diagram composed of symbols and words. The painting makes sense to an observer only after its parts have been analyzed and the logic of their connection has been understood. In some respects it is like the diagrammatic chart shown in table 7 that lists, in a spatially significant way, the different realms of the universe. Such diagrams offer a coded summary or condensation of the soteriologically relevant aspects of the cosmos. They are comprehensive, they list things in order, they provide measurements, and they use technical terms. Like other diagrams, the wheel of rebirth aims to be complete: it shows all Five (or Six) Paths, and it includes reference to nirvāṇa as well as saṃsāra. The symbols contained in the composition are designed to encourage analysis, not empathy. The viewer is not supposed to imagine himself or herself as united with, or brought into the presence of, the monkey in the chain of causation, for instance. Rather, the monkey is a symbol that urges the viewer to reflect on the nature of what it represents, namely, consciousness. According to the Buddha's instructions in the vinaya, upon seeing the round, white altar outside the wheel of rebirth, the viewer is not simply supposed to think about its referent, nirvāṇa. He or she should also reflect on how the symbolic qualities of roundness and whiteness stand for the properties of completion and purity, respectively. Having taken apart the wheel and unpacked the meaning of its symbols, the observer is supposed to gain a deeper, more detached, and objective understanding of life and death. Far from being a sop for the unenlightened masses, paintings of the wheel of rebirth encourage critical reflection and explanation. According to L. Augustine Waddell, who wrote one of the first Western scholarly articles on the saṃsāracakra, the wheel of rebirth piqued the interest of its audience in nineteenth-century Tibet. He writes, "Its strange objects and varied scenes strongly excite the curiosity of the junior monks and laity, whose inquisitiveness is only to be satisfied, or whetted, by a short explanatory sermon."[27]

27. Waddell, "Buddhist Pictorial Wheel of Life," p. 134.

Whatever their differences, all of these representations of saṃsāra—stories about the wheel of rebirth as well as artistic renderings of it—demonstrate that talk about the other world is linked to action. Discourse about the wheel usually begins with mortality and ends with morality. In the canonical account of the creation of the wheel, the reaction of Maudgalyāyana's audience confirms this reading: they respond to his stories of the other world not simply by being amused and returning to hear him preach again, but by becoming Buddhists. Their actions are marked as Buddhist: they cultivate merit, perform deeds with an awareness of their consequences, and lead others to achieve nirvāṇa. Maudgalyāyana's followers are converted not to Buddhist dogma but to Buddhist ethics. So too in the case of paintings of the wheel of rebirth. They are diagrams that contain not only symbols but also words, the two stanzas that push the viewer toward renunciation and the lessening of desire. The saṃsāracakra is, thus, a form of Buddhist moralizing. Without exemplification in symbols or explanation by preachers, a simple map of the other world is useless.

At Ajaṇṭā the painting of the wheel on the porch prefaces the story of the bodhisattva told in the *vihāra*. In this context, the wheel introduces the narrative of the deeds of the Buddha-to-be over many lifetimes as he moves closer to perfection. His actions are depicted for emulation, just as his presence is portrayed in the inner shrine for worship. At Kumtura the wheel of rebirth is painted in a tiny cave memorializing a virtuous monk. In the cave temples at Yulin the wheel of rebirth and the story of Maudgalyāyana are situated before the viewer's entry into paradise, which is protected by guardians of the Law and made possible for all sentient beings by following the dictates of Buddhist morality. In the temple at Tabo the wheel of rebirth is a preface to a highly structured ritual program involving purification, invocation, visualization, and identification. Similarly, the niche depicting the wheel of rebirth at Baodingshan is placed within a program which not only teaches about saṃsāra, nirvāṇa, and Tantric techniques, but which also recommends a two-tiered system of morality, consisting of filial piety for householders and austerities for religious professionals. The Baodingshan composition explains the laws of karmic retribution and holds up the deeds of Buddhas, bodhisattvas, and holy men as examples for all to follow. Wherever they are painted in the Buddhist world, then, pictures of life and death achieve their purpose only when deployed within a system of morality.

TABLE 7. Diagram of Buddhist cosmology according to the *Abhidharmakośa*. After Kloetzli, *Buddhist Cosmology*, pls. 3, 4.

				Distance Above or Below Golden Earth (in *yojanas*)
Realm of Non-Form (Ārūpyadhātu)	Neither Consciousness nor Not-Consciousness			
	Realm of Nothingness			
	Infinity of Intellect			
	Infinity of Space			
Realm of Form (Rūpadhātu)	(Beyond Desire)	Fourth Meditation (Dhyāna)	Not Youngest	167,772,160,000
			Well-Seeing	83,886,080,000
			Beautiful	41,943,040,000
			No Heat	20,971,520,000
			Effortless	10,485,760,000
			Abundant Fruit	5,242,880,000
			Merit-Born	2,621,440,000
			Cloudless	1,310,720,000
		Third Meditation	Complete Beauty	655,360,000
			Immeasurable Beauty	327,680,000
			Limited Beauty	163,840,000
		Second Meditation	Radiant	81,920,000
			Immeasurable Splendor	40,960,000
			Limited Splendor	20,480,000
		First Meditation	Great Brahmā	10,240,000
			Brahmā-Priest	5,120,000
			Retinue of Brahmā	2,560,000
	Realm of Desire (Kāmadhātu)	Gods of Desire (Kāmadeva)	Rulers over Things Created by Others	1,280,000
			Those Who Have Their Pleasure in Creation	640,000
			Blissfull Gods	320,000
			Yāma	160,000
			Gods of Thirty-three	80,000
			Four Great Kings	40,000
		Humans (Manuṣya)		0
		Animals (Tiryagyoni)		0
		Ghosts (Preta)		–500
		Hell Beings (Naraka)		
			Reviving	–1,000
			Black String	
			Crushed	
			Weeping	
			Great Weeping	
			Heating	
			Great Heating	
			No Release	–20,000

Golden Earth (320,000 *yojanas* tall)
Disc of Water (800,000 *yojanas* tall)
Disc of Wind (1,600,000 *yojanas* tall)
Space

Character Glossary

ai	愛
“Anle xing”	安樂行
An Lushan	安祿山
Anxi	安西
anxing (official tour)	案行
anxing (comfortable conduct)	安行
banan	八難
Baiguansi	百官寺
bai yuan tan	白圓壇
Baizhang Huaihai	百丈懷海
Baodingshan	寶頂山
baoshen	報身
bei	悲
benchao	本朝
bi’an	彼岸
bijian	碧澗
bianxiang	變相
bing	病
Busa	布灑
Cao	曹
Cao Yangong	曹延恭
Cao Yijin	曹議金
Cao Yuande	曹元德
Cao Yuanshen	曹元深
Cao Yuanzhong	曹元忠
chenhui	瞋恚
Chengdu	城都
chizhai	持齋
“Chongxiu Baodingshan Shengshouyuan ji”	重修寶頂山聖壽院記
chujia	出家
Chujiang wang	初江王
chuli	出離
ci	刺
Dafowan	大佛灣
Dalun	大輪
dalun wubu mizhou	大輪五部秘咒
Dashizhi	大勢至
Dazu	大足
Dazu xianzhi	大足縣志
Daocheng	道誠
Daoguang	道光
Daoming	道明
Daoshou	道首
Disa	底灑
diyu bianxiang	地獄變相

diyu tubian 地獄圖變
Dizang pusa 地藏菩薩
Dingji 頂髻
Duli 都吏
Duyou 督郵
Dunhuang pusa 敦煌菩薩
duomen 多門

e-fu-luo-he 阿嚩囉訶
Emeishan 峨嵋山
Emituo fo 阿彌陀佛
e-wan-lan-han-qian 阿鋄籃唅欠
Ennin 圓仁
etoki 絵解き

Facheng 法成
falun 法輪
fashen 法身
Fazong 法宗
fanxing 梵行
fangzhang shinei 方丈室內
fenshao 焚燒
Foming jing 佛名經
Fuhui 福惠
Fu Xi 傅翕
"Fu xinyuan suo liuhao tu" 縛心猿鎖六耗圖

Ganzhou 甘州
ge 鴿
Genbenshuoyiqieyoubu 根本說一切有部
Gulusi (Li) 骨祿思力
Gua 瓜
Guazhou 瓜州
Guanshiyin 觀世音
Guanghan 廣漢
"Guangming" 光明
Gui Wen 歸文
Guiyijun jiedushi 歸義軍節度史
guizhen 歸真
guizhong 歸鍾
guo 果

Hexi 河西
Hexi duhufu 河西都護府
huaji 化跡
huashen 化身
Huayan sansheng 華嚴三聖
huihuhua 回鶻化

Jiaduoyanna 迦多演那
Jiazhou 嘉州
Jianjiao taibao 檢校太保
Jiedu liuhou shi 節度留後使
Jiedushi 節度史
Jingangjie mantuoluo 金剛界曼陀羅
Jingang jing 金剛經
Jing'ai 淨藹
jingjin 精進
jingtu 淨土
jingxiu 精修

"Kanshin jūkai zu" 觀心十界圖
ku 苦
Kumutula 库木吐拉

lao 老
lao si 老死
lian 煉
Liang 涼
Lingyou 靈祐
Liu Benzun 柳本尊
liuchu 六處

Liuhou	留後
"Liuqu weixin tu"	六趣唯心圖
liushu	柳樹
Liu Tianren	劉畋人
liuzei	六賊
Lu Ban	魯班
mie	滅
Miliangxiang	米粮鄉
Mimeng	彌濛
Mimou	彌牟
ming se	名色
Mingwang	明王
Mingxiang ji	冥祥記
Mingzong	明宗
Mokuren kyūbo kyō	目連救母経
nao	腦
Pishamen	碧沙門
Pinsheng	貧生
poyidijia	波逸底迦
Pushe	僕射
Puxian pusa	普賢菩薩
qibao	七寶
qizhen	七珍
Qiuci	龜茲
qu	取
Rengui	仁貴
Rongyang	滎陽
sandu	三毒
sanjian	三堅
sanjianfa	三堅法
sanzhongxing	三種形
sanzhou	三晝
Shaxi	沙溪
Shazhou	沙洲
Shansheng	善生
shejia	捨家
shentong	神通
shenzu	神足
sheng	生
shengguo	勝果
Shengshou Benzunyuan	聖壽本尊院
Shengshouyuan	聖壽院
shengsi	生死
shengsi jun	生死軍
shengsi lun	生死輪
shi	識
shicong (disciples)	侍從
shicong (events follow)	事從
shi'e	十惡
shi'eryinyuan	十二因緣
shi'erzhi yuanqi	十二支緣起
shilian	十煉
shiliuguan	十六觀
Shisong lü	十誦律
Shiwang jing	十王經
shou	受
Shuwang	蜀王
si	死
Sifen lü	四分律
Si gao	寺誥
Sikong	司空
simen wuxia	寺門屋下
simenxia	寺門下
sishamenguo	四沙門果
Sita ji	寺塔記
sitianwang	四天王
sizhong (Four Orders)	四眾
sizhong (hosts of death)	死眾
su (fashion)	塑
su (simplify)	素
Su	肅

tanran	貪染	xueren shi'er yinyuan yuan	學人十二因緣院
Tangchao minghua lu	唐朝名畫錄		
"Tang Liu Jushi zhuan"	唐柳居士傳	Yanlu	延祿
Tianqingwen jing	天請問經	Yanluowang	閻羅王
		Yanshouming jing	延壽命經
waihu	外護	Yaoshiwang pusa	藥師王菩薩
wanxiang	萬象	yebao chabie	業報差別
Wang Bing	王秉	yejing	業鏡
Wang Jian	王建	Yijing	意淨
Wang Yan	王琰	yiku zhi zhong	一窟之中
weixin	唯心	yiqieyou	一切有
Wenshu pusa	文殊菩薩	yiqie you xin zao	一切由心造
Wuchang dagui	無常大鬼	yishu	異熟
wuchang jun	無常軍	ying	癭
Wu Daozi	吳道子	ying'er	嬰兒
wufu	五福	Yongxi	壅溪
wulou	無漏	you (becoming)	有
wulun	物論	you (sadness)	憂
wuming	無明	Youtuoxian	優陀羨
wuqu	五趣	yuchi	愚癡
wuqu shengsi lun	五趣生死輪	Yu Jiangmo	諭江末
wuqu shengsi zhi lun	五趣生死之輪	Yulin	榆林
wuwei	無為	Yueguang	月光
wuxin	物信		
wuyi	無異	"Zashi"	雜事
		Zhai	翟
xifang	西方	Zhai Fengda	翟奉達
xirong	西戎	zhanzhuan shi	展轉食
Xizhou	西州	Zhang Chengfeng	張承奉
Xiandao	仙道	Zhang Huaishen	張淮深
xianshenli	現神力	Zhang Min	張岷
Xiaofowan	小佛灣	Zhang Yichao	張義朝
Xie Lingyun	謝靈運	Zhao Zhifeng	趙智風
"Xinwang ming"	心王銘	Zhaozong	昭宗
xing	行	Zheng	鄭
Xuye	續業	zhi	支
Xuanzang	玄奘	Zhi	稚

zhiguai	志怪	zhongxin tazhu shi	中心塔柱式
zhihui	智慧	zhou	州
zhijie	制戒	Zhu Fahu	竺法護
Zhisheng	智昇	zhuanlun wang	轉輪王
Zhi Yan	智嚴	Zizhou	梓州
Zhongguo difangzhi zongmu tiyao	中國地方志總目提要	Zujue	祖覺
Zhongshu ling	中書令		

Bibliography

Abbreviations

AA	*Artibus Asiae*
AAA	*Archives of Asian Art*
BÉFEO	*Bulletin de l'École Française d'Extrême-Orient*
CEA	*Cahiers d'Extrême-Asie*
DY	*Dunhuang yanjiu* 敦煌研究
HJAS	*Harvard Journal of Asiatic Studies*
IBK	*Indogaku bukkyōgaku kenkyū* 印度學佛教學研究
JA	*Journal Asiatique*
JAOS	*Journal of the American Oriental Society*
JAS	*Journal of Asian Studies*
JIABS	*Journal of the International Association of Buddhist Studies*
JIP	*Journal of Indian Philosophy*
SW	*Sichuan wenwu* 四川文物
T	*Taishō shinshū daizōkyō*
TP	*T'oung Pao*
WW	*Wenwu* 文物
Z	*Dainihon zokuzōkyō*

Primary Sources in Chinese and Japanese

Beiduoshuxia siwei shi'eryinyuan jing 貝多樹下思惟十二因緣經. Trans. Zhi Qian 支謙 (220–252). *T* no. 713.

Bieza ahan jing 別雜阿含經 (*Saṃyuktāgama*). Anon. (350–431). *T* no. 100.

Chuyao jing 出曜經. Trans. Buddhasmṛti (Zhu Fonian 竺佛念, ca. 365). *T* no. 212.

Dainihon zokuzōkyō 大日本續藏經. 750 vols. in 150 cases. Kyoto: Zōkyō shoin, 1905–12. Reprint, Shanghai: Commercial Press, 1923.

Daloutan jing 大樓炭經. Trans. Fali 法立 (ca. 290–306) and Faju 法炬 (ca. 290–306). *T* no. 23.

Dapiluzhena chengfo jing shu 大毘盧遮那成佛經疏. Yixing 義行(673–727). *T* no. 1796.

Dapiluzhena chengfo shenbian jiachi jing 大毘盧遮那成佛神變加持經 (*Mahāvairocana [abhisambodhi vikurvita ādhiṣṭhāna vaipulya] sūtra*). Trans. Śubhakarasiṃha (Shanwuwei 善無畏, ca. 716–735) and Yixing 義行 (673–727). *T* no. 848.

Dasheng bensheng xindi guan jing 大乘本生心地觀經. Trans. Prajñā (Bore 般若, 744–ca. 810). *T* no. 159.

Datang xiyu ji 大唐西域記. Xuanzang 玄奘 (602–664). *T* no. 2087.

Datang xiyu qiufa gaoseng zhuan 大唐西域求法高僧傳. Yijing 義淨 (635–712). *T* no. 2066.

Dizang pusa benyuan jing 地藏菩薩本願經. Trans. Śikṣānanda (Shichanantuo 實叉難陀, 652–712). *T* no. 412.

Eyuwang zhuan 阿育王傳 (*Aśokarājasūtra*?). Saṃghabhara? (Sengqiepoluo 僧伽婆羅, 460–524). *T* no. 2043.

Fa jiyao song jing 法集要頌經. Trans. Fajiu 法救 (Dharmatrāta?, dates unknown) and Tianxizai 天息災 (fl. 980–1000). *T* no. 213.

Fayuan zhulin 法苑珠林. Daoshi 道世 (d. 683). *T* no. 2122.

Foding zunshengxin podiyu zhuanyezhang chusanjie mimi sanshen foguo sanzhongxidi zhenyan yigui 佛頂尊勝心破地獄轉業障出三界祕密三身佛果三種悉地貞言儀規. Trans. Śubhakarasiṃha (Shanwuwei 善無畏, ca. 716–735). *T* no. 906.

Foding zunshengxin podiyu zhuanyezhang chusanjie mimi tuoluoni 佛頂尊勝心破地獄轉業障出三界祕密陀羅尼. Trans. Śubhakarasiṃha (Shanwuwei 善無畏, ca. 716–735). *T* no. 907.

Genbenshuoyiqieyoubu bichuni pinaiye 根本說一切有部苾芻尼毘奈耶 (*Mūlasarvāstivāda vinaya bhikṣuṇī vibhaṅga*). Trans.Yijing 義淨 (635–713). *T* no. 1443.

Genbenshuoyiqieyoubu jie jing 根本說一切有部戒經 (*Mūlasarvāstivāda prātimokṣa sūtra*). Trans. Yijing 義淨 (635–713) in 710. *T* no. 1454.

Genbenshuoyiqieyoubu pinaiye 根本說一切有部毘奈耶 (*Mūlasarvāstivāda vinaya vibhaṅga*). Trans. Yijing 義淨 (635–713). *T* no. 1442.

Genbenshuoyiqieyoubu pinaiye chujia shi 根本說一切有部毘奈耶出家事 (*Mūlasarvāstivāda pravrajāvastu*). Trans. Yijing 義淨 (635–713). *T* no. 1444.

Genbenshuoyiqieyoubu pinaiye poseng shi 根本說一切有部毘奈耶破僧世 (*Mūlasarvāstivāda saṃghabhedakavastu*). Trans. Yijing 義淨 (635–713). *T* no. 1450.

Genbenshuoyiqieyoubu pinaiye yaoshi 根本說一切有部毘奈耶藥事 (*Mūlasarvāstivāda bhaiṣajyavastu*). Trans. Yijing 義淨 (635–713). *T* no. 1448.

Genbenshuoyiqieyoubu pinaiye zashi 根本說一切有部毘奈耶雜事 (*Mūlasarvāstivāda vinaya kṣudrakavastu*). Trans. Yijing 義淨 (635–713) in 710. *T* no. 1451.

Guanfo sanmei hai jing 觀佛三昧海經 (**Buddhānusmṛti samādhisāgara sūtra*). Trans. Buddhabhadra (Fotuobatuoluo 佛陀跋陀羅, 359–429). *T* no. 643.

Jiucheng yu jing 舊城喻經. Trans. Faxian 法賢 (aka Tianxizai 天息災, fl. 980–1000). *T* no. 715.

Kaiyuan shijiao 開元釋教錄. Zhisheng 智昇 (669–740). *T* no. 2154.

Lidai minghua ji 歷代名畫記. Zhang Yanyuan 張顏遠 (fl. 847–874). In *Huashi congshu* 畫史叢書, vol. 1. 4 vols. Shanghai: Shanghai renmin meishu chubanshe, 1963.

Liaoben shengsi jing 了本生死經 (*Śālistambhaka sūtra*). Trans. Zhi Qian 支謙 (ca. 220–252). *T* no. 708.
Miaofa lianhua jing 妙法蓮華經 (*Saddharmapuṇḍarīka*). Trans. Kumārajīva (Jiumoluoshi 鳩摩羅什, 350–409). *T* no. 262.
Pusa yingluo jing 菩薩瓔珞經. Trans. Buddhasmṛti (Zhu Fonian 竺佛念, fl. 365). *T* no. 656.
Qishi jing 起世經. Trans. Jñānagupta (Shenajueduo 闍那崛多, 523–600). *T* no. 24.
Qishi yinben jing 起世因本經. Trans. Dharmagupta (Damojiduo 達摩笈多, ca. 590–619). *T* no. 25.
Sanzhong xidi podiyu zhuanyezhang chusanjie mimi tuoluoni fa 三種悉地破地獄轉業障出三界祕密陀羅尼法. Trans. Śubhakarasiṃha (Shanwuwei 善無畏, ca. 716–735). *T* no. 905.
Shiji jing 世紀經. Trans. Buddhayaśas (Fotuoyeshe 佛陀耶舍, ca. 384–417) and Buddhasmṛti (Zhu Fonian 竺佛念, ca. 365), in 412–413. In *Chang ahan jing* 長阿含經 (*Dīrghāgama*), *T* no. 1.
Shishi yaolan 釋氏要覽. Daocheng 道誠 (ca. 1017–1021), in 1019. *T* no. 2127.
Song gaoseng zhuan 宋高僧傳. Zanning 贊寧 (919–1001). *T* no. 2061.
Taishō shinshū daizōkyō 大正新修大藏經. 100 vols. Edited by Takakusu Jinjirō 高楠順次郎, Watanabe Kaigyoku 渡邊海旭, and Ono Gemmyō 小野玄妙. 1924–34. Reprint, Taibei: Xinwenfeng chuban gongsi, 1974.
Wang Wutianzhuguo zhuan 往五天竺國傳. Hye-č'o 慧超 (704–ca. 780). In *Youfang jichao* 遊方記抄. *T* no. 2089.
Weimojie suoshuo jing 維摩詰所說經 (*Vimalakīrti nirdeśa*). Trans. Kumārajīva (Jiumoluoshi 鳩摩羅什, 350–409). *T* no. 475.
Xu gaoseng zhuan 續高僧傳. Daoxuan 道宣 (596–667). *T* no. 2060.
Yuanqi shengdao jing 緣起聖道經. Trans. Xuanzang 玄奘 (602–664). *T* no. 714.
Za ahan jing 雜阿含經 (*Saṃyuktāgama*). Trans. Guṇabhadra (Qiunabatuoluo 求那跋陀羅, 394–468). *T* no. 99.
Za baozang jing 雜寶藏經. Trans. Kiṃkārya (Jijiaye, 吉加夜 ca. 472) and Tanyao 曇曜(ca. 453–462). *T* no. 203.
Zengyi ahan jing 增一阿含經 (*Ekottarāgama*). Trans. Gautama Saṃghadeva (Qutan Sengqietipo 瞿曇僧伽提婆, fl. 383–398). *T* no. 125.
Zheng fahua jing 正法華經. Trans. Dharmarakṣa (Zhu Fahu 竺法護, fl. 265–313). *T* no. 263.
Zhong Tianzhu Sheweiguo Qihuansi tujing 中天竺舍衛國祇洹寺圖經. Daoxuan 道宣 (596–667), in 667. *T* no. 1899.

Secondary Sources and Translations

Acker, William R. B. *Some T'ang and Pre-T'ang Texts on Chinese Painting*. 2 vols. Leiden, The Netherlands: E. J. Brill, 1954, 1974.
Akanuma Chizen 赤沼智善. *Indo bukkyō koyū meishi jiten* 印度佛教固有名詞辭典. Kyoto: Hōzōkan, 1967.

Alabaster, Henry. *The Wheel of the Law: Buddhism Illustrated from Siamese Sources by "The Modern Buddhist," "A Life of Buddha," and "An Account of the Phrabat."* London: Trubner and Co., 1871.

Almond, Philip C. *The British Discovery of Buddhism*. Cambridge: Cambridge University Press, 1988.

Bai Ziran 白自然. *Zhongguo Dazu shiku* 中國大足石窟*: Les sculptures millénaires de Dazu*. Beijing: Waiwen chubanshe, 1985.

Bakker, Hans T. *The Vākāṭakas: An Essay in Hindu Iconology*. Gonda Indological Studies 5. Groningen, The Netherlands: Egbert Forsten, 1997.

Bareau, André. "Chūu." In *Hōbōgirin: Dictionnaire encyclopédique du bouddhisme d'après les sources chinoises et japonaises*, edited by Paul Demiéville and Jacques May, pp. 558b–63b. 6 vols. to date. Tokyo: Maison Franco-Japonaise, 1929–.

———. *Recherches sur la biographie du Bouddha dans les sūtrapiṭaka et les vinayapiṭaka anciens*. 3 vols. Publications de l'École Française d'Extrême-Orient 53, 77, 178. Paris: École Française d'Extrême-Orient, 1963–1995.

———. *Les sectes bouddhiques du petit véhicule*. Publications de l'École Française d'Extrême-Orient 38. Paris: École Française d'Extrême-Orient, 1955.

Batt, Jill Crossley, and Irving Baird. *"Sipa Khorlo" (The Tibetan Wheel of Life)*. New York: Python Publishing Co., 1955.

Beal, Samuel, trans. *Si-yu-ki: Buddhist Records of the Western World*. 2 vols. London: Kegan Paul, Trench, Trübner and Co., 1884.

Beckwith, Christopher I. *The Tibetan Empire in Central Asia: A History of the Struggle for Great Power among Tibetans, Turks, Arabs, and Chinese during the Early Middle Ages*. Princeton, NJ: Princeton University Press, 1987.

Béguin, Gilles. *Les peintures du bouddhisme tibétain*. Paris: Réunion des Musées Nationaux, 1995.

Behl, Benoy K. *The Ajanta Caves: Artistic Wonder of Ancient Buddhist India*. New York: Harry N. Abrams, 1998.

Blackburn, Anne M. *Buddhist Learning and Textual Practice in Eighteenth-Century Lankan Monastic Culture*. Princeton, NJ: Princeton University Press, 2001.

Boucher, Daniel. "The *Pratītyasamutpāda gāthā* and Its Role in the Medieval Cult of Relics." *JIABS* 14, no. 1 (1991): 1–27.

Brown, Percy. *Indian Architecture (Buddhist and Hindu)*. 3rd ed. Bombay: D. E. Taraporevala, 1956.

Brown, Robert. *The Dvāravatī Wheels of the Law and the Indianization of South East Asia*. Studies in Asian Art and Archaeology 18. Leiden, The Netherlands: E. J. Brill, 1996.

Bucknell, Roderick S. "Conditioned Arising Evolves: Variation and Change in Textual Accounts of the *Paticca-samuppāda* Doctrine." *JIABS* 22, no. 2 (1999): 311–42.

Burgess, James. *Report on the Buddhist Cave Temples and Their Inscriptions: Being Part of the Results of the Fourth, Fifth, and Sixth Seasons' Operations of the Archaeological Survey of Western India, 1876–77*, 1877–78, 1878–89. Archaeological Survey of Western India 4. London: Trubner, 1883.

Campany, Robert Ford. *Strange Writing: Anomaly Accounts in Early Medieval China.* Albany, NY: SUNY Press, 1996.

Chandra, Lokesh, ed. *Sarva-Tathāgata-Tattva-Sangraha.* Delhi: Motilal Banarsidass, 1987.

Chao Huashan 晁华山. "Kumutula shiku chutan 库木吐喇石窟初探." In *Kumutula shiku* 库木吐喇石窟, edited by Xinjiang Weiwu'er zizhiqu wenwu guanli weiyuanhui 新疆维吾尔自治区文物管理委员会, Kuchexian wenwu baoguansuo 库车县文物保管所, and Beijing daxue kaogusuo 北京大学考古所, pp. 170–202. Beijing: Wenwu chubanshe, 1992.

———. "Kumutula shiku de dongku fenlei yu siyuan zuhe 庫木吐拉石窟的洞窟分類與寺院組合." In *Kuche Kumutula shiku* 庫車庫木吐拉石窟, edited by Xinjiang Weiwu'er zizhiqu bowuguan 新疆維吾爾自治區博物館 and Xinjiang renmin chubanshe 新疆人民出版社, pp. 236–46. Shanghai: Xinjiang renmin chubanshe, Shanghai meishu chubanshe, 1992.

———. "Xinjiang shiku bihuazhong de Qiuci fengge 新疆石窟中的龜玆風格." In *Xinjiang shiku bihua* 新疆石窟壁畫, edited by Zhongguo meishu quanji bianji weiyuanhui 中國美術全集編輯委員會, pp. 1–30. Zhongguo meishu quanji, huihua bian 中國美術全集, 繪畫編 16. Beijing: Wenwu chubanshe, 1986.

Chavannes, Édouard. *Cinq cents contes et apologues: Extraits du tripitaka chinois et traduits en français.* 3 vols. Paris: Ernest Leroux, 1911.

Chen, Jinhua. "The Birth of a Polymath: The Genealogical Background of the Tang Monk-Scientist Yixing (673–727)." *Tang Studies* 18–19 (2000–2001): 1–39.

———. "The Construction of Early Tendai Esoteric Buddhism: The Japanese Provenance of Saicho's Transmission Documents and Three Esoteric Buddhist Apocrypha Attributed to Subhakarasimha." *JIABS* 21, no. 1 (1998): 21–76.

———. "The Formation of Early Esoteric Buddhism in Japan: A Study of Three Japanese Esoteric Apocrypha." Ph.D. dissertation, McMaster University, 1997.

Chen Fangying 陳芳英. *Mulian jiumu gushi zhi yanjin ji qi youguan wenxue zhi yanjiu* 目蓮救母故事之演進及其有關文學之研究. History and Literature Series 65. Taibei: Taiwan National University, 1983.

Chen Mingguang 陈明光. "Sichuan moyan zaoxiang Liu Benzun huadao 'shilian tu' youlai ji niandai tansuo 四川摩岩造像柳本尊化道十炼图由来及年代探索." *SW*, 1996, no. 1:33–39.

———. "Song ke 'Tang Liu Benzun zhuan' bei jiaobu 宋刻唐柳本尊传碑校补" *Shijie zongjiao yanjiu* 世界宗教研究, 1985, no. 2:107–11.

Chen Xishan 陈习删. *Dazu shike zhilue jiaozhu* 大足石刻志略校注. In *Dazu shike yanjiu* 大足石刻研究, edited by Liu Changjiu 刘长久 et al. Chengdu: Sichuansheng shehui kexueyuan chubanshe, 1985.

Chongqing Dazu shike yishu bowuguan 重庆大足石刻艺术博物馆, and Chongqingshi shehui kexueyuan Dazu shike yishu yanjiusuo 重庆市社会科学院大足石刻艺术研究所, eds. *Dazu shike mingwen lu* 大足石刻名纹录. Chongqing: Chongqing chubanshe, 1999.

Chūgoku gaibun shuppansha 中国外文出版社, ed. *Daisoku sekkoku geijutsu* 大足石刻芸術. Kyoto: Bi no bi, 1981.

Clarke, Shayne. "The *Mūlasarvāstivāda Vinaya Muktaka.*" *Bukkyō kenkyū* 仏教研究 30 (2001): 81–108.
Cohen, Richard Scott. "Setting the Three Jewels: The Complex Culture of Buddhism at the Ajaṇṭā Caves." Ph.D. dissertation, University of Michigan, 1995.
Coolidge, Usher P., ed. *Religious Wood-Block Prints of the Far East: An Exhibition of Chinese, Korean, and Japanese Religious Wood-Block Prints dating from the Seventh to the Nineteenth Century*. Cambridge, MA: The Fogg Museum of Art, 1948.
Collins, Steven. "On the Very Idea of a Pāli Canon." *Journal of the Pāli Text Society* 15 (1990): 89–126.
Conze, Edward. *Buddhist Thought in India: Three Phases of Buddhist Philosophy*. London: George Allen and Unwin, 1962.
Cowell, Edward B., and Robert A. Neil. *The Divyāvadāna: A Collection of Early Buddhist Legends*. Cambridge: Cambridge University Press, 1886.
Daizōkyō gakujutsu yōgo kenkyūkai 大藏經學術用語研究會, ed. *Taishō shinshū daizōkyō sakuin* 大正新修大藏經索引. 45 vols. Tokyo: Taishō shinshū daizōkyō kankōkai, 1975–78.
De Caroli, Robert. "An Analysis of Daṇḍin's *Daśakumāracarita* and Its Implications for both the Vākāṭaka and Pallava Courts." *JAOS* 115, no. 4 (Oct.–Dec. 1995): 671–78.
Dehejia, Vidya. *Discourse in Early Buddhist Art: Visual Narratives of India*. New Delhi: Munshiram Manoharlal Publishers Private, 1997.
———. *Early Buddhist Rock Temples: A Chronological Study*. Studies in Ancient Art and Archaeology. London: Thames and Hudson, 1972.
de Jong, J. W. "Les *Sūtrapiṭaka* des Sarvāstivādin et des Mūlasarvāstivādin." In *Mélanges d'indianisme à la mémoire de Louis Renou*, pp. 395–402. Publications de l'Institut de Civilization Indienne, series 8, fascicle 28. Paris: Editions E. de Boccard, 1968.
Deng Zhijin 邓之金. "Dazu Baodingshan Dafowan 'liuhao tu' kan diaocha 大足宝顶山大佛湾六耗图龛调查." *SW*, 1996, no. 1:23–32.
Denwood, Philip. "Tibetan Architecture." In *On the Path to the Void: Buddhist Art of the Tibetan Realm*, edited by Pratapaditya Pal, pp. 26–65. Mumbai: Marg Publications, 1996.
Deshpande, M. D. "Buddhist Art of Ajanta and Tabo." *Bulletin of Tibetology* 10 (1973): 1–44.
DeWoskin, Kenneth J. "The Six Dynasties *Chih-kuai* and the Birth of Fiction." In *Chinese Narrative: Critical and Theoretical Essays*, edited by Andrew H. Plaks, pp. 21–52. Princeton, NJ: Princeton University Press, 1977.
Ding Mingyi 丁明夷. "Chuanbei shiku zhaji 川北石窟札记." *WW*, 1990, no. 6:41–53.
———. "Sichuan shiku zashi 四川石窟杂识." *WW*, 1998, no. 8:46–58
Du Doucheng 杜斗城. "'Diyu bianxiang' chutan 地狱变相初探." *Dunhuangxue jikan* 敦煌学辑刊 16 (1989): 73–84.
———. *Dunhuangben foshuo shiwang jing jiaolu yanjiu* 敦煌本佛说十王经校录研究. Lanzhou: Gansu jiaoyu chubanshe, 1989.

Duan Wenjie 段文杰. "Mogaoku wanqi de yishu 莫高窟晚期的艺术." In *Dunhuang Mogaoku* 敦煌莫高窟, edited by Dunhuang yanjiusuo 敦煌研究所, 5:161–74. Zhongguo shiku 中国石窟. Beijing: Wenwu chubanshe, 1987.

———. "Yulinku de bihua yishu 榆林窟的壁画艺术." In *Anxi Yulinku* 安西榆林窟, edited by Dunhuang yanjiuyuan 敦煌研究院, pp. 161–76. Zhongguo shiku 中国石窟. Beijing: Wenwu chubanshe, 1997.

Dunhuang yanjiusuo 敦煌研究所, ed. *Dunhuang Mogaoku* 敦煌莫高窟. 5 vols. Zhongguo shiku 中国石窟. Beijing: Wenwu chubanshe, 1982–87.

Dunhuang yanjiuyuan 敦煌研究院, ed. *Anxi Yulinku* 安西榆林窟. Zhongguo shiku 中国石窟. Beijing: Wenwu chubanshe, 1997.

———. *Dunhuang shiku neirong zonglu* 敦煌石窟内容总录. Beijing: Wenwu chubanshe, 1996.

Dunhuang yanjiuyuan 敦煌研究院 and Jiangsu meishu chubanshe 江苏美术出版社, eds. *Dunhuang shiku yishu: Mogaoku di si'erbaku (Bei Zhou)* 敦煌石窟艺术：莫高窟第四二八窟（北周）. Nanjing: Jiangsu meishu chubanshe, 1998.

———. *Dunhuang shiku yishu: Mogaoku di yiwubaku* 敦煌石窟艺术：莫高窟第一五八窟（中唐）. Nanjing: Jiangsu meishu chubanshe, 1998.

Dunnington, Jacqueline Orsini. *The Tibetan Wheel of Existence: An Introduction*. Edited by Robert Thurman and Thomas Yarnall. New York: Tibet House, 2000.

Dutt, Sukumar. *Buddhist Monks and Monasteries of India: Their History and Their Contribution to Indian Culture*. London: George Allen and Unwin, 1962.

Edgerton, Franklin. *Buddhist Hybrid Sanskrit Grammar and Dictionary*. 2 vols. New Haven, CT: Yale University Press, 1953.

Enoki Kazuo 榎一雄. *Tonkō no rekishi* 敦煌の歴史. Kōza Tonkō 講座敦煌 2. Tokyo: Daitō shuppansha, 1970.

Enomoto, Fumio. "'Mūlasarvāstivāda' and 'Sarvāstivāda.'" In *Vividharatnakarundaka: Festgabe für Adelheid Mette*, edited by Christine Chojnacki, Jens-Uwe Hartmann, and Volker M. Tschannerl, pp. 239–50. Indica et Tibetica 37. Swisstal-Odendorf, Germany: Indica et Tibetica Verlag, 2000.

Eracle, Jean. *L'art des thanka et le bouddhisme tantrique, d'après les peintures du Musée d'ethnographie de Genève et quelques autres pièces*. Geneva: Musée d'ethnographie, 1970.

Essen, Gerd-Wolfgang, and Tsering Tashi Thingo. *Die Götter des Himalaya: Buddhistische Kunst Tibets: Die Sammlung Gerd-Wolfgang Essen*. 2 vols. München: Prestel-Verlag, 1989.

Fan Jinshi 樊锦诗. *Dunhuang shiku* 敦煌石窟藝術: *Three Great Caves of the Dunhuang Grottoes*. Lanzhou: Gansu wenhua chubanshe, 1998.

———. "Yulinku 榆林窟." In *Dunhuangxue dacidian* 敦煌学大辞典, edited by Ji Xianlin 季羡林 pp. 11–12. Shanghai: Shanghai cishu chubanshe, 1998.

Fan Jinshi 樊錦詩, and Mei Lin 梅林. "An Interpretation of the Maudgalyayana Murals in Cave 19 at Yulin." *Orientations* 27, no. 10 (Nov. 1996): 70–75.

———. "Yulinku dishijiuku Mulian bianxiang kaoshi 榆林窟第十九窟目蓮變相考釋." In *Duan Wenjie Dunhuang yanjiu wushinian jinian wenji* 段文傑敦煌研究五十

年紀念文集, edited by Dunhuang yanjiuyuan 敦煌研究院, pp. 46–60. Beijing: Shijie tushu chuban gongsi, 1996.

Fang Guangchang 方广锠. *Fojiao dazangjing shi (ba-shi shiji)* 佛教大藏经史（八–十世纪）. Beijing: Zhongguo shehui kexueyuan chubanshe, 1991.

Fergusson, James, and James Burgess. *The Cave Temples of India*. London: W. H. Allen and Co., 1880.

Foley, Caroline A. [Caroline A. F. Rhys Davids.] "Correspondence." *Journal of the Royal Asiatic Society of Great Britain and Ireland* (Apr. 1894): 388–90.

Fontein, Jan. *The Pilgrimage of Sudhana: A Study of Gaṇḍavyūha Illustrations in China, Japan, and Java*. The Hague and Paris: Mouton and Co., 1967.

Forte, Antonino. *Mingtang and Buddhist Utopias in the History of the Astronomical Clock: The Tower, Statue and Armillary Sphere Constructed by Empress Wu*. Serie Orientale Roma 59, Publications de l'École Française d'Extrême-Orient 145. Rome: Istituto Italiano per il Medio ed Estremo Oriente, Paris: École Française d'Extrême-Orient, 1988.

Francke, August Hermann. *Antiquities of Indian Tibet*. Pt. 1, *Personal Narrative*. Pt. 2, *The Chronicles of Ladakh and Minor Chronicles*. 1914, 1926. Reprint, Archaeological Survey of India, New Imperial Series 38, 50. New Delhi: S. Chand and Co., 1992.

Fraser, Sarah E. "The Manuals and Drawings of Artists, Calligraphers, and Other Specialists from Dunhuang." In *Images de Dunhuang: Dessins et peintures sur papier des fonds* PELLIOT *et* STEIN, edited by Jean-Pierre Drège, pp. 55–104. Mémoires archéologiques 24. Paris: École Française d'Extrême-Orient, 1999.

———. *Performing the Visual: The Practice of Buddhist Wall Painting in China and Central Asia, 618–960*. Stanford, CA: Stanford University Press, 2004.

Frauwallner, Erich. *The Earliest Vinaya and the Beginnings of Buddhist Literature*. Trans. Luciano Petech. Serie Orientale Roma 8. Rome: Istituto Italiano per il Medio ed Estremo Oriente, 1956.

Freemantle, Francesca. *Luminous Emptiness: Understanding the "Tibetan Book of the Dead."* Boston: Shambhala, 2001.

Fujieda Akira 藤枝晃. "Shashū kigigun setsudoshi shimatsu 沙州歸義軍節度史始末." *Tōhō gakuhō* 東方學報 (Kyoto) 12, no. 3 (Dec. 1941): 59–98; 12, no. 4 (Mar. 1942): 42–75; 13, no. 1 (June 1942): 63–95; 13, no. 2 (Jan. 1943): 46–98.

———. "Tonkō zenbutsudō no chūkō: Chōshi shokutsu o chūshin to shita kyū seiki no butsukutsu zōei 敦煌千佛洞の中興：張氏諸窟お中心とした九世紀の佛窟造營." *Tōhō gakuhō* 東方學報 (Kyoto) 35 (1964): 9–140.

Funayama, Toru. "The Acceptance of Buddhist Precepts by the Chinese in the Fifth Century." *Journal of Asian History*, forthcoming.

Gabain, Annemarie von. *Das Leben im uigurischen Königreich von Qočo (850–1250)*. Veröffentlichungen der Societas Uralo-Altaica 6. Wiesbaden, Germany: Otto Harrassowitz, 1973.

Gimello, Robert M. "Random Reflections on the 'Sinicization' of Buddhism." *Society for the Study of Chinese Religions Bulletin* 5 (1978): 52–89.

Gjertson, Donald E. "The Early Chinese Buddhist Miracle Tale: A Preliminary Survey." *JAOS* 101 (1981): 287–301.

Gnoli, Raniero, ed. *The Gilgit Manuscripts of the Sanghabhedavastu*. 2 pts. Serie Orientale Roma 49, nos. 1–2. Rome: Istituto Italiano per il Medio ed Estremo Oriente, 1977–78.
Goepper, Roger. *Alchi: Ladakh's Hidden Buddhist Sanctuary, the Sumtsek*. Photography by Jaroslav Poncar. Boston: Shambhala Publications, 1996.
Gokhale, Balkrishna Govind. "Buddhism in the Gupta Age." In *Essays in Gupta Culture*, edited by Bardwell L. Smith, pp. 129–53. Delhi: Motilal Banarsidass, 1983.
Gombrich, Richard, and Gananath Obeyesekere. *Buddhism Transformed: Religious Change in Sri Lanka*. Princeton, NJ: Princeton University Press, 1988.
Gordon, Antoinette K. *The Iconography of Tibetan Lamaism*. Rev. ed. Rutland, VT: Charles E. Tuttle, 1959.
Govinda, Angarika Brahmacari. *Foundations of Tibetan Mysticism*. London: Rider and Co., 1969.
Griffiths, John. *The Paintings in the Buddhist Cave-Temples of Ajaṇṭā, Kandesh, India*. 2 vols. 1896–97. Reprint, Delhi: Caxton, 1983.
Grünwedel, Albert. *Alt-Kutscha: Archäologische und religionsgeschichtliche Forschungen in tempera-gemälden aus Buddhistischen Höhlen der ersten acht Jahrhunderte nach Christi geburt*. Berlin: O. Elsner Verlagsgesellschaft, 1920.
Gupta, Chandrashekhar. "Authorship of Ajaṇṭā Caves 17 to 20." In *The Art of Ajaṇṭā: New Perspectives*, edited by Ratan Parimoo et al., 1:100–104. New Delhi: Books and Books, 1991.
Gyatso, Tenzin. *Answers: Discussions with Western Buddhists*. Rev. ed. of *The Bodhgaya Interviews*, 1988. Edited by José Ignazio Cabezón. Ithaca, NY: Snow Lion Publications, 2001.
———. *The Meaning of Life from a Buddhist Perspective*. Translated and edited by Jeffrey Hopkins. Boston: Wisdom Publications, 1992.
———. *The World of Tibetan Buddhism: An Overview of Its Philosophy and Practice*. Trans. Geshe Thupten Jinpa. Boston: Wisdom Publications, 1995.
Hackin, J. "Les scènes figurées de la vie du Buddha d'après des peintures tibétaines." *Mémoires concernant l'Asie Orientale (Inde, Asie Centrale, Extrême-Orient) publiés par l'Académie des Inscriptions et Belles-Lettres*, vol. 2. Paris: Ernst Leroux, 1916.
Hagiwara, Tatsuo 萩原龍夫. *Miko to bukkyō shi: Kumano bikuni no shimei to tenkai* 巫女と仏教史：熊野比丘尼の使命と展開. Tokyo: Yoshikawa kōbunkan, 1983.
Hallisey, Charles. "Apropos the Pāli Vinaya as Historical Document: A Reply to Gregory Schopen." *Journal of the Pali Text Society* 15 (1991): 197–208.
Hamilton, James Russell. *Les Ouïghours à l'époque des Cinq Dynasties d'après les documents chinois*. Bibliothèque de l'Institut des Hautes Études Chinoises 10. Paris: Imprimerie Nationale, Presses Universitaires de France, 1955.
Han Xiang 韩翔, and Zhu Yingrong 朱英荣. *Qiuci shiku* 龟兹石库. Qiuci wenhua yanjiu 龟兹文化研究. Urumqi: Xinjiang daxue chubanshe, 1990.
Handa, O. C. *Buddhist Western Himalaya*. Pt. 1, *A Politico-Religious History*. New Delhi: Indus Publishing Co., 2001.
———. *Tabo Monastery and Buddhism in the Trans-Himalaya: Thousand Years of Existence of the Tabo Chos-khor*. New Delhi: Indus Publishing Co., 1994.

Hao Chunwen 郝春文. *Tanghouqi Wudai Songchu Dunhuang sengni de shehui shenghuo* 唐后期五代宋初敦煌僧尼的社会生活. Beijing: Zhongguo shehui kexue chubanshe, 1998.

Harle, James C. *The Art and Architecture of the Indian Subcontinent*. 2nd ed. Pelican History of Art. New Haven, CT: Yale University Press, 1994.

Härtel, Herbert, and Marianne Yaldiz. *Along the Ancient Silk Routes: Central Asian Art from the West Berlin State Museums*. New York: The Metropolitan Museum of Art, 1982.

Hartmann, Gerda. "Symbols of the *Nidānas* in Tibetan Drawings of the Wheel of Life." *JAOS* 60 (1940): 356–60.

Hay, Jonathan. "Toward a Theory of the Intercultural." Editorial in special issue on "Intercultural China." *Res* 35 (Spring 1999): 5–9.

Hayashi Masahiko 林雅彦. *Nihon no etoki: Shiryō to kenkyū* 日本の絵解き：資料と研究. Tokyo: Miyai shoten, 1984.

He Shizhe 贺世哲. "Cong gongyangren tiji kan Mogaoku bufen dongku de yingjian niandai 从供养人题记看莫高窟部分洞窟的营建年代." In *Dunhuang Mogaoku gongyangren tiji* 敦煌莫高窟供养人题记, edited by Dunhuang yanjiuyuan 敦煌研究院, pp. 194–236. Beijing: Wenwu chubanshe, 1986.

Hegel, Robert E. "Heavens and Hells in Chinese Fictional Dreams." In *Psycho-Sinology: The Universe of Dreams in Chinese Culture*. Edited by Carolyn T. Brown. Washington, DC: Asia Program, Woodrow Wilson International Center for Scholars, 1988.

Heller, Amy. "Eighth- and Ninth-Century Temples and Rock Carvings of Eastern Tibet." In *Tibetan Art: Towards a Definition of Style*, edited by Jane Casey Singer and Philip Denwood, pp. 86–103. London: Laurence King Publishing, 1997.

Henss, Michael. "Wall-Paintings in Western Tibet: The Art of the Ancient Kingdom of Guge, 1000–1500." In *On the Path to the Void: Buddhist Art of the Tibetan Realm*. Edited by Pratapaditya Pal. Mumbai: Marg Publications, 1996.

Hertz, Robert. *Death and the Right Hand*. Trans. Rodney Needham and Claudia Needham. Glencoe, IL: Free Press, 1960.

Hirakawa Akira 平川彰. *Ritsuzō no kenkyū* 律蔵の研究. Tokyo: Sankibo busshorin, 1960.

———. "Shibunrisshū no shutsugen to jūjuritsu 四分律宗の出現と十誦律." 1986. Reprinted in *Hirakawa Akira chosakushū: Nihon bukkyō to Chūgoku bukkyō* 平川彰著作集：日本仏教と中国仏教, pp. 157–87. Tokyo: Shunjūsha, 1991.

Hiraoka Mihoko 平岡三保子. "Indo no shōjirin zu—Ajantā hekiga no sakurei ni tsuite インドの生死輪図—アジャンター壁画の作例について." In *Mandara to rinne: Sono shisō to bijutsu* 曼荼羅と輪廻：その思想と美術, edited by Tachikawa Musashi 立川武蔵, pp. 278–96. Tokyo: Kōsei shuppansha, 1993.

Hiraoka, Satoshi. "The Relation between the *Divyāvadāna* and the *Mūlasarvāstivāda vinaya*." *JIP* 26, no. 5 (1998): 419–34.

———. "The Relation between the *Divyāvadāna* and the *Mūlasarvāstivādavinaya*: The Case of *Divyāvadāna* Chapter 31." *IBK* 39, no. 2 (Mar. 1991): 17–19 (Japanese pagination 1038–36).

Ho, Puay-peng. "The Ideal Monastery: Daoxuan's Description of the Central Indian Jetavana Vihara." *East Asian History* 10 (Dec. 1995): 1–18.
———. "Setting for the Faith: Icons in Space in Early Chinese Monasteries." In *In the Footsteps of the Buddha: An Iconic Journey from India to China*, edited by Rajeshwari Ghose, pp. 127–37. Hong Kong: University Museum and Art Gallery, University of Hong Kong, 1998.
———. "The Symbolism of the Central Pillars in Cave-Temples of Northwest China." In *Sacred Architecture in the Traditions of India, China, Judaism, and Islam*, edited by Emily Lyle, pp. 59–70. Edinburgh: Edinburgh University Press, 1992. Also published as *Cosmos* 8 (1992).
Holt, John C. "Protestant Buddhism?" Review of *Buddhism Transformed: Religious Change in Sri Lanka*, by Richard Gombrich and Gananath Obeyesekere. *Religious Studies Review* 17, no. 4 (1998): 307–12.
Hopkins, Jeffrey. *The Tantric Distinction: An Introduction to Tibetan Buddhism*. Edited by Anne C. Klein. Boston: Wisdom Publications, 1984.
Howard, Angela Falco. "The Development of Buddhist Sculpture in Sichuan: The Making of an Indigenous Art." In *The Flowering of a Foreign Faith: New Studies in Chinese Buddhist Art*, edited by Janet Baker, pp. 118–33. Mumbai: Marg Publications, 1998.
———. *The Imagery of the Cosmological Buddha*. Studies in South Asian Culture 13. Leiden, The Netherlands: E. J. Brill, 1986.
———. "The Monumental 'Cosmological Buddha' in the Freer Gallery of Art: Chronology and Style." *Ars Orientalis* 14 (1984): 53–73.
———. *Summit of Treasures: Buddhist Cave Art of Dazu, China*. Trumbull, CT: Weatherhill, 2001.
———. "In Support of a New Chronology for the Kizil Mural Paintings." *AAA* 44 (1991): 68–83.
———. "Tang Buddhist Sculpture of Sichuan: Unknown and Forgotten." *Bulletin of the Museum of Far Eastern Antiquities (Östasiatiska Museet), Stockholm* 60 (1988): 1–164.
Hu Wenhe 胡文和. "Anyue Dazu 'Liu Benzun shilian tu' tike he Song li 'Tang Liu Jushi zhuan' bei de yanjiu 安岳大足柳本尊十炼图题刻和宋立唐柳居士传碑的研究." *SW*, 1991, no. 3:42–47.
———. "Lun diyu bianxiang tu 论地狱变相图." *SW*, 1988, no. 2:20–26.
———. *Sichuan daojiao fojiao shiku yishu* 四川道教佛教石窟艺术. Chengdu: Sichuan renmin chubanshe, 1994.
———. "Sichuan shikuzhong 'diyu bianxiang' tu de yanjiu 四川石窟中地獄變相圖的研究." *Yishuxue* 藝術學 19 (Mar. 1998): 41–80.
Hu Zhaoxi 胡照曦. "Dazu Baodingshan shike qianlun 大足宝顶山石刻浅论." 1983. Reprinted in *Dazu shike yanjiu* 大足石刻研究. Edited by Liu Changjiu 刘长久 et al. Chengdu: Sichuansheng shehui kexueyuan chubanshe, 1985.
Huang Wenbi 黄文弼. "Lueshu Qiuci ducheng wenti 略述龟兹都城问题." 1962. Reprinted in *Xibei shi di luncong* 西北史地论丛, pp. 261–67. Shanghai: Shanghai renmin chubanshe, Xinhua shudian Shanghai faxingsuo, 1981.

———. *Talimu pendi kaogu ji* 塔里木盆地考古记. Beijing: Kexue chubanshe, 1958.
Huang Yongwu 黄永武, ed. *Dunhuang baozang* 敦煌寶藏. 140 vols. Taibei: Xinwenfeng, 1981–86.
Huber, Édouard. "Études bouddhiques: III. Le roi Kaniska dans le Vinaya des Mūlasarvāstivādins." *BÉFEO* 14 (1914): 18–19.
———. "Études de litterature bouddhique: V. Les sources du *Divyāvadāna*." *BÉFEO* 6 (1906): 1–37.
Hucker, Charles O. *A Dictionary of Official Titles in Imperial China*. Stanford, CA: Stanford University Press, 1985.
Huntington, Susan L. "Aniconism and the Multivalence of Emblems: Another Look." *Ars Orientalis* 22 (1977): 111–56.
Ikeda On 池田温. *Chūgoku kodai shahon shikigo shūroku* 中國古代寫本識語集錄. Tōyō bunka kenkyūjo sōkan 東洋文化研究所叢刊 11. Tokyo: Tōkyō daigaku tōyō bunka kenkyūjo, 1990.
Itō Chūta 伊東忠太. "Gion shōja zu to Ankoru Watto 祇園精舎圖とアンコルワット." *Tōyō kenchiku no kenkyū* 東洋建築の研究. 2 vols. 1937. Reprinted in *Itō Chūta chosakushū* 伊東忠太著作集 3:365–406. Tokyo: Hara shobō, 1982.
Iwamoto Yutaka 岩本裕 *Jigoku meguri no bungaku* 地獄めぐりの文学. Bukkyō setsuwa kenkyū 佛教說話研究, vol. 4. Tokyo: Kaimei shoten, 1979.
Iyanagi, Nobumi. "Récits de la soumission de Maheśvara par Trilokyavijaya d'après les sources chinoises et japonaises." In *Tantric and Taoist Studies in Honour of R. A. Stein*, edited by Michel Strickmann, 3:633–45. Brussels: Institut Belge des Hautes Études Chinoises, 1985. Also published as *Mélanges chinois et bouddhiques* 22 (1985).
Ji Xianlin 季羨林, ed. *Dunhuangxue dacidian* 敦煌学大辞典. Shanghai: Shanghai cishu chubanshe, 1998.
———. "Qiuci de fojiao mizong 龜茲的佛教密宗." *Hualin* 華林 2 (2002): 1–10.
Jia Yingyi 賈應逸, and Musha Maimaiti 目沙買買提. "Lishi hualang: Kumutula bihua yanjiu 歷史畫廊：庫木吐拉壁畫研究." In *Kumutula* 庫木吐拉, edited by Zhongguo bihua bianji weiyuanhui 中國壁畫編輯委員會, pp. 1–26. Zhongguo meishu fenlei quanji 中國美術分類全集, Zhongguo Xinjiang bihua quanji 中國新疆壁畫全集. Urumqi: Xinjiang meishu sheying chubanshe, 1995.
Jiang Boqin 姜伯勤. *Tang Wudai Dunhuang sihu zhidu* 唐五代敦煌寺戶制度. Beijing: Zhonghua shuju, 1987.
Kanaoka Shōkō 金岡昭光. "Tonkōbon jigoku bunken kanki awasete bakkōkutsu no seikaku o ronzu 敦煌本地獄文献管窺併せて莫高窟の性格お論ず." *Komazawa daigaku bukkyō gakubu ronshū* 駒澤大學佛教教部論集 13 (Oct. 1982): 31–52.
Kapstein, Matthew T. *The Tibetan Assimilation of Buddhism: Conversion, Contestation, and Memory*. New York: Oxford University Press, 2000.
Karetsky, Patricia Eichenbaum. "The First Sermon." *East and West* 45, nos. 1–4 (Dec. 1995): 127–47.
Karmay, Heather. *Early Sino-Tibetan Art*. Warminster, England: Aris and Phillips, 1975.
Karmay, Samten Gyaltsen. "A Discussion on the Doctrinal Position of rDzogs-chen from the Tenth to the Thirteenth Centuries." *JA* 263 (1975): 147–56.

———. "The Ordinance of lHa Bla-ma Ye-shes-'od." In *Tibetan Studies in Honour of Hugh Richardson: Proceedings of the International Seminar on Tibetan Studies, Oxford 1979*, edited by Michael Aris and Aung San Suu Kyi, pp. 150–62. Warminster, England: Aris and Phillips, 1980.

Karunaratne, T. B. *The Buddhist Wheel Symbol*. The Wheel, no. 137–38. Kandy, Sri Lanka: Buddhist Publication Society, 1969.

Kegasawa Yasunori 氣賀澤保規. *Chūgoku bukkyō sekkyō no kenkyū: Bōsan Unkoji sekkyō o chūshin ni* 中國佛教石經の研究：房山雲居寺石經お中心に. Kyoto: Kyōto daigaku gakujutsu shuppankai, 1996.

Khandalavala, Karl. "The Chronology of Caves 16, 17, 19, 26, and 2 at Ajaṇṭā and the Ghatotkacha Cave." In *The Art of Ajaṇṭā: New Perspectives*, edited by Ratan Parimoo et al., 1:105–29. New Delhi: Books and Books, 1991.

Khantipalo, Bhikkhu. *The Wheel of Birth and Death*. The Wheel, nos. 147–49. Kandy, Sri Lanka: Buddhist Publication Society, 1970.

Khosla, Romi. *Buddhist Monasteries in the Western Himalaya*. Bibliotheca Himalayica, series 3, vol. 3. Kathmandu: Ratna Pustak Bhandar, 1979.

Kinnard, Jacob N. *Imaging Wisdom: Seeing and Knowing in the Art of Indian Buddhism*. London: Curzon Press, 1999.

Kipling, Rudyard. *Kim*. Edited by Edward W. Said. London: Penguin Books, 1989.

Klimburg-Salter, Deborah E. *The Silk Route and the Diamond Path: Esoteric Buddhist Art on the Trans-Himalaya Trade Routes*. Los Angeles: UCLA Arts Council, 1982.

———. *Tabo: A Lamp for the Kingdom, Early Indo-Tibetan Buddhist Art in the Western Himalaya*. New York: Thames and Hudson, 1998.

Kloetzli, Randy. *Buddhist Cosmology: From Single World System to Pure Land: Science and Theology in the Images of Motion and Light*. Delhi: Motilal Banarsidass, 1983.

Kornman, Robin, ed. "Forum: The Law of Karma." *Buddhadharma: The Practitioner's Quarterly* 1, no. 1 (Fall 2002): 30–39.

Krom, Nicolaas Johannes. *Barabuḍur: Archaeological Description*. 2 vols. The Hague: Martinus Nijhoff, 1927. Reprint, 5 vols. Delhi: Gyan Publishing House, 1986.

Kucera, Karil J. "Cliff Notes: Text and Image at Baodingshan." Ph.D. dissertation, University of Kansas, 2002.

Lamotte, Étienne. *Histoire du bouddhisme indien: Des origines à l'ère Śaka*. Publications de l'Institut Orientaliste de Louvain 14. Louvain-la-neuve, Belgium: Université de Louvain, Institut Orientaliste, 1976.

———. *Le traité de la grand vertu de sagesse de Nāgārjuna (Mahāprajñāpāramitāśāstra)*. 5 vols. Publications de l'Institut Orientaliste de Louvain 25, 26, 2, 12, 24. Louvain-la-neuve, Belgium: Université de Louvain, Institut Orientaliste, 1981, 1981, 1970, 1976, 1980.

Lauf, Detlef Ingo. *Tibetan Sacred Art: The Heritage of Tantra*. Trans. Ewald Osers. Berkeley: Shambhala, 1976.

La Vallée Poussin, Louis de. "Cosmogony and Cosmology (Buddhist)." In *Encyclopaedia of Religion and Ethics*, edited by James Hastings, 4:129b–38a. New York: Charles Scribner's Sons, 1921.

———. "Deux notes sur le Pratîtyasamutpâda." *In Actes du XIVe Congrès International des Orientalistes, Alger, 1905*, vol. 1, sec. 1, pp. 193–203. Paris: Ernst Leroux, 1906.
———. "Théorie des douze causes: Bouddhisme, études et matériaux." *Université de Gand, Recueil de travaux publiées par la faculté de philosophie et lettres.* Ghent, Belgium: Librairie Scientifique F. van Goethom, 1913.
Leach, Edmund. "Two Essays Concerning the Symbolic Representation of Time." In *Rethinking Anthropology*, pp. 124–36. London School of Economics Monographs on Social Anthropology 22. London: Athlone Press, 1961.
Leoshko, Janice. "About Looking at Buddha Images in Eastern India." *AAA* 52 (2000–2001): 63–82.
———. "What Is in *Kim*? Rudyard Kipling and Tibetan Buddhist Traditions." *South Asia Research* 21, no. 1 (2001): 51–75.
Lévi, Sylvain. "L'*Apramāda-varga*: Étude sur les récensions des *Dharmapadas*, Documents de l'Asie centrale (Mission Pelliot)." *JA*, 10th series 20 (1912): 203–94.
———. "Les élements de formation du Divyāvadāna." *TP*, 1st series 8 (1907): 105–22.
Li Chongfeng 李崇峰. *Zhong Yin fojiao shikusi bijiao yanjiu: yi tamiaoku wei zhongxin* 中印佛教石窟寺比較研究：以塔廟窟為中心. Xinzhu: Caituan faren juefeng fojiao yishu wenhua jijinhui, 2002.
Liang Zhixiang 梁志祥 and Ding Mingyi 丁明夷. "Xinjiang Kumutula xin faxian de jichu dongku 新疆库木吐喇新发现的几处洞窟." *WW*, 1985, no. 5:1–6.
Lin, Fu-shih. "Religious Taoism and Dreams: An Analysis of the Dream-Data Collected in the *Yün-chi ch'i-ch'ien*." *CEA* 8 (1995): 95–112.
Linrothe, Robert. "Mapping the Iconographic Program of the Sumtsek." In *Alchi: Ladakh's Hidden Buddhist Sanctuary, the Sumtsek*, edited by Roger Goepper, pp. 269–72. Photography by Jaroslav Poncar. Boston: Shambhala Publications, 1996.
Liu Changjiu 刘长久 et al., eds. *Dazu shike yanjiu* 大足石刻研究. Chengdu: Sichuansheng shehui kexueyuan chubanshe, 1985.
———. *Dazu shike yanjiu wenxuan* 大足石刻研究文选. In *Dazu shike yanjiu* 大足石刻研究, edited by Liu Changjiu 刘长久 et al. Chengdu: Sichuansheng shehui kexueyuan chubanshe, 1985.
Liu, Mau-Tsai. *Kutscha und seine Beziehungen zu China vom 2 Jh.v.bis zum 6 Jh.n. Chr.* 2 vols. Asiatische Forschungen 27. Wiesbaden, Germany: Otto Harassowitz, 1969.
Lopez, Donald S., Jr., ed. *Curators of the Buddha: The Study of Buddhism under Colonialism*. Chicago: University of Chicago Press, 1995.
———. *A Modern Buddhist Bible: Essential Readings from East and West*. Boston: Beacon Press, 2002.
Lu Xun 鲁迅. *Gu xiaoshuo gouchen* 古小说勾沉. In *Lu Xun quanji* 鲁迅全集. Beijing: Renmin wenxue chubanshe, 1973.
Luo Zhufeng 羅竹風 et al., eds. *Hanyu dacidian* 漢語大詞典, 13 vols. Hongkong: Sanlian shudian; Shanghai: Shanghai cishu chubanshe, 1987–95.
Luczanits, Christian. "Another Rin chen bzan po Temple?" *East and West* 44, no. 1 (1994): 83–98.

———. *Buddhist Sculpture in Clay: Early Western Himalayan Art, Late 10th to Early 13th Centuries*. Chicago: Serindia Publications, 2004.

———. "Minor Inscriptions and Captions in the Tabo Gtsug Lag Khan." In *Inscriptions from the Tabo Main Temple: Texts and Translations*, edited by Luciano Petech and Christian Luczanits, pp. 95–187. Serie Orientale Roma 83. Rome: Istituto Italiano per l'Africa et l'Oriente, 1999.

Ma Shichang 马世长. "Kezi'er zhongxinzhuku zhushi quanding yu houshi de bihua 克孜尔中心柱窟主室券顶与后室的壁画." In *Kezi'er shiku* 克孜尔石窟, edited by Xinjiang Weiwu'er zizhiqu wenwu guanli weiyuanhui 新疆维吾尔自治区文物管理委员会 et al., 2:174–226. Beijing: Wenwu chubanshe, 1989–97.

———. "Kumutula de hanfeng dongku 库木吐喇的汉风洞窟." In *Kumutula shiku* 库木吐喇石窟, edited by Xinjiang Weiwu'er zizhiqu wenwu guanli weiyuanhui 新疆维吾尔自治区文物管理委员会, Kuchexian wenwu baoguansuo 库车县文物保管所, and Beijing daxue kaogusuo 北京大学考古所, pp. 203–30. Beijing: Wenwu chubanshe, 1992.

———馬世長. "Xinjiang shikuzhong de hanfeng dongku he bihua 新疆石窟中的漢風洞窟和壁畫." In *Xinjiang shiku bihua* 新疆石窟壁畫, edited by Zhongguo meishu quanji bianji weiyuanhui 中國美術全集編集委員會, pp. 31–51. Zhongguo meishu quanji, huihua bian 中國美術全集, 繪畫編 16. Beijing: Wenwu chubanshe, 1986.

Mair, Victor H. "Records of Transformation Tableaux (*Pien-hsiang*)." *TP* 72, nos. 1–3 (1986): 3–43.

———. *Tun-huang Popular Narratives*. Cambridge Studies in Chinese History, Literature, and Institutions. Cambridge: Cambridge University Press, 1983.

Makita, Tairyō 牧田諦亮. *Gikyō kenkyū* 疑經研究. Kyoto: Kyōtō daigaku jinbun kagaku kenkyūjo, 1976.

Malalasekera, G. P., O. H. De A. Wijesekera, W. G. Weeraratne et al., eds. *Encyclopaedia of Buddhism*. 6 vols. to date. Peradeniya and Colombo: The Government Press of Ceylon, 1961–.

Masefield, Peter. *Divine Revelation in Pali Buddhism*. Colombo, Sri Lanka: Sri Lanka Institute of Traditional Studies; Boston: G. Allen and Unwin, 1986.

Mei Lin 梅林. "Sibailiushijiuku yu Mogaoku shishi jingzang de fangwei tezheng 469 窟與莫高窟石室經藏的方位特徵." *DY*, 1994, no. 4:186–97.

Mibu Taishun 壬生台舜. "Rokudōsetsu ni kan suru nisan no mondai ni tsuite 六道説に関する二三問題について." In *Nakagawa Zenkyō sensei shōtoku kinen ronshū: Bukkyō to bunka* 中川善教先生頌徳記念論集：仏教と文化, edited by Kōyasan daigaku bukkyōgaku kenkyūshitsu 高野山大学仏教学研究室, pp. 539–52. Kyoto: Dōhōsha, 1983.

Migot, André. "Un grand disciple du Bouddha, Śāriputra: Son rôle dans l'histoire du bouddhisme et dans le développement de l'*Abhidharma*." *BÉFEO* 46, no. 2 (1954): 405–554.

Mirashi, Vasudev Vishnu. "Historical Data in Dandin's *Daśakumāra charita*." In *Studies in Indology*, 1:182–94. 2nd ed. Nagpur: Vidarbha Samshodhan Mandal, 1968.

———. *Inscriptions of the Vākāṭakas*. Archaeological Survey of India, Corpus Inscriptionum Indicarum, 5. Ootacamund, Tamil Nadu: Government Epigraphist for India, 1963.

Miya Tsugio 宮次男. "Mokuren kyūbo setsuwa to sono kaiga: Shutsugen ni yonde 目連救母説話とその繪畫：出現に因んで." *Bijutsu kenkyū* 美術研究 no. 255 (Jan. 1968): 1–24.

Mochizuki, Shinkō 望月信亨. *Bukkyō daijiten* 佛教大辞典. 3rd rev. ed. 10 vols. Edited by Tsukamoto Zenryū 塚本善隆. Tokyo: Sekai seiten kankō kyōkai, 1954–63.

Moerman, D. Max. *Localizing Paradise: Kumano Pilgrimage and the Landscape of Premodern Japan*. Harvard East Asian Monographs 235. Cambridge, MA: Harvard University Press, 2004.

Monier-Williams, Sir Monier. *A Sanskrit-English Dictionary Etymologically and Philologically Arranged with Special Reference to Cognate Indo-European Languages*. 2nd ed. Oxford: Oxford University Press, 1899.

Mori Shōji 森章司. *Bukkyō hiyū reiwa jiten* 仏教比喻例話辞典. Tokyo: Tōkyōdō shuppan, 1987.

Morohashi Tetsuji 諸橋徹治. *Dai kan wa jiten* 大漢和辞典. 13 vols. Tokyo: Taishūkan, 1955–1960.

Mukherjee, Biswadeb. "On the Relationship between the Sarvāstivāda Vinaya and the Mūlasarvāstivāda Vinaya." *Journal of Asian Studies* (Madras) 2, no. 1 (1984): 139–65.

———. "Shih-sung-lu and the Reconstruction of the Original Sarvāstivāda Vinaya." *Buddhist Studies* 15 (1991): 46–52.

Muller, Charles. *Digital Dictionary of Buddhism*. http://www.acmuller.net/ddb/.

Murakami Shinkan 村上真完. *Seiiki no bukkyō: Bezekuriku seiganga kō* 西域の仏教：ベゼクリク誓願画考. Tokyo: Daisan bunmeisha, 1984.

Murray, Julia. "Buddhism and Early Narrative Illustration in China." *AAA* 48 (1995): 17–31.

Mus, Paul. *Barabuḍur: Sketch of a History of Buddhism Based on Archaeological Criticism of the Texts*. Trans. Alexander W. Macdonald. New Delhi: Indira Gandhi National Centre for the Arts, Sterling Publishers Private, 1998.

———. *La lumière sur les six voies: Tableau de la transmigration bouddhique d'après les sources sanskrites, pāli, tibétaines, et chinoises en majeure partie inédites*. Travaux et Mémoires de l'Institut d'Ethnologie, Université de Paris, 35. Paris: Institut d'Ethnologie, 1939.

Myer, Prudence M. "The Great Temple at Bodh-Gayā." *The Art Bulletin* 40, no. 4 (Dec. 1958): 277–98.

Naba Toshisada 那波利貞. "Rokuchō Zui Tō no hekiga 六朝隋唐の壁画." *Gibun* 藝文 9, no. 1 (Jan. 1932): 114–27.

Nakamura Hajime 中村元. *Bukkyōgo daijiten* 佛教語大辭典. 3 vols. Tokyo: Tōkyō shoseki kabushiki kaisha, 1975.

Nanjiu, Bunyiu. *A Catalogue of the Chinese Translation of the Buddhist Tripiṭaka, the Sacred Canon of the Buddhists in China and Japan*. Oxford: Clarendon Press, 1883.

Nara, Kōmei 奈良康明. "Shigo no sekai 死後の世界." In *Kōza bukkyō shisō* 講座仏教思想, edited by Mitsuyoshi Saigusa 三枝充悳, vol. 7, pp. 63–116. Tokyo: Risōsha, 1975.

Narain, A. K. "Religious Policy and Toleration in Ancient India with Particular Reference to the Gupta Age." In *Essays in Gupta Culture*. Edited by Bardwell L. Smith. Delhi: Motilal Banarsidass, 1983.

Nebesky-Wojkowitz, Réne de. *Oracles and Demons of Tibet: The Cult and Iconography of Tibetan Protective Deities*. 's Gravenhage, The Netherlands: Mouton and Co., 1956.

Neumann, Helmut F. "The Wheel of Life in the Twelfth Century Western Tibetan Cave Temple of Pedongpo." In *Buddhist Art and Tibetan Patronage, Ninth to Fourteenth Centuries: PIATS 2000, Tibetan Studies: Proceedings of the Ninth Seminar of the International Association for Tibetan Studies*. Edited by Deborah Klimburg-Salter and Eva Allinger. Brill's Tibetan Studies Library, vol. 2, no. 7. Leiden, The Netherlands: E. J. Brill, 2002.

Ng, Zhiru. "The Formation and Development of the Dizang Cult in Medieval China." Ph.D. dissertation, University of Arizona, 2000.

Ning Ke 寧可 and Hao Chunwen 郝春文. *Dunhuang sheyi wenshu jijiao* 敦煌社邑文書輯校. Nanjing: Jiangsu guji chubanshe, 1997.

Ning Qiang. *Art, Religion, and Politics in Medieval China: The Dunhuang Cave of the Zhai Family*. Honolulu: University of Hawai'i Press, 2004.

Nishimoto Ryōsen 西本龍山, trans. "Konponsetsuissaiubu binaya 根本說一切有部毘奈耶." In *Kokuyaku issaikyō, Indo senjutsu bu* 國譯一切經, 印度撰述部. Ritsu bu 律部 19–21. Tokyo: Heibonsha, 1975.

Nobel, Johannes, trans. *Udrāyana, König von Roruka: Eine buddhistische Erzählung*. 2 vols. Wiesbaden, Germany: Otto Harrassowitz, 1955.

Norman, K. R., trans. *Poems of Early Buddhist Monks: Theragāthā*. Rev. ed. Oxford: Pali Text Society, 1997.

Ñyāṇamoli, Bhikkhu, trans. *The Path of Purification (Visuddhimagga) by Bhadantācariya Buddhaghosa*. 2nd ed. Colombo, Sri Lanka: A. Semage, 1964.

Ñyanaponika, Thera, and Hellmuth Hecker. *Great Disciples of the Buddha: Their Lives, Their Works, Their Legacy*, edited by Bhikkhu Bodhi. Boston: Wisdom Publications and Buddhist Publication Society, 2003.

Obermiller, Evgenii Evgenevich, trans. *History of Buddhism (Chos-hbyung) by Bu-ston*. 2 vols. Materialien zur Kunde des Buddhismus 18, 19. Heidelberg, Germany: Otto Harrassowitz, 1931–32.

Okano, Kiyoshi 岡野潔. "Chūki Avadaana bunken no kenkyū shi 中期 Avadaana 文献の研究史." In *Kyūshū Indo bukkyōgaku* 九州印度佛教学. http://member.nifty.ne.jp/OKANOKIYOSHI/. Accessed Apr. 17, 2003.

Olschak, Blanche Christine, in collaboration with Geshé Thupten Wangyal. *Mystic Art of Ancient Tibet*. London: George Allen and Unwin, 1973.

Oltramare, Paul. *La formule bouddhique des douze causes: Son sens original et son interprétation théologique*. Geneva: Georg, 1909.

Ono Gemmyō 小野玄妙. *Bussho kaisetsu daijiten* 佛書解說大辭典. 15 vols. Tokyo: Daitō shuppansha, 1933–36, 1964–78, 1988.
Orzech, Charles D. "Maṇḍalas on the Move: Reflections from Chinese Esoteric Buddhism Circa 800 C.E." *JIABS* 19, no. 2 (Winter 1996): 209–44.
Ōsaka shiritsu hakubutsukan 大阪市立博物館, ed. *Shaji sankei mandara* 社寺参詣曼荼羅. Tokyo: Heibonsha, 1987.
Ostertag, Ernst. *Der Grottenzyklus von Dazu: Ein buddhistischer Initiationsweg*. Vienna: Octopus Verlag, 1988.
Owen, Lisa Nadine. "Constructing Another Perspective for Ajaṇṭā's Fifth-Century Excavations." *JIABS* 24, no. 1 (2001): 27–59.
Pachow, Wayne. "A Comparative Study of the Prātimokṣa." *Sino-Indian Studies* 4, nos. 1–4 (1951): 18–46, 51–114, 115–93; 5, no. 1 (1955): 1–45.
Pal, Pratapaditya. *Art of the Himalayas: Treasures from Nepal and Tibet*. New York: Hudson Hills Press, 1991.
———. *A Buddhist Paradise: The Murals of Alchi, Western Himalayas*. Photographs by Lionel Fournier. Basel: Ravi Kumar, 1982.
———, ed. *On the Path to the Void: Buddhist Art of the Tibetan Realm*. Mumbai: Marg Publications, 1996.
Pan Yushan 潘玉闪 and Ma Shichang 马世长. *Mogaoku kuqian diantang yizhi* 莫高窟窟前殿堂遗址. Beijing: Wenwu chubanshe, 1985.
Panglung, Jampa Losang. *Die Erzählstoffe des Mūlasarvāstivāda-Vinaya: Analysiert auf Grund der tibetischen Übersetzung*. Studia Philologica Buddhica 3. Tokyo: Reiyukai Library, 1981.
Pauly, Bernard. "Fragments sanskrits de Haute Asie (Mission Pelliot)." *JA* 248, no. 2 (1959): 203–49.
Petech, Luciano. "Western Tibet: Historical Introduction." In *Tabo: A Lamp for the Kingdom, Early Indo-Tibetan Buddhist Art in the Western Himalaya*, by Deborah Klimburg-Salter. New York: Thames and Hudson, 1998.
Pinks, Elisabeth. *Die Uiguren von Kan-chou in der frühen Sung-Zeit (960–1028)*. Asiatische Forschungen 24. Wiesbaden, Germany: Otto Harrassowitz, 1968.
Pinsky, Robert. "The Figured Wheel." *Ploughshares* 9, no. 1 (Spring 1983): 45–47.
Pommaret, Françoise. *Les revenants de l'au-delà dans le monde tibétain: Sources littéraires et tradition vivante*. Paris: Éditions du Centre National de la Recherche Scientifique, 1989.
Prebish, Charles S. *Buddhist Monastic Discipline: The Sanskrit Pratimoksa Sūtras of the Mahāsāmghikas and Mūlasarvāstivādins*. University Park and London: The Pennsylvania State University Press, 1975.
———. *A Survey of Vinaya Literature*. The Dharma Lamp Series 1. Taibei: Jin Luen Publishing House, 1994.
———. "Theories Concerning the *Skandhaka*: An Appraisal." *JAS* 32, no. 4 (1973): 669–78.
———. "The Vinaya Piṭaka." In *Buddhism: A Modern Perspective*. Edited by Charles S. Prebish. University Park and London: The Pennsylvania State University Press, 1975.

Prinsep, James. "Facsimiles of Ancient Inscriptions, Part IV." *Journal of the Royal Asiatic Society of Bengal* 5, no. 57 (Sept. 1836): 554–61.

Pritzker, Thomas J. "Tabo Monastery: The Sacred Precinct." In *On the Path to the Void: Buddhist Art of the Tibetan Realm*, edited by Pratapaditya Pal, pp. 66–81. Mumbai: Marg Publications, 1996.

———. "The Wall Paintings in the Dukhang of Tabo." In *Tibetan Art: Towards a Definition of Style*, edited by Jane Casey Singer and Philip Denwood, pp. 150–59. London: Laurence King Publishing, 1997.

Przyluski, Jean. "Fables in the Vinaya-Piṭaka of the Sarvāstivādin School." *Indian Historical Quarterly* 5 (1929): 1–5.

———. "Le nord-ouest de l'Inde dans le *Vinaya* des Mūla-sarvāstivādin et les texts apparentés." *JA* 11th series 4 (1914): 493–537.

———. "La roue de la vie à Ajaṇṭā." *JA* 11th series 16 (1920): 313–31.

Reischauer, Edwin O., trans. *Ennin's Diary: The Record of a Pilgrimage to China in Search of the Law*. New York: Ronald Press Co., 1955.

Reynolds, Valrae, et al. *Catalogue of the Newark Museum Tibetan Collection*. 2nd ed. 3 vols. Newark, NJ: Newark Museum, 1983–86.

———. *From the Sacred Realm: Treasures of Tibetan Art from the Newark Museum*. Munich: Prestel, 1999.

Rhie, Marylin Martin. *Early Buddhist Art of China and Central Asia*. Vol. 2, *The Eastern Chin and Sixteen Kingdoms Period in China and Tumshuk, Kucha and Karshahr in Central Asia*. Handbook of Oriental Studies, Section 4, China 12. Leiden, The Netherlands: E. J. Brill, 2002.

———. *The Fo-kuang ssu: Literary Evidences and Buddhist Images*. New York: Garland Publishing, 1977.

———. "Tibetan Painting: Styles, Sources, and Schools." In *Worlds of Transformation: Tibetan Art of Wisdom and Compassion*, edited by Marylin M. Rhie and Robert A. F. Thurman, pp. 45–74. New York: Tibet House, 1999.

Rhie, Marylin Martin, and Robert A. F. Thurman, eds. *Worlds of Transformation: Tibetan Art of Wisdom and Compassion*. New York: Tibet House, 1999.

Rhys Davids, Caroline A. F., F. H. Woodward, and Sūriyagoda Sumangala Thera, trans. *The Book of the Kindred Sayings (Sanyutta-Nikaya) or Grouped Sayings*. 5 vols. London: Oxford University Press, 1917–30.

Rhys Davids, Thomas M., and Caroline A. F. Rhys Davids, trans. *Dialogues of the Buddha, Translated from the Pali of the Dīgha Nikāya*. 4th ed. 3 vols. Sacred Books of the Buddhists 2–4. London: Oxford University Press, 1889, 1921; London: Luzac and Co., 1959.

Richardson, Hugh E. "Monuments of the Yarlung Dynasty." In *On the Path to the Void: Buddhist Art of the Tibetan Realm*, edited by Pratapaditya Pal, pp. 26–45. Mumbai: Marg Publications, 1996.

Roerich, George N., trans. *The Blue Annals*. 2 vols. Royal Asiatic Society of Bengal, Monograph Series 7. Calcutta: Royal Asiatic Society of Bengal, 1949, 1953.

Rong Xinjiang 榮新疆. *Guiyijun shi yanjiu: Tang Song shidai Dunhuang lishi kaosuo* 歸義軍史研究：唐宋時代敦煌歷史考索. Shanghai: Shanghai guji chubanshe, 1996.

Rotman, Andrew. "Wheel of Existence." Translation of portion of "Sahasodgata-avadāna" in *Divyāvadāna*. E-mail letter to Ken O'Neill, posted to Buddha-L electronic discussion group, Mar. 25, 2000.

Ruegg, David Seyfort. "On a Yoga Treatise in Sanskrit from Qïzïl." *JAOS* 87, no. 2 (1967): 157–65.

Ryder, Arthur W., trans. *The Ten Princes: Dandin's Dasha-kumara-charita*. Chicago: University of Chicago Press, 1927.

Sadakane Keiji 定金計次. "Ajantā daijūshichikutsu no 'goshu shōjirin' hekiga: Kakkuga no shudai hitei to shomondai Ajantā 第17窟の「五趣生死輪」壁画ー各区画の主題比定と諸問題." *Seinan ajia kenkyū* 西南アジア研究 42 (Mar. 1995): 20–43.

———. "Ajantā hekiga no sezokuteki seikaku アジャンター壁画の世俗的性格." In *Geijutsu no riron to rekishi* 芸術の理論と歴史, edited by Kyōto daigaku bigaku bijutsu shigaku kenkyūkai 京都大学美学美術史学研究会, pp. 221–30. Kyoto: Shibunkaku shuppan, 1990.

———. "Ajantā Hekiga wa dare no tame ni kakareta ka? Ajantā 壁画は誰のために描かれたか?" *Kyōto shiritsu geijutsu daigaku bijutsu gakubu kenkyū kiyō* 京都市立芸術大学美術学部研究紀要 40 (Mar. 1996): 35–54.

———. "Indo bukkyō kaiga no tenkai: Hekiga no henten to reihaiga no seiritsu インド仏教絵画の展開ー壁画の変転と礼拝画の成立." *Bukkyō geijutsu* 仏教芸術 214 (May 1994): 75–131.

Scherrer-Schaub, Cristina A. "Was Byang chub sems dpa' a Posthumous Title of King Ye śes 'od?" In *Tabo Studies II: Manuscripts, Texts, Inscriptions, and the Arts*, edited by Cristina A. Scherrer-Schaub and Ernst Steinkellner, pp. 207–25. Serie Orientale Roma 87. Rome: Istituto Italiano per l'Africa e l'Oriente, 1999.

Schlingloff, Dieter. *Ein buddhistisches Yogalehrbuch: Textband*. Deutsche Akademie der Wissenschaften zu Berlin, Institut für Orientforschung, Veröffentlichung 59. Sanskrittexte aus den Turfanfunden 7. Berlin: Akademie Verlag, 1964.

———. *Erzählende Wandmalereien*. 3 vols. Ajaṇṭā, Handbuch der Malereien 1. Wiesbaden, Germany: Harassowitz, 2000.

———. *Guide to the Ajaṇṭā Paintings*. Trans. Miriam Higgins. New Delhi: Munshiram Manoharlal Publishers Private, 1999.

———. "Das Lebensrad in Ajaṇṭā." *Asiatische Studien/Études Asiatiques* 25 (1971): 324–34.

———. *Studies in the Ajaṇṭā Paintings: Identifications and Interpretations*. Delhi: Ajaṇṭā Publications, 1987.

Schopen, Gregory. "The Bones of a Buddha and the Business of a Monk: Conservative Monastic Values in an Early Mahāyāna Polemical Tract." *JIP* 27 (1999): 279–324.

———. "The Buddha as an Owner of Property and Permanent Resident in Medieval Indian Moasteries." *JIP* 18 (1990): 181–217.

———. "Death, Funerals, and the Division of Property in a Monastic Code." In *Buddhism in Practice*, edited by Donald S. Lopez Jr., pp. 473–502. Princeton, NJ: Princeton University Press, 1995.

———. "Hierarchy and Housing in a Buddhist Monastic Code: A Translation of the

Sanskrit Text of the *Śayanāsanavastu* of the *Mūlasarvāstivāda-vinaya*—Part One [from the Sanskrit]." *Buddhist Literature* 2 (2000): 92–196.

———. "The Lay Ownership of Monasteries and the Role of the Monk in Mūlasarvāstivādin Monasticism." *JIABS* 19, no. 1 (1996): 81–126.

———. "On Avoiding Ghosts and Social Censure: Monastic Funerals in the Mūlasarvāstivāda-Vinaya." *JIP* 20, no. 1 (1992): 1–39.

———. "Ritual Rights and Bones of Contention: More on Monastic Funerals and Relics in the *Mūlasarvāstivāda-Vinaya*." *JIP* 22, no. 1 (1994): 31–80.

Seckel, Dietrich. *The Art of Buddhism*. Trans. Ann E. Keep. New York: Crown Publishers, 1963.

Sharf, Robert H. "Buddhist Modernism and the Rhetoric of Meditative Experience." *Numen* 42, no. 3 (1995): 228–83.

———. *Coming to Terms with Chinese Buddhism: A Reading of the "Treasure Store Treatise."* Kuroda Institute, Studies in East Asian Buddhism 14. Honolulu: University of Hawai'i Press, 2002.

Sharf, Robert H., and Elizabeth Horton Sharf, eds. *Living Images: Japanese Buddhist Icons in Context*. Stanford, CA: Stanford University Press, 2001.

Shashibala, Dr. Mrs. *Comparative Iconography of the Vajradhātu-Maṇḍala and the Tattva-Saṅgraha*. Śata-Pitaka Series 344. New Delhi: Sharada Rani, 1986.

Shi Weixiang 史苇湘. "Dunhuang Mogaoku dashi nianbiao 敦煌莫高窟大事年表." In *Dunhuang Mogaoku* 敦煌莫高窟, ed. Dunhuang yanjiusuo 敦煌研究所, 5:236–44. Zhongguo shiku 中國石窟. Beijing: Wenwu chubanshe, 1987.

Shinkyō Uiguru jichiku bunbutsu kanri iinkai 新疆ウイグル自治区文物管理委員会, Haijōken Kijiru Senbutsudō bunbutsu hōkanjo 排城県キジル千仏洞文物保管所, and Chūgoku sekkutsu Kijiru sekkutsu henshū iinkai hokanjo 中国石窟キジル石窟編集委員会保管所, eds. *Kijiru sekkutsu* キジル石窟. 3 vols. Chūgoku sekkutsu 中国石窟. Tokyo: Heibonsha, 1983. See also Xinjiang Weiwu'er zizhiqu wenwu guanli weiyuanhui.

Shinkyō Uiguru jichiku bunbutsu kanri iinkai 新疆ウイグル自治区文物管理委員会 and Kushaken bunbutsu hokanjo 庫車県文物保管所, eds. *Kumutora sekkutsu* クムトラ石窟. Chūgoku sekkutsu 中國石窟. Tokyo: Heibonsha, 1985.

Shinohara, Koichi. "Imaging the Jetavana Monastery in Medieval China: An Exploratory Discussion of Daoxuan's Jetavana Diagram Scripture." Unpublished paper presented at the Thirty-fourth International Congress of Asian and North African Studies, Hong Kong, Aug. 1993.

Sichuansheng shehui kexueyuan 四川省社会科学院, eds. *Dazu shike neirong zonglu* 大足石刻内容总录. In *Dazu shike yanjiu* 大足石刻研究. Edited by Liu Changjiu 刘长久 et al. Chengdu: Sichuansheng shehui kexueyuan chubanshe, 1985.

Singer, Jane Casey. "Painting in Central Tibet, ca. 950–1400." *AA* 54, nos. 1–2 (1994): 87–136.

Singhal, Sudarshana Devi. "Identification of Sculptures in the Central Hall of the Tabo Monastery." In *Bauddha adhyayana kī Bhāratīya patrika (The Indian Journal of Buddhist Studies)* 3, no. 1 (1991): 25–33.

Skorupski, Tadeusz. *A Catalogue of the Stog Palace Kanjur*. Bibliographia Philologica Buddhica, Series Maior 4. Tokyo: International Institute for Buddhist Studies, 1985.

Snellgrove, David L. "Buddhism in North India and the Western Himalayas—Seventh to Thirteenth Centuries." In *The Silk Route and the Diamond Path: Esoteric Buddhist Art in the Trans-Himalayan Trade Routes*, edited by Deborah E. Klimburg-Salter, pp. 64–80. Los Angeles: UCLA Arts Council, 1982.

———. *Indo-Tibetan Buddhism: Indian Buddhists and Their Tibetan Successors*. 2 vols. Boston: Shambhala, 1987.

———. Introduction to *Sarva-Tathāgata-Tattva-Saṅgraha: Facsimile Reproduction of a Tenth-Century Sanskrit Manuscript from Nepal*. Edited by David L. Snellgrove and Lokesh Chandra. Śata-Pitaka Series 269. New Delhi: Mrs. Sharada Rani, 1981.

Snellgrove, David L., and Lokesh Chandra, eds. *Sarva-Tathāgata-Tattva-Saṅgraha: Facsimile Reproduction of a Tenth-Century Sanskrit Manuscript from Nepal*. Śata-Pitaka Series 269. New Delhi: Mrs. Sharada Rani, 1981.

Snellgrove, David L., and Tadeusz Skorupski. *The Cultural Heritage of Ladakh*. Vol. 1, *Central Ladakh*. Vol. 2, *Zangskar and the Cave Temples of Ladakh*. Warminster, England: Aris and Phillips, 1977, 1980.

Somers, Robert M. "The End of the T'ang." In *The Cambridge History of China*.Vol. 3, *Sui and T'ang China, 589–906*. Edited by Denis C. Twitchett. Cambridge: Cambridge University Press, 1979.

Song Langqiu 宋郎秋. "Dazu shike fenqi shulun 大足石刻分期述论." *DY*, 1996, no. 3:64–75.

Sopa, Geshe. "The Tibetan 'Wheel of Life': Iconography and Doxography." *JIABS* 7, no. 1 (1984): 125–45.

Soper, Alexander C. "Northern Liang and Northern Wei in Kansu." *AA* 21, no. 2 (1958): 131–64.

Sorenson, Henrik, H. *A Survey of the Religious Sculptures of Anyue*. Copenhagen: East Asian Institute Occasional Papers, University of Copenhagen, 1989.

Sørenson, Per K. *Tibetan Buddhist Historiography: The Mirror Illuminating the Royal Genealogies: An Annotated Translation of the XIVth Century Tibetan Chronicle: rGyal-rabs gsal-ba'i me-long*. Asiatische Forschungen 128. Wiesbaden, Germany: Harrassowitz Verlag, 1994.

Soucek, Svat. *A History of Inner Asia*. Cambridge: Cambridge University Press, 2000.

Spink, Walter M. *Ajaṇṭā: A Brief History and Guide*. Ann Arbor: Asian Art Archives of the University of Michigan, 1993.

———. "Ajaṇṭā's Chronology: The Crucial Cave." *Ars Orientalis* 10 (1975): 143–69.

———. "The Archaeology of Ajaṇṭā." *Ars Orientalis* 21 (1991): 67–94.

———. "Notes on Buddha Images." In *The Art of Ajaṇṭā: New Perspectives*, edited by Ratan Parimoo, 1:213–41. New Delhi: Books and Books, 1991.

———. "Review of *Ajaṇṭā Paintings: Identifications and Interpretations*, by Dieter Schlingloff." *Ars Orientalis* 19 (1989): 119–20.

———. "The Vākāṭaka's Flowering and Fall." In *The Art of Ajaṇṭā: New Perspectives*, edited by Ratan Parimoo, 1:71–99. New Delhi: Books and Books, 1991.

Stein, Rolf A. *Une chronique ancienne de bSam-yas: sBa-bžed*. Textes et Documents, Publications de l'Institut des Hautes Études Chinoises 1. Paris: Institut des Hautes Études Chinoises, 1961.

Steinhardt, Nancy Shatzman. "Early Chinese Buddhist Architecture and Its Indian Origins." In *The Flowering of a Foreign Faith: New Studies in Chinese Buddhist Art*, edited by Janet Baker, pp. 38–53. Mumbai: Marg Publications, 1998.

———. "The Mizong Hall of Qinglong Si: Space, Ritual, and Classicism in Tang Architecture." *AAA* 44 (1991): 27–50.

Steinkellner, Ernst. "Notes on the Function of Two 11th Century Inscriptional Sūtra Texts in Tabo: *Gaṇḍavyūhasūtra* and *Kṣitigarbhasūtra*." In *Tabo Studies II: Manuscripts, Texts, Inscriptions, and the Arts*, edited by Cristina A. Scherrer-Schaub and Ernst Steinkellner, pp. 243–74. Serie Orientale Roma 87. Rome: Istituto Italiano per l'Africa e l'Oriente, 1999.

———. *Sudhana's Miraculous Journey in the Temple of Ta pho: The Inscriptional Text of the Tibetan Gandavyūhasūtra, Edited with Introductory Remarks*. Serie Orientale Roma 76. Rome: Istituto Italiano per l'Africa e l'Oriente, 1995.

Steinkellner, Ernst, and Christian Luczanits. "Appendix: A New Translation of the Renovation Inscription in the Tabo Main Temple (*gtsug-lag-khang*)." In *Tabo: A Lamp for the Kingdom, Early Indo-Tibetan Buddhist Art in the Western Himalaya*, by Deborah Klimburg-Salter, pp. 257–59. New York: Thames and Hudson, 1998.

Stoddard, Heather [Heather Karmay]. "Early Tibetan Paintings: Sources and Styles (Eleventh–Fourteenth Centuries A.D.)." *AAA* 49 (1996): 26–50.

Strickmann, Michel. "Dreamwork of Psycho-Sinologists: Doctors, Taoists, Monks." In *Psycho-Sinology: The Universe of Dreams in Chinese Culture*, edited by Carolyn T. Brown, pp. 25–46. Washington, DC: Asia Program, Woodrow Wilson International Center for Scholars, 1988.

Strong, John. *The Experience of Buddhism: Sources and Interpretations*. Belmont, CA: Wadsworth Publishing Co., 1995.

———. "Filial Piety and Buddhism: The Indian Antecedents to a 'Chinese' Problem." In *Traditions in Contact and Change: Selected Proceedings of the XIVth Congress of the International Association for the History of Religions*, edited by Peter Slater and Donald Wiebe, pp. 171–86. Waterloo, Ontario: Wilfrid Laurier Press, 1983.

———. *The Legend and Cult of Upagupta: Sanskrit Buddhism in North India and Southeast Asia*. Princeton, NJ: Princeton University Press, 1992.

———. *The Legend of King Aśoka: A Study and Translation of the Aśokāvadāna*. Princeton, NJ: Princeton University Press, 1983.

Stryk, Lucien, ed. *World of the Buddha: An Introduction to Buddhist Literature*. New York: Grove Press, 1968.

Su Bai 宿白 "Liangzhou shiku yiji yu 'Liangzhou moshi' 涼州石窟遺迹與涼州模式." 1986. Rev. ed. in *Zhongguo shikusi yanjiu* 中國石窟寺研究, pp. 39–51. Beijing: Wenwu chubanshe, 1996.

———. "Xinjiang Baicheng Kezi'er shiku bufen dongku de leixing yu niandai 新疆拜

城克孜爾石窟部份洞窟的類型與年代." 1990. Reprinted in *Zhongguo shikusi yanjiu* 中國石窟寺研究, pp. 21–38. Beijing: Wenwu chubanshe, 1996.

Suzuki, Daisetz Teitaro. "Zen as Chinese Interpretation of the Doctrine of Enlightenment." In *Essays in Zen Buddhism*, 1st series, pp. 39–117. London: Rider, 1949.

Takakusu, Junjirō, trans. *A Record of the Buddhist Religion as Practised in India and the Malay Archipelago (A.D. 671–695) by I-tsing*. Oxford: Clarendon Press, 1896.

Tan, Zhihui. "Daoxuan's Vision of Jetavana: Imagining a Utopian Monastery in Early Tang (China, India)." Ph.D. dissertation, University of Arizona, 2002.

Tang Changru 唐長儒. "Guanyu guiyijun jiedu de jizhong ziliao ba 關於歸義軍節度的幾種資料跋." *Zhonghua wen shi luncong* 中華文史論叢 1 (1962): 275–98.

Tang Geng'ou 唐耕耦. "Cao Rengui jiedu Shazhou guiyijun shimo 曹仁贵节度沙洲归义军始末." *DY*, 1987, no. 2:14–19.

Tang Yongtong 湯用彤. *Han Wei Liangjin Nanbeichao fojiao shi* 漢魏兩晉南北朝佛教史. Reprint, Taibei: Dingwen shuju, 1976.

Tatelman, Joel, trans. *Glorious Deeds of Pūrna: A Translation and Study of the Pūrnāvadāna*. Curzon Critical Studies in Buddhism. Richmond, Surrey: Curzon Press, 2000.

Teiser, Stephen F. "Chinese Buddhism before China." Paper presented at the conference, "Religion and Chinese Society: The Transformation of a Field and Its Implications for the Study of Chinese Culture," Chinese University of Hong Kong, May 2000.

———. "Comparing Wheels: Concepts of Rebirth in Ancient Indian Buddhism, Rudyard Kipling, and Robert Pinsky." Paper presented at the conference, "Reflections on the Study of Religion: A Conference in Honor of John F. Wilson," Princeton University, Oct. 2003.

———. [Taishi Wen 太史文]. "Difangxing yu jingdianxing: zai Gansu Sichuan jingnei faxian de liudao lunhui tu 地方性與經典性: 在甘肅四川境內發現的六道輪迴圖." In *Fojiao wuzhi wenhua: siyuan caifu yu shisu gongyang* 佛教物質文化:寺院財富與世俗供養 (*Buddhist Material Culture: Monastic Wealth and Secular Offerings*), *Guoji yantaohui lunwenji* 國際研討會論文集, edited by Hu Suxin 胡宿馨 [Sarah E. Fraser], pp. 221–45. Shanghai: Shanghai Fine Arts Publishers, 2003.

———. *The Ghost Festival in Medieval China*. Princeton, NJ: Princeton University Press, 1988.

———. "'Having Once Died and Returned to Life': Representations of Hell in Medieval China." *HJAS* 48, no. 2 (Dec. 1988): 433–64.

———. "The Growth of Purgatory." In *Religion and Society in T'ang and Sung China*, edited by Patricia B. Ebrey and Peter N. Gregory, pp. 115–45. Honolulu: University of Hawai'i Press, 1993.

———. "The Local and the Canonical: Pictures of the Wheel of Rebirth in Gansu and Sichuan." *Asia Major*, 3rd series 17, part 1 (2004): 73–122.

———. *"The Scripture on the Ten Kings" and the Making of Purgatory in Medieval Chinese Buddhism*. Kuroda Institute, Studies in East Asian Buddhism 9. Honolulu: University of Hawai'i Press, 1994.

Thakur, Laxman S. *Buddhism in the Western Himalaya: A Study of the Tabo Monastery*. New Delhi: Oxford University Press, 2000.

———. "The Earliest Tibetan Inscriptions from Tabo and Their Historical Significance." *Tibet Journal* 25, no. 2 (Summer 2000): 42–51.

———. "Nako Monastery: Archaeological Notes from an Account of the Western Himalayan Expeditions." *East and West* 46, nos. 3–4 (1996): 337–52.

Thapar, Romila. "Patronage and Community." In *The Powers of Art: Patronage in Indian Culture*, edited by Barbara Stoler Miller, pp. 19–34. Delhi: Oxford University Press, 1992.

Tharchin, Sermey Geshe Lobsang. *King Udrayaṇa and the Wheel of Life: The History and Meaning of the Buddhist Teaching of Dependent Origination*. Howell, NJ: Mahayana Sutra and Tantra Press, 1984.

Tokuno, Kyoko. "The Evaluation of Indigenous Scriptures in Chinese Buddhist Bibliographical Catalogues." In *Chinese Buddhist Apocrypha*, edited by Robert E. Buswell Jr., pp. 31–74. Honolulu: University of Hawaii Press, 1990.

Tokushi Yūshō 禿氏祐祥 and Ogawa Kan'ichi 小川貫弌. "*Jūō shōshichi kyō* sanzuken no kōzō 十王生七經讃圖卷の構造." In *Chūō ajia bukkyō to bijitsu* 中央アジア佛教と美術, edited by Seiiki bunka kenkyūkai 西域文化研究會, vol. 1, pp. 255–96. Kyoto: Hōzōkan, 1963.

Trungpa, Chögyam. *Cutting through Spiritual Materialism*. Edited by John Baker and Marvin Casper. Berkeley: Shambhala, 1973.

Tso, Sze-bong [Cao, Shibang]. "The Transformation of Buddhist Vinaya in China." Ph.D. dissertation, Australian National University, 1982.

Tucci, Giuseppe. *The Religions of Tibet*. Trans. Geoffrey Samuel. Berkeley: University of California Press, 1980.

———. *Rin c'en bzan po e la rinascita del Buddhismo nel Tibet intorno al mille. Indo-Tibetica*, vol. 2. Reale accademia d'Italia, Studi e documenti 1. Rome: Reale accademia d'Italia, 1933. Translated as *Rin-chen-bzan-po and the Renaissance of Buddhism in Tibet around the Millennium* by Nancy Kipp Smith, under the direction of Thomas J. Pritzker. Edited by Lokesh Chandra. Śata-Pitaka Series, Indo-Asian Literatures 348. New Delhi: Aditya Prakashan, 1988.

———. *Templi del Tibet Occidentale e il lorosimbolismo artistice*. Pt. 1, *Spiti e Kunavar*. *Indo-Tibetica*, vol. 3. Reale accademia d'Italia, Studi e documenti 1. Rome: Reale accademia d'Italia, 1935. Translated as *The Temples of Western Tibet and Their Artistic Symbolism: The Monasteries of Spiti and Kunavar*. *Indo-Tibetica* 3, no. 1. Edited by Lokesh Chandra et al. New Delhi: Aditya Prakashan, 1988.

———. *The Theory and Practice of the Mandala*. Trans. Alan Houghton Broderick. London: Rider and Co., 1961.

———. *Tibetan Painted Scrolls*. Trans. Virginia Vacca. 2 vols. Rome: Libreria dello Stato, 1949.

Turner, Terence S. "Transformation, Hierarchy and Transcendence: A Reformulation of Van Gennep's Model of the Structure of Rites de Passage." In *Secular Ritual*, edited by Sally F. Moore and Barbara G. Myerhoff, pp. 53–72. Assen, The Netherlands: Van Gorcum, 1977.

Tworkov, Helen, ed. "Reincarnation: A Debate, Batchelor v. Thurman." *Tricycle: The Buddhist Review* 6, no. 4 (Summer 1997): 24–27, 109–16.

Ueno Ryūzō 上野隆三. "Shisen ni okeru Tō Sō jiki no sekkoku zōzō sekkyō jigyō 四川における唐宋時期の石刻造像石經事業." In *Chūgoku bukkyō sekkyō no kenkyū: Bōsan Unkoji sekkyō o chūshin* ni中國佛教石經の研究：房山雲居寺石經お中心に, edited by Kegasawa Yasunori 氣賀澤保規. Kyoto: Kyōtō daigaku gakujutsu shuppankai, 1996.

Umezu Jirō 梅津次郎. "Goshu shōjirin zu ni tsuite: Etoki no kaigashiteki kōsatsu, sono ichi 五趣生死輪図について－絵解きの絵画史的考察、その一." 1928. Reprinted in *Emakimono sōkō* 絵巻物叢考, pp. 9–24. Tokyo: Chūō kōron bijutsu shuppansha, 1968.

Upreti, Kalpana. *India as Reflected in the Divyāvadāna*. New Delhi: Munshiram Manharlal Publishers Private, 1995.

Vaidya, Parasurama Lakshmana, ed. *Divyāvadāna*. Buddhist Sanskrit Texts 20. Darbhanga, Bihar: Mithila Institute of Post-Graduate Studies and Research in Sanskrit Learning, 1959.

van Buitenen, J. A. B. *The Maitrāyanīya Upaniṣad: A Critical Essay, with Text, Translation, and Commentary*. Disputationes Rheno-Trajectinae 6. 's Gravenhage, The Netherlands: Mouton, 1962.

van Gennep, Arnold. *The Rites of Passage*. Trans. Monika B. Vizedom and Gabrielle L. Caffee. Chicago: University of Chicago Press, 1960.

Vitali, Roberto. *Early Temples of Central Tibet*. London: Serindia Publications, 1990.

———. *The Kingdoms of Gu.ge Pu.hrang According to mNga'.ris rgyal.rabs by Gu.ge mkhan.chen Ngag.dbang grags.pa*. Dharamsala: Tho.ling gtsug.lag.khang lo.gcig.stong 'khor.ba'i rjes.dran.mdzad sgo'i go.sgrig tshogs.chung, 1996.

———. *Records of Tho.Ling: A Literary and Visual Reconstruction of the "Mother" Monastery in Gu.ge*. Dharamshala: Amnye Machen Institute, 1999.

von Le Coq, Albert. *Die buddhistische Spätantike in Mittelasien*. 7 vols. Berlin: Dietrich Reimer, Ernst Vohsen, 1922–33.

Waddell, L. Augustine. "Buddha's Secret from a Sixth-Century Pictorial Commentary and Tibetan Tradition." *Journal of the Royal Asiatic Society of Great Britain and Ireland* (Apr. 1894): 367–84.

———. "The Buddhist Pictorial Wheel of Life." *Journal of the Royal Asiatic Society of Bengal* 61, pt. 1, no. 3 (1892): 133–55.

Waldschmidt, Ernst. *Gandhara, Kutscha, Turfan: Eine Einführung in die frühmittelalterliche Kunst zentralasiens*. Leipzig: Klinkhardt und Biermann, 1925.

Walshe, Maurice, trans. "*Mahāparinibbāna Sutta*: The Great Passing." In *The Long Discourses of the Buddha: A Translation of the Dīgha Nikāya*. Boston: Wisdom Publications, 1995.

Wang Bangwei 王邦維. *Nanhai jigui neifa zhuan jiaozhu* 南海寄歸内法傳校注. Zhongwai jiaotong shiji congkan 中外交通史籍叢刊. Beijing: Zhonghua shuju, 1995.

Wang, Eugene Yuejin. "Grotto-Shrine as Chronotope and the Working of Analogous Iconography: The Sixth-Century Sculptural Program in Cave 38 at Yungang in Perspective." In *Han Tang zhi jian de zongjiao yishu yu kaogu* 漢唐之間的宗教藝術與考古, edited by Wu Hong 巫鴻, pp. 279–312. Beijing: Wenwu chubanshe, 2000.
Wang Guangzhao 王光照. "Tangdai Chang'an fojiao siyuan bihua 唐代长安佛教寺院壁画." *Dunhuangxue jikan* 敦煌学辑刊 23, no. 1 (1993): 77–83.
Wang Jiayou 王家祐. "Liu Benzun yu mijiao 柳本尊与密教." In *Dazu shike yanjiu wenxuan* 大足石刻研究文选. In *Dazu shike yanjiu* 大足石刻研究, edited by Liu Changjiu 刘长久 et al., pp. 168–74. Chengdu: Sichuansheng shehui kexueyuan chubanshe, 1985.
Wang Zhongmin 王重民, ed. *Dunhuang bianwen ji* 敦煌變文集. 2 vols. Beijing: Renmin wenxue chubanshe, 1957.
Wang-Toutain, Françoise. *Le Bodhisattva Kṣitigarbha en Chine du Ve au XIIIe siècle.* Presses de l'École Française d'Extrême-Orient, Monographies 185. Paris: École Française d'Extrême-Orient, 1998.
Weidner, Marsha. *Latter Days of the Law: Images of Chinese Buddhism, 850–1850.* Lawrence: Spencer Museum of Art, University of Kansas, Honolulu: University of Hawai'i Press, 1994.
Weiner, Sheila L. *Ajaṇṭā: Its Place in Buddhist Art.* Berkeley: University of California Press, 1977.
Weitzmann, Kurt. *Illustration in Roll and Codex: A Study of the Origin and Method of Text Illustration.* 2nd ed. Princeton, NJ: Princeton University Press, 1970.
Whitfield, Roderick. *The Art of Central Asia: The Stein Collection in the British Museum.* 3 vols. Tokyo: Kodansha International, 1982–1985.
Wille, Klaus. *Die handschriftliche Überlieferung das Vinayavastu der Mūlasarvāstivādin.* Verzeichnis der orientalischen Handscrhiften in Deutschland, Supplementband 30. Stuttgart: Steiner, 1990.
Willemen, Charles. *The Chinese Udānavarga: A Collection of Important Odes of the Law, Fa Chi Yao Sung Ching.* Published as *Mélanges chinois et bouddhiques* 19. Brussells: Institut Belge des Hautes Études Chinoises, 1978.
———. *The Storehouse of Sundry Valuables.* BDK English Tripiṭaka 10–1. Berkeley: Numata Center for Buddhist Translation and Research, 1994.
Willemen, Charles, Bart Dessein, and Collett Cox. *Sarvāstivāda Buddhist Scholasticism.* Handbook of Oriental Studies, Section 2, South Asia 11. Leiden, The Netherlands: E. J. Brill, 1998.
Williams, Joanna Gottfried. *The Art of Gupta India: Empire and Province.* Princeton, NJ: Princeton University Press, 1982.
———. "Vākāṭaka Art and the Gupta Mainstream." In *Essays in Gupta Culture.* Edited by Bardwell L. Smith. Delhi: Motilal Banarsidass, 1983.
Winternitz, Maurice. *A History of Indian Literature.* 2 vols. Trans. S. Ketkar and H. Kohn. Calcutta: University of Calcutta, 1927, 1933.
Wu, Hung. [Wu Hong]. "What is *Bianxiang*?—On the Relationship between Dunhuang Art and Dunhuang Literature." *HJAS* 52, no. 1 (June 1992): 111–92.

Wu Zhuo 吴焯. "Kezi'er shiku xingfei yu Weiganhe gudao jiaotong 克孜爾石窟興廢與渭干河谷道交通." In *Han Tang zhi jian de zongjiao yishu yu kaogu* 漢唐之間的宗教藝術與考古, edited by Wu Hong 巫鴻, pp. 183–208. Beijing: Wenwu chubanshe, 2000.

———. "Kumutula shiku bihua de fengge yanbian yu gudai Qiuci de lishi xingshuai 库木土拉石窟壁画的风格演变与古代龟兹的历史兴衰." *Zhongya xuekan* 中亚学刊 3 (1990): 77–94.

Xiao Mo 萧默. *Dunhuang jianzhu yanjiu* 敦煌建筑研究. Beijing: Wenwu chubanshe, 1989.

Xie Zhiliu 謝稚柳. *Dunhuang yishu xulu* 敦煌藝術敘錄. 1957. Reprint, Shanghai: Shanghai guji chubanshe, 1996.

Xinjiang Qiuci shiku yanjiusuo 新疆龟兹石窟研究所, ed. *Kezi'er shiku neirong zonglu* 克孜尔石窟内容总录. Urumqi: Xinjiang meishu sheying chubanshe, 2000.

Xinjiang Weiwu'er zizhiqu bowuguan 新疆维吾尔自治区博物馆 and Xinjiang renmin chubanshe 新疆人民出版社, eds. *Kuche Kumutula shiku* 庫車庫木吐拉石窟. Xinjiang shiku 新疆石窟. Shanghai: Xinjiang renmin chubanshe, Shanghai meishu chubanshe, 1992.

Xinjiang Weiwu'er zizhiqu wenwu guanli weiyuanhui 新疆维吾尔自治区文物管理委员会, Baichengxian Kezi'er Qianfodong wenwu baoguansuo 拜城县克孜尔千佛洞文物保管所, and Beijing daxue kaoguxi 北京大学考古系, eds. *Kezi'er shiku* 克孜尔石窟. 3 vols. Beijing: Wenwu chubanshe, 1989–97.

Xinjiang Weiwu'er zizhiqu wenwu guanli weiyuanhui 新疆维吾尔自治区文物管理委员会, Kuchexian wenwu baoguansuo 库车县文物保管所, and Beijing daxue kaogusuo 北京大学考古所, eds. *Kumutula shiku* 库木吐喇石窟. Beijing: Wenwu chubanshe, 1992.

Yaldiz, Marianne. *Archäologie und Kunstgeschichte chinesisch-zentralasians (Xinjiang)*. Handbook of Oriental Studies, Section 7 Art and Archaeology, Central Asia 2. Leiden, The Netherlands: E. J. Brill, 1987.

Yamabe, Nobuyuki. "Practice of Visualization and the *Visualization Sūtra*: An Examination of Mural Paintings at Toyok, Turfan." *Pacific World*, 3rd series, no. 4 (Fall 2002): 123–52.

———. "The Signficance of the 'Yogalehrbuch' for the Investigation into the Origin of Chinese Meditation Texts." *Bukkyō bunka* 仏教文化 9 (1999): 1–74.

———. "The Sūtra on the Ocean-Like Samādhi of the Visualization of the Buddha: The Interfusion of the Chinese and Indian Cultures in Central Asia as Reflected in a Fifth-Century Apocryphal Sūtra." Ph.D. dissertation, Yale University, 1999.

Yan Juanying 顏娟英. "Fojiao yishu fangfaxue de zai jiantao 佛教藝術方法學的再檢討." In *Zhonghua minguo shi zhuanti lunwenji, di sijie taolunhui* 中華民國史專題論文集第四屆討論會, edited by Zhonghua minguo shi zhuanti taolunhui 中華民國史專題討論會. Taibei: Guoshiguan, 1998.

Yang Fuxue 楊富學. *Huihu zhi fojiao* 回鶻之佛教. Urumqi: Xinjiang renmin chubanshe, 1998.

———. "On the Sha-chou Uighur Kingdom." *Central Asiatic Journal* 38, no. 1 (1994): 80–107.

Yang, Han-sung, Yün-hua Jan, Shotaro Iida, and Laurence W. Preston. *The Hye Ch'o Diary: Memoir of the Pilgrimage to the Five Regions of India*. Religions of Asia Series 2. Berkeley: Asian Humanities Press, 1984.

Yazdani, Ghulam. *Ajaṇṭā: The Colour and Monochrome Reproductions of the Ajaṇṭā Frescoes Based on Photography*. Introduction by Laurence Binyon. 4 vols. of text, 4 vols. of plates. London: Oxford University Press, 1930–55.

Yifa. *The Origins of Buddhist Monastic Codes in China*. Kuroda Institute Classics in East Asian Buddhism. Honolulu: University of Hawai'i Press, 2002.

Yuan, Yanhe 園延鶴. "Qiucifeng bihua de xingcheng yu fazhan 龜茲風壁畫的形成與發展." In *Kezi'er* 克孜爾, edited by Zhongguo bihua quanji bianji weiyuanhui 中國壁畫全集編輯委員會, pp. 1–22. Zhongguo meishu fenlei quanji 中國美術分類全集, Zhongguo Xinjiang bihua quanji 中國新疆壁畫全集, 2. Tianjin and Urumqi: Tianjin renmin meishu chuban, Xinjiang meishu sheying chubanshe, 1995.

Yun Anzhi 员安志. "Sichuan Bazhongxian shiku diaocha ji 四川巴中县石窟调查记." *Kaogu yu wenwu* 考古与文物, 1986, no. 1:50–57, 45.

Zhang Boyuan 张伯元. *Anxi Yulinku* 安西榆林窟. Chengdu: Sichuan jiaoyu chubanshe, 1995.

———. "Anxi Yulinku 'liudao lunhui tu' kaoshi 安西榆林窟六道轮回图考释." *DY*, 1998, no. 1:20–23, pl. 1.2.

Zhang Hua 张划. "Songdai Dazu shike jueqi neiyin tantao 宋代大足石刻崛起内因探讨." *SW*, 1991, no. 2:40–44.

Zhang Qiyun 張其昀. *Zhongwen dacidian* 中文大辭典. Rev. ed. 10 vols. Taibei: Huagang chuban youxian gongsi, 1979.

Zhang Yushu 張玉書. *Peiwen yunfu* 佩文韻府. 7 vols. Shanghai: Wanyou wenku, 1937.

Zhongguo bihua bianji weiyuanhui 中國壁畫編輯委員會, ed. *Kumutula* 庫木吐拉. Zhongguo meishu fenlei quanji 中國美術分類全集, Zhongguo Xinjiang bihua quanji 中國新疆壁畫全集 4. Urumqi: Xinjiang meishu sheying chubanshe, 1995.

Zhongguo fojiao renming dacidian bianji weiyuanhui 中國佛教人名大辭典編輯委員會, ed. *Zhongguo fojiao renming dacidian, Zhenhua Fashi yigao* 中國佛教人名大辭典, 震華法師遺稿. Shanghai: Shanghai cishu chubanshe, 1999.

Zhongguo meishu quanji bianji weiyuanhui 中國美術全集編輯委員會, ed. *Sichuan shiku diaosu* 四川石窟雕塑. Zhongguo meishu quanji, diaosu bian 中國美術全集, 雕塑編, 12. Beijing: Renmin meishu chubanshe, 1988.

Zhongguo shehui kexueyuan kaogu yanjiusuo shiyanshi 中国社会科学院考古研究所实验室. "Xinjiang Tulufan he Nanjiang diqu bufen dongku niandai ceding baogao 新疆吐鲁番和南疆地区部分洞窟年代测定报告." *Kaogu* 考古, 1991, no. 11:1039–45.

Zhu Yingrong 朱英荣. *Qiuci shiku yanjiu* 龟兹石窟研究, edited by Xinjiang Qiuci shiku yanjiusuo 新疆龟兹石窟研究所. Urumqi: Xinjiang meishu sheying chubanshe, 1993.

Zin, Monika. *Devotionale und ornamentale Malereien*. 2 vols. Ajaṇṭā: Handbuch der Malereien 2. Wiesbaden, Germany: Harrassowitz, 2003.

Zou Chonghua 邹重华, and Hu Zhaoxi 胡昭曦. "Qianshu Houshu yu zhongyuan zhengquan de guanxi 前蜀后蜀与中原政权的关系." In *Qian Hou Shu de lishi yu wen-*

hua: Qianhoushu lishi yu wenhua xueshu taolunhui lunwenji 前后蜀的历史与文化：前后蜀历史与文化学术讨论会论文集, edited by Chengdu Wang Jian mu bowuguan 成都王建墓博物馆, pp. 10–17. Chengdu: Ba Shu shushe chuban, 1994.

Zürcher, Erik. "Buddhist Art in Medieval China: The Ecclesiastical View." In *Function and Meaning in Buddhist Art: Proceedings of a Seminar Held at Leiden University 21–24 October 1991,* edited by K. R. van Kooij and H. van der Veere, pp. 1–20. Groningen, The Netherlands: Egbert Forsten, 1995.

Index

abhidharma (treatises on the Dharma), 51
Abhidharmakośa, 156n14; cosmology according to, 271 table 7
Account of Temples and Pagodas (*Sita ji*; ninth century), 145
Adhikaraṇavastu, 106n
Āgamas (Collections), 31, 33, 34
Ajaṇṭā (Maharashtra, India), 43, 44, 79–87, 92, 100, 184, 237
  Cave 16: 82–83 fig. 3.1, 92n
  Cave 17, 64; compared with *vinaya* accounts, 101; donors of, 87, 100, 102; images of the Buddha in, 84, 86, 94, 101, 103 fig. 3.8; inscriptions in, 87; wheel of rebirth in, 27 pl. 8, 43, 60–61, chap. 3, 221, 242–43, 256–58, 263, 265, 270; plan of, 85 fig. 3.3
Ajātaśatru, 128
Ākāśagarbha, 210
Akṣobhya, 199, 200
Alabaster, Henry, 42
A-lci, 204; wheel of rebirth at, 218
All exists (*sarvam asti*, Ch.: *yiqieyou*), 74
Amāravatī (Andhra Pradesh), 35; wheel of dharma sculpture at, 37 fig. 1.15
American Museum of Natural History: no. 70/11044 (wheel of rebirth), 20 pl. 5, 21 fig. 1.10; no. 70.0/6931 (wheel of rebirth), 22 pl. 6, 23 fig. 1.11, 24 fig. 1.12
Amitābha, 125, 127–28, 142, 173–74, 186, 200, 209–10, 225, 229, 237–38, 244, 246
Amitāyus, 199; depicted in the wheel of rebirth, 16, 21
Amoghasiddhi, 200
Amoghavajra (705–774), 149
Analysis of the Vinaya of the Mūlasarvāstivāda (*Mūlasarvāstivāda vinaya vibhaṅga*, *Genbenshuoyiqieyoubu pinaiye*), 53, 58n20, 59, 65, 66–67, 67n47, 104–5n1, 105n3, 112n, 120, 262; structure of, 73. See also under *vinaya*
Anāthapiṇḍika, 31, 57, 74, 174–75
anātman. *See* lack of soul
animals. *See* paths of rebirth
anitya. *See* impermanence
An Lushan rebellion (755–763), 44, 167
Aparagodānīya (western continent), 95. *See also* Four Continents
architecture: relation to audience, 254–60. *See also* temple design
arhat (worthy one or saint), 54n12, 57, 59, 79, 110, 112–16, 119; depicted in the wheel of rebirth, 79. *See also* Four Fruits
arhat caves, 153
army of impermanence (*wuchang jun*), 65
army of life and death (*shengsi jun*, *macuno sena*), 65
Ārya Śūra (third century?), 85
Asaṅga (sixth century), 26
Aśoka, King (r. 273–232 B.C.E.), 35, 81, 93, 117
Aśokarājasūtra? See *Eyuwang jing*
Aśokāvadāna. See *Legend of King Aśoka*
asuras (demigods), 131, 155, 244; in the wheel of rebirth, 6, 14, 60, 214, 218, 232, 243, 254. *See also under* paths of rebirth
Atiśa (Jo-bo-rje, 982–1054), 26, 199
audience, 254–60
avadāna, 77, 104, 105, 117, 152
Avadānakalpalatā, 105n2
Avalokiteśvara Bodhisattva (Guanshiyin pusa), 123, 124n11, 125, 128, 169, 170–71 table 4, 174, 209, 210n18; depicted in the wheel of rebirth, 12, 16; with one thousand arms, 229; Six-Armed, 218n31
Avataṃsaka sūtra. See *Flower Garland Scripture*
Avīci Hell, 113, 182

Baizhang Huaihai (720–814), 262
Bakker, Hans, 81
Baodingshan, 64, 259–60; Dafowan (Larger Buddha Bay), 228n10, 232; Dafowan Niche 3, 230 fig. 9.4, 233 fig. 9.5, 235 fig. 9.6, 236

Baodingshan *(continued)*
fig. 9.7; Dafowan Niche 11, 222 fig. 9.1, 223 fig. 9.2; Dafowan Niche 19, 231; Dafowan Niche 22, 225, 225n4, 226 fig. 9.3; Dafowan Niche 27, 225; donors of, 237; Liu Benzun depicted at, 225–26; structure and content of, 229; wheel of rebirth at, 32 pl. 14, 48, 61, chap. 9, 243, 246, 256, 260, 264–65, 270; Xiaofowan (Smaller Buddha Bay), 228n10
Bao'en jing. See *Scripture on Repaying Kindness*
Barabuḍur (ninth century, Java), 220, 220n; Kātyāyana depicted at, 108–9 fig. 4.2, 109; Rudrāyaṇa story depicted at, 105, 105n2, 113, 114–15 fig. 4.4
Benzun (Original Honored One), 225, 225n3
Bhaiṣajyaguru Bodhisattva (Yaoshiwang pusa), 142, 173; paradise of, 143, 173, 186, 244
bhakti (devotion), 102
Bhaktin, Mikhail, 257
bhavacakra. See wheel of rebirth
bianwen. See transformation texts
bianxiang. See transformation scenes
Bieza ahan jing (*Saṃyuktāgama*), 33n7
Bimbisāra, 105, 106, 108, 109, 112, 116–18
Birth of Good (Shansheng), 69, 69n48. *See also* Born in Poverty; Sahasodgata
Bishamen. *See* Vaiśravana
bKra-shis-mgon (r. ca. 950–975), 196, 199
bKra-shis-'od. *See* Byang-chub-'od
bKra-shis-rtsegs, 199
Bodhidharma, 232
bodhisattva, 40, 86, 124, 137–38, 158, 206, 268; in the wheel of rebirth, 7
Bön, 6
Born in Poverty (Pinsheng), 67–72, 118–19. *See also* Birth of Good; Sahasodgata
Boys of Good and Evil, 244
Brahmā, 55, 151, 158
British Museum: Illustration of the Realms of the Ten Directions of Mind Contemplation, 248 fig. 10.4
Brooklyn Museum of Art: L25.5 (wheel of rebirth), 18 pl. 4, 19 fig. 1.9
Brown, Percy, 83–84
Buddha. *See* Akṣobhya; Amitābha; Amitāyus; Amoghasiddhi; Maitreya; Ratnasambhava; Śākyamuni; Vairocana; Vajradhara
Buddha-fields (Buddha-*kṣetras*), 205
Buddhaghosa, 34–35
buddhakṣetra. See Buddha realm
Buddhānusmṛti samādhisāgara sūtra. See *Guanfo sanmei hai jing*
Buddha realm (*buddhakṣetra*), 127
Buddhas of the Ten Directions, 206, 209, 216n28
Buddhasmṛti (Zhu Fonian, ca. 365), 65n40, 95n32, 124n11
Buddhavaṃsa Commentary, 229n14
Burgess, James, 99
Byang-chub-'od, 199, 210, 212

caityas (halls for worship): at Ajaṇṭā, 82–83, 102
cakra. See wheels
cakravartin rāja. See wheel-turning king
Campany, Robert, 124
Candraprabhā (Ch.: Yueguang), 104–5n1, 110, 111 fig. 4.3
Cao family, 165, 168, 172, 187, 258; chronology of, 170–71 table 4
Cao Yanlu, 169, 170–71 table 4
Cao Yijin, 170–71 table 4, 172, 187
Cao Yuanzhong, 48, 165, 168, 169, 170–71 table 4, 172; depicted in Yulin Cave 19, 172 fig. 7.2, 175
Catalogue of the Buddhist Teachings during the Kaiyuan Era (*Kaiyuan shijiao lu*), 51n3, 53n7, 169, 261n19
central Asia, x, 44, 168, 184, chap. 6, 195; literacy in, 40; map of ca. 850, 148; *vinaya* in, 52
central stūpa-pillar style (*zhongxin tazhu shi*), 151–53, 165, 184, 250
chain of causation. *See* dependent origination
Chan (Zen), 268
Chang ahan jing (*Dīrghāgama*), 95n32
Chang'an, 44, 127, 142, 149, 167, 264
China, x, 13, 16–17, 42–43, 64, 165, 195–96; cave temples in, 44, 48, 143–45, 184–88; fluid boundaries of, xii, 43–49; influence in the Hexi Corridor, 165–68; influence on Kumtura, 146, 152; map of late tenth century, 166; *vinaya* in, 50–52, 78, 261–63; wheel of rebirth in, chap. 5, chap. 7, chap. 9, 256, 265
Chongxiu Baodingshan Shengshou yuan ji. *See* Record of the Repair of the Cloister of the Sagely and Long-Lived at Baodingshan
Čhos-grub (Facheng, 832–865), 167
Chu Guangxi, 190n31
Chuyao jing, 65nn40–41
circle of the wheel of rebirth (*saṃsāracakrasya maṇḍala*). *See* wheel of rebirth
circles, 8, 13, 162, 179, 242–54
Cloister of the Twelve Causes and Conditions for the Educated (*xueren shi'er yinyuan yuan*), 137
Collection of Auspicious Signs from the Dark World (*Mingxiang ji*), 121, 123n7
conditioned coarising (*pratītyasamutpāda*). *See* dependent origination
Consecration Sūtra (*Guanding jing*), 147
cosmological Buddha, 130–31, 132 fig. 5.2, 133 fig. 5.3, 134 fig. 5.4, 135 fig. 5.5, 249 fig. 10.5, 250–52

Dafowan (Larger Buddha Bay). *See under* Baodingshan

Dalai Lama, Fourteenth (Tenzin Gyatso) 38–39, 64
Daloutan jing, 95n32. See also *Sūtra on the Arising of the World*
Daocheng (ca. 1017–1021), 120–21, 121n1, 262
Daoming, 244
Daoshi (d. 683), 64n36, 123n7, 142n24
Daoshou, 169
Daoxiu, 158–59, 159n18
Daoxuan (596–667), 64n36, 127n14, 136–42, 258, 262; temple homologies of, 142 table 2
Dapiluzhena chengfo jing shu, 156n14
Dapiluzhena chengfo shenbian jiachi jing. See *Mahāvairocana Sūtra*
Daśakumāracarita, 81n9
Dasheng bensheng xindi guan jing. See *Mahāyāna Scripture on Previous Lives*
Dashizhi pusa. *See* Mahāsthāmaprāpta Bodhisattva
Datang xiyu ji, 147n2
Datang xiyu qiufa gaoseng zhuan, 51n3
Dayun Temple, 149–50
Dazu, 221, 227
demigods. See *asuras*
Demon of Impermanence. *See* Great Demon of Impermanence
Deng Zhijin, 232
Denwood, Philip, 217
dependent origination (or conditioned coarising, *pratītyasamutpāda*), 10–11 table 1, 61–62; depicted in Yulin Cave 19, 163, 178
  with Twelve Conditions (*nidāna*), 55n14, 137–38, 252–54; in Kumtura Cave 75, 146, 161; at Pedongpo, 218; in the Rudrāyaṇa story, 104, 106, 107, 109, 116, 118–19, 220, 256; in the wheel of rebirth, 9–10, 13, 15, 16, 19, 55, 61–64, 76, 78, 116, 118, 161, 212–13, 242
  with Eighteen Conditions (*nidāna*), 62–63, 98–99, 232
devotion. See *bhakti*
dhāraṇīs. *See* spells
dharmacakra. *See* wheel of Dharma
Dharmagupta vinaya. See under *vinaya*
Dharmapāda (*Verses on the Law*, aka *Udānavarga*), 65, 65n40
Dharmarakṣa (Zhu Fahu, fl. 265–313), 124n11, 167
Dhe-ba ra-tsa (Devarāja), 196, 216
Diamond Realm maṇḍala, 193, 200, 202 fig. 8.3, 206, 208–10, 210n18, 212, 217, 219–20, 226n, 259
Diamond Sūtra, 169, 170–71 table 4
Dīpaṃkara. *See* Three Buddhas
Dīpaṃkara Śrījñāna. *See* Atiśa
Dīrghāgama. See *Chang ahan jing*
discursive practice, 41–42, 49, 239, 254–56, 262
Divyāvadāna (*Avadānas of Gods*), 58n21, 60n23, 65n40, 66n44, 69n48, 74, 77n1, 93, 102; account of the wheel of rebirth in, 77–78, 87–88n18, 99–100, 255; compared with the Mūlasarvāstivāda vinaya, 77–78, 77n2; Rudrāyaṇa story in, chap. 4
Dizang pusa. *See* Kṣitigarbha Bodhisattva
Dizang pusa benyuan jing, 244n
Dizang pusa jing, 244n
donor(s), 150, 151, 168–69, 254–55; of Ajaṇṭā Cave 17, 87, 100, 102; of Baodingshan, 237; of Kumtura Cave 75, 146, 156, 158–60; of Mogao Cave 94, 187–88; Rudrāyaṇa as, 109; of Tabo, 204, 210–12, 216–18, 237; of Yulin Cave 19, 163–65, 169, 170–71 table 4, 172, 175
Dpal-ldan bkra-shis bde-gnas, 211
dreams: in medieval Chinese literature, 125n; of Wang Qiu, 124–25
Du Fu, 190n31
duḥkha. *See* suffering
Dunhuang, 4, 53n, 126, 128, 129 fig. 5.1 (Amitābha's pure land), 130–31, 142, 142n25, 143, 147, 165–68, 170–71 table 4, 174, 184, 186, 242, 258, 264–65. *See also* Mogao; Yulin
Durkheim, Emile, 266

eastern continent. *See* Pūrvavideha
Eight Difficulties (or Eight Unfortunate [Places], *aṣṭa akṣaṇāḥ*, Ch.: *banan*), 92–93, 94
Eightfold Path, 12, 40
eight forms of life, 94
Ekottarāgama. See *Zengyi ahan jing*
Ennin, 142
Eyuwang jing (*Aśokarājasūtra*?), 66n42

Fahai, 149
Fa jiyao song jing, 65nn40–41
Fan Jinshi, 180–83
Faxian (aka Tianxizai, fl. 980–1000), 62n28, 65n40
Fayuan zhulin, 64n36, 123n7, 142n24
Fazong, 170–71 table 4
Five Blessings, 189, 191
Five Dynasties period, 142, 165–67, 169, 187, 237
Five Paths of rebirth (*wuqu*, *pañcagatayaḥ*). *See* paths of rebirth
Five Precepts, 67, 70, 106, 107, 116
Flower Garland Scripture (*Avataṃsaka Sūtra*), 52, 130, 205
Foding zunshengxin podiyu zhuanyezhang chusanjie mimi sanshen foguo sanzhongxidi zhenyan yigui, 226–27n5
Foding zunshengxin podiyu zhuanyezhang chusanjie mimi tuoluoni, 226–27n5
Foming jing. See *Scripture of the Buddhas' Names*
Fontein, Jan, 205
Fotudeng (232–348?), 147

Four Continents, 94, 94n31. *See also* Aparagodānīya; Jambudvīpa; Pūrvavideha; Uttarakuru
Four Elements, 158
Four Fruits (*catvāri śramaṇa-phalāni*), 59–60, 59n22, 69–70, 79, 110, 267. See also *arhat*; non-returner; once-returner; stream-enterer
Four Heavenly Kings (*catvāsraḥ mahārājikāḥ*, Ch.: *sitianwang*), 175
Four Noble Truths, 35, 38, 69, 138, 174, 196
Four Orders (*sizhong, catasraḥ parṣadaḥ*), 54, 54n8, 59
Freemantle, Francesca, 39
Freer Gallery of Art: F1900.25 (cosmological Buddha), 134 fig. 5.4; F1900.26 (storyteller at the Sumiyoshi Shrine), 247 fig. 10.3; F1980.86.1–.8 (rubbing of the cosmological Buddha), 135 fig. 5.5
Fundamental Observations on the Śākya Clan (*Shishi yaolan*), 120–21, 121n1
Fu Xi (497–569), 232
Fu xinyuan suo liuhao tu. *See* Illustration of the Binding of the Monkey of the Mind and Locking up the Six Sources of Waste

Gaṇḍavyūha Sūtra, 205
Gansu, 165–68, 195, 265
Garbhadhātu maṇḍala. *See* Womb Realm maṇḍala
Gar-log, 199, 218
Gautama Saṃghadeva (Qutan Sengqietipo, fl. 383–398), 62n28, 93n27
Genbenshuoyiqieyoubu. *See* Mūlasarvāstivāda sect
Genbenshuoyiqieyoubu jie jing (*Mūlasarvāstivāda prātimokṣa sūtra*), 67n46. See also under *vinaya*
Genbenshuoyiqieyoubu pinaiye. See *Analysis of the Vinaya of the Mūlasarvāstivāda*
Genbenshuoyiqieyoubu pinaiye chujia shi (*Mūlasarvāstivāda pravrajyāvastu*), 57n18. See also under *vinaya*
Genbenshuoyiqieyoubu pinaiye poseng shi (*Mūlasarvāstivāda saṃghabhedakavastu*), 57n19. See also under *vinaya*
Genbenshuoyiqieyoubu pinaiye yaoshi (*Mūlasarvāstivāda bhaiṣajyavastu*), 58n21. See also under *vinaya*
Genbenshuoyiqieyoubu pinaiye zashi. See *Miscellaneous Matters*
Genghis Khan (1155–1227), 48
Ghost Festival, 182
giving up the family (*shejia* or *chujia, pravrajya*), 65
Glang Dar-ma (d. 842), 196
gods. *See* paths of rebirth
Government Museum, Madras: no. 21.1505 (worship of the wheel of Dharma), 37 fig. 1.15
Great Demon of Impermanence (Wuchang dagui), 10, 13, 56, 64, 233; symbolizing ignorance, 99. *See also* Yama, King
Gresley, Captain, 88–89
Griffiths, John, 88
Grünwedel, Albert (1856–1935), 150
Guanding jing. See *Consecration Sūtra*
Guanfo sanmei hai jing (**Buddhānusmṛti samādhisāgara sūtra*), 33n9
Guanshiyin pusa. *See* Avalokiteśvara Bodhisattva
Guanzhong chuangli jietan tujing, 137n21, 138–39 fig. 5.6
Guazhou (Gua Prefecture), 165–68, 170–71 table 4
Guge, 196–98, 210
Guiyijun. *See* Returning to Righteousness Army
guizhong (those who take refuge in the bell), 142n24
Gulusi, 159
Guṇabhadra (Qiunabatuoluo, 394–468), 33n7, 62n28
Guṇaprabha (sixth-century?), 66, 66n43
Gupta dynasty, 43, 79, 81, 102

Hall of Benzun (Benzun dian), 228, 228n10
Hariṣena, 87
Hayagrīva, 216n27
Heart Sūtra, 169
heavens. *See* paths of rebirth
Hedin, Sven (1865–1952), 150
hells, 92; depicted at Baodingshan, 227n8, 229, 237; in Buddhist cosmology, 38; illustrated in China, 126–27; illustrated in the *Scripture on the Ten Kings*, 179 fig. 7.5, 181 fig. 7.6, 242; Maudgalyāyana in, 53–54, 56–57, 126, 163, 180–82, 183 fig. 7.7, 184 fig. 7.8, 240–42, 259, 263–64, 268. *See also* paths of rebirth
Hertz, Robert, 266
Hexi Corridor, 142, 165–68, 182, 185, 187, 258
Hinduism, 6, 34, 57, 81, 84, 102, 214
Hopkins, Jeffrey, 38
hosts of death (*sizhong*), 65
Howard, Angela, 130, 250
humans. *See* paths of rebirth
hungry ghosts. *See* paths of rebirth
Hye-č'o (704–ca. 780), 149–50

Illustrated Scripture on Jetavana Monastery in Śrāvastī in Central India (*Zhong Tianzhu Sheweiguo Qihuansi tujing*), 136–42
Illustration of the Binding of the Monkey of the Mind and Locking up the Six Sources of Waste (Fu xinyuan suo liuhao tu), 231
Illustration of the Ten Realms of Mind Con-

templation (Kanshin jūkai zu), 246, 247 fig. 10.3, 248 fig. 10.4
impermanence (*anitya*), 3, 33, 61, 64, 79, 233. *See also* Three Marks
India, x, 34, 42–43, 44, 63, 105, 170–71 table 4; Buddhism in, 4–5, 27, 31, 50–52, 62, 64, 105–6, 196, 199; fluid boundaries of, xii, 43–49; literacy in, 40; map of ca. 500, 80; "Middle Period" religion of, 101–2; *vinaya* in, 26, 50, 52; wheel of rebirth in, chap. 3
Indianization, 42
Indra, 81, 93, 94, 151; heaven of, 93
Instructions on Temples (*Si gao*), 138–39
intermediate existence, state of (*antarābhava*, Ch.: *zhongyou*), 74–75

Jambudvīpa (southern continent), 55, 59, 95, 206. *See also* Four Continents
Japan, x, xii, 26, 53n, 240–41, 246–48
Jātakamāla, 85–86
Jātaka tales, 130, 151–52, 263
Java (Indonesia), 105, 199
Jetavana monastery: according to Daoxuan, 136–42
Jing'ai (534–578), 127, 127n14
Jiucheng yu jing, 62n28
Jung, Carl Gustav, 204, 206

Kaiyuan shijiao lu. See *Catalogue of the Buddhist Teachings during the Kaiyuan Era*
kalyāṇamitras. *See* mentors
Kamalaśīla, 195
Kaṇherī (Maharashtra), 81, 99, 99n38
Kanthaka, 131
karma (action), 4, 6, 27, 39, 74–75, 101, 108, 117–18, 124, 125, 127, 196, 220, 270
karmadāna (assigner of duties), 149
karma mirror. *See* Mirror of Deeds
karmavācanā, 73
Kāśyapa, 4, 221n
Kātyāyana (Ch.: Jiaduoyanna), 109–10, 113, 114, 116
'Khor-re (ca. 959–1036?, r. 975–985?). *See* Ye-shes-'od
Khosla, Romi, 256
Khri Strong-lde'u-btsan (756–797?), 195
Kim, ix-xii, 24
king of ascetics (*munirāja*), 84
Kipling, Rudyard, ix–xii, 24, 26n4
Kizil, 52, 105, 150, 151, 157, 184, 250; Cave 83, 110, 110n6, 111 fig. 4.3; Cave 175, 249 fig. 10.5 (cosmological Buddha), 249–52
Klimburg-Salter, Deborah, 200, 206–8, 214
Kṣitigarbha Bodhisattva (Dizang pusa), 156, 156n12, 180–82, 210, 243–46
Kṣmendra (eleventh century), 105n2
Kṣudrakavastu. See *Miscellaneous Matters*
Kucha, 44, 52, 79, 105, 146–51, 157, 159, 161, 249, 250n9
Kumārajīva (Jiumoluoshi, 350–409), 124n11, 147, 191n32
Kumtura (Xinjiang, China), chap. 6, 220, 237, 249
  Cave 20 plan of, 152 fig. 6.1
  Cave 45, 153
  Cave 75, 153, 154 fig. 6.3; donors of, 146, 156, 158–60; hungry ghosts in, 155 fig. 6.4; structure of, 153–54, 160; wall painting of meditating monk, 28 pl. 9, 146, 155–62, 243, 258; wheels of rebirth in, 29 pl. 10, 44, 61, 146, 160–62, 242–43, 256, 258, 263, 270
  Cave 78: Daoxiu's name in, 159n18

lack of soul (*anātman*), 64. *See also* Three Marks
land of bliss. *See* pure land
Laufer, Berthold (1874–1934), 16
Leach, Edmund, 266
Le Coq, Albert von (1860–1930), 150
Legend of King Aśoka (*Aśokāvadāna*), 65–66, 93
Lha-lde (r. 1000–1025?), 198–99
Liang Wudi (r. 502–550), 232
Liaoben shengsi jing (*Scripture on Understanding the Fundamentals of Birth and Death*). See *Rice-Seedling Scripture*
Liao dynasty, 48, 168
Lidai minghua ji, 127n15
lines, 239–54
Lingyou (518–605), 138
Liu Benzun (844–907), 48, 222–29, 232, 237; austerities of, 225–28
Liu-Song dynasty (420–479), 43, 123
Liu Tianren, 227
Lord of Death (gShin-rje), 11.
Losang Samten (b. 1953), 23
Lotus Sūtra, 124n11, 169
Luoyang, 44, 127, 147

Mādhyamika, 196
Mahākātyāyana. *See* Kātyāyana
Mahānidāna suttanta, 62n28
Mahāsāṃghika vinaya. See under *vinaya*
Mahāsthāmaprāpta Bodhisattva (Dashizhi pusa), 123, 124n11, 125, 128, 174, 209
Mahāvairocana. *See* Vairocana
Mahāvairocana Sūtra (*Dapiluzhena chengfo shenbian jiachi jing*): visualizations in, 156–58, 157 table 3, 160
Mahāyāna Scripture on Previous Lives and the Contemplation of the Stages of Mindfulness (*Dasheng bensheng xindi guan jing*), 33, 33n8
Mahīśāsaka vinaya. See under *vinaya*

Maitrāyaṇīya Upaniṣad, 4n
Maitreya, 126, 152, 169, 170–71 table 4, 225, 232, 238, 244, 252; depicted in the wheel of rebirth, 15; paradise of, 142, 143, 186. *See also* Three Buddhas
maṇḍala, 23–24, 25 pl. 7, 34, 157, 158, 199, 204, 214, 237, 268–69. *See also* Diamond Realm maṇḍala
Mañjuśrī Bodhisattva (Wenshu pusa), 170–71 table 4, 175, 175n11, 205. *See also* Three Sages of Huayan
mantras. *See* spells
Māra, 102; defeat of, 130, 151, 250; and the wheel of rebirth, 79, 99
Marīci, 58, 169
Ma Shichang, 187
Maudgalyāyana, 66, 77, 79, 175, 192, 218n31, 260, 270; associated with filial piety, 58; depicted in the wheel of rebirth, 12; preaching on the paths of rebirth, 26–27, 53–56, 60, 72, 78, 119, 163, 239, 255, 266, 270; spiritual powers of, 57–59; tour of hell, 53–54, 56–57, 126, 163, 180–82, 183 fig. 7.7, 184 fig. 7.8, 240–42, 259, 263–64, 268
meditation, xi, 57, 81, 180, 220; depicted at Baodingshan, 229, 231–32; depicted in Kumtura Cave 75, 28 pl. 9, 146, 155–62, 243, 258
Mei Lin, 180–83
memorial caves (*yingku*), 153
mentors (*kalyāṇamitras*), 205
merit, xi, 70, 75–76, 84, 86–87, 191, 196, 204, 208, 210, 212, 257–58, 270
Miaofa lianhua jing (*Saddharmapuṇḍarika*). See *Lotus Sūtra*
Miliang Village, 227, 227n7
Mimou (or Mimeng), 222n, 223
mind only (*weixin*), 231
Mingxiang ji. See *Collection of Auspicious Signs from the Dark World*
Mingzong (r. 926–934), 223, 228
miracle tales (or recording anomalies, Ch.: *zhiguai*), 121, 123
Mirror of Deeds (or karma mirror, *yejing*), 180
Miscellaneous Matters (*Kṣudrakavastu*, Ch.: *Zashi*), 64n37, 74, 74nn53–54, 93n27, 101. See also under *vinaya*
Mogao (Dunhuang, Gansu), 4, 165–68, 175, 186–87, 191; Cave 5, 170–71 table 4; Cave 25, 170–71 table 4; Cave 38, 170–71 table 4; Cave 53, 170–71 table 4; Cave 55, 170–71 table 4; Cave 61, 170–71 table 4; Cave 94, 168, 187–91; Cave 96, 168, 170–71 table 4; Cave 98, 170–71 table 4, 187, 188 fig. 7.11 (structural diagram); Cave 100, 170–71 table 4; Cave 123, 170–71 table 4; Cave 124, 170–71 table 4; Cave 125, 170–71 table 4; Cave 146, 144 fig. 5.9 (Bhaiṣajyaguru paradise); Cave 158, 4 fig. 1.1 (*parinirvāṇa*), 5 fig. 1.2 (*parinirvāṇa*); Cave 196, 176–77 fig. 7.3 (Śāriputra and Raudrakṣa); Cave 220, 170–71 table 4; Cave 231, 126; Cave 256, 170–71 table 4; Cave 285, 185 fig. 7.9 (structural diagram); Cave 326, 186 fig. 7.10 (structural diagram); Cave 387, 170–71 table 4; Cave 412, 170–71 table 4; Cave 423, 143 fig. 5.8 (sketch of Buddha hall in Maitreya paradise); Cave 427, 170–71 table 4; Cave 428, 130–31, 132 fig. 5.2 (cosmological Buddha), 133 fig. 5.3 (cosmological Buddha); Cave 469, 170–71 table 4
Moheyan, 195
Mokuren kyūbo kyō. See *Scripture on Maudgalyāyana Saving His Mother*
morality, 266–70
Mount Sumeru, 93, 94, 131, 155, 175, 243
mTho-lding (Tholing in the Guge region), 198–99, 210, 214, 218
mudrā, 200. See also *samādhi mudrā*; *varāda mudrā*
Mūlasarvāstivāda bhaiṣajyavastu. See *Genbenshuoyiqieyoubu pinaiye yaoshi*
Mūlasarvāstivāda prātimokṣa sūtra. See *Genbenshuoyiqieyoubu jie jing*
Mūlasarvāstivāda pravrajyāvastu. See *Genbenshuoyiqieyoubu pinaiye chujia shi*
Mūlasarvāstivāda saṃghabhedakavastu. See *Genbenshuoyiqieyoubu pinaiye poseng shi*
Mūlasarvāstivāda sect (Genbenshuoyiqieyoubu), 27, 50; in relation to the Sarvāstivāda, 50n, 74–75
Mūlasarvāstivāda vinaya. See under *vinaya*
Mūlasarvāstivāda vinaya kṣudrakavastu. See *Miscellaneous Matters*
Mūlasarvāstivāda vinaya vibhaṅga. See *Analysis of the Vinaya of the Mūlasarvāstivāda*
Müller, F. W. K., 151
Musée Guimet: EO 3580 (Kṣitigarbha and the pure land), 245 fig. 10.2; no. 16541 (Buddha posing for a portrait), 107 fig. 4.1; no. 17673 (Amitābha's pure land), 129 fig. 5.1
Mus, Paul, 254

Na-ga ra-tsa (Nāgarāja), 196
Nāgārjuna (second century), 26, 196
nāgas (serpentlike creatures), 7–8, 120, 131, 175, 216
Nālandā, 102
Neumann, Helmut, 218
Nidāna vagga, 62n28
Nikāyas (Collections), 34, 62n28, 65, 65n40, 95n32
Ning Qiang, 173
nirvāṇa (extinction), 4, 12, 59–60, 64, 65, 102, 212, 232, 238, 267; as distinct from the paths of rebirth, 3, 13, 131, 252, 254; in the Rudrāyaṇa story, 104, 109, 112, 117; symbol-

ized in the wheel of rebirth, 56, 66, 71, 99, 234, 269
non-returner (*anāgāmi*), 59, 79. *See also* Four Fruits
northern continent. *See* Uttarakuru
Northern Wei dynasty (386–534), 44, 130

'Od-lde (r. ca. 1025–1060), 199
once-returner (*sakṛdāgāmi*), 59, 79. *See also* Four Fruits
One Thousand Buddhas, 210, 218
other shore (*bi'an*, *pārimaṃtīraṃ*), 65
Owen, Lisa, 84

Pad-ma'i-sdong-po. *See* Pedongpo
Padmasambhava (Padma-'byung-gnas), 195
Pad-sdong-po. *See* Pedongpo
Pan Yushan, 187
parinirvāṇa, 206; depicted at Baodingshan, 221, 222 fig. 9.1, 223 fig. 9.2, 229; depicted at Kizil, 250, 250n10; depicted at Kumtura, 152; depicted in Mogao Cave 158, 4 fig. 1.1, 5 fig. 1.2; depicted in Mogao Cave 428, 130
paths of rebirth, 127, 131, 242, 252–54, 269
  numbering five, 6, 31, 54, 59–60, 69, 71, 74, 125, 139, 242; depicted in eight segments in the wheel of rebirth, 94, 97–98, 242–43; in Kumtura Cave 75, 146, 161, 242–43; in the Rudrāyaṇa story, 107
  numbering six, 6, 8, 10–13, 15–16, 27, 33, 38, 40, 267; at Baodingshan, 232, 246; depicted on the cosmological Buddha, 130; emanating from Kṣitigarbha Bodhisattva, 156, 244–45; in illustrations of the Ten Realms, 246; in Kumtura Cave 75, 146, 155, 158, 161; at Pedongpo, 218; at Tabo, 214; in Yulin Cave 19, 163, 178
patron(s). *See* donor(s)
Pauly, Bernard, 79
pāyantika (or *pāyattika*, Ch.: *poyidijia*), 67, 67n45
Pedongpo, 64; wheel of rebirth at, 31 pl. 13, 61, 218, 219 fig. 8.9
Pelliot, Paul, 79
Pelliot manuscripts: no. 2762, 189n24; no. 3451, 265n
perfection of wisdom (*prajñāpāramitā*), 199
picture explainers (Ja.: *etoki*), 26, 100
pictures: in *Kim*, x–xi
pilgrimage, 205, 221, 227–29, 232, 237–38, 259–60
Pinsky, Robert, 255
prajñāpāramitā. *See* perfection of wisdom
Prasenajit, King, 174
pratimokṣa (emancipation), 51, 66–67, 73
pratītyasamutpāda. *See* dependent origination
pratyekabuddha, 94, 137–38, 246; in the Mūlasarvāstivāda *pratimokṣa*, 70; in the Rudrāyaṇa story, 114–15; slandered, 72, 77
Prince of Shu (Shuwang). *See* Wang Jian (847–918)
Przyluski, Jean, 93–94
Purang, 196–99
pure land, 125–26, 127–30, 142, 152–53, 173–74, 206, 209–10, 244, 257, 268; depicted in the wheel of rebirth, 21
Pūrvavideha (eastern continent), 95. *See also* Four Continents
Pusa yingluo jing, 124n11
Puṣya (Ch.: Busa), 110, 113
Puxian pusa. *See* Samantabhadra Bodhisattva

Qishi jing, 95n32, 97n. See also *Sūtra on the Arising of the World*
Qishi yinben jing, 95n32. See also *Sūtra on the Arising of the World*
Qočo (Gaochang, Xinjiang), 44, 147, 150

Rahula, 86
Rājagṛha, 53, 57, 68, 69, 71, 105, 108, 110, 112
rakṣa (demon), 55, 79, 98–99
Ralph, Mr., 88–89
Ratnasambhava, 200
Raudrakṣa, 174–75, 176–77 fig. 7.3
rDo-rje-chen-mo (Skt.: Mahāvajra Devi), 206–9, 214, 217
rebirth. See *saṃsāra*
recording anomalies. *See* miracle tales
Record of Famous Painters of the Tang Dynasty (*Tangchao minghua lu*; eighth century), 145
Record of the Repair of the Cloister of the Sagely and Long-Lived at Baodingshan (Chongxiu Baodingshan Shengshou yuan ji), 227–28
reincarnation. See *saṃsāra*
renunciation (*chuli*, *naiṣkramya*), 12, 39, 56, 56n15, 65, 116
Returning to Righteousness Army (Guiyijun), 167, 170–71 table 4
Rice-Seedling Scripture (*Liaoben shengsi jing* [*Scripture on Understanding the Fundamentals of Birth and Death*], *Śālistambhaka sūtra*), 62, 62n26
Rin-chen-bzang-po (958–1055?), 197–99, 202, 204, 208
Roruka, 104, 105, 108, 113–17
Rubin Museum of Art: item no. 591, acc. no. F1997.40 10 (wheel of rebirth), 17 pl. 3; item no. 65356 (wheel of rebirth), ii pl. 1, 7 fig. 1.3, 8 fig. 1.4, 9 fig. 1.5, 12–13 fig. 1.6
Rubin, Shelley and Donald: item no. 78, acc. no. P1994.3.6 (wheel of rebirth), 2 pl. 2, 14 fig. 1.7, 15 fig. 1.8
Rudrāyaṇa, King (var.: Udrāyaṇa, Ch.: Xiandao or Youtuoxian), 26n6, chap. 4, 220, 256

Sadakane Keiji, 94–99
Saddharmapuṇḍarika. See *Lotus Sūtra*
Sahasodgata (Suddenly Arisen), 69n48, 77. *See also* Birth of Good; Born in Poverty
Śākyamuni (historical Buddha), 3, 4, 26, 60, 62, 128, 189, 244, 253–54; defeat of Māra, 130; depicted in the wheel of rebirth, 6, 7, 8, 12, 13–14, 15, 16, 61, 79, 116, 252, 267–68; images of at Ajaṇṭā, 84, 86, 94, 101, 103 fig. 3.8; images of at Baodingshan, 221, 222 fig. 9.1, 229, 237–38; images of in Kizil Cave 175, 250–52; images of at Kumtura, 151; images of at Tabo, 205–6, 209, 213 fig. 8.7, 216n28; instructions for painting the wheel of rebirth, 12, 26–27, 60–66, 72, 121, 212, 214, 239, 255, 260, 261–62, 269; in *Kim*, ix; in Mogao Cave 428, 130–31; in the Rudrāyaṇa story, 104, 105–9, 114–15, 116–19, 220, smile of, 66; symbolized by the wheel of Dharma, 35; in Yulin Cave 19, 173. *See also* cosmological Buddha; Three Buddhas
Śālistambhaka sūtra. See *Rice-Seedling Scripture*
samādhi mudrā, 209
Samantabhadra Bodhisattva (Puxian pusa), 175, 175n11, 205. *See also* Three Sages of Huayan
saṃsāra (to undergo transmigration), 3, 4 ,11, 31, 204, 211, 217, 230, 232, 236, 238; as illustrated by the wheel of rebirth, 6, 61, 222, 254, 269–70; metaphors for, 33; release from, 12, 40, 65, 118–19, 231, 244; represented by a wheel, 31, 33–34, 252
saṃsāracakra. *See* wheel of rebirth
Saṃyuktāgama. See *Bieza ahan jing; Za ahan jing*
Saṃyutta-Nikaya, 62n28
Sanskrit seed syllables: depicted in the wheel of rebirth, 21
Śāntarakṣita (Zhi-ba-'tsho), 195
Sanzhong xidi podiyu zhuanyezhang chusanjie mimi tuoluoni fa, 226–27n5
Śāriputra, 57, 78, 165, 174–75, 176–77 fig. 7.3
Sārnāth (Uttar Pradesh), 35, 102
Sārnāth Museum: lion sculpture, 36 fig. 1.14
Sarvāstivāda sect, 27, 95, 147, 161, 243; in relation to the Mūlasarvāstivāda, 50n, 74–75
Sarvāstivāda vinaya. See under *vinaya*
Sarvatathāgata-tattva-saṃgraha, 202, 204
Schlingloff, Dieter, 158
Schopen, Gregory, 84, 101
Scripture of the Buddhas' Names (*Foming jing*), 170–71 table 4
Scripture of the God Asking Questions (*Tian qingwen jing*), 173–74
Scripture on Maudgalyāyana Saving His Mother (*Mokuren kyūbo kyō*), 240–41
Scripture on Prolonging Life (*Yanshouming jing*), 170–71 table 4
Scripture on Repaying Kindness (*Bao'en jing*), 173
Scripture on the Ten Kings (*Shiwang jing*), 179; courts of hell illustrated in, 179 fig. 7.5, 181 fig. 7.6, 242
Seven Buddhas of the Past, 249–50
Seven Rare Jewels (*qizhen*), 189, 191
Sha Creek (Shaxi), 227, 227n7
Shazhou (Sha Prefecture), 165–68, 170–71 table 4, 264–65
shengsi (birth and death). *See* saṃsāra
shengsi lun. *See* wheel of rebirth
Shiji jing, 95n32. See also *Sūtra on the Arising of the World*
Shishi yaolan. See *Fundamental Observations on the Śākya Clan*
Shisong lü. See under *vinaya*
Shiwang jing. See *Scripture on the Ten Kings*
Shōzō en'yū sandai zusetsu, 246n7
Sichuan, 48, 61, 121, 126, chap. 9, map of ca. 1250, 224, 264–65
Sifen lü. See under *vinaya*
Si gao. See *Instructions on Temples*
Sikhaṇḍi, King (Ch.: Dingji), 104, 112–13, 115–16
Śikṣānanda (652–710), 52, 244n
Silk Road, 147, 196, 249
Siṃhalāvadāna, 101
Sinification, 43
Sita ji. See *Account of Temples and Pagodas*
Sitātapatra: depicted in the wheel of rebirth, 16
Six Bandits (*liuzei*). *See* six senses
Six Paths of rebirth. *See* paths of rebirth
Six Perfections (*ṣaṭpāramitā*), 123n3, 174
six senses, 231
Six Sources of Waste. *See* six senses
skandhaka, 73
Snellgrove, David, 63
Somendra (eleventh century), 105n2
Somers, Robert, 237
Song dynasty, 121, 142, 165–68, 170–71 table 4, 227–29, 237, 262
Song gaoseng zhuan, 51n3
soteriology, 15–16, 39, 59, 60, 72, 79, 254; in the Rudrāyaṇa legend, 110, 116–17
Southeast Asia, x, xii, 51, 229n14
southern continent. *See* Jambudvīpa
spells (*dhāraṇīs* and *mantras*), 223, 226, 226–27n5, 237
Spink, Walter, 89–91
spiritual feet (*ṛddhi pāḍāḥ, shenzu*), 57
Śraddhākaravarman, 198–99
Śrāvastī, 31, 74, 101, 136, 174
Śrīmitra (Bo Shilimiduoluo, ca. 307–342), 147
Steinkellner, Ernst, 205

Stein manuscripts: no. 3329, 189n24; no. 6161, 189n24; no. 6973, 189n24
stream-enterer (*śrotāpati*), 58, 59, 69–70, 79, 109, 110, 119. *See also* Four Fruits
Strong-btsan-sgam-po (d. 649), 195
Strong-nge (r. 985–1000?), 196
Śubhakarasiṃha (Shanwuwei, ca. 716–735), 156n14, 226, 227n5
Sudatta. *See* Anāthapiṇḍika
Sudhana (Tib.: Nor-bzang), 205–6, 209, 216n28, 220
suffering (*duḥkha*), 38, 64. *See also* paths of rebirth; *saṃsāra*; Three Marks
Sui dynasty (581–618), 131, 143, 167, 185
sukhāvatī. *See* pure land
Sumatra, 52
Sumiyoshi Shrine, 246
Sūtra on the Arising of the World (**Loka-upapatti sūtra*), 94–95
Suzuki, D. T. (1870–1966), 37–38

Tabo: design of main temple, 200–201, 209–10, 212, 216–17; donors of, 204, 210–12, 216–18, 237; Mahāvairocana statue at, 203 fig. 8.4; wall painting of Buddha and verses, 213 fig. 8.7; wall painting of deities of Vajradhātu maṇḍala, 202 fig. 8.3; wall painting of rDo-rje-chen-mo, 207 fig. 8.5; wall painting of red deity, 30 pl. 12; wall painting of sponsors, 211 fig. 8.6; wall painting of Ye-shes-'od and Devarāja, 198 fig. 8.1; wheel of rebirth at, 44, chap. 8, 221, 243, 259, 263, 270
Taklamakan Desert, 147, 165
taming of the ox, 229
Tangchao minghua lu. See *Record of Famous Painters of the Tang Dynasty*
Tang dynasty (618–907), 4, 4 fig. 1.1, 5 fig. 1.2, 44, 52, 64n36, 120, 126–28, 136, 138, 142, 142n24, 145, 147, 150, 165–67, 173, 185–86, 190, 221, 225, 236–37, 256, 258, 264; map of, 122
Tantric Buddhism, 48, 130, 152–53, 162, chap. 8, 229
Tarim Basin, 43–44, 146–49
temple design, 40; according to Daoxuan's plan for the Jetavana monastery, 136–42; evolution of in China, 143–45, 184–88; at Kumtura, 151–54, 160; at Tabo, 200–201, 209–10, 212, 216–17; Tibetan, 48; at Yulin, 163, 173–75, 191–92
Ten Acts of Refining (*shilian*). *See under* Liu Benzun
Ten Evil Deeds (*shi'e, daśākuśala*), 54n9
Ten Kings of Hell, 244
Ten Precepts, 191
Ten Realms, 246, 247 fig. 10.3, 248 fig. 10.4, 254
Ten Virtues, 189, 191
Tenzin Gyatso. *See* Dalai Lama
Teshoo Lama, ix–xi
Theragātha, 65, 65n40
Three Bodies of the Buddha, 189, 190n29, 208n16
Three Buddhas of the past (Dīpaṃkara), present (Śākyamuni), and future (Maitreya), 222, 234, 264
Three Certainties (*sanjian*), 189, 191
Three Jewels, 35, 54, 58, 59, 70, 87, 107, 116–17, 121, 139, 195
Three Marks (*trilakṣana*), 64. *See also* impermanence; lack of soul; suffering
Three Poisons (*sandu, tridoṣāpaha*), 11, 13, 16, 55n13, 61, 146, 160, 218, 232, 252, 253
Three Refuges, 106, 116, 138
Three Sages of Huayan (Huayan Sansheng), 237
Three Symbols (*sanzhongxing*). *See* Three Poisons
Three Vehicles (*sansheng*), 137, 137n22
Thus Come One (Tathāgata). *See* Buddha
Tian qingwen jing. See *Scripture of the God Asking Questions*
Tianxizai (fl. 980–1000). *See* Faxian
Tibet, xii, 38, 259; burial custom of, 15, 19; fluid boundaries of, xii, 43–49; influence in the Hexi Corridor, 165–67; influence on Kumtura, 146, 150, 152; kings of, 197 table 5; map of in eleventh century, 194; *vinaya* in, 51, 52–53, 76, 78, 262; wheel of rebirth in, ii pl. 1, x, 2 pl. 2, chap. 1, 61, 64, chap. 8, 269
Tiṣya (Ch.: Disa), 110, 113
transformation scenes (*bianxiang*), 126, 189
transformation texts (*bianwen*), 174n, 182, 240, 264
Trungpa, Chögyam, 39
Tso Szebong, 52, 262
Tucci, Giuseppe, 200, 202, 204
Turfan, 52, 147, 159
Tuṣita Heaven, 142, 205
Twelve Conditions or Underlying Factors (*nidānas*). *See* dependent origination
Two Truths, 38

Udānavarga. See *Dharmapāda*
Udrāyaṇa. *See* Rudrāyaṇa
Uighurs, 44, 158–59, 162, 168, 170–71 table 4, 258, 264; influence in the Hexi Corridor, 165, 167; influence on Kumtura, 146, 150, 153–55
Upagupta, 102
Upaniṣads, 2n, 63
Upendragupta, 87
ūrṇākeśa, 230
Uṣṇīṣavijaya: depicted in the wheel of rebirth, 16
Uttarakuru (northern continent, Ptolemy's Ottorokorra), 95–97. *See also* Four Continents

Vaidehī, Queen, 128
Vairocana, 130, 152, 193, 199–200, 203 fig. 8.4, 204, 208–10, 210n18, 212, 217, 219–20; depicted at Baodingshan, 225, 229, 230, 238. *See also* Three Sages of Huayan
Vaiśravana (Bishamen), 170–71 table 4
Vajrabodhi (662–732), 149
Vajradhara: depicted in the wheel of rebirth, 16
Vajradhātu maṇḍala. *See* Diamond Realm maṇḍala
Vajrapāni, 216n27
Vajrasattva Bodhisattva, 210n18
Vākāṭaka empire, 43, 79–81, 87, 102, 257
Van Gennep, Arnold, 266
varāda mudrā, 212
Vasudhāra: depicted in the wheel of rebirth, 16
Vasumitra (fourth century), 260
Verses on the Law. See *Dharmapāda*
Vidyārājas (Mingwang), 229
vigor (*jingjin*, Skt.: *vīrya*), 123n3, 124
vihāras (residence halls for monks), 99, 163, 184–85; at Ajaṇṭā, 82–87, 88, 94, 100–101, 102, 256, 270
Vimalakīrti Sūtra (*Weimojie suoshuo jing*), 191n32
vinaya, 26, 31, 50–52, 101, 116
 of the Dharmagupta sect (*Shisong lü*), 51, 52, 120, 261
 of the Mahāsāṃghika sect, 52, 261
 of the Mahīśāsaka sect, 52, 261
 of the Mūlasarvāstivāda sect, 27, 50–51, 64, 73–74, 76, 101; compared with the *Divyāvadāna*, 77–78, 77n2; Eight Difficulties in, 93, 93n27; in Chinese translation, 50–51, 52, 78; in Tibetan translation, 51, 52–53; *pratimokṣa* of, 66–67; Rudrāyaṇa story in, chap. 4; wheel of rebirth origin myth in, 26–27, chap. 2, 86, 99–100, 121, 127, 161, 161n20, 163, 179–82, 212, 214, 221, 238, 255–56, 260, 261–64, 266, 269. See also *Adhikaraṇavastu*
 of the Sarvāstivāda sect (Ch.: *Sifen lü*), 51–52, 261
Vinayasūtra, 66n43
Vinaya vibhaṅga. See *Analysis of the Vinaya of the Mūlasarvāstivāda*
Viśvantara jātaka, 101
voice-hearer (*śrāvaka*), 94

Waddell, L. Augustine, 94, 269
Wang, Eugene, 257
Wang Jian (847–918), 225, 237
Wang Qiu, 121, 123, 125–26
Wang Wei, 190n31
Wang Wutianzhuguo zhuan, 149n
Wang Yan (ca. 454–501), 121, 125, 256
Weigan River, 150, 151, 153
Weimojie suoshuo jing. See *Vimalakīrti Sūtra*
Wenshu pusa. *See* Mañjuśrī Bodhisattva
western continent. *See* Aparagodānīya
wheel having five sections (*pañcagaṇḍaka cakra*). *See* wheel of rebirth
wheels (*cakra*): and circular time, 266–70; formal structure of, 242–43, 252–54; indicating repetition, 242; as mnemonic teaching devices, 35; as objects of meditation, 157–58; representing the sun, 34; symbolizing Buddhist doctrines, 34, 35; various kinds of, 34
wheel of birth and death (*shengsi lun*, *saṃsāracakra*). *See* wheel of rebirth.
wheel of birth and death in the five paths (*wuqu shengsi lun*, *pañcagati saṃsāracakra*). *See* wheel of rebirth
wheel of Dharma (*dharmacakra*), 35; depicted in the wheel of rebirth, 12, 27; sculpture at Amāravatī, 37 fig. 1.15; symbolizing the Buddha, 35; symbolizing the Buddha's first sermon, 35
wheel of the Five Paths. *See* wheel of rebirth
wheel of rebirth, x, 4n, 24, 31, 34–35, 44, 64, 65, 101, 104, 239–40, 242–43, 250, 252–54; at Ajaṇṭā Cave 17, 27 pl. 8, 43, 60–61, chap. 3, 221, 256–58, 263, 265, 270; at Baodingshan, 32 pl. 14, 48, 61, chap. 9, 243, 246, 256, 260, 264–65, 270; in central Asia, chap. 6; compared with other forms of Buddhist art, 267–69; in China, chap. 5, chap. 7, chap. 9, 256, 265; compared with the Rudrāyaṇa painting, 116–19; diversity in its depictions, 100; in India, chap. 3; inscriptions in, 65; as introduction to Buddhist teachings, 229, 237, 265; in *Kim*, ix–xii; at Kumtura Cave 75, 29 pl. 10, 44, 61, 146, 160–62, 242–43, 256, 258, 263, 270; origin story in the *Divyāvadāna*, 12, 77–78; origin story in the Duldur-aqur fragments, 79; origin story in the *vinaya*, 12, 26–27, chap. 2, 86, 99–100, 121, 255–56, 260, 261–64, 266, 270; as pan-Buddhist symbol, 42, 260; at Pedongpo, 31 pl. 13, 61, 218, 219 fig. 8.9; as preface to Tantric ritual, 193, 200, 219–20, 257–60, 270; ritual context of, 41, 193, 200, 219–20, 257; as sand *maṇḍala*, 23–24, 25 pl. 7, 25 fig. 1.13; in the story of Born in Poverty, 67, 71; at Tabo, 44, chap. 8, 221, 243, 259, 263, 270; at temple entrances, 60, 74, 78, 88, 100–101, 118, 145, 162, 163, 182–83, 187, 191–92, 193, 212, 218, 238, 256–60, 265, 270; in Tibetan painting, ii pl. 1, 2 pl. 2, 6–12, 7 fig. 1.3, 8 fig. 1.4, 9 fig. 1.5, 12–13 fig. 1.6, 13–23, 15 fig. 1.8, 17 pl. 3, 18 pl. 4, 19 fig. 1.9, 20 pl. 5, 21 fig. 1.10, 22 pl. 6, 23 fig. 1.11, 24 fig. 1.12, 61, chap. 8; at Yulin

Cave 19, 29 pl. 11, 48, 61, 64, 126, chap. 7, 193, 214, 221, 233, 238, 240, 243, 256, 258–59, 263–65, 270
wheel of *saṃsāra*. *See* wheel of rebirth
wheel-turning king (*cakravartin rāja*), 35, 94, 107
White Tārā: depicted in the wheel of rebirth, 16
Wi-nyu-myin. *See* rDo-rje-chen-mo
Womb Realm maṇḍala, 210n18
Wuchang dagui. *See* Great Demon of Impermanence
Wu Daozi (fl. 713–755), 126
Wu, Empress, 52

Xiaofowan (Smaller Buddha Bay). *See under* Baodingshan
Xiao Mo, 187
Xie Lingyun (385–433), 190
Xinjiang, 44, 61, 79, 146, 151, 159
Xiuxing, 149
Xizong (r. 873–888), 237
Xuanzang (602–664), 52, 62n28, 86, 147, 147n2, 161, 261
Xuanzong (r. 712–756), 228, 237, 264
Xu gaoseng zhuan, 127n14

Yama, King (Yanluo wang), 64, 127, 180, 182, 246; depicted in the wheel of rebirth, 7, 10–11, 19, 21
Yanluo wang. *See* Yama, King
Yanshouming jing. See *Scripture on Prolonging Life*
Yaoshiwang pusa. *See* Bhaiṣajyaguru Bodhisattva
yejing. *See* Mirror of Deeds
Ye-shes-'od (Skt.: Jñānaprabha), 196–99, 204, 210–11, 216–17, 259
Yijing (635–713), 50–52, 53, 53n7, 57nn18–19, 58nn20–21, 64n37, 67n46, 69n48, 74, 78, 93n27, 104–5n1, 120, 261–62
yingku. *See* memorial caves
Yixing (673–727), 156n14, 157
Yogācāra school, 231
Yogalehrbuch, 158
Yong Creek (Yongxi). *See* Sha Creek
Youfang jichao, 149n
Yuan dynasty, 48, 167, 228
Yuanqi shengdao jing, 62n28
Yulin, 165–69, 175, 186, 191, 237
  Cave 12, 169
  Cave 19: design of, 163, 164 fig. 7.1, 173–75, 219; donors of, 163–65, 169, 170–71 table 4, 172, 175; Maudgalyāyana shown in, 180–82, 183 fig. 7.7, 184 fig. 7.8, 218n31, 240, 259, 263–64, 270; wheel of rebirth in, 29 pl. 11, 48, 61, 64, 126, chap. 7, 193, 214, 221, 233, 238, 240, 243, 256, 258–59, 263–65, 270
  Cave 25, 175n11

Za ahan jing (*Saṃyuktāgama*), 33n7, 62n28
Za baozang jing, 104–5n1
Zengyi ahan jing (*Ekottarāgama*), 62n28, 93n27
Zhai Fengda, 170–71 table 4
Zhang Huaishen, 168, 187, 264–65
Zhang Min, 222n
Zhang Yichao, 167, 187
Zhang Yu, 136
Zhao Zhifeng (1159–1249), chap. 9, 259
Zhaozong (r. 889–904), 225
Zheng fahua jing. See *Lotus Sūtra*
zhiguai. *See* miracle tales
Zhi Qian (ca. 220–252), 62n26, 62n28
Zhisheng (669–740), 51n3, 169, 261n19
Zhiyan, 170–71 table 4
Zhong Tianzhu Sheweiguo Qihuansi tujing. See *Illustrated Scripture on Jetavana Monastery in Śrāvastī in Central India*
Zhongzong, Emperor (r. 705–710), 52
Zhu Fonian (ca. 365). *See* Buddhasmṛti
Zin, Monika, 93, 99